The Life And Times Of Duncan Farrar Kenner

Oil portrait of Duncan Kenner in his later years by Thomas Corner
Courtesy of Dr. and Mrs. Robert C. Judice

A LEADER AMONG PEERS

The Life And Times
Of Duncan Farrar Kenner

Craig A. Bauer

University of Louisiana at Lafayette Press

Library of Congress Catalog Number: 91-77438
ISBN Number: 978-1-935754-58-9
Copyright 1993

University of Louisiana at Lafayette Press
P.O. Box 40831
Lafayette, LA 70504-0831
http://ulpress.org

For *Betsy And Charlotte*

TABLE OF CONTENTS

INTRODUCTION 1

CHAPTER I
    The Early Years 3

CHAPTER II
    The Grand Tour and a Grand Manor 28

CHAPTER III
    The Estate 43

CHAPTER IV
    Family and Society 70

CHAPTER V
    The Political Arena 98

CHAPTER VI
    Whig Leader 112

CHAPTER VII
    Decade of Challenge and Change 131

PHOTO ESSAY 158

CHAPTER VIII
    Service to the Cause 169

CHAPTER IX
    The Home Front 189

CHAPTER X
    The Mission 211

CHAPTER XI
    Post War Survival 238

CHAPTER XII
　　Reconstruction and Redemption 260

CHAPTER XIII
　　"Inter Pares Dux" 283

ENDNOTES 292

BIBLIOGRAPHY 327

INDEX 351

INTRODUCTION

The history of Louisiana is replete with many prominent personalities who were instrumental in guiding the social and political direction of the state through the portentous decades of the nineteenth century. This book undertakes an examination of a major contributor to events in Louisiana and the South during the last century who has been largely overlooked by historians. Though some attention has been given to Duncan Farrar Kenner's Civil War exploit of undertaking a hazardous diplomatic mission to Europe during the war's final days in a last desperate attempt by the South to stave off defeat, this work is the first in-depth examination of his life and contributions.

There were individuals in Louisiana who rose for periods of time to greater levels of political and social influence; however, no other individual in nineteenth-century Louisiana sustained as high a position of influence for a longer period of time than Duncan Kenner. From the 1840s until his retirement four decades later, Kenner was involved with virtually every major issue relating to Louisiana's social and political history, as well as the development of the state's sugar and horse-racing industries. On first view his life appears to personify much of the glamorized "moonlight and magnolias" culture which has characterized so much of the literature on the nineteenth-century South. However, this examination of Kenner reveals a far more capitalistic and multi-dimensional existence than the seignorial lifestyle often associated with the Southern planter.

The researching and writing of this book has taken several years to complete. During that time, I was sometimes asked why so significant a historical figure as Duncan Kenner had been so long neglected by historians delving into the history of nineteenth-century Louisiana. The answer to this important question is simple. Though he was a well-read person who possessed a large personal library and who kept detailed records of his large financial and agricultural holdings, after his death there appeared to be little serious effort by his descendants to preserve his notes and records. As a result of this all too common practice of families failing to appreciate the significance of their personal collections, there is today a dearth of primary materials relating to Kenner. No large repository of Kenner material exists. What primary sources do survive are largely scattered throughout many works and collections located in several different institutions, with holdings at the archives collections at the Historic New Orleans Collection and at Louisiana

State University having some of the most useful materials.

In a study such as this, the author could never have brought the work to fruition without the assistance and encouragement of many individuals. Sincere appreciation is extended to Dr. William K. Scarborough, Dr. Orazio Ciccarelli, Dr. John Guice, Dr. Glenn Harper, and Dr. Ronald Marquardt, for their guidance and assistance during the preparation of much of this work while a graduate student at the University of Southern Mississippi. A very special thanks is expressed to Dr. William K. Scarborough, who served as the writer's major professor and doctoral committee chairman. His advice, encouragement, enriching criticisms, and infinite patience were indispensable ingredients in the completion of this study.

Though their identities remain unknown to me, I am grateful to the numerous archival librarians of the many institutions where research for this work took place. Without their generous assistance and cooperation in obtaining materials, this biography could not have been written. Particular thanks are extended to the staffs of the Howard-Tilton Memorial Library at Tulane University, the Louisiana State Museum, the Historic New Orleans Collection, and the National Archives.

I am indebted to Mr. Engel H. Schmidt, Robert and Joan McKee, and Robert and Susan Judice for their encouragement and advice, and for generously sharing their privately held materials which provided invaluable pieces to the puzzle of understanding the man Duncan Kenner.

Gratitude is also extended to Mr. Glenn Conrad and the capable staff at the Center for Louisiana Studies at the University of Southwestern Louisiana. Without their support, guidance, and assistance this book would not have been possible.

Heartfelt appreciation and thanks to my mother and father, Joyce and Rudy Bauer, for their support and the many sacrifices they made which allowed their six children to pursue their diverse personal and educational goals.

Finally, an especially large and special debt of gratitude is owed to the writer's wife Betsy. Over the years which the preparation of this project spanned, and in spite of the many sacrifices and demands in time and effort that the researching and writing of this worked placed upon the family of the writer, her support and encouragement was unwavering and inexhaustible. Her tireless review of drafts, criticisms of style, assistance in rewriting and rethinking awkward formulations, countless suggestions, and hours of research assistance all made an immeasurable contribution to the completion of this manuscript.

I

THE EARLY YEARS

As the nineteenth century dawned, Louisiana was a colony in transition. Little more than a hundred years old, Louisiana at the turn of the century was a thinly populated French-speaking Spanish possession. Within twelve short years the situation changed radically, as Louisiana went from a Spanish colony to become one of the United States. Yet, even before the dramatic change from autocratic to republican government occurred, the transition in the population from Old World colonists to Americans had begun.

Among the many salient changes brought to the American continent by the Treaty of Paris of 1783 was the permanent lowering of the political barriers which had hampered the development of lands in the trans-Appalachian territory. After the Revolution, Americans in ever-increasing numbers began to desert their homesteads in the original thirteen states for the lands to the west of the eastern mountain ranges. The surge of settlers into the trans-Appalachian region soon spread into the areas of the Ohio River Valley, and to the south, into the soon-to-be-established Mississippi Territory. A few individuals chose to locate in the already established settlements of Spanish West Florida.[1]

One such emigrant from the older provinces of the South was young William Kenner. Except for a few family traditions, little is known of his life in the years which preceded his migration to Spanish Natchez. Born on June 4, 1776, William, like so many of his fellow Virginians, at an early age sought wealth and adventure in lands to the west of his native state.[2]

Although some individuals made their way west by sailing from East Coast ports to New Orleans on the Gulf Coast and then upriver from there, the majority of those who headed west did so by means of the overland routes which followed the narrow valleys and gorges through the eastern mountain ranges to the valleys of the tributaries of the Ohio and Mississippi rivers. It was this overland route that young William Kenner most likely followed during the waning years of the century on his trek to find fortune in the developing lands of the West. Ambitious and anxious to make a success of his effort, Kenner continued his journey until he reached what was then considered to be the extreme western point of the frontier. This was the settlement of Natchez, built atop high bluffs on the east bank of the Mississippi. Though a Spanish possession, Natchez attracted the young entrepreneur because of the many business opportunities it seemed to offer.[3]

There were several sound reasons for such an optimistic prognosis by a young American moving into the Natchez District during the waning years of the eighteenth century. Located at the center of a thinly populated area that stretched along the eastern bank of the Mississippi River and on the western border of the Indian territory, Natchez was the southern anchor of the only direct overland route in the trans-Appalachian section of the South, the Natchez Trace. This five-hundred-mile path served as passage for thousands of individuals who traveled between New Orleans and the settlements of Tennessee and Kentucky. The town also served as a dispersal center for the smaller settlements of the area.[4]

Besides having an advantageous location, Spanish Natchez offered the entrepreneur a favorable business climate. Realizing that the great influx of Americans into trans-Appalachia might precipitate future problems between their country and the United States, Spanish authorities attempted various means to stem the inevitable American expansion into their lands. Not able to stop the influx by military action and failing in its efforts to negotiate a means to keep the Americans away from the Mississippi, the Spanish crown actively sought to protect its holdings by forming alliances with regional Indian tribes who also feared the land-grabbing Americans. Spanish authorities realized too that a needed ingredient in any plan to halt American expansionism was the support of loyal subjects in the disputed areas. Heretofore Spanish policy discouraged migration of subjects other than a few Spaniards, officials and soldiers, to the colony. Now, if they were going to stop the Americans, Spain must counter-colonize with individuals loyal to the crown. As a consequence, the Spanish adopted a more tolerant stand towards emigrants from the United States. Americans were encouraged to settle in Spanish-held areas and to become loyal subjects of Spain. To this end, the crown enticed settlers by allowing goods to be imported free of duty into the colony and generous land grants and a ready market through New Orleans for their produce were offered as enticements by the crown. Furthermore, Spanish authorities, aware of the great discontent that many Westerners had for their federal government, actively fomented dissatisfaction among the frontiersmen who remained on American soil. Additionally, to make living under Spanish rule more attractive, Spain modified its traditional controls on the economy, government, and religion.[5]

Although the overtures did attract many new settlers such as William Kenner to the colony, the Spanish were disappointed in the overall results of their efforts. The numbers of immigrants were small in comparison to what they had anticipated. During the thirteen-year period from 1784 to 1797, the population of the Natchez District only increased from approximately 1,600 to about 4,500 whites and blacks. Failure of the Spanish project was largely due to the fact that many Americans were unfamiliar with Spanish laws and considered the government to be totalitarian. Moreover, many individuals did not trust the Spanish position on religious freedom. Although permitted to enter the colony, Protestants were not allowed public worship. The imagined threat of eventual forced conversion to Catholicism frightened away many would-be colonists.[6]

Despite this prejudiced American view regarding life under Spanish rule, William Kenner chose to settle in Natchez sometime during the waning years of Spain's occupation of the settlement. The lightly populated frontier community exhibited characteristics considerably different from some of the wilderness towns which lay to the north and west. Since many of the post-American Revolution immigrants to Natchez were educated individuals, the settlement was somewhat more cultivated than its neighbors. As had been the case throughout Spanish dominion, the Natchez District was populated predominantly by Anglo-Americans along with a few Frenchmen and an even smaller number of Spaniards. The lax nature of Spanish authorities in Natchez permitted goods to be imported free of duty, and this lack of economic restrictions resulted in considerable prosperity for the area. For example, the merchant John McDonogh included the following items on an 1801 manifest of imported goods: 720 casks of claret, 2,400 bottles of Medoc wine, 15 pipes of brandy, 70 dozen of men's white stockings, 312 dozen kid gloves, 18 gross white playing cards, 96 reams of "faint blue" paper, wall paper of various kinds, including "nine muses dark grounded."

The list also included such hard-to-find luxuries as sweet oil, almonds, soap, cambrices, and linen.[7]

Most settlers cultivated the rich soils of the region and exported bountiful crops of tobacco, indigo, and most importantly, cotton to ready market by way of New Orleans. A few merchants also made their homes in the growing community on the Mississippi River bluffs. Seeing the potential in each activity, William Kenner invested both in the mercantile business and in land. Possessing much business acumen, the young Virginian, with the aid of his brilliant business partner, James C. Wilkins, was eventually able to control much of the commerce of Mississippi. Kenner's land speculation was also extremely lucrative. One of his holdings on St. Catherine's Creek alone totaled 764 arpents of valuable real estate.[8]

As a successful businessman, Kenner early became associated with the social and political leaders of the Natchez District. Excluding the full-time bureaucrats of the Spanish and the American regimes, political leadership was usually limited to a small number of wealthy planters and merchants with the money, leisure, and inclination necessary to sustain a position of influence in the community.[9]

During the years of Spanish domination, Kenner established a close relationship with the adjutant major of Natchez, Stephen Minor. A native of Pennsylvania, Minor was a close friend of the Spanish governor and served as interim governor during the final months of Spanish occupation. In light of the Spanish practice of taking care of local favorites, the close relationship between Kenner and Minor no doubt assisted the former in his financial dealings in the colony.[10]

With the signing of the Treaty of San Lorenzo on October 17, 1795, Spain relinquished its control over the Natchez District to the United States. Despite this change in governments, Kenner continued for some time to enjoy input into the highest levels of local authority. Spanish forces did not evacuate the area until March, 1798. Congress then created the Territory of Mississippi and gave it the same boundaries as the Spanish Natchez District. With American control, there developed among community leaders a period of factionalism based on political loyalties, family connections, and economic interests. It was an era characterized by intense jealousies and suspicions. Though some wealthy planters were also financiers, political alignments, for the most part, were divided between the merchant-creditor faction and the agrarian-debtor class.[11]

The Early Years 7

The new American government was headed by Winthrop Sargent, a New England Federalist appointed by President John Adams. The administration also included a secretary and three judges; however, most officials were delayed in arriving in the territory, thereby forcing Sargent to govern by executive decree. For assistance in running the settlement, the governor turned to community leaders. Seeking recommendations for suitable men for office, Sargent spoke with Andrew Ellicott, the United States boundary commissioner who had preceded him to the territory, and acted on many of Ellicott's suggestions. Among those who obtained appointments was twenty-two-year-old William Kenner who was named justice of the peace for Adams County.[12]

Although no direct evidence exists to explain Sargent's selection of the young Virginian for this position, Kenner's close association with Stephen Minor no doubt was a factor in his appointment. The willingness of Natchez merchant class to support policies of New England Federalist governor, along with their experience and desire for stability, contributed to Sargent's policy of appointing members of the old Spanish power structure to positions of authority in the new American bureaucracy. This practice, however, did much to alienate the members of the agrarian debtor class who were generally Jeffersonian in their political philosophy.[13]

Kenner's position as justice of the peace was one of considerable importance. The major local subdivision of government in the South of that period was the county. Among the most prominent officials of this basic unit of local government was the justice of the peace. Individuals named to this position were usually members of the area's more prominent and wealthy families. Serving with Kenner as a county justice was Daniel Clark, a member of the influential Clarkesville, Tennessee, family. The post had both judicial and administrative functions. The county court had the responsibility of keeping the peace in the county and the power to adjudicate both felonies and misdemeanors. The two justices frequently held court together and were not lax in carrying out their duties. Most offenses were settled by fining the guilty party; however, the unlucky defendant once fined was usually incarcerated until the fine, which averaged about twenty dollars, was paid, as was the case when Thomas Lovelass was fined twenty dollars for selling liquor to Indians. Where they felt justified, Kenner and Clark did not hesitate to issue harsher sentences. Hence, for taking a horse without permission, Alex Johnson was fined fifty dollars for the value of the animal and was ordered to receive twenty-five lashes on his back at the public whipping post.[14]

Throughout his years in Natchez, Kenner maintained a close association with Stephen Minor. Eventually, the dealings between the two men went beyond political and financial affairs. They also shared a social relationship which led to Kenner's marriage to the ex-governor's daughter, Mary. A delicate individual who possessed a girlish figure and with pretty childish features, Mary was the only surviving child from Minor's marriage to Martha Ellis, who had died in 1791. Besides Mary, Minor had four other children, all from his third wife, Catherine Lintot. Born in Natchez on July 4, 1787, Mary was only fourteen years old when she married Kenner on November 19, 1801, at Concord, the Minor family estate in Natchez. Little more is known of the courtship between the couple, but it is likely that their courtship followed the social conventions of the day.[15]

Though Southern women on average married at an earlier age than their Northern counterparts, marriage at age fourteen was somewhat unusual. Catherine Clinton's study of the women's world in the Old South reveals that the median age of marriage for women (based upon a sample of planters born from 1765 to 1815) was twenty, whereas the median age for Southern men at the time of marriage was twenty-eight. This compares to twenty-four for Northern females and twenty-six for Northern men. Clinton's study also reveals just how far from the norm was Mary's marriage at such an early age. Only .5 percent of the Southern females in her statistical sample married at Mary's young age of fourteen.[16]

In most cases the selection of the marriage partner was a young man's or woman's prerogative. Southerners traditionally only courted individuals who were of their own social stratum. Besides the proper social credentials, acceptable suitors had to possess adequate wealth. When discussing members of the opposite sex, Southern men commonly described women in terms of their financial holdings. In writing of a Southern belle who had caught his eye, for example, one frustrated suitor wrote: "If she were not guilty of the unpardonable crime..., to wit, poverty [she] would be a great belle."[17] It is highly unlikely that such thoughts crossed William Kenner's mind during his courtship of Mary, for as part of her dowry, William's young bride brought into the marriage her share of her father's estate which amounted to the substantial sum of $70,000.[18]

Shortly after their wedding, the Kenners migrated to New Orleans in Spanish-controlled Louisiana, a move seemingly motivated primarily by business and economics. Political considerations, however, may have entered into the decision of the Kenners to abandon their Natchez homestead. With most of the planters of the Natchez region being Jeffersonians, Governor Sargent's Federalist administration was studded with political controversy. Considered by many area residents as being arrogant and arbitrary, Sargent was replaced by William C. C. Claiborne shortly after Thomas Jefferson became president in 1801. This change in the political power structure marked a decline in the influence of many individuals, including Kenner, who had supported Sargent.[19]

Despite his political activities in Natchez, Kenner was, above all else, an entrepreneur. Simultaneously with political changes in Natchez, economic opportunities elsewhere caught the attention of the young Mississippi merchant. In the years immediately after the United States was granted the right of deposit in New Orleans by Pinckney's Treaty of 1795, the trade of the city greatly expanded. Though the treaty stipulated that nothing was to be sold by Americans in the city because their property was officially merely goods in transit, ambitious Americans were able to make handsome profits because of the lax enforcement policies of the Spanish. Furthermore, because of the lack of industries in Mississippi at the time, many consumer items had to be imported into the territory, and high prices brought by these imported goods offered American businessmen the incentive to become part of this lucrative trade. It was this promising atmosphere of large and quick profits which enticed William Kenner and his young bride to leave their comfortable lifestyle, family, and friends of Natchez to begin a new life in the Crescent City.[20]

New Orleans at the beginning of the nineteenth century was rapidly becoming one of the leading communities of North America. Spain's lenient financial policies had energized the city's economy. Already a cosmopolitan community with a population of approximately 5,000 whites, 2,000 free-persons-of-color, and 3,000 slaves, the great majority of the city's white population was of French descent. The years of Spanish control of the city did little to diminish the French influence in New Orleans. Both the business and social life of the Crescent City was dominated by the old French inhabitants. It was this French power structure that the new and more aggressive elements in the community, namely the Americans and refugees from Napoleonic France, began to challenge for economic and political supremacy. Culturally, New Orleans had already gained a reputation as a carefree and colorful city. Most of the elements

of the Crescent City's future fame, including its architecture of low brick and plaster structures constructed around patios and its Creole food with its unique combination of French, Spanish, Indian, and African influences, were already in place. About half of the residents were said to be able to read and write; however, only about two hundred could do it well. Furthermore, the moral standards of the community were notoriously loose, with concubinage
looked upon as a normal practice.[21]

Physically, the city had many unusual characteristics. Because it was below sea level, New Orleans' existence was made possible only by building of levees to hold back the muddy waters of the Mississippi River. So wet was the area that it was impossible for the inhabitants to have basements or below ground graves. Water for drinking had to be collected either from the river or from cisterns which collected rainwater. Most individuals lived within the stockaded area, known today as the Vieux Carré.[22]

Like most other immigrants of the time in the city, the Kenners chose the Vieux Carré as the location of their new home. Residing at Number Seventeen Bienville Street, Kenner established his business office a short distance away on Chartres Street. Shortly after his arrival in the Crescent City, he established a partnership with Stephen Henderson in a general mercantile and commission business. Dealing extensively with the developing trade areas of the West, Kenner and Henderson soon became one of the city's leading general mercantile and commission enterprises.

The partnership was able to profit greatly from the unsettled political conditions of the times. With Europe mired in the Napoleonic wars, there existed many excellent opportunities for American businessmen in New Orleans. The foreign conflicts created a huge demand for American goods of such magnitude that the Spanish were forced to relax their traditional trade restrictions. While official relaxation of trade barriers on upriver goods made life easier for New Orleans merchants, the opportunity to make large profits was such that competition was fierce among local merchants to gain access to the lucrative market. Shepherd Brown, a protégé of the wealthy merchant John McDonogh, informed his colleague that he had attempted to do business with most of the principal planters of Natchez but had failed because their crops had already been engaged. Much of this trade was going to the firm of Kenner and Henderson. No doubt Kenner's friendship with the Natchez planters and his father-in-law's connections had provided an advantage over his competitors in this profitable trade.[23]

The advantageous commercial atmosphere of the Spanish colony changed dramatically in 1802 when the warring parties in Europe agreed to the Treaty of Amiens. This temporary halt in the fighting between France and its adversaries enabled Spain once again to tighten trade restrictions in Louisiana. In October, 1802, after receiving authorization from King Carlos IV, the Spanish intendant at New Orleans withdrew the American right of deposit in the port city. The Spanish king also prohibited all commerce between Spanish and American citizens and terminated land grants to Americans. These new restrictions caused havoc among many of the American commission agents in New Orleans. Nevertheless, despite the imposition of these crippling restrictions, Kenner escaped any long-term financial damage. He continued to act as commercial agent for his in-laws and other clients at Natchez and continued to operate several of the financial holdings he had acquired there before removing to New Orleans. Most notable among these were his real estate enterprises, which included the transferring of properties as well as the collecting of many minor debts which were owed to him.[24]

Fortunately for New Orleans merchants, the economic recession caused by the cessation of hostilities in Europe was shortlived. Within a few months, war again broke out between France and its neighbors, thus renewing the demand and necessity for American products from the Mississippi Valley. American commercial interests in Louisiana were bolstered even further by the deteriorating political situation in Europe. With renewed war threatening, Bonaparte decided that France should give up control of the recently ceded colony of Louisiana rather than attempt to defend it from invasion during the approaching hostilities. Accordingly, to nearly everyone's surprise, Bonaparte agreed to sell his vast Louisiana holdings to the United States.[25]

Transfer of the colony to the Americans occurred in New Orleans on December 20, 1803. The acquisition of control of the colony was for the most part well received by the residents of New Orleans. Pierre Clément Laussat, Bonaparte's envoy at the transfer ceremonies, wrote that the Americans in the city were ecstatic over the news, while the Spanish residents were pleased that the colony would not be returned to the French. On the other hand, many French inhabitants, who had looked forward to a return to French rule, voiced disapproval of American acquisition of the colony.

Despite widespread popular acquiescence in the American takeover, United States officials were concerned about the Spanish government's response to the event. When Spain transferred the colony to Bonaparte, it was stipulated that Louisiana was not to be transferred to any other country.

Hence, to forestall objections by Spain, President Jefferson moved quickly to take possession of the newly acquired territory. The nearest American military force of any strength was at Natchez. Therefore, the president directed Governor William C. C. Claiborne of the Mississippi Territory and General James Wilkinson, the ranking general of the army, to take formal possession of the Louisiana territory. To provide security for the transfer, a company of volunteer cavalry under the command of Captain Benjamin Farrar, Mary Minor Kenner's uncle, escorted Claiborne to New Orleans.[26]

During the first months of American control of Louisiana, Claiborne served as civil governor and Wilkinson as military commander of the territory; however, the largely Catholic and French population was not satisfied with the actions of the thirty-year-old Protestant governor. Many objected to the introduction of English, which few understood, as the official language and were plagued by the governor's inability to understand the French language. Furthermore, some felt slighted because the prospect for early statehood was not very promising. Finally, French Louisianians found aspects of the American legal system to be confusing, and they resented the United States ban on the importation of slaves.

Realizing the importance of winning the support of the local inhabitants, Congress, in March, 1804, established the Territory of Orleans, which nearly paralleled the present boundaries of Louisiana, and the Territory of Louisiana, which consisted of the rest of the vast region acquired by the United States from France. Claiborne was appointed governor of Orleans Territory, with broad executive powers. Legislative authority under the new government was vested in the governor and in a unicameral legislative body called the Legislative Council, whose thirteen members were appointed annually by the president. Judicial authority was held by a federal district judge, three judges of a Superior Court, and several justices of the peace, all of whom were presidential appointees. Congress retained for itself the authority to rescind any laws the territorial government might enact.[27]

When selecting individuals to serve on the Legislative Council, President Jefferson relied heavily upon Governor Claiborne's recommendations. In a letter to the governor dated July 7, 1804, Jefferson stated that the council should be "composed of men of integrity, of understanding, of clear property and influence among the people, well acquainted with the laws, customs, and habits of the country." The president asked that a majority of the council members should be "of sound American characters long established and esteemed there, and the rest of French or Spaniards, the most estimable and well affected." However, despite the broadness of the guidelines, Claiborne had difficulty finding people to fill the positions on the Legislative Council. Because they were not permitted to elect any official in the new government, many residents of the territory opposed that government and refused to take part in it. As late as December, 1804, Claiborne was only able to find eight individuals who were willing and qualified to serve on the lawmaking council.[28]

Among the eight citizens who accepted appointments to the Legislative Council was William Kenner. Through his Natchez background, Kenner had been acquainted with Governor Claiborne for some time before he arrived in New Orleans. Although there had been differences between the two men in the past, stemming from Kenner's appointment to public office by Governor Sargent, a political adversary of Claiborne's, the two men demonstrated mutual respect and willingly put past disagreements to rest. In a letter to Thomas Jefferson on October 5, 1804, Claiborne recommended the New Orleans businessman for the legislative post because he was "a native of the United States, an honest man and a respected merchant." In an earlier communication to the president, Claiborne had also commended Kenner. Calling him a man of "sense and property," the territorial governor downplayed an item which could have affected Kenner's appointment. The questionable issue concerned Kenner's dealings with the Spanish in Florida. In his August 30, 1804, communication to the president, Claiborne wrote that Kenner and some of his other choices for the Legislative Council were "moderate, prudent men" who were to "a small degree interested in the Florida purchases, and indeed . . . there are few Americans of fortune who resided in New Orleans previous to the Treaty, but were more or less engaged in the speculation." Jefferson agreed with Claiborne, and Kenner and the others were duly appointed members of the legislative body.[29]

Despite the efforts of Jefferson and Claiborne to choose only able and honest men for the Legislative Council, the people of the territory continued to oppose it. The Creoles, natives of Louisiana regardless of their ethnic background, believed that the new government showed partiality to Americans. With public dissatisfaction and official frustration mounting over the failure to establish an effective government, Congress on March 2, 1805, took action to address the problem by authorizing the president to establish a new government patterned after that of the Mississippi Territory. Thus, a bicameral legislature was created, with the twenty-five member house being elected for a two-year term and a five-member legislative council being appointed by the president. This governmental organization remained in effect until Louisiana was granted statehood in 1812.[30]

Although this reorganization of the territorial government marked the end of the Legislative Council and of William Kenner's career in public office, it did not signify the end of his community service. For example, he provided valuable assistance to the government during the War of 1812. When Gen. Ferdinand Leigh Claiborne was given the responsibility of protecting much of the Gulf Coast from British attack, he frequently received little assistance from the government. Ordered to provide the needed medicine and supplies to transfer a force of 600 troops from Baton Rouge to the Alabama River, Claiborne had insufficient means to carry out his orders. Hearing of the plight of the general, Kenner, along with John and Stephen Minor, advanced sufficient funds to pay for the upkeep of the military force in question.[31]

Kenner also played an active role in the affairs of his church. When he and Mary first arrived in New Orleans, the Spanish authorities prohibited all non-Roman Catholic services. Except for clandestine and furtive visits by a few Protestant ministers, the non-Catholic residents of Louisiana were unable to attend services of their own choosing. So successful had been the Spanish prohibition on non-Catholic religious groups that at the time of the transfer of the territory to the United States there was not a single Protestant church or Jewish synagogue in Louisiana. This soon changed. On June 2, 1804, fifty-three Protestants of New Orleans held an organizational meeting in the boarding house of Madame Fourage. At this meeting they voted in favor of establishing an Episcopal religion as the guide to their heavenly reward. Highly dignified, the Episcopal Church lacked much of the evangelical zeal which attracted the masses to the Baptist and Methodist denominations. Despite the fact that this first Protestant congregation to be organized in Louisiana never appealed to more than a small fraction of the people of the territory, it was an important organization, for among its members were many of the territory's most prominent Americans. Included among its membership were John McDonogh; Edward Livingston; Maunsel White, one of the dominant figures in the commercial and banking interest in

New Orleans; Thomas Urquhart, president of Louisiana Bank; B. Chew and R. D. Shepherd, both directors of the Bank of the United States; and even Judah Touro, the wealthy philanthropic Jew who contributed impartially to many religious organizations. In 1805, when the congregation was officially organized and a minister was provided, fifteen individuals, including William Kenner, were chosen as members of the original vestry. Naming itself Christ Church, the congregation held its services at the historic Cabildo located on the Place D'Armes until able to construct a church.[32]

Despite his interests in community affairs, Kenner's primary interest remained his mercantile and commission business. His partnership with Stephen Henderson developed into one of the territory's leading commercial enterprises. Involved in many moneymaking activities, including the profitable real-estate market, the partnership's main line of business was serving as commercial agents or factors for the region's planters. It was to the factors that growers sent their crops either to be sold to buyers from Northern or English houses or for forwarding directly to New York or Liverpool. As factors, Kenner and Henderson were men of versatility in business who performed many different functions for the planter besides just selling his crops. Among their typical duties were the purchasing and selling of slaves for their clients, the giving of advice concerning the condition of the market, the purchasing of supplies and equipment; and on occasion, they even arranged for the schooling of the children of their customers. Factors also performed the valuable service of furnishing credit to planters until their crops were marketed. For their services the commercial agents were usually paid a percentage commission on the varied services they provided to the planter.[33]

The factorage business in New Orleans was highly competitive. To keep ahead of the competition, it was important for a factor to have the support of prominent planters. Hence, Kenner was able to use his relationship and business dealings with Stephen Minor and his brother-in-law John Minor to draw additional clients to his firm, including members of the prominent Bringier family.[34]

An ambitious entrepreneurial capitalist, Kenner was always interested in expanding his business activities. In 1805 he was chosen to serve as one of only thirteen members of the local board of directors of the United States Bank of Philadelphia when that prestigious institution opened a branch in New Orleans. With his mercantile and commission business firmly established, Kenner's interest next turned to the rapidly developing sugar industry. In partnership with different associates, he acquired two sugar plantations. With Theophilus Minor he obtained part of the Linwood Plantation in Ascension Parish, and with Benjamin Morgan he purchased a section of land at the Cannes Brûlées settlement, now the site of the city of Kenner. While most of his time was spent in New Orleans, William's attention nevertheless increasingly turned to his agricultural holdings. Eventually acquiring full ownership of the Cannes Brûlées property, he ended his partnership with Stephen Henderson in 1811. However, he remained in the factorage business, reorganizing his affairs under the name of William Kenner and Company.[35]

Kenner's new company proved to be just as successful as his first. An example of the new firm's business prowess was demonstrated in 1812 when the first steamboat to arrive in the Crescent City, the side-wheeler *New Orleans*, contained a consignment for Kenner's new company. In a letter to Stephen Minor, William described the impressive appearance of the vessel in the city. According to Kenner, "He [the vessel] has been astonishing and amusing the multitude here by going down to the extremity of the English turn, returning in five hours, without setting any sail." William concluded with the observation that the vessel's "manouvring [sic] in the River . . . has exceeded the most sanguine expectations that had been formed by any person here."[36]

Named after plantations he had known and admired in the Natchez region, Kenner's Linwood Plantation in Ascension Parish and Oakland at Cannes Brûlées became two of the most productive sugar estates in the state. So successful were these agricultural enterprises that they soon surpassed the firm in New Orleans as a source of revenue. One reason for the high productivity of the sites was Kenner's insistence on using the most up-to-date equipment and scientific methods for sugar production.[37]

Of their two rural properties, Kenner and his family preferred the Oakland estate. Named after the Natchez plantation of Dr. William N. Mercer, the husband of Mary Kenner's cousin Anna Farrar, Oakland's location approximately twelve miles upriver from New Orleans made it convenient for frequent family visits by riverboat. Situated on a tract of land which stretched from the river to Lake Pontchartrain, Kenner only cultivated the portion of land nearest the Mississippi River. As was the case on most sugar plantations, other crops were also produced at Oakland. In an 1813 letter to Stephen Minor from his home in New Orleans, Kenner yearned for a return to Oakland "where things really look charmingly" and boasted that he had "the finest crop of corn in Louisiana and about ninety acres of prime cane."[38]

Located about one hundred yards from the river, the main house was raised off the ground because of the danger of flooding. Constructed of hand-hewn cypress timbers, the whitewashed plantation house was said to have been beautifully enhanced by Mary Kenner's magnificent flower garden. In addition to the family house, there were several other major buildings on the property, including an office and sugar mill. William also maintained sizable work forces on his plantations. Papers filed after his death recorded 148 slaves working at Linwood and sixty-three at Oakland, eight of whom were house servants.[39]

Although comfortable in comparison to the lifestyles of most Southerners, Kenner's life as a planter was far from the serene and leisured existence depicted in the romantic legend of the Old South. In reality, the great majority of plantation owners were working farmers who supervised the labor on their farms themselves with the aid of either a Negro driver or an overseer. Kenner seems to have used a manager at Linwood Plantation and personally supervised events at Oakland. The close proximity of the Cannes Brûlées site to New Orleans made it possible for him to boat up to the property whenever his presence was needed.[40]

Naturally, Kenner was often accompanied by his family on his visits to Oakland. William and Mary Kenner had seven children, three girls and four boys. All lived to middle age except for their first born, Maria, who died in October, 1806, at the age of three. The other daughters were Martha and Frances Ann. Martha was born on September 28, 1804, while her mother was visiting her family at their Concord estate in Natchez. Before her death in 1873, she would wed three times, including a marriage to John B. Humphreys, a nephew of James Brown—one of Louisiana's first U.S. senators and owner of Roseland Plantation in St. Charles Parish. Her second husband was a Mr. Bruce of whom little is known; and the third was Charles Oxley, a New Orleans merchant originally from Liverpool, England. Frances Ann was born in New Orleans in 1806. She married John Dick, an attorney who later served as United States attorney for Louisiana. Two years after his death in 1824, she wed George Currie Duncan. An Englishman by birth, Duncan was one of the Crescent City's leading bankers. Until her death in 1875, Frances Ann remained one of the social leaders of glamorous New Orleans.[41]

The Kenner's first son was born in New Orleans on February 18, 1808. Stephen Minor Kenner, named for his grandfather, eventually married Eliza Davis and farmed Belle Grove Plantation in Jefferson Parish. The second son, William Butler, was born in the Crescent City on March 11, 1810. He married Ruhamsh Riske of Cincinnati, Ohio, and settled on the family estate at Oakland. George, the third son, was born in New Orleans on January 18, 1812, and was the only one of the Kenner children to leave Louisiana permanently. After spending some time at Linwood, he lived in Kentucky near Cincinnati, where he married Charlotte Riske Jones, the sister of Ruhamsh. The couple eventually removed to Matagorda County, Texas, where he died in 1852.[42]

The Kenners' youngest child was born at their New Orleans home on Bienville Street during the difficult times brought about by the War of 1812. A British blockade of the mouth of the Mississippi River had greatly reduced trade into the city from other ports. Despite the depressing news of American military setbacks in the war and declining business opportunities, William's spirits were lifted with the birth of his fourth son on a chilly February 11, 1813. Tradition in the Old South dictated that the husband had the right to name the child. Hence, in naming his new son Duncan Farrar, William honored two close acquaintances, Dr. Stephen Duncan of Natchez and Captain Benjamin Farrar, who had escorted Governor Claiborne to New Orleans to accept the transfer of the territory from France.[43]

The Kenners were a close family with Mary and William being devoted to one another and to their children. However, as sometimes happens in large families, the Kenner children seemed to have developed special rela-tionships among themselves, with the two daughters—Martha and Frances Ann—the two oldest sons—Minor and William Butler—and the two young-est children—George and Duncan—pairing off. The familial closeness of the Kenners extended beyond the immediate family. Although, as previously noted, William Kenner had little if any contact with his family in Virginia, just the opposite was true about his relations with Mary's relatives in Mississippi. The Kenners and their Natchez kin corresponded often and paid frequent and occasionally long visits to one another. In addition to Mary's father and brother, Stephen and John Minor, the Kenners were close to Benjamin Farrar's family, particularly his daughters Mary and Ann. The close relationship between the Kenners and Minors was not an unusual phenomenon. More than in any other part of the country, the

The Early Years 19

closely knit family unit with its widespread kinship ties was a common, if not dominant, folk characteristic of the Old South.⁴⁴

The coming of fall in 1814 brought with it more than just the passing of another summer. For this time of change in the weather and growing season also brought with it tragedy which would forever temper the close and happy ways of the Kenners. Death was no stranger to the families of nineteenth-century New Orleans. The humid, semitropical climate often had a devastating effect upon the residents of the Crescent City. Traveler Josiah Gregg amply summarized conditions when he wrote that "it is no wonder that the air of New Orleans should be generally so unhealthy, and in autumn quite pestilential, for the town is built in a complete swamp." He added that it was "never intended by nature [to be] the abode of men. . . . It is the Churchyard of the United States."⁴⁵

Once before, on an autumn day in October, 1806, death had visited the Kenner family and taken little three-year-old Maria. Nearly eight years to the day after that tragic event, death again called. Although Mary Kenner enjoyed a standard of living which was better than that experienced by the average Southern female, burdens of being a mother and wife in nineteenth-century Louisiana took their toll on the delicate frame of the twenty-seven-year-old mother of seven. Perhaps most damaging of all to Mary's health was the region's sickly climate. William Kenner wrote to his father-in-law in June of the fateful year that nearly everyone in his family was "sick with violent colds and soreness in the breast." He added that Mary was the sickest because her illness was accompanied by fever. Though she recovered from the June illness, she was again stricken during the final days of summer while at the family's Oakland home. Dr. Cochrane, the family physician, reassured the family that although "severe," Mary's condition "was not very dangerous." Unfortunately, things did not improve. On Tuesday, October 4, her condition worsened so much that Dr. Flood, a more experienced physician, was summoned to the plantation from his home in New Orleans. Hopes began to rise the next morning when her condition seemed to stabilize; however, by mid-afternoon it was evident to all that death was near. Her six young children were called to her bedside, where they remained with their father until death came at approximately three o'clock on the afternoon of October 5, 1814.⁴⁶

In accordance with her wishes, Mary was laid to rest the next morning in a grave in New Orleans. A participant at the sad event later wrote that "perhaps no event of the same nature has occurred here for many years which excited more sensibility, or was generally lamented."[47]

The Southern proclivity for clannishness was never more evident than at the time of a loved one's death. Just as William had reported Mary's illness to her family in Natchez, with the onset of any serious illness of a family member, cousins, aunts, and uncles were notified as well as the immediate family circle. Friends and neighbors also joined in the sick watch and offered their assistance. Such was the case with Mary's death. Kenner was so affected by the death of his beloved wife that his friends were worried about his health and state of mind. He was said to be "inconsolable," and friends attempted to persuade him to accompany them with his children to their homes. When he refused to leave his home, his friends arranged for a week of alternating visits among themselves so that he would not be left without companionship.[48]

Word of Mary's death also greatly saddened her family in Natchez. Family members were particularly worried about the welfare of the Kenner children. It was fairly common practice in the Old South for motherless children to move to the home of a relative, frequently a maternal aunt. When her husband, Benjamin Farrar, who was staying in New Orleans at the time, notified her of her niece's death, Mary Farrar wrote her spouse a sorrowful letter on the loss of the Kenner children's mother. She added that, "When I think of the lost [sic] [William's] poor little children have met with I feel almost heart broken. What will become of them at there [sic] tender years to be deprived of their affectionate mother?" She then suggested the possibility of the Kenner children moving in with them: "Shall I, my beloved husband, request Mr. Kenner to let us have them to know that they do not suffer for anything in my power to do for them would be great satisfaction [sic] to me."[49] The Farrar's daughter also favored the idea. Her letter to her father was similar to her mother's. After commenting on how good Mary was to her children, Mary Farrar asked her father to allow the Kenner children to stay with them provided their father did not object. She concluded with the observation that she had much leisure time to devote to the children and that it would be beneficial for the Kenner children to stay with them because "New Orleans is not considered as safe as Natchez."[50]

Kenner's emotional state was such that he made no quick decision concerning his children's status. As late as January, 1815, Ann Farrar wrote to her father that she was anxious, "to know what Cousin Kenner intends doing with his children."[51] Kenner eventually decided to keep his family together as much as practicality would allow. One of the salient factors in his decision was his concern to provide all of his children with a proper education. In nearly all correspondence between the Kenners and their friends and relatives, the education of the Kenner children was one of the most frequent topics of discussion. Even the letter from William Kenner's associate, R. Claque, to Stephen Minor telling of Mary's death contained a discussion of the educational needs of the young Kenners.

The Kenner family's concern for their children's education was not uncharacteristic of the attitudes of other individuals of their social class in the Old South. Members of the South's upper class traditionally were concerned about obtaining adequate educational opportunities for their children. Sons had to be appropriately educated so that they could someday assume their role as society's leaders and business managers of their family estates. However, interest in the training and education of the daughters of the South's elite also played an increasingly prominent role during the early years of the nineteenth century. Until the waning years of the eighteenth century, daughters of planters, as well as their Northern sisters, mostly studied the Scriptures and other pious texts. By contrast, their brothers received wide-ranging training in the classics, philosophy, history, and mathematics. With the close of the American Revolution, however, there was a dramatic transition in the attitude of Southerners towards their daughters' training. The shift in opinion on female education did not reflect a decline in piety or chauvinism but rather an increased tide of republicanism caused by the spread of Enlightenment values and the increased patriotism of the time. Education was now looked upon as a needed ingredient in the building of a democratic nation.[52]

Attitudes in Louisiana on education did not differ greatly from those in the rest of the South. Throughout its colonial period, except for the work of a few Catholic religious orders, little attention was given to the question of education. With the advent of the American regime, a greater effort was made to provide schools for the people. Despite these attempts to educate the children of Louisiana, as in most Southern states, public education in southern Louisiana customarily bore the stigma of charity. Hence, when the German traveler Karl Postl visited New Orleans in 1826, he observed that public education in the Crescent City was inferior to "any city of equal extent and less wealth" in the United States.[53]

With public education in Louisiana in such a state of neglect, parents such as William Kenner who aspired to provide their children with a proper education were forced to patronize the private schools of the area or to send their children to more reputable institutions in other parts of the country. There was also the option of hiring a tutor. This was a choice open primarily only to wealthy individuals. Sometimes planters employed schoolmasters who worked for several planters, staying with various families by rotation. Although popular with the colonial aristocracy in the Old South, the tutorial system did not adequately meet the needs of the antebellum period and declined markedly during the latter part of this time frame. Instead of employing tutors, the upper class Southerners turned increasingly to "old field schools" and academies.[54]

Even before Mary's untimely death, the decision had been made to send the Kenner children away for proper schooling. Because there were "no good schools" in the area for young children, the Kenners enrolled their two oldest children, Martha and Frances Ann, in an out-of-town institution referred to as only Mrs. Florians' Seminary.[55] Several months after the death of their mother, William determined that the needs of his "dear little girls" were not being met adequately at the old school. Instead, the girls were transferred to Mrs. Mallon's Seminary in Philadelphia, which William considered to be "one of the first Seminaries in the country." In a letter to the girl's grandfather in Natchez, Kenner explained some of the benefits the new school offered to his children. He was impressed with the fine faculty and Mrs. Mallon's ability to engage "the affection of her children." He added that the headmistress had working for her "the best of teachers for every branch of useful and polite education."[56]

Reading and writing were the primary ingredients of the "polite education" of Southern females. Girls took courses in grammar and composition and were given special instruction in the form and style of letter writing; letters home were frequently supervised exercises. However, because of the controversial nature of popular-novel reading at the time, most schools avoided courses in literature. Instead, emphasis was given to the study of Scriptures. Female students were also taught the fundamentals of arithmetic to aid them in their household accounts and in understanding plantation ledgers. Other common topics of study for the academy student included ancient and modern geography, languages, natural history, and astronomy. Moreover, Southern girls were usually encouraged in their studies with stiff doses of discipline.[57]

The cost of educating a daughter away from home was an expensive undertaking that only the wealthier families could afford. Tuition varied from $2.50 to $4.00 a month for day pupils to the unusually high rate of $772.52 that John Couper of Saint Simon's Island, Georgia, paid for his daughter Anne's year of schooling in 1811 at Miss Datty's institution in Charleston. Mrs. Mallon charged Kenner a fee between the two extremes. The annual tuition per child for all expenses was $340. Kenner was quite pleased with the amount, for not only did he consider the school to be of such quality that it was "impossible to have [his children] in a better place" but the cost was less than he had previously paid for less satisfactory schooling in New Orleans. Martha and Frances Kenner remained enrolled at Mrs. Mallon's for several years.[58]

Unlike Martha and Frances Ann, Kenner's four sons received a considerable portion of their education closer to home. The Kenner boys went to schools in the New Orleans area. George and Duncan, the two younger children, were enrolled at a "French school" a couple of miles below the city. Although close to home, the young boys boarded at the facility and visited home on the average of once every two weeks. Not totally satisfied with the schooling being provided to his young sons, William considered transferring them to other institutions, including an unnamed facility in the North which his two older boys attended or possibly Mr. Shute's school in New Orleans. A rector of the Episcopal church, Shute operated a facility which was considered by many to be the best school in the Crescent City during the time the Kenner boys were obtaining their elementary schooling.[59]

It is more than likely that the boys attended several different schools during the time they were acquiring their education. During most of the first half of the nineteenth century the private schools and academies of the region operated on a marginal basis. The majority of these facilities were short-lived and existed for only a few semesters. Tuition at these local institutions for day students ranged from $2 to $5 per month, depending on the school, level of instruction, and qualifications of the faculty; whereas, pupils who boarded paid an average of $100 to $200 a year for room, board, laundry, and tuition. Instruction in special subjects such as music and dance usually cost extra. However, not all Southerners looked with favor upon these extracurricular activities for their sons. When the son of prominent New Orleans merchant, Maunsel White, wrote his father from a boarding school asking for permission to take piano lessons, the elder White replied that "drumming" on a piano was a waste of precious time and ordered "let me hear no more of pianos."[60]

As with female students, life in a boys' school could be Spartan. Long hours of study was the general rule. The early Louisiana historian Charles Gayarré recalled that, after rising before dawn at his childhood boarding school,

> they then had breakfast, which consisted of a half loaf of dry bread, which each boy procured, on hearing his name called, by going to an aperture whence it was dealt out. From half past seven until twelve students were engaged with their books and recitations; an hour was then given for dinner, which was a more generous meal than breakfast, and for recess. From one o'clock until about seven they were back again at books. Then came supper and the evening was devoted to recreation.[61]

The curriculum at boys' institutions was not altogether dissimilar to that which was offered at girls' schools of that time. Masters at the boys' facilities usually offered courses in reading, writing, arithmetic, English grammar, geography, and history. On occasion, Latin, Greek, or a modern foreign language was added to the list of subjects offered. One confident French master promised that he could teach his students to read, write, and perform the elementary functions in arithmetic "in two months at the soonest and three months at the latest and to correct the most vicious handwriting in eight lessons.[62]

Besides their lengthy stays away from home at schools, the Kenner children also frequently visited their relatives in Natchez. While there, the young Kenners were under the tutorship of their aunts and uncles, to whom their father gave the authority to "do to them as you wish me to yours."[63]

The Kenners reciprocated the hospitality of their Natchez kin by serving as gracious hosts for their relatives' frequent visits to New Orleans. Life on the plantation was often mundane and unexciting. Those who could afford it sometimes turned to travel to enliven their uneventful lives. With Natchez but a relatively short trip away by steamboat from New Orleans, the Kenners' Mississippi friends and relatives often visited the Crescent City. Among those who visited the Kenners frequently were William's brother-in-law John Minor and Captain Benjamin Farrar of Laurel Hill Plantation in Natchez. While in New Orleans, the Kenners' guests, like most visitors, took advantage of their stay in the bustling community to enjoy the prosperity and variety of the city's marketplace. After one such visit, Captain Farrar's expense account clearly revealed the extravagance in which planters indulged. Farrar's ledger included such items as $100 for a bonnet and gown for his wife Mary and another $100 for "certain furnishings." Most surprising of all was the unexplained notation, "Benjamin Farrar, incidental expenses, $10,000.00."[64]

Because of business and custom, men had the opportunity to travel and visit more in the Old South than did their female counterparts. Still, female relatives also paid their share of visits to New Orleans and the Kenner household. Their shopping trips and visits, particularly before Mary Kenner's death, were occasions of great social gaiety during which the latest styles of clothing and the latest social fads were eagerly sought. So enjoyable were these outings for the Mississippians that both the Minors and Mercers as well as Farrar's daughter and son-in-law eventually bought houses in New Orleans.[65]

At the same time that their acquaintances from Natchez were building and purchasing homes in the Crescent City, the Kenners also moved to a new house. The economic ups and downs of the time, including the decline in cotton and sugar prices, had little negative effect on Kenner's business. His keen instincts for business enabled him to avoid the large-scale economic reverses that the uncertain market conditions caused other businessmen in the community. So successful were Kenner's business undertakings that he was able to purchase 1200 acres from Wade Hampton and add it to Linwood Plantation. In 1822, as the country recovered from a serious economic depression, Kenner constructed an elegant new home for himself and his children in the Vieux Carré. Located on Royal Street and built in the style common at that time, the Kenners' new home was a spacious three-story brick structure with a flat roof and wrought iron railing along the second-story balcony.[66]

Ironically, it was at this time, when the country was recovering from the serious economic problems which he had avoided, that Kenner's prosperity began to decline. John Oldham, a trusted associate, whom William had hired in 1819 with the expectation that his "mercantile knowledge, ability, and activity [would] afford . . . great additional aid in transacting to the best advantage the concerns of our friends," absconded with a large portion of the company's assets and valuables. Despite determined efforts, Kenner was unable to continue to meet the financial obligations of the firm and consequently was forced to declare bankruptcy. However, he was fortunate to have capable legal representation. His attorney, Etienne Mazureau, a state senator and attorney general (1820-1823), was able to save a sufficient portion of Kenner's fortune to allow him and his family to continue to live comfortably. Though heavily mortgaged, both Linwood and Oakland plantations remained in his hands.[67]

Although Kenner survived his financial troubles without losing everything, the experience weighed heavily upon him. A stout, florid gentleman, with mild blue eyes and large spectacles, Kenner had always pursued his business interests energetically. With the near collapse of his life's work, William was determined not only to rebuild his financial holdings but also to pay back anyone who might have lost money from Oldham's scheme. Kenner, however, never obtained his goal of repairing all of the financial damage caused by his employee's dishonesty. In spite of his determined personal effort and months of work, William's endeavor was cut short when the forty-eight-year-old businessman's health unexpectedly failed. In early March, 1824, only days before the wedding of his eldest child Martha, Kenner was stricken with a paralytic stroke. So debilitating was the attack that, for the first twenty-four hours after being stricken, he could not speak. There was considerable doubt whether the once robust and energetic planter and businessman would survive. Fortunately, his determination again proved itself, and by the second day following the seizure William was beginning to attempt to speak. Some progress in his health continued to be made; however, it was evident to his children and his many friends that there would be no complete recovery.[68]

Realizing the seriousness of her father's illness, Martha decided to proceed with her wedding plans so that he would be able to witness her marriage. On the day of the nuptials William, still partially paralyzed on his left side and mentally disordered, requested that the ceremony take place in the morning. This was done. Sadly, by mid-afternoon he had totally lost all recollection of the event and wondered when the marriage was going to take place. Never regaining his presence of mind, William's condition gradually worsened until his death at eleven-thirty on the evening of May 10, 1824.[69]

As was traditional, the burial quickly followed. At five o'clock on the following evening the family's friends and relatives gathered at the Kenner home on Royal Street for the funeral. The burial of his father marked not only a major turning point in young Duncan's development but also his business maturation. Only a youth of eleven years, William Kenner's youngest child now faced a difficult and challenging future. Not only were he and his brothers and sisters faced with a task of managing their father's business holdings, they also were saddled with the difficult responsibility of clearing up the unresolved financial problems which had continued to plague William during his final months. The innocent happy-go-lucky days of a young boy growing up in early New Orleans and on his family's plantations were now, at least partially, stripped away for the reality of life as an orphan having to deal with the death of his father and the harsh demands of the dual role of nineteenth-century businessman and plantation owner.[70]

II

THE GRAND TOUR
AND A GRAND MANOR

With the death of his father, eleven-year-old Duncan Kenner turned to relatives and friends to fill the void created by the tragic loss. Ever since the death of their mother, ten years before that of William Kenner, the Kenner children had relied frequently upon the assistance of relatives and family friends during the sometimes long absences of their father because of business trips. In his will William Kenner made provisions for his estate to be divided equally among his children. However, because of the financial problems which plagued him during his final years, many of William Kenner's holdings remained involved in legal entanglements for some time following his death.[1]

In spite of their father's nagging debts, each of William Kenner's six surviving children eventually received substantial assets from his estate. Relatives and friends of the family, including the able attorney Etienne Mazureau, assisted young Duncan and his siblings in reorganizing their father's holdings. So successful were their efforts that assets of over $277,000 were ultimately shared by William's children. Most of the inheritance was in the form of real estate holdings which included the heavily mortgaged Oakland and Linwood plantations and valuable properties in the Vieux Carré in New Orleans. Cash reserves for the family were secured by the sale of some of the two hundred slaves owned by William at the time of his death.[2]

Records do not reveal any specific details as to the custody and disposition of the Kenner children during the years following their father's death. In view of their ages, the frequent long separations from their father that they had previously experienced when he was away on business, and their extended absences from home for educational purposes, it is possible that the living arrangements of the Kenner children were not seriously altered after William's death. It is likely that they continued with their schooling and, when needed, that they received business and personal guidance and assistance from the family's relatives and friends.

During the months and years following his father's death, circumstances forced young Duncan Kenner to assume many of the responsibilities and duties normally associated with older individuals. A number of decisions on the management and disposition of their numerous holdings had to be made by the Kenner children and their counselors. By observing and being involved in some of the business decisions needed to clear up his father's financial involvements and in deciding the division of the inheritance among the heirs, Duncan learned many valuable lessons which would be of great value to him later in life.

One of the important decisions that Kenner made after his father's death concerned his future education. It was not long before Duncan exhausted the educational offerings which were available to him in the New Orleans area. As a member of the upper class it was always taken for granted by family members that the Kenner boys would receive the best possible education, including studies at the college level. The family's interest in higher education was not uncommon for Southerners of the stature of the Kenners, as demonstrated by the fact that although the title college was loosely used, the antebellum South boasted a larger proportion of college-trained men than any other section of the country.[3]

Because there were only a handful of colleges and universities in the South of the 1820s, many young Southerners went north or to Europe to receive their advanced schooling. Duncan Kenner followed both paths to higher learning. Enrolling at Miami University of Oxford, Ohio, he completed his studies at the school in 1831. Though located in the North, Miami University drew many of its students from the South. Of the 192 students enrolled in the school in 1831, nearly half, including eleven from Louisiana, were from slaveholding states.[4] In Kenner's senior class there were seventeen students. Of these, six were from the South or from border states, with only one other student besides Kenner being a resident of New Orleans. Other classmates of the young Louisianian included Theophilus Lyle Dickey and Charles Anderson. Dickey later served for two years during the Civil War on the staff of General Ulysses S. Grant and for a time as chief of cavalry; Anderson, a sophomore in 1831, later served as governor of Ohio. His brother, Robert, would win fame as the defender of Fort Sumter.[5]

With the classics making up the core of most courses of study, curriculum offerings in the majority of colleges during the nineteenth century were essentially the same. At Miami University students were able to choose a curriculum from one of three departments—Ancient Languages, Mathematics and Natural Science, and Moral Science. Although existing records do not indicate which of the three courses of study Duncan Kenner followed while he was enrolled at the Ohio school, his interest in the law probably led him to the curriculum offered by the Department of Moral Science. Senior level courses in this department included moral philosophy, philosophy of the mind, jurisprudence and the first principles of natural and revealed religion, forensics, political economy, Alexander's Evidence of Divine Revelation, Faber's Difficulties of Infidelity, English, American history, logic, and supplemental courses of French and Spanish.[6]

The cost of attending Miami University was not extravagant. Tuition was $10.00 a term with boarding costing an additional $1.25 per week. Board and lodging together increased the price to $1.50 a week. In comparison, the cost of board and lodging at the University of North Carolina ranged from $13 to $15 a month, with tuition for a year being $30. Although the cost of a college education was beyond the reach of most Southerners, both university tuitions listed above paled in comparison to the $340 a year William Kenner had paid for his daughters to attend Mrs. Mallon's Seminary in Philadelphia.[7]

Duncan Kenner completed his studies at Miami in 1831. As was common practice for young Southern gentlemen of the day, Kenner sailed to Europe shortly thereafter to experience the cultural and social offerings of the Europeans. For over two years between the spring of 1832 and the fall of 1834, he traveled in Western Europe and studied the customs of the people. Often journeying with friends from America, including his sister and her husband, Mr. and Mrs. Currie Duncan, Kenner at times experienced mixed feelings about some of his encounters. For example, though he found the city of Edinburgh to be the "finest city I have seen," he found the eternal city of Rome totally to his dislike. As noted in his diary of April 1, 1834, he "left Rome with but little regret. Independent of its antiquities and its paintings and statues . . . it is at best but a dull and dirty town, with a miserable, poor and filthy population, whose palled features fully attest the unhealthiness of its climate." He experienced similar feelings of vexation during his visit to Monaco. He was amazed over the plight of the people of the little state, whom he pitied—somewhat ironically in view of his feelings toward slavery in America—because they enjoyed "about as much liberty as the negroes and are slaves in all but the name."[8]

Among the more memorable events of Kenner's grand tour was his attendance at a ball given by Baron Rothschild for European royalty which he characterized in his diary as "one of the finest I have ever seen in my life." However, the most unforgettable experience of his stay occurred shortly after he first arrived on the Continent when on June 4, 1834, Kenner and a friend were able to obtain a private meeting in Vienna at the Austrian Palace with the venerable Prince Klemens von Metternich. During the brief meeting the wily veteran politician and the young Southerner spoke mainly about the United States. The former expressed admiration for the young nation and alluded to the great number of Germans who had chosen to leave their homeland to resettle in America.[9]

Upon his return to Louisiana following the completion of his studies in Europe, Kenner settled in New Orleans and returned to his study of the law. He entered the law firm of John Slidell. A friend of William Kenner, Slidell was a shrewd and sophisticated New Yorker who had emigrated to New Orleans in 1819. A Democrat and a man destined to become a major figure in both Louisiana and national politics, Slidell not only gave young Kenner guidance and direction in the practice of law, but his ambition and love of the political game also struck a responsive chord in the young apprentice attorney which would develop and mature further in later years. Many of the skills Kenner acquired during his tutelage with Slidell later served him well in the many business and political battles which awaited him in the future.[10]

Though it consumed much of his time, studying the law was only one of Kenner's interests. Having inherited a large amount of valuable real estate from his father, his landholdings demanded much of his attention. In addition to the valuable real estate they inherited, Duncan and his brothers also had acquired much of their father's considerable business prowess. This was particularly true in the area of real estate acquisition and management. At first with the advice of family friends and relatives and later on their own, the Kenner brothers made impressive gains in the real estate market.[11]

The majority of Duncan Kenner's most valuable landholdings were acquired at the time of his father's death. When William Kenner's sizable holdings were divided equally among his children, the Kenner brothers concentrated their interest on their father's two sugar plantations, Oakland in Jefferson Parish and Linwood in Ascension Parish. The ambitious young men were anxious to expand their own acreage. Since neither plantation was sufficiently large to satisfy the needs of the four men, as soon as they were financially able they began to acquire lands adjacent to their properties.[12]

Gradually the Kenners consolidated their holdings. The Kenner girls did not have much interest in the plantations and were content to transfer their inherited portions to their brothers. The Kenners also decided that it would be beneficial if they reorganized their plantation interests. Thus, the two eldest sons, Stephen Minor and William Butler, concentrated their efforts on the sugar lands in Jefferson Parish, with their holdings being divided into two plantations. William Butler acquired the family estate at Oakland, and Stephen Minor established his Belle Grove Plantation on family-owned land downriver and adjacent to his brother's property. Minor, as he was called, would later use part of his estate plus lands obtained from a later acquisition of the neighboring Pasture Plantation to establish the town of Kennerville, which eventually expanded to become the city of Kenner.[13]

Being only a year apart in age, the two youngest of William Kenner's sons were much attached to one another. Up until the time that Duncan went away for his schooling, the two young men did almost everything together including attending school, making long visits with family friends and relatives, and, as young entrepreneurial businessmen, purchasing property. Hence, George and Duncan Kenner united to develop the holdings they had inherited at Linwood Plantation in Ascension Parish.[14]

Duncan Kenner's interest in his landholdings and the crops he grew on them gradually consumed more and more of his time and energy. Eventually, as the profits from the production of sugar increased, he decided to leave Slidell's law firm and to concentrate his energies on his estate in Ascension Parish. Located on the east bank, then usually referred to as the left bank, of the Mississippi River approximately seven miles above and across the river from the town of Donaldsonville, Linwood Plantation was originally part of the Minor family holdings in Louisiana. William Kenner, Theophilus and Philip Minor, were among the first to work the area. With William Kenner's death and the subsequent consolidation of their real estate holdings by the Kenner brothers, ownership of the large Linwood tract passed to George and Duncan and Philip Minor. Desiring to solidify their holdings even further, the two young Kenner men agreed with their great uncle to divide formally the tract, with Minor taking the upper half and with the lower half of slightly over 2,429 acres going to George and Duncan Kenner.[15]

With their holdings consolidated, these two Kenner brothers turned their efforts to increasing the productivity and profitability of their lands. At the time southeastern Louisiana, particularly the areas along the Mississippi River and Bayou Lafourche, was undergoing a transformation from diversified crop production to concentration upon the production of a single commodity— sugarcane. The area's principal settlements were situated along the borders of major waterways. Here the lands were extremely fertile and had been used for years to produce a variety of products, including oranges, figs, peaches, plums, indigo, cotton, and some sugarcane. As a consequence of insect-induced failures of the indigo and cotton crops and the simultaneous increase in sugar prices, most of the productive lands of the region were converted to the cultivation of cane and the production of sugar. The expansion of the sugar economy was so rapid that the number of sugar plantations in the state jumped from 300 in 1827 to over 1500 in 1849.[16]

William Kenner had been among the earliest to realize the economic potential of the cane crop. His efforts to be in the forefront of the cane industry had turned his Oakland and Linwood properties into lucrative financial ventures. Duncan and George Kenner were determined to follow in their father's footsteps. To do so required a great amount of capital because only individuals of considerable wealth could afford to acquire, outfit, and stock a plantation of notable size. An inhabitant of St. Martin Parish reported in 1830 that a 1,250-acre sugar plantation, approximately half the size of the Kenner's Ascension Parish tract, required about $90,000 in capital. Fortunately for the two Kenners, their father's investments in the production of sugar at Linwood spared them the necessity of having to outfit their plantation from scratch. However, their efforts to bring improvements to the site and to add to its size were such that the two brothers had to pool their resources to accomplish their goals.[17]

Although they were very close, the partnership between Duncan and George Kenner was only temporary. Having renamed their share of the Linwood tract "Ashland," in honor of Henry Clay's home, the two brothers worked together to improve their holdings. Their joint effort ended in March, 1844, when Duncan paid George $18,200 for his portion of the property. The dissolution of shared endeavor was on friendly terms. It was George's desire to marry and establish a family which led to the two men ending their longstanding partnership. George Kenner met and married Charlotte Jones, a member of a wealthy Cincinnati, Ohio, family. The opportunity of doing business with his new in-laws along with his wife's desires to remain near her family prompted George to give up his share of Ashland. After selling out in Louisiana, George and his new bride returned to the Cincinnati area where they purchased part of a Kentucky estate belonging to Charlotte's half-brother Israel Ludlow. However, when the sugar culture in Texas began to show promise shortly after that area was admitted to the Union, George acquired a tract of land on the Caney River in Matagorda County and again attempted the growing of cane. Unfortunately, his efforts met with only limited success. When he died in 1852 his Texas holdings were yielding only 125 hogsheads of the product.[18]

Duncan Kenner met and married his wife, Nanine Bringier, even before his older brother George married. Before their marriages the two brothers shared residence in whatever structure existed at the Ascension Parish plantation from the time their father had owned the property. When he and his fiancée decided to marry in 1839, Duncan made the decision to give his new bride a home of which she would be proud. A member of the well-to-do Bringier family, Nanine had always been accustomed to a standard of living few could match. Despite the impressive stature of his in-laws, the proud and self-confident twenty-six-year-old bridegroom resolved to build a house second to no other dwelling existing in Louisiana's cane country.[19]

Construction on their grand home started even before Duncan and Nanine's nuptials. At the time of the wedding in early June, 1839, the foundation and part of the first story had been built. Though Nanine's family's estates were only a short distance downriver from the construction site, the young couple preferred to live at the site of their future home instead of with Nanine's family. They set up housekeeping in a small house near the lower line of the plantation's front pasture. Located next to a fine live oak tree near the road which ran alongside the levee bordering the Mississippi River, the little home was comfortable and aptly suited the couple's needs during their first months of marriage. As they watched their new home being constructed, Nanine and Duncan carefully supervised the work so that everything that was done met their specifications. Even when the mansion became inhabitable, Nanine preferred to remain in her temporary quarters until the grand house was finished and furnished in every particular.[20]

The care and attention put into the construction of the Kenner home was not uncommon. For besides the fact that the structure was an expensive investment, it symbolized much more. To most planters their home served as the showpiece of their estate; it was the most visible symbol of an individual's wealth and status. Though the style and size of Southern mansions varied from region to region and period to period, each dwelling was usually as impressive and lavish a monument as the owner could afford.[21]

In the sugar-growing region of South Louisiana which stretched along the banks of the region's many streams, particularly the Mississippi River and Bayous Lafourche and Teche, there existed a large concentration of majestic and beautiful plantation homes which reflected the gracious life that the region's planter society enjoyed. For the most part, the design of the houses followed the Louisiana Classic style of architecture which usually took the form of Greek Revival styling modified by important characteristics peculiar to Louisiana. Usually great rounded brick columns surrounded the dwellings with broad encircling verandas extending from the pillars to the house, this presenting an imposing facade. The structures were more often than not topped with hipped and dormered roofs. The floor plans of these mansions followed simple patterns, usually a wide central hall flanked by large rooms, an arrangement repeated on the second floor. Designed to provide maximum comfort to the residents in the hot and humid climate of South Louisiana, the grand manor of the sugar grower was essentially functional.[22]

To properly plan and design their showpiece dwellings, plantation owners often turned to architects for assistance. Because the title of "architect" had little legal meaning until relatively recent times, anyone wishing to do so could call himself an architect. Hence, the title was seldom used in the Old South. The artisans who sold their services to the planters and assisted in the construction of the great houses were usually called by terms which denoted their particular skill, such as "carpenter" or "surveyor." Of the individuals who actually used the title architect, there were a few whose work stood out from others who plied the trade. Most noted among these individuals were those exponents of the popular modified Greek Revival style of architecture, including Henry Howard, Charles and James Dakin, and the most famous of all, James Gallier and his son, James Gallier, Jr.[23]

There is little doubt that Duncan Kenner, in his determination to build a grand home, turned to a professional for assistance. However, the identity of the designer of Ashland remains uncertain. Nearly every author who has written on the subject gives credit for the work to either James Gallier or his son. Despite the popularity of the notion of the Gallier involvement in the building, the designer's identity remains elusive. The Gallier speculations are based largely upon his family's tradition that James Gallier did the house. Since practically every other structure in South Louisiana with similar columns has been attributed to Gallier, this is hardly reliable evidence. For example, although Belle Grove Plantation for years was credited to James Gallier, it is now known that the structure was the work of Henry Howard, the architect of both Woodlawn and Madewood plantation houses.

Contradicting the argument in support of the Gallier influence on Ashland is the fact that his and his son's styles were usually dissimilar to that found at the Kenner home. Although at least one drawing by Gallier exists which shows characteristics similar to Ashland, the square columns and details of the Kenner plantation are unlike anything done by Gallier in the region. Similarly, since James Gallier, Jr., was only fourteen years old when the mansion was completed, it is fairly certain that he was not its designer.[24]

Though the evidence does not positively eliminate James Gallier as the designer of Ashland, a more plausible candidate for the role is another pioneer architect of the region, James Dakin. There is circumstantial evidence which points to Dakin as Kenner's architect at Ashland. The dwelling's large square columns and massive entablature, the assemblage supported by the columns are more characteristic of the New York Greek Revival style of architecture than the more common Louisiana Classic style discussed above. This method of design is similar to buildings constructed and drawn by Dakin and his brother Charles. At the time of construction the columns of the plantation were very similar to those of the Arsenal Building in New Orleans and to the side pilaster treatment of the Presbyterian Church in Troy, New York. Both of these structures were completed by Dakin before the construction of Ashland was commenced in 1839. Dakin's later work, including the Old State Capitol in Baton Rouge, frequently included design characteristics not unlike those of Ashland. Furthermore, it is known that at the time of his death in June, 1839, Charles Dakin was staying in Ascension Parish even though his residence was in New Orleans. It is possible that his absence from the city was due to the fact that he was supervising a job for the Dakin firm. This job may have been the construction of Ashland.[25]

Arthur Scully, James Dakin's biographer, supports the contention that Dakin was the designer of Ashland with the observation that Nanine

Kenner's father, Michel Doradou Bringier, did considerable business with the firm of Dakin and Dakin. Several large checks to the two brothers from Bringier indicate that they designed the Bringier family plantation mansions. Furthermore, a story persists among the Bringier descendants that Michel Bringier gave each of his six daughters a new house as a wedding present. Perhaps Ashland was such a gift. Checks from Bringier to Dakin and Dakin are dated 1839, 1840, and 1841, the years that the Kenner home was under construction.[26]

Further confusion regarding the identity of the architect of Ashland can be found by examining the debates of the Louisiana senate in 1847. At that time the legislative body was debating the question of hiring an architect to design the new capitol in Baton Rouge. The new Louisiana Constitution of 1845 had transferred the seat of government to that city. Shortly afterwards, a commission was appointed by the governor to oversee the construction of the capitol. When the commission recommended to the legislature that James Dakin be hired to design the building, strong opposition arose from some members of the law-making body. Chief antagonist to the appointment of Dakin was Duncan Kenner, at that time a member of the senate. With two of the three members of the governor's capitol commission members of the Whig party, Kenner's political party, it is unlikely that his criticisms were based on partisan politics. Kenner attacked the project for its potential cost overruns and luxurious designs and suggested that additional commissioners be appointed to supervise the building's construction and thus eliminate the need for an architect. Supporters of Dakin quickly denounced Kenner's efforts as "a mere introductory scene in a ludicrous farce."[27]

Several days later when the question was again discussed by the senate, the issue of an appropriate salary for the architect was broached. Kenner immediately renewed his criticism of the project with an attack on architects in general and Dakin in particular. When an amount was suggested for the salary, Kenner pointed out that a state supreme court justice received an equal amount and questioned whether an architect deserved a salary on a par with that of a state judge. When the debate moved to the question of hiring Dakin, Kenner launched a blistering attack on the designer, claiming that "this cabinet man should be set aside for one of sound practical knowledge who understands the simple fact of putting brick and mortar together.[28]

Kenner's opposition to Dakin met with only limited success. Although the architect's salary was drastically reduced, Dakin was given the job of designing the new capitol. Kenner's vicious attack upon the architect would seem out of place against someone who designed one of his most precious possessions. Such comments would have adversely reflected upon the quality of his own home. Furthermore, considering the invidious nature of the debate, if Kenner's criticisms of Dakin had been based upon some parting of the ways over a spoiled business arrangement between the two men, it is probable that Kenner's opponents would have used this information to counter his attack on Dakin. Thus, despite some interesting possibilities, the identity of the designer of the Ashland plantation house remains an uncertainty.

Once ground was broken for the house, construction continued at a steady pace. Whereas individuality of design and appearance varied among the grand homes of the region, construction techniques were fairly similar. To build a dwelling such as Ashland required a varied labor source. To meet the demand, contractors often owned highly skilled and valued slaves who, with a few white mechanics, performed the technical and skilled jobs at the construction site. These craftsmen were assisted by the planter's own unskilled slave labor force. The slaves were used everywhere at the site as laborers and to perform simple crafts, including forming the lumber and molding the many bricks which were needed in the plantation's construction.[29]

As was the general practice, materials for the construction of the grand manor were obtained almost entirely from local sources. Most builders used hard-heart pine and cypress for their lumber needs with the latter being preferred by the workmen at the Kenner home site. Very little iron was used in the construction. Except for hinges, door knobs, gutters, and locks, which were imported either from the North or Europe, Ashland was constructed without extensive use of iron. Even the fastening of lumber was done, for the most part, by means of wooden pegs. In addition to the lumber being produced at the Ashland site, the many thousands of bricks used in the construction of the building were produced on the plantation.[30]

Builders of Louisiana mansions relied on the prevalent construction procedures to form the walls of the buildings. Early structures were built of heavy hand-hewn cypress framing arranged in vertical angles extending from sills to ceiling plates. The framing was then packed with mud mixed with moss. Called *bousillage entre poteaux*, the mix was allowed to harden and was then either plastered or boarded on its sides. The second popular method used was similar to the first. Instead of the mud and moss mixture to pack the walls, bricks were placed between the hewn framework. This *briquette entre poteaux* process was also plastered over and was more popular with later homes. However, the builders of Ashland chose neither of these common techniques. No cypress supports, except for an all-wood wall which contains sliding doors, have ever been located in the structure's interior and exterior walls. The walls of Ashland are simply solid brick. Approximately sixteen inches thick, the massive masonry walls of the stately structure were all plastered. To enhance the aesthetics of the new home, the plaster on the exterior walls is marked off in fifty-six by eighteen inch ashlar courses.[31]

Though worn by years of wear and tear and with the exception of a relatively new metal roof, Ashland remains today much the way it appeared at the time of its construction. With each side of the building having eight enormous pillars of brick and stucco reaching thirty feet into the air, the four facades of the house are all alike. The twenty-eight large square columns support at their midpoint a twelve-foot gallery, which is set off by the customary simple wooden balustrade. Capping off the large pillars is an exceptionally heavy entablature. The hipped roof is unlike those found on most Louisiana plantations because it was built with only a forty-degree pitch so that it would be hidden by the large entablature and not be seen from the ground. As originally constructed, the roof was covered with either cypress or slate shingles and had four dormers which provided light and ventilation to the attic and access to the roof.[32]

The two-story structure is laid out in the form of a perfect square with each side sixty feet long. Unlike the exterior of the house with its many unique design characteristics, the interior design of the building is basic and not unlike other mansions constructed at the time. Large doorways decorated by sidelights, transoms, and pilasters open to a twelve-foot-wide central hall which runs the length of the building. The corridor is flanked on either side by three rooms, the four larger of which measured twenty-feet square. Two of these rooms on the right side of the house were used by the Kenners as parlors and the two on the opposite side of the building as the family's library and dining room. A beautiful spiral staircase with solid cypress steps and hand-carved mahogany balustrades completes the plan of the mansion's first floor.[33]

As was occasionally the practice in the plantation homes of the Old South, the plan of the second floor of the Kenner house is basically the same as that of the first. The only differences between the two levels relate to the original use of the rooms on the second floor as bedrooms. As such, there are no sliding doors dividing rooms as are used on the lower level of the house. Also, the twelve-foot ceilings of the second floor are two feet lower than the fourteen-foot ones of the mansion's first level. As on the lower floor of the house, a large hallway runs the length of the house and connects two identical, simply decorated entrances. The portals of the two levels open to broad upper and lower verandas which extend out twelve feet from the walls.[34]

Adaptability to climate was a major concern for the designers of plantation mansions. The semitropical climate of South Louisiana made it imperative for both health and comfort that the region's contractors design their structures to provide as much protection from the adverse weather conditions as possible. Among the common techniques used by builders and incorporated into the construction of Ashland were solid thick walls as well as breezy outdoor living space. Since the winters were usually short and mild and the summers long and hot, the builders of the Kenners' home made extensive use of windows. Extending down to the floor, the large windows facilitated the flow of air through the dwelling and were often used interchangeably with the doors as passageways in and out of the house. With only a moderate need for heating facilities, most planters gave only slight architectural emphasis to their home's fireplaces and chimneys. However, this was not the case with Kenner and his design for Ashland. The eight main rooms of the building were all enhanced with fireplaces surrounded by elegant black Italian marble mantels.[35]

The exterior appearance of Ashland and its surrounding grounds followed the simpler classic elements of design which characterized the interior of the house. Planters enjoyed the use of color in their homes, and many of the grand structures with stuccoed walls were decorated with brilliant colors. Tinting the walls a light lemon, the shutters of the large windows greenish-blue, and the pillars and entablature white, Kenner and his builders took a simpler approach to the popular trend of brightly colored homes. The creators of Ashland also differed slightly from their counterparts in the way the plantation's grounds were laid out. The house was situated several hundred yards from the banks of the Mississippi River, with a broad meadow stretching from the front of the house to the levee. Unencumbered by large trees, this open space gave the inhabitants of the house a grand panorama of the river and the many vessels that plied its turgid waters. Conversely, the site of Ashland standing temple-like in the center of a green plain and backed with huge trees was one of the most stunning scenes experienced by individuals traveling on the lower Mississippi.[36]

With its live-oak alleys situated to the rear of the mansion, Ashland's setting differed from most other Louisiana plantation homes where the oaks were usually located in the front of the home. In addition to the large oaks, most planters preferred to surround their homes with various other types of greenery. Blooming shrubs, flowering magnolia trees, cedars, and live oak trees were all commonly found on the sugar estates of South Louisiana. Many of these plants were also used by the Kenners to beautify the grounds at Ashland.[37]

The typical popular conception of a plantation home carries the connotation of a grand structure adorned with beautifully landscaped gardens. However, the propensity of the Kenners and other sugar planters to landscape the grounds around their homes was, for the time, looked upon as a rather unique custom by residents of other areas of the country. New Englanders preferred a more formal, clipped, and restrained style of landscaping. On the other hand, most other Southerners seldom landscaped their homes at all. The Southern practice of giving livestock free range made the maintenance of a flower garden and the care of shrubbery a trying task. Furthermore, trees and shrubbery around a house were considered to be unhealthy by many Southerners. For example, *The Southern Cultivator*, as late as 1857, discussed a man who had lost his wife and three small children by a disease caused by barren mulberry trees which grew thickly in his yard.[38]

Though the mansion and its surrounding greenery served as the centerpiece of the plantation, it was just one of many structures on the estate. As a commodity-producing agricultural business unit with a large work force, the Southern plantation typically included a variety of other buildings. Among the accessory structures at Ashland was the kitchen. As was the practice on most plantations, this half-brick and half-frame building was located a few feet away from the main structure so that the heat, noise, and odors of this little building would not invade the main structure. Additionally, there was a crenelated two-story brick pigeonnier, a carriage house, offices, blacksmithies, hospital, overseer's house, and a small cottage, which housed the trainer of Kenner's race horses.[39]

Though there were at least three wells on the estate to supply water, old photographs reveal that most water for the mansion was obtained in the region's traditional method of collecting run-off rainwater from the roof of the main house in a large cistern. Besides the structures and greenery which were located on the property, there were broad fields for growing the cash crop as well as smaller plots for special purposes, including a vegetable garden, a deer lot, a large chicken yard, and a paddock. A large fruit and pecan orchard, as well as a horse racetrack located not far from the main house, completed the layout of the estate.[40]

Ashland was not the Kenners' only residence. As his father had done, Duncan Kenner continued to maintain a place of residence in New Orleans even after the construction of his mansion in Ascension Parish. Many of the planters of the river parishes followed the same practice. Their proximity to the Mississippi River provided them with a quick and economical means of transportation back and forth to the Crescent City. Few details are known about the Kenners' antebellum town home except that it was a large structure and that the family spent a considerable amount of time visiting it.

In agricultural civilizations such as existed in the antebellum South, the country mansion was of far greater importance than the town home. Not only was the planter's home frequently a magnificent structure resplendently designed and furnished, it was also the social and cultural pivot of the planter's world. It served as a tangible statement by the agrarian aristocrat of his position in the society of the Old South. So it was with Duncan Kenner and his beloved Ashland. When construction was finally finished after two years of labor, the event was marked with a lavish ball which served to demonstrate to all the size and splendor of the Kenners' new home and its claim as one of the area's most celebrated structures. Similarly, the housewarming was indicative of Duncan's rise to prominence. For as Ashland assumed its place as one of the most prominent homes of the time, the event also signaled Kenner's emergence, at twenty-eight years of age, as a leading member of the area's agrarian elite.[41]

III

THE ESTATE

Just as the manor house served as the social and cultural pivot of the plantation, the production of sugar was the economic focal point of Ashland. All other activities of those who lived and worked on the estates of the region were secondary to their efforts to produce a successful cane crop. Because of the nature of the crop there was seldom an idle time on the well-managed sugar estate of the period. When the crop itself did not require attention, there were many other related duties which kept all hands quite busy throughout the year.[1]

On most plantations the major planting season for cane was in late December or early January. This varied depending upon the end of the grinding season which preceded the planting. On some of the larger farms, including Ashland, where the labor force was sufficient, some cane was planted in the fall and served as seed cane for future crops. In order to plant the cane considerable effort went into preparing the soil. Soon after the harvesting of the previous crop and when the weather permitted, the ground for the new crop was thoroughly plowed. Deep furrows several feet apart were cut to create rows, and the seed cane was placed lengthwise in them and covered with several inches of soil. Because of the nature of the crop, planters did not have to replant all of their fields every year. A second- or even third-year crop could be obtained from rejuvenated growth from the stubble left after the first year's crop was harvested. Techniques of cultivation varied widely from year to year and from planter to planter. However, the character of the preceding winter primarily determined whether the stubble might be profitably used another year. Unlike the planters of the West Indies, it was extremely rare for a planter in the South to use the same plants, or ratoons, for more than three seasons. Though records are skimpy for Ashland, it appears that Kenner usually replanted half of his fields each year. For example, in 1852 his overseer reported that there were 266 acres of "solid cane" and 300 acres of ratoons planted.[2]

The cane planting was a laborious task which consumed a large amount of time and effort on the plantation. Usually completed by early March, the job was sometimes extended because of poor weather conditions, including everything from monsoon-like rains to bitter cold and, on rare occasions, even snow. A cold wave in 1852 brought extremely trying conditions to the residents of South Louisiana and had the unusual effect of putting a temporary stop to nearly all the work at Ashland. On January 13 of that year the region experienced an unprecedented snowfall of four inches which stayed on the ground for three days before melting. To compound problems, less than a week after the snow, the area was hit with another cold snap even worse than the first. W. G. Wade, Kenner's overseer at Ashland, was so taken aback by the chill that he labeled the wintry blast as being the "coldest day that was saw in Louisiana." Despite the frosty conditions of this second front, the slaves were ordered into the fields to continue their work.[3]

When the planting of the cane was completed, other work was undertaken until the crop was ready for cultivation. Among the most common tasks assigned to the field hands at this time was the repairing of the estate's roads, levees, and wharf. Another important task which was usually addressed at this time was the cleaning of the plantation's many ditches. Proper drainage was a major factor in the production of a successful sugar crop. Therefore, to insure that all surplus water was rapidly carried away and not allowed to damage the growing cane by damp rot, all plantation ditches were thoroughly cleaned on a regular basis.[4]

It was also common practice at this time of the year to take some rudimentary steps to fertilize the soil. After a crop was harvested, great quantities of leaves and unused joints remained in the fields. This trash was usually left on the ground throughout the winter months to protect the stubble cane from the weather. In the early spring when it became necessary to remove the trash because of the needs of the new crop, Kenner had his workers burn the rubbish. Often done at night, these fires illuminated the sky in a picturesque glow which one observer of the event at another estate called "the most sublime sight that I have ever beheld." The ashes from these burnings were then relied upon to add to the fertility of the soil.[5]

March and April marked the period when cultivation of the cane crop began in earnest. Field hands were set to work plowing and hoeing to keep the cane free of grass and weeds and to keep the soil loose to encourage the rapid growth of the young cane plants. Depending upon the variety of cane used, plant growth varied considerably. The newly planted cane usually grew more rapidly than the stubble and had to be cultivated sooner. Cultivating the fields remained the main interest on the sugar estate throughout the spring until the crop was laid by around the middle of the summer. Until this took place, the rows had to be plowed and hoed approximately every two weeks. These activities had to be repeated five or more times before the crops were laid by. One other task remained before the crop could be laid by. This was the ridging up of rows in such a manner that any water which might accumulate during the summer rainy season would rapidly drain away.[6]

Often the demands of the cane crop could be met by only a portion of the plantation's work force. This, however, did not result in the slackening of work assignments for the estate's slaves. There were always other jobs on Ashland to keep the hands busy. Though sugarcane was the principal crop, it was by no means the only one cultivated on the property. Large amounts of sweet potatoes, hay, Irish potatoes, and, most important of all the auxiliary crops, corn, were grown primarily for consumption on the plantation. Beginning in early March and followed by successive plantings until midsummer, the farm hands at Ashland planted corn in nearly every available plot of open land. So determined was Kenner to produce enough corn to meet the needs of the plantation that on at least one occasion he even had it planted around his beloved racetrack. At the same time that the corn crop was cultivated, peas were also planted, sometimes even between the rows of corn so that the soil could be enriched for the important food crop.[7]

Through the steamy months of the Louisiana summer, work continued to make everything ready for the fall harvest and grinding season. Repairs were made on plantation buildings and machinery, ditching continued, as did the never-ending efforts to keep the weeds under control. Another time-consuming task for Ashland's slaves was the making of bricks. With all hands engaged in that endeavor, the work force at the estate was able to make 8,500 bricks in a single work day.[8]

An adequate fuel supply for the upcoming grinding season and winter was another critical need which had to be addressed. Whenever the growing crops did not need attention or the weather made work in the fields impossible, Kenner had his gangs collecting the needed fuel. There were two principal sources for the wood fuel consumed at Ashland. One was the driftwood which was found in abundance along the levee which held back the waters of the Mississippi River. This was particularly true during the early summer following the ebbing of the river after its late spring crest. The other major source of wood for the plantation was the vast forest which covered the swamp in the rear of the estate.[9]

August and September at Ashland was a time of final preparations for the fall harvest season. The various vegetables planted on the plots around the plantation had to be gathered, and fodder for the estate's stock had to be stored in the barns. Much of the hay used on the farm was obtained from the waste lands at the rear of the property. Some additional plowing also took place at this time to clear the areas where the vegetables had grown and to prepare the spaces for the upcoming cane-planting season.[10]

October marked the beginning of the harvest season and the busiest time of all for the residents of Ashland. From that time until the sugar-making process was completed in late December or early January, there were no idle hands and very little free time for the inhabitants of the Kenner estate. Planters preferred to leave the cane they intended to mill in the field as long as possible so that its saccharine content would increase and thus produce more sugar. Since cane intended to be used as seed did not have to stand that long in the field, the plots where it was grown were usually the first areas to be harvested. After being cut, the seed cane was stored in large mats to protect it from the weather and the possible danger of freezing. During these early days of the harvest at Ashland, when the hands had not yet started cutting the mill cane, Kenner usually put his workers to planting some of the seed crop for the next season's harvest.[11]

To insure a constant supply of cane for the mill, the slaves were put to work cutting the cane in the fields three or four days before the actual grinding process got under way. Once begun, every effort was made to proceed as quickly as possible towards the completion of the project. Grinding usually continued day and night until all of the crop was manufactured. Typically at Ashland on the days that the mill and kettle were operating, there would be forty or fifty hands in the fields cutting the cane, while still others used six carts and wagons to haul the harvested crop to the mill.[12]

Harvesting was the most expensive and bothersome aspect in the production of sugar. The entire crop had to be cut within a period of ninety days or run the risk of suffering devastating losses from an early-winter cold snap. The mill generally set the pace for the cutters. However, with the approach of a threatening cold front, all available hands were ordered into the fields to protect the cane against loss from freezing. This was done by a procedure known as windrowing in which the crop was protected by cutting it, laying it down in the furrows between the ridges in the field, and covering it with the trash in the field. Usually performed in a state of urgency, windrowing efforts often continued around the clock. One such exercise took place during late November, 1852, when the threat of a severe cold snap forced Kenner to send his workers into the fields, where they labored in the cold past midnight windrowing the crop.[13]

The nature of the sugar-manufacturing process discouraged the use of centrally located custom mills, with the consequence that every plantation of any size had its own sugarhouse. At Ashland, not unlike most of the other large estates of the region, the sugarhouse was located near the center of the property not far from the slave quarters. (By 1859 a second sugarhouse was added nearby.) This site was chosen to shorten the distance from the various fields where the cane was grown, which, in turn, facilitated the work of supplying the harvested crop to the mill during the grinding season. The facilities were also located next to the estate's main road so that the finished product could be moved to the pier on the river for shipment elsewhere. As with most sugarhouses in South Louisiana the Ashland plants were constructed largely of wood. A believer in doing things first class, Kenner extensively used bricks manufactured on the estate to add to the strength and appearance of his sugarhouses. When completed, the structures were second only to the manor house in size and impressiveness on the estate.[14]

At the sugarhouse as much juice as possible was extracted from the cane by passing the crop through a series of rollers. Once collected, the juice ran into a kettle where it was processed into sugar. Technology gradually improved the sugar-making process used by the area's sugar planters. Before 1830 planters used an open kettle procedure to make the product. From that date on, technology, including the vacuum pan, greatly improved the sugar manufacturing process. The vacuum pan process was refined further in 1843 by a French-educated black named Norbert Rillieux. His apparatus needed less labor and fuel than the older methods by using the vapor of one kettle to heat another and improved both the quality and quantity of the sugar.[15]

The equipment needed to properly outfit a sugarhouse was among the most expensive items a planter had to obtain for his estate. When first introduced to the region a planter could outfit his mill with a vacuum pan for under $10,000. As improvements were added to the equipment the cost of outfitting a sugarhouse greatly increased, with some of the larger units costing over $100,000. However, the average cost of equipping a sugarhouse was $50,000.

The equipment at Ashland consisted of a large grinder and vacuum pan which Kenner estimated weighed nearly fifty-two tons. The cost of the sugar-making equipment alone, without the price of the building or other tools and equipment needed to produce the sugar, was $7,500. So impressive was the machinery Kenner chose for Ashland that his father-in-law, Michel Doradou Bringier, one of the most prosperous planters in the region and the proprietor of the neighboring Hermitage Plantation, ordered one exactly like it because, as Kenner later wrote, the "mills and engines are the best." Commenting in a letter to William Minor in Natchez that although his machinery cost more than that of others, Kenner noted that it was worth it because "they are more substantial [with] more iron out and in and [are] better finished." Kenner continued to upgrade his methods of production. As noted above, a second sugar mill equipped with the updated Rillieux apparatus was added to the estate.[16]

Besides the expensive machinery which was needed to outfit the sugarhouse, sugar planting required a large investment in sundry other items, including livestock, slaves, and farm implements. For example, a partial listing of the farm utensils used on Ashland included plows, carts, cultivators, spades, shovels, sickles, a mowing machine, tarpaulins, hay forks, axes, scythes, and dirt scrapers. In addition to the assortment of farm implements needed to keep an estate operating, a varied group of animals also was an essential component of plantation life. A livestock inventory made in July, 1852, by Ashland's overseer revealed the following: 20 work horses, 16 colts, 83 work mules, 12 cows, 12 calves, 6 pigs, 340 sheep, and 78 oxen.[17]

As on most large agricultural operations of the time, horses, oxen, and mules were the most important work animals in the antebellum sugar region. Though the horse played an important role in the work scheme of the sugar plantation, in the early nineteenth century the ox was the prevailing draft animal. The ox was well suited for the heavy tasks of plowing, hauling heavy loads, and clearing out stumps which were everyday activities on the antebellum plantation. Many planters gradually replaced their oxen with mules. Kenner, however, continued to rely on the oxen to make up approximately one-half of his draught animal herd at Ashland. The toilsome tasks which these animals had to perform during cultivation and harvesting often made replacement necessary. Costing upwards of $180 to $200 each to replace, it is not surprising that W. G. Wade boasted in his journal in July, 1852, that despite a severe winter the mules and oxen at Ashland "looked remarkably well," and Kenner would not have to buy a horse, mule, or ox because not a single animal had been lost that year.[18]

In order to operate his plantation successfully, the sugar planter had to maintain a large work force. Negro slaves furnished most of the labor on sugar plantations, which required a much larger proportion of prime field hands than were needed on most other types of large agricultural units, including cotton plantations. In 1840 Ashland had a working force of 117 slaves, of whom 100 were reported as engaged in agriculture. Ten years later the number of slaves owned by Kenner had more than doubled to 125 male and 138 female slaves for a total of 263 workers. Like other planters, Kenner continually sought to increase his labor force. So successful was he that by 1860, with a total of 473 hands, he was the eleventh largest owner in Louisiana and one of the largest slaveholders in the country, being one of the relatively small number of individuals in the nation that year to own nearly 500 slaves.[19]

One factor which contributed to the great increase in the size of the Ashland labor force between 1850 and 1860 was the death of George Kenner. At the time of his death in 1853, George Kenner was attempting to establish a sugar plantation in Matagorda County in southern Texas. Though never really successful, George had acquired a sizeable slave force. The exact number is not known; however, when Duncan obtained these laborers either by inheritance or by purchase from his brother's estate, they formed a large enough body that he was able to set them up as a separate work force. Kenner had his workers construct a row of brick quarters near the edge of his Ashland property for his newly acquired Texan slaves. These hands were managed and employed separately from the plantation's main work force and, though never officially listed as such, the land they worked was generally called the "Texas" plantation.[20]

The rapid expansion of the sugar industry led to an increased demand for slaves. With few exceptions, planters in the region followed Kenner's example and continually worked to expand their operations throughout the antebellum period. Seldom was there a surplus of field hands on the slave market. The increased demand also brought about a rapid increase in the prices planters were forced to pay to obtain additions to their labor forces. Sugar planters in Louisiana usually purchased their Negroes on the New Orleans market. Prices varied from about $600 for a prime field hand at the end of the 1820s to $1200 to $1500 in the 1850s. Skilled blacks such as carpenters and blacksmiths brought even higher prices, with some selling for as much as $2,000 to $3,000 in the period shortly before the secession of the Southern states. With such a demand, it was rare, except as a disciplinary measure, for a sugar planter to sell any of his slaves.[21]

In addition to those slaves bought on the open market, planters were able to add to their labor force through the natural reproduction of their slave population. This was a somewhat unique phenomenon for a slave society. In his study of the nation's sugar industry, historian J. Carlyle Sitterson found that on most plantations the population more than reproduced itself. This appears to have been the situation at Ashland. Overseer Wade recorded in his journal in July, 1852, that since January of that year there had been ten births on the plantation. During the same period he listed the deaths of three Negroes, including Paris from dropsy, Tizi from consumption, and "Jakes child" from influenza. Kenner's manager concluded his observations with the comment that between January 1, 1845, and January 1, 1852, "there has been eighty-six births and forty-seven of them is now dead." Though these figures support the contention that the birthrate of the slaves on the typical sugar estate outstripped the number of deaths, they also reveal the devastating mortality rate of slave children at the Kenner estate. With nearly fifty-five percent of the slave children of Ashland dying before their seventh birthday, the young Negroes of the Kenner plantation experienced a death rate not unlike many of their counterparts on other estates. Such devastating mortality rates were found by Robert W. Fogel and Stanley L. Engerman in their study, *Time on the Cross*, to be the norm. Though they concentrated their study only on infants—those less than a year old—the two cliometricians concluded that the average mortality rate of slave infants in the plantation South in 1850 was 183 for every 1000 births or eighteen percent of the newborns during only the very first year following birth.[22]

Because of the sparseness of primary materials on the subject, it is not possible to define with certainty the reasons for the high child mortality rate experienced by the Ashland slave population. Similarly, except for the vague statements that there was little evidence that masters neglected the care of infants and that the South was less healthy than the North, Fogel and Engerman also failed to identify definitive reasons for the high infant mortality rate on the South's plantations. Obviously, like free infants, slave deaths during the early years of life were commonly caused by diseases such as whooping cough, pneumonia, cholera, and disorders of the gastrointestinal system. Of the two slave children deaths mentioned by Kenner's overseer W. G. Wade, in his journal for 1852, "Aliza's child" was listed as dying from inflammation of the chest, and the cause of death for "Jakes child" was recorded as influenza. Contributing to the survival difficulties of the slave young was the reality of a plantation routine which prevented the lavishing of care upon the infant. At an early age the children were usually placed in the plantation's nursery where they were cared for by the old slave women or placed in the hands of their elder siblings. This arrangement often resulted in the child receiving only minimal care, thus rendering him susceptible to the variety of ills which afflicted the children of the South.[23]

For those slave children who survived the perils which accompanied their first months of existence, life on the sugar plantation for the next few years was not one of great demands. Most plantation masters required little work of their young slaves before the age of eight. Apart from looking after those younger than themselves, the tasks given to the young blacks were not unlike those given to the children of free parents of the time. Somewhere between the ages of eight and twelve slave children began to take on added work responsibilities around the estate, such as cleaning yards, helping in the vegetable gardens, and carrying water to the field hands. Their hardest work came during the harvest season when they, like everyone else on the plantation, were called upon to assist. The breaking-in process for slave children on a plantation was a gradual procedure. Though young plantation blacks began to take on various duties at a relatively early age, the courts and public opinion in the South usually considered slaves to be children until about twelve years of age and adolescents until their late teens. At Ashland the age of fourteen seems to have been the point when young slaves began to be counted as members of the adult work force. Surviving plantation journal excerpts divide Ashland's blacks into two age groups, with all hands up to the age of fourteen being labeled as children and everyone else being included in the journal's adult listings.[24]

The work at Ashland was not unlike that on most other large sugar estates of the region. The field hands were kept busy at arduous and continuous tasks from sunup to sundown six days a week throughout most of the year. During the grinding season and other periods when the work load was especially heavy, the field gangs were also required to work on Sundays. During the grinding season the pressure to get the cane out of the fields before it could be damaged by cold weather was so great that often the field and grinding activities went on uninterrupted through the Christmas season. This was the case in 1852 when the Ashland overseer's entry for Christmas day simply was the notation that "all hands engaged as on Wednesday," which meant that the plantation's workers "finished grinding all the standing cane at twelve o'clock last night and commenced to winrow [sic]"—hardly festive holiday activities.[25]

Slaveholders in the Old South used two basic methods of managing their laborers: the gang or time-work system and the task or piece-work system. Virtually all sugar planters, including Kenner, relied primarily on the gang system to direct the work of their slaves. Under this system the field hands of the estate worked in gangs commanded by Negro drivers for a specified period of time each day. However, because of the diverse nature of many of the tasks needed to be completed on the sugar plantation, some planters found it expedient to deviate from the gang method. Planters on occasion applied the task system of labor in which individual workers were given specific duties to perform. Among the slave groups which sometimes worked under the task system were the coopers, woodcutters, and ditch-diggers of the estate's work force.[26]

Besides sometimes turning to the task system to obtain maximum work and good behavior from their slaves, the sugar planters of the region also tried more creative methods to encourage their Negroes to perform their duties. One of the more innovative incentive systems attempted was used by the Bringier plantations in Ascension and St. James parishes. Meat, flour, shoes, calico, tobacco, and handkerchiefs were stocked in a plantation store where slaves were able to purchase items with credits earned from performing small tasks such as chopping wood and making hogsheads. Though Kenner and his wife remained close to the Bringier family and shared ideas with them on ways to improve their sugar production, there is no evidence that Kenner or any other planter adopted the Bringier's unique labor-incentive program.[27]

Instead of the innovative methods of distribution used by his wife's relatives on their neighboring estates, Kenner relied on the more traditional methods of allocating food and clothing to his slaves. In order to keep their labor force viable, most planters provided them with a reasonably adequate supply of the basic essentials of subsistence, including food, clothing, and shelter. On most sugar estates of the period the basic rations consisted of meat, cornbread, and molasses. At Ashland, Kenner also provided his workers with additional staples of salt, coffee, and oil. Locally produced crops of corn, sweet potatoes, peas, and turnips were also provided to the members of the plantation's work force. Slaves were able to supplement their diets further with vegetables, chickens, and other fowls which they were encouraged to raise on small personal garden plots near their cabins.[28]

Most masters would have preferred to distribute food supplies to their Negroes on Monday or Tuesday rather than on the weekends. Yet Kenner and the vast majority of planters dispensed their supplies on weekends in response to pressure from their slaves. To the black bond servant the weekend, especially Sunday, was a time of festivity which called for a special culinary effort. Even though Kenner had his overseer make food allocations to his slaves on Sunday, there was always the fear that too much of the week's ration would be used up in a few days and that either hunger or stealing would result.[29]

Though the diets of sugar plantation slaves lacked variety, the amount of food was usually quite adequate. Kenneth Stampp, however, maintains in his work *The Peculiar Institution* that the diet of most slaves was improperly balanced and consequently caused the Negroes of the South to suffer from dietary deficiencies.[30] Though there were undoubtedly situations, such as when a planter became so preoccupied with his staple crops that he neglected to produce enough food, in which the slaves suffered, the usual practice was to provide reasonable amounts of nutritional foodstuffs to the laborers. Keeping the slaves in good health was obviously the best economic policy. In their study of the diet of the Southern slave, Robert Fogel and Stanley Engerman concluded that not only was the slave diet adequate, but it actually exceeded modern recommended daily levels of the chief nutrients. The two cliometricians contend that a careful reading of plantation documents shows that the slave diet included many nutritional foods not always listed in the plantation journals, which were used by earlier scholars to formulate their views on the deficiency of plantation victuals. A review of the surviving records of Ashland tends to support the position of Fogel and Engerman. In his entries for the days when supplies were distributed to the Negroes of the estate, Ashland's overseer usually listed only pork and molasses as being dispensed. However, an inspection of the overseer's record book reveals that a variety of foodstuffs, including various types of vegetables, meats, and grains, were either produced on the plantation or were purchased and kept in storehouses on the estate in such quantities as to indicate that they were intended to be used to feed the estate's slaves.[31]

Clothing for Ashland's Negroes consisted mainly of pants, shirts, jackets, hats, handkerchiefs and shoes. Women were also issued frock-type garments called joseys. The few existing records from the Kenner estate make no mention of small clothing items such as socks and underclothes. However, surviving documents suggest that the distribution of clothes at Ashland was not unlike that of most of the other large plantations of the area. Although a few slaveholders bought clothing for their Negroes, others, especially those with larger slave populations, purchased material for plantation manufacture. Even those units which purchased clothing for their slaves expected them to make some of their own accessories and socks. This seems to have been the practice followed on the Kenner estate.[32]

Clothes were distributed twice a year—during the winter and spring. Although on occasion complete outfits were given to some of Ashland's slaves, it was customary to furnish only partial outfits. Fogel and Engerman's review of records from large plantations indicates that a fairly standard annual issue for adult male slaves was four shirts, four pairs of pants, and one or two pairs of shoes; Negro women usually were issued four dresses or the material needed to make them. Blankets were given once every two or three years. These allotments of clothing generally were sufficient to keep the slaves warm through most of the year. However, slave clothing sometimes proved to be inadequate to protect the plantation workers against the bitter cold fronts that periodically struck southern Louisiana.[33]

Little is known of the living quarters of Ashland's Negroes. Like most of the surviving journals of antebellum sugar plantations, no descriptions of the estate's slave quarters are to be found in the remaining records of the Kenner plantation. However, a postbellum diagram of the estate shows thirty-five structures which obviously had served as slave housing. Located several hundred feet directly behind the estate's Big House and near the sugar mill and other work buildings, the dwellings were situated in two rows with a tree-lined center lane separating the rows of houses. It is reasonable to suppose that, as with other aspects of the Kenner plantation, there was little or no difference between the slave quarters of Ashland and those of other sugar estates. Commonly, these dwellings consisted of one- or two-room whitewashed cabins of wood arranged in rows similar to that at

Ashland. With the large supply of bricks available at the Kenner plantation, it is likely that the estate's slaves quarters contained more bricks in their construction than were typically used on other plantations of the region.[34]

Though inadequate, when judged by modern standards, for good health and morality, the cabin of the Negro slave varied little in size and comfort from homes of many of the poor whites of the antebellum South. The small cabins of the blacks were frequently overcrowded. Fogel and Engerman's study shows an average of 5.2 slaves per house on a large plantation as compared to 5.3 individuals per free household. The average number of people housed in Ashland's slave dwellings is unknown because it cannot be determined what portion of Kenner's slave force was housed in the thirty-five cabins located near the manor house, or, indeed, how many slave houses there were at Ashland during the prewar years. However, if thirty-five is an accurate figure for the number of slave cabins and if the 1860 slave population of 473 is considered, it would mean that there would have been the unusually high average of 13.5 slaves per cabin.[35] This is not likely to have been the case, for the 1860 numbers included the slaves Duncan Kenner had acquired from his brother's estate. These Negroes were housed in brick cabins separate from those which were located near the Big House.[36]

Not surprisingly, the plantation slave often suffered from a variety of ailments. The hot, humid climate of South Louisiana, along with the ever-present hordes of mosquitoes, swamps, and lack of sanitation facilities, resulted in some sickness nearly always being present among the inhabitants of the region's large sugar plantations. Planters and their overseers usually tried to protect the health of their human property by acting in the capacity of amateur doctor for most minor slave ailments. However, in cases of more serious sickness, professional physicians were called to provide the needed medical services. Cholera, yellow fever, smallpox, chills, colds, whooping cough, measles, and dysentery were all among the common ailments which afflicted the South's inhabitants, with pneumonia and diseases of the gastrointestinal tract being the greatest killers of the members of the sugar estate's work force. The overseer's journal for 1852, the most important surviving document which sheds light on day-to-day life at Ashland, makes little mention of sickness among the estate's slaves. Nevertheless, four deaths among the Ashland slave force are listed by the overseer, with dropsy, consumption, influenza, and inflammation of the chest given as the causes of the deaths.[37]

On Ashland, as on most other estates of considerable size, a hospital to care for ill workers was maintained. Better care could be given to sick individuals by this means because healthy people on the plantation had jobs to perform and were not available to nurse the sick in their own cabins. Furthermore, if each family had been allowed to care for its own sick, it would have been more difficult to control contagious diseases. Facilities for the treatment of sick Negroes varied with the size of the estate. The larger the number of slaves on the plantation the more substantial the hospital. Little is known of the medical facility at Ashland; however, considering the large number of slaves which inhabited the estate, the medical building must have been fairly large. The only comment about the clinic which appears in the plantation's records is a notation by one of the overseers that he was assigning three hands to plant trees around the estate's hospital, an obvious attempt to add to the comfort of the sick during the warmer months of the year.[38]

Though primitive and lacking in many ways when compared to contemporary standards, the medical deficiencies of the plantation were characteristic of the era—not the institution. Both blacks and whites suffered from the crude medical practices of the time. However, if the medical treatment of the plantation black is compared to his white counterparts, there is evidence that the health of slaves was a prime concern of the sugar planter. Fogel and Engerman's statistical studies reveal that, although the life expectancy of the slaves in 1850 was twelve percent below the average of white Americans, it was nearly identical with that of the people of France and Holland and was much longer than the life expectations of the free urban industrial workers in both the United States and Europe.[39]

Like slaves on other large estates, Ashland's field hands lived a regimented life. Though the particular details of the daily regulations for the workers of the Kenner plantations are not known, it is reasonable to assume that the management techniques used by Kenner did not vary greatly from those in use by proprietors of other large sugar estates. The absence of sufficient alternative motivators for the plantation slave led Kenner and most other planters to rely upon punishment for misdeeds to bring about effective crop production and community life on their estates. Punishment for misdeeds varied from plantation to plantation and master to master. However, it was generally administered in the form of extra or more distasteful work assignments. The more serious problems were often penalized by forms of corporal punishment including flogging, the most common single form of punishment, or confinement in stocks. Sunday work was also a common punishment throughout the sugar region. In those rare instances when a particular Negro could not be made to conform, the recalcitrant black was sold. This was not a common practice, for the sugar plantations of the region were usually short of labor and tried to avoid decreasing their labor force.[40]

Ashland's labor force was occasionally depleted by slave truancy. Nearly all antebellum plantations were bothered to some extent by runaways. Despite the large number of Negroes used on the Kenner property, unauthorized absences by members of the work force seem not to have been a major problem at Ashland. For example, in 1852, the only year for which detailed records are available, there is only one reference to the problem. In his journal entry for Monday, May 24, 1852, overseer W. G. Wade listed George Brecks as having "ran off today." In most instances such truancies were not long-lasting offenses. The missing slaves usually either returned voluntarily within a few days or were apprehended by the authorities. Relatively few slave escapees made good their bids for freedom. During the final decade before the outbreak of hostilities between the Northern and Southern states only about a thousand blacks a year successfully ran away to the North, Canada, or Mexico, with only a few of this number being from the sugar region of the lower South.[41]

The reasons for the truancies were varied. According to historian J. Carlyle Sitterson, a leading authority on the sugar plantation, the causes for runaways on sugar estates could be grouped into three major categories. They included the slave's fear of being punished for a misdeed he had committed, a newly acquired bondsman's homesickness and adjustment difficulties with his new surroundings, and a slave's desire to escape the regular routine of the plantation.[42]

As on most Southern plantations, life on Ashland was a paternalistic existence. Most day-to-day activities of the estate's Negroes were determined or controlled by Kenner and the other whites who resided on the plantation. Despite the effort to supply the bondsmen of the estate with their needs, including food, clothing, and housing, the paternalism of Ashland and of the antebellum South as a whole had little to do with the benevolence, kindness, or good cheer of Duncan Kenner or any other planter. Instead, it was an outgrowth of the system of exploitation which existed on the sugar estates of the region for the financial advantage of the planters.[43]

An example of the economic pragmatism which permeated Ashland's paternalistic society was demonstrated in the way Kenner regulated the use of his slaves' personal garden plots. Although he followed the common practice of providing his Negroes with small patches of land for their personal use, Kenner insisted that he be given a share of their gains. The slaves were allowed to fence in their little gardens, which they worked enthusiastically into the night. Besides vegetables, the blacks raised poultry and hogs, using the money received from their sales to buy little comforts such as tea and clothes. At Ashland large numbers of chickens were produced by the blacks on their personal plots; however, Kenner required that all the chickens be sold to him at the rate of twenty cents a pair. He then resold the birds for thirty cents. Shortly after leaving the plantation in 1863, one ex-slave complained that, besides the obvious economic benefit the practice brought to Kenner, the main reason the Negroes of the estate were forced to sell their products to their master was so that Kenner could keep track of how much money each of his slaves had because he did not want them to accumulate any personal property. However, it is more likely that Kenner's interest in the slaves' chicken market was based on an effort to prevent the blacks from stealing birds from the estate's flock or from other bondsmen.[44]

The comments of Kenner's former slave reveal a resentment toward his master and his master's authority which was not uncommon among slaves. Since the master possessed virtually all power and authority on the estate, he defined the institutional rules and roles of all the individuals who resided on the plantation. Incidents such as Kenner's attempt to regulate the amount of personal property his slaves accumulated underscored the salient fact of life on the antebellum plantation. A slave was property. He belonged to his master, just as did the horses, cows, and other farm animals of the estate. He could be purchased, sold, or rented, and his personal wishes counted only as much as his owner chose to regard them.[45]

Though many slaves resented their subservient status and resisted their masters, many others reacted differently to their condition of servitude. The paternal master who treated his bondsmen with a degree of kindness usually got better cooperation from them. This seems to have been the atmosphere which prevailed at Ashland. For although the work force at the Kenner estate included its share of unhappy and resentful slaves, the evidence suggests that discontent among the blacks of the estate was kept to a minimum. Many, if not most, of the slaves accepted their lifestyle and living conditions. The estate was not plagued by an excessive number of runaways. Even during the Civil War when the estate was raided by Federal soldiers, the Kenners were protected from capture and harm by members of the estate's slave force.[46]

Unfortunately, few records remain which shed any light upon the master-slave relationship as it existed on the Kenner plantation. However, the only existing slave account of any extent which deals with the question does give some insight into the complexities which sometimes arose between the black man and the aristocratic whites who controlled his life. This account reveals the stoic pragmatism of Duncan's approach to his bondsmen as opposed to that of his brother George, who obviously took a much more personal interest in the estate's slaves. The document also demonstrates the varying attitudes that some blacks held toward their servitude.

Interviewed in Kentucky during the Civil War, Alexander Kenner claimed to be one of seven children born of a union between George Kenner and an unnamed female slave. According to the ex-slave, the affair between George and the slave girl had continued for years until the white planter met and married his wife, Charlotte Jones. At that time George Kenner released the black woman along with four of her children. The newly freed family traveled north to St. Louis where they worked at washing clothes. When George sold his share of the plantation to Duncan, he also transferred ownership of the remaining three children of his ex-paramour to his brother for $1800. Over the next few years the family members who had made their way to St. Louis prospered and were even able to purchase several thousand dollars worth of property.[47]

As the former slave family gained in wealth, efforts were made to obtain the freedom of its separated members who remained in bondage at Ashland. The family made an offer of $2,000 to Kenner to buy the release of their enslaved relatives. Ignoring humanitarian considerations, Kenner callously contended that, since one of the slaves in question had become valuable to him as a trainer of his racehorses, he would only sell the slave for the right price—a figure equal to that of "the whole of the mother's property." The black family rejected this offer and countered with a proposal of $2,500 for the trainer alone. Though the amount offered was a very respectable price for a single slave, Kenner insisted that, in addition to the price discussed, the slave would continue to work at Ashland for three years at $15 a month to pay the balance of his exorbitant asking price of $3400.[48]

The agreement between Kenner and the former slave family did not mark the end of the dealings between the two parties. As demonstrated above, Kenner, always the shrewd and calculating businessman looking for a way to add to his fortune, was not above taking advantage of a situation. This was again evidenced when the former lover of George Kenner and the mother of the trainer mentioned earlier died. Duncan succeeded in getting himself appointed executor of her estate. Since several of her children were minors at the time of her death, Kenner received control of their shares of their mother's property. When one of the young blacks reached adulthood, he approached Kenner for his share of his mother's holdings. Kenner again demonstrated his insensibility to rights and needs of blacks by refusing to give the young Negro his share. Despite the imposing stature Kenner held in the community, the young black did not retreat from his demand for the legal portion of his mother's inheritance.[49]

As a resident of Louisiana, the young free black had options that his counterparts in most other Southern and some Northern states did not enjoy. For, although he could not vote or hold office, serve on juries, belong to the militia, or intermingle with whites at public places, the free black in Louisiana did possess some civil rights. He could serve as witness, hold all forms of property, and inherit property. Free blacks also could sue and be sued. Hence, when Kenner failed to meet his demands for his inheritance, the son of the former slave girl turned to the courts for help and was able to win a judgment against the wealthy and influential planter.[50]

Although Kenner's effort to take advantage of the plight of the black family typifies some of the negative aspects of the relationship between the black man and his white master in antebellum Louisiana, the same event serves to illustrate how many blacks were comfortable with life as it existed for them on the large estates of the time. After winning his case in court against Kenner, Alexander, the ex-slave who had brought the litigation, approached Kenner with an offer to trade all of his share of the court judgment for the freedom of his brother William. However, both Kenner and William declined the overture. So devoted was William to his master that he not only rejected the offer of assistance from his brother, but, during the war when the area was occupied by Federal troops and many of the slaves abandoned their estates, William remained at Ashland.[51]

William's decision to remain on the plantation is not the only example which can be cited of loyalty by the blacks who lived and worked at Ashland. At a time during the war when all of the white men on the estate had either been forced to flee the area or had been arrested by the occupation forces, Mrs. Kenner and her children were left without protection from the many slaves on the estate and the dozens of other bondsmen who had fled from neighboring plantations and were wandering throughout the region. If the slaves of Ashland had wanted to do evil to the Kenners, no better opportunity could have presented itself. However, instead of harming anyone or causing great damage to the property, some of the male slaves acted as guards for the family and protected them and the estate from any serious damage.[52]

The apparent contentment of a large portion of the Ashland slave force, as demonstrated by their complacency during the confusing time which accompanied the Federal invasion of this region during the Civil War and the scarcity of remarks in the overseer's journal concerning slave truancy and disobedience, supports the notion that the blacks of the estate generally received paternalistic treatment as long as they remained in their place and did not challenge the system. Such paternalism was not uncommon among Southern slave estates. Though there were individuals who fit historian Kenneth Stampp's contention that the policy of the planter towards his slaves was "to make them stand in fear," they were the exceptions. Kenner and his cohorts wanted to make money in order to maintain their status in the community. Keeping their expensive labor force healthy and contented was obviously the wisest economic policy.[53]

Despite the paternal atmosphere which existed on many of the slave estates of the South, the majority of planters believed in maintaining firm discipline among their laborers. Though many planters like Jefferson Davis and Joseph A. S. Acklen, who owned one of Louisiana's greatest and most pretentious estates, cautioned against its use, the majority of plantation owners occasionally used the whip to enforce discipline among their Negroes. With the lash being a common means of correction on the plantations of the South, Northern abolitionists propagandized the idea of widespread savagery among the planters. Although some neo-abolitionist writers of the present day continue to support this belief, available records suggest that the abolitionists' accusations of savage treatment of the laborers were overstated. For example, Frederick Law Olmsted, considered by historians to be one of the most objective Northerners to visit the South during the antebellum period, disagreed with the abolitionists of his day. He concluded from his three visits to the slave states in the 1850s that the slaves were better fed and housed than any other proletarian class in existence at that time. He noted that, although he occasionally saw negligent and lazy workers being urged along by having whips cracked over their heads, he seldom saw slaves actually whipped.[54]

On those occasions when it was necessary to chastise a defiant slave the task was not normally carried out by the planter. Instead, on most estates the responsibility for disciplining wayward Negroes was given to the overseer. Most masters limited the types and severity of the punishments which could be administered by their subordinates. To help insure that their hands were not abused by assistants, many planters issued detailed instructions to their employees regulating the treatment of their slaves. Typical of these rules were those issued by Kenner's uncle, William J. Minor, for the overseers of his various plantations. Minor included among his guidelines the order that the overseer "must not strike the Negroes with anything but his whip, except in self defense." He went on to direct that "when necessary to punish, he will inflict it, in a serious, firm gentlemanly manner and endeavor to impress the culprit that he is punished for his bad conduct only and not for revenge or passion."[55] Overseers who were found to have brutalized their slaves were usually dismissed by their employer. Though many planters made efforts to prevent cruel treatment of their Negroes, records reveal numerous examples of slave maltreatment by overseers and other subordinates of the planters. However, despite the presence of those who abused their workers, historian William K. Scarborough concludes, in his extensive study on the overseers of the Old South, that "the majority of southern overseers treated the Negroes in their charge fairly well."[56]

Although maintaining discipline among the slaves of the plantation was a major responsibility of the antebellum overseer, as plantation manager he was usually required to perform numerous other duties. Among the additional major responsibilities which were typically assigned to an estate's overseer were the care of the livestock and agricultural implements and the production of the estate's crops. He was also expected to see that the slaves were fed and kept clean, and he had to treat most of the minor illnesses which afflicted members of the slave force. Finally, the overseer was expected to provide security for the whites of the area against any harm by their slaves.[57]

The amount of authority and responsibility delegated to an overseer varied from one estate to another. Properties with at least thirty slaves usually had overseers to supervise the Negroes. The amount of power given to these managers ranged from almost complete control on absentee estates, where the owner was seldom present, to little more than seeing that the routine work of the labor force was carried out. However, because of the complicated nature of cane cultivation and the process of manufacturing sugar, the successful operation of most large sugar plantations depended heavily upon the overseer.[58]

The complex nature of the job, with its multifarious responsibilities which often called for exceptional talents and abilities, frequently resulted in the overseer falling short of his employer's expectations. One of the most common complaints voiced by planters of the antebellum period was the difficulty they encountered in finding what they considered to be a good overseer. The low social status of the position, relatively low pay (which in the 1850s ranged from $500 for small plantations to $2000 a year for the larger estates), and the insecurity of tenure all resulted in an environment where the removal of an overseer was looked upon as being commonplace. Though many examples of the rapid turnover in the profession could be cited, one of the more telling examples of the practice was Captain John Nevitt of Clermont Plantation near Natchez. During the seven-year period from 1826 to 1832, Nevitt changed overseers a total of nineteen times. Conversely, there were plantation managers such as J. A. Randall of Effingham Lawrence's large Magnolia Plantation in Plaquemines Parish who successfully administered estates for many years.[59]

Though few records from his plantations survive, the data contained in them suggest that Duncan Kenner's relations with his overseers were not unlike those experienced by many other planters of the time. The overseers mentioned in the surviving Ashland records did not enjoy tenures any longer than most of their counterparts on other estates. Census records from 1850 indicate that forty-year-old A. C. Antel was serving as the estate's manager. Only two years later Antel had been replaced by W. G.Wade, the individual whose record book provides important insight into the day-to-day operations of the plantation. By 1860 the overseer position had again changed hands, with thirty-one-year-old J. A. Braud, Jr., serving as Kenner's manager.[60]

The sheer size of the Kenner plantation seems to have contributed to the managerial difficulties of the estate's overseers. By the eve of the Civil War, Kenner's holdings had grown to include more than 2,000 improved and 1,600 unimproved acres. Along with a work force of 473 slaves and $65,000 worth of farm implements, Kenner's agricultural holdings in Ascension Parish alone were worth approximately a quarter of a million dollars. To address the need for improved management on his holdings, Kenner divided his Ascension Parish property into three separate tracts, each of which had its own independent organization of overseer, hands, animals, equipment, and structures. Given separate names, the three land parcels included Ashland, containing most of Kenner's original holdings; Texas, the area where the slaves obtained from George Kenner's estate were settled; and Bowden. This latter parcel was part of the estate of H. Browse Trist, Kenner's brother-in-law. Duncan purchased the property in 1858 for $210,000 in order to assist his wife's family, who were experiencing some financial problems following the death of Trist.[61]

The overseer was not the only employee to assist Kenner in the operation of his estate. It was a common practice among planters to hire additional help when needed. Although it was not uncommon for some proprietors to hire additional Negro hands to supplement their work force, planters generally turned to skilled white laborers when they needed assistance in completing jobs their work force was not able to accomplish. On most sugar plantations the most important white employees, excluding the overseer, were the sugarmaker and the engineer. These individuals necessarily possessed considerable skill and experience and were usually engaged only during the four or five months of the grinding season each year.[62]

In addition to the sugarmaker and engineer, plantation owners occasionally employed other skilled white artisans. Carpenters, coopers, and bricklayers were among the more common artisans hired. Kenner, like his peers, also employed white workers on his estate. However, because of the large size of his standing labor force, he was not as dependent upon outside help as others. For example, most carpentry work at Ashland was performed by skilled members of the estate's slave force. However, Kenner did employ a white trainer for his extensive stable of thoroughbred horses and, for at least a short period of time, a school teacher for the education of his children.[63]

Most planters also used Negroes to assist in the management of their estates. The drivers, who were themselves slaves, were key figures both in the work of the plantation labor force and in the society of the estate's slaves. Acting as foremen of the labor gangs and as supervisors of behavior in the quarters, these individuals were among the most important slaves on the estate. Utilized mostly to assist the overseer in carrying out the routine duties of the plantation, the driver was the individual who handled the many minor problems that arose in the everyday life of the slaves. Among the more common activities of the driver were befriending the sick and preventing quarrels and feuds from disrupting the slave community.[64]

On the Kenner estate, as on most other plantations, blacks who were used as servants in the planter's residence or Big House were considered above even the driver in social status. Because they lived in close proximity to the planter's family, it is not surprising that they often were able to gain the favor of their master. Slaves selected to serve as house servants were usually chosen because of their intelligence, training, appearance, and reliability. Another group of slaves who enjoyed special status at Ashland were those individuals who were associated with Kenner's extensive racing stable. A few blacks, such as the light mulatto Henry Hammond, were able to progress from one position to another. Starting in the stables where he excelled as a jockey, he eventually became too heavy to continue that role. Next he served as coachman, and gradually he took on the additional tasks of cook, butler, and gardener.[65]

Though the work force on Ashland was large and somewhat diverse, its goal was sharply defined. Like most other plantations of the time, the Kenner estate was a highly specialized agricultural unit with the primary economic objective of producing a marketable crop of sugar and its by-product molasses. From Kenner and his family who resided in the Big House to the slaves in their small cabins, one common thread which connected their lives was the fact that their individual well-being, to a large degree, was tied to the success or failure of the cane crop.

Success and profitability were by no means guaranteed to the residents of Ashland or any other agricultural unit in the region. Misfortunes such as hurricanes, freezes, fires, epidemics, and—perhaps most damaging of all—floods, constantly threatened the growers in South Louisiana. Of these feared occurrences, it was flooding which had the greatest potential for causing damage to Kenner and his neighbors. Fortunately for Kenner, Ashland never experienced the degree of inundation that some of the neighboring estates experienced. The most damaging of the floods to affect the plantation took place during the 1851-1852 growing season when a rise in the level of the Mississippi caused a crevasse in the levees protecting Hardtimes Plantation, five miles upriver from Ashland. So large was the break that, not only was Hardtimes severely damaged by the overflowing waters, but Ashland also was partly flooded. Despite the damage to his estate, Kenner was more fortunate than his brothers. For, just the year before Ashland experienced its problems, William Butler Kenner's Oakland and Minor Kenner's Belle Grove and Pasture plantations were severely damaged. Oakland's production was decreased from nearly 500 hogsheads the year before the flood to only 95. Damage was even worse on Minor Kenner's Belle Grove estate, where the output was reduced from 409 hogsheads to zero because of the overflow.[66]

In spite of the misfortunes which on occasion threatened their crops, the region's planters were able to produce large quantities of sugar each year. Once made, the sugar was put into wooden hogsheads which held about 1,000 to 1,100 pounds of the product. In the process of curing the sugar there was also some drainage of molasses which was placed in barrels with a capacity of forty to fifty gallons. Both sugar and molasses would then be ready for market.[67]

The following table shows the production and gross return for Ashland during several years of the antebellum period in which statistics are available. The return is figured on the average price per pound earned by the sugar planters of the region.[68]

TABLE 1

SUGAR PRODUCTION, PRICES, AND RETURNS, 1844-1862

Year	Sugar (hhds of 1,000 lbs.)	Average price per lb.)	gross return
1844	1156	—	—
1846	956	—	—
1850	580	—	—
1851	859	5.5	$47,245.00
1852	710	5.5	39,050.00
1853	1169	5.5	64,295.00
1854	1370	6.5	89,050.00
1855	1397	6.0	83,820.00
1856	570	10.0	57,000.00
1857	342	8.5	29,070.00

1858	1080	8.5	91,800.00
1859	2002	8.5	170,170.00
1860	1500	7.5	112,500.00
1861	940	7.5	70,500.00
1862	2150	—	—

With such production totals, Ashland was usually among the top one percent of the sugar-producing units in the state. In both 1851 and 1860 the output of the Kenner plantation was surpassed by only one other unit in the state. Over the antebellum years listed in the table Ashland's annual production averaged 1,116 hogsheads. The low production years of 1856 and 1857 were caused by poor growing conditions. The former crop was damaged by a dry spring which greatly reduced the sugar content in the cane, and the latter was ravaged by an unusually cold and wet winter.[69]

Once packed into large hogsheads, the crop was ready to be marketed. Although on some sugar plantations it took considerable effort to move the crop to the market because the location of the estate was remote from efficient transportation arteries, at Ashland it was relatively easy to haul the sugar and molasses along the plantation's roads to the estate's wharf on the river. At the steamboat landing it was stockpiled and later picked up by riverboat. Kenner usually shipped on the steamer *New Zatoma* every few days. For example, in 1852, a year when production was below average, twenty-one shipments were made between January and April.[70]

As was the normal practice among Louisiana's sugar planters, Kenner sold most of his crop through his New Orleans factor, Martin Gordon, Jr., who was also his brother-in-law. Though often criticized by Southern planters for being outrageous exploiters, the antebellum factor played a vital role in the agricultural economy of the period. Developed in conjunction with the South's scheme of specialized labor, the factorage system relieved the planter of the responsibility of marketing his crop, thus enabling him to devote his energies to the problems of slave management and the production of staple crops. The factors of the antebellum period performed more valuable services than just that of marketing the planter's crops. They also extended credit to their planter clients, purchased his supplies, and acted as his agent in the city. Additionally, factors frequently rendered such services as insuring a plantation owner's crop and sugarhouse, paying his bills, and informing him of business conditions in general.[71]

Unfortunately, the paucity of records concerning sugar production at Ashland makes it impossible to compute a reliable estimate of the profitability of the entire operation. As can be seen from the table above, the gross return from the sale of sugar produced on the Kenner estate in the period from 1851 to 1861 averaged approximately $85,000 annually. However, the lack of records concerning the estate's expenses during the same period makes it impossible to derive an accurate total of Kenner's profits from his sugar crop. As with other aspects of plantation life, it is likely that Kenner's profits approximated those of the other large sugar growers of the period. Very probably they were exceptionally high in good years and were poor in bad years.[72]

In addition to their desire to show an annual profit, Kenner and his fellow plantation owners also subscribed to a second major financial consideration. Next to wanting a sufficient annual income to make possible a standard of living commensurate with his social position, the planter wanted the valuation of his property to increase. For it was the land value of his land which determined the amount of credit he could depend upon when additional money was needed. Adequate credit was a major concern to nearly all sugar planters, even to those of the status of Kenner. The nature of the industry, with its fluctuations in product, prices, and income resulting from occurrences beyond his control, made it necessary for nearly every planter to seek loans from time to time. With respect to the valuation, the figures concerning Ashland are impressive. By 1860, Kenner's estate in Ascension Parish alone was estimated to be worth $440,000.[73]

Skillful management and direction were the keys to profitability on the sugar plantation, with the successful planter being the one who achieved economy in his expenditures and a high product per working hand and per acre of cane. Though ineffective sugar operations were not rare, the industry as a whole during the antebellum period was profitable.[74]

Thus, events on the Kenner estate of Ashland during the antebellum period resembled those of most other large sugar plantations of the region. Though looked upon by its inhabitants primarily as a large agricultural unit, Ashland and its sister estates were much more. The large antebellum sugar plantation was nearly as much a manufacturing enterprise as it was a farm. Furthermore, its unique labor force made it much more than just a large agricultural production unit attempting to compete in a capitalistic environment. Ashland and its counterparts with their bonded laborers were little worlds unto themselves. They were small paternalistic civilizations, which not only exhibited characteristics of capitalistic enterprise but also the paternalistic and languorous traits common to the seigniorial societies of the Western World.[75]

IV

FAMILY AND SOCIETY

Despite a wealth of historical evidence and literature on the realities of the plantation culture of the South, many inaccurate notions concerning life during the antebellum era have received wide acceptance. The mint julep and magnolia romanticism has infected much of the popular literature written on the subject of the Old South. Some of the more tenacious and damaging conceptions on the subject date back to the antebellum period when abolitionists' attacks upon the planter class presented the belief that the slaveholders did little but live off of the fruits of the back-breaking labors of their Negro workers. It is true that rich planters, like rich industrialists, had time and money for leisure activities. However, the wealth had to be made. The sugar plantation was a large and complex business which required a great deal of effort and skill by its owner to keep it functioning smoothly. The operation of an estate was a twelve-month undertaking which required sophisticated business and management skills to which Duncan Kenner and most of his planter colleagues gave much personal attention.[1]

Though most sugar planters worked hard at advancing their interest by good management, they did not usually put much effort into taking joint action with others in finding common solutions to some of the problems faced by members of their profession. A few agricultural societies were formed to promote the common interests of the sugar growers, yet they seldom accomplished much and usually just languished until they ceased to exist. The typical antebellum sugar planter was an individual who, when it came to managing his affairs, looked to himself for his needs. Similarly, most planters took a narrow approach to the pursuit of other economic activities. The majority of the region's sugar growers did not seek other financial investment opportunities.[2]

Duncan Kenner did not subscribe to the limited economic perspectives held by the majority of his planter colleagues. He frequently shared with others ideas on ways to improve their craft. Kenner was also among the relatively few planters who had both the capital and insight to broaden his activities to include other financial endeavors. Although he read the law for some time after he returned from his European studies, Kenner, unlike Judah P. Benjamin, the proprietor of Bellechasse Plantation in Plaquemines Parish and one of the South's leading barristers, used his legal training primarily to meet his own needs. One area, however, where Kenner invested his time and capital was in real estate speculation.[3]

Kenner's involvement in the real estate market started early in his life. With the death of his father when he was only eleven years old, Kenner inherited a considerable amount of land. From that time on in his life, Kenner was continually involved in the buying and selling of properties. Though he purchased holdings in various sections of both Mississippi and Louisiana, Kenner concentrated his real estate interests in the New Orleans area.

Although only a secondary business interest of his, Kenner's real estate investments were a major source of income for him throughout his life. At the time of his father's death, the family's finances were slowly recovering from a severe setback. Much of William Kenner's legacy to his children consisted of his extensive property holdings. Fortunately for Duncan and his siblings, at the time they acquired their holdings the area was undergoing a rapid population increase. Following the War of 1812, a constant stream of settlers from other areas of the country and from Europe landed at New Orleans. While most of these newcomers moved up the Mississippi and settled in the Mid-West, many remained in the area. By 1840 the population of Louisiana had reached 350,000, and New Orleans had become the fourth largest city in the United States, challenging New York for the title of the country's largest port. So extensive and long lasting was this period of prosperity that the five decades between the ending of the War of 1812 and the outbreak of the Civil War are referred to by historians as the golden years of New Orleans.[4]

As the Old Quarter of the city filled with the influx of new residents, many of the newcomers looked to the less populated areas to the west of the city for places to live. Settled mostly by Americans, these little communities or faubourgs expanded rapidly. Eighteenth-century sugar plantations and many small farms with modest structures were replaced with high density residential and commercial areas. The real estate boom of the city's golden years brought with it opportunities of which only a few of the area's planters took advantage. In the wheelings and dealings which accompanied the boom times, fortunes were quickly made and sometimes just as quickly lost. Among those planters who successfully speculated in the Crescent City's land boom was Duncan Kenner, who continued to buy and sell property in the city and elsewhere until the eve of the Civil War. Among his more valuable city holdings were thirteen lots and residences located in some of the community's more prestigious neighborhoods; the Three Sisters, an imposing columned structure on Canal Street; and the valuable city square bounded by the streets of Carondelet, Common, Baronne, and Gravier.[5]

Kenner also was careful to invest resources in other money-making activities. Though his investments became much more diversified after the war than they were before, nevertheless, during the antebellum period he did go beyond the common practice of many planters of investing their surplus funds almost exclusively in additional slaves and land. Primarily as a hobby, Kenner invested heavily in thoroughbred race horses. He also purchased stock in promising companies, including the Southern Pacific Railroad. Kenner also derived a modest income from the interest he charged on loans of money which he made to acquaintances. Surviving records reveal dozens of transactions over a span of years between Kenner and other individuals, often including members of his wife's family. Although most of these loans were obviously made by Kenner to his wife's relatives as an act of kindness to help them through financially difficult times, most loans earned Kenner respectable interest income which usually ranged from eight to ten percent.[6]

An important factor in helping him survive the periodic economic setbacks which afflicted the sugar economy of the region, Kenner's diverse financial holdings were somewhat extraordinary for a large-scale sugar planter. Some sugar growers did not attempt to diversify their holdings simply because they lacked the capital and time to do so; others simply were content with their life style and were averse to making any changes in the way they carried on their business. Chief among this latter group of planters were those individuals who were descendants of settlers of the region before it became American territory. Often inaccurately labeled by postbellum writers as "Creoles,"[7] these *anciennes'* outlook on life was often considerably different than that of the many newcomers who entered Louisiana following its acquisition by the United States in 1803.

The cultural differences between the *anciennes* and the newcomers were of such magnitude that they remained one of the major themes which affected the political, cultural, and social history of the region during much of the antebellum period in Louisiana. The aristocratic *anciennes* generally held themselves aloof from the Americans and built a social barrier of bitter resentment between themselves and the newcomers. Theirs was more of a seigniorial existence than that of their American neighbors. Not unlike their slave-owning counterparts in Brazil and elsewhere, the *anciennes* worked to preserve the good life and shied away from the pursuit of material gains or highly intellectual activities which might prove detrimental to their slow and pleasant rhythm of existence. They objected to the use of English as the official language of the state and many refused to learn it. Most were resentful and contemptuous of their American neighbors and looked upon those who were Protestants as being irreligious and evil.[8]

The Americans on the other hand, including Duncan Kenner and his father William, added a capitalistic flavor to their pursuit of the good life in Louisiana. Most had come to their new home with the hope of adding to their fortunes, and they aggressively pursued this objective. Architect Benjamin Henry B. Latrobe noted in his journal in early 1819 that the new American immigrants to the Crescent City were "in an eternal bustle . . . [with] their limbs, their heads, and their hearts, [moving] to that sole object, . . . buying and selling, and all the rest of the occupations of a money-making community."[9] The assertiveness of the Americans often put them at odds with the *anciennes*. The concerns of the *anciennes* over the possible loss of their way of life were dismissed by the newcomers, who accused them of being backward, ignorant, and innocent of the sophisticated ways of the modern world.[10]

So involved became the rivalry between the two groups that at times bemused visitors to the region joined in the fray. While visiting New Orleans in the 1820s, the Duke of Saxe-Weimar expressed displeasure with the American populace because they seemed only motivated "by the desire to accumulate wealth." By contrast, he considered the *anciennes* of the city to be "a warm hearted generation." Timothy Flint, who visited the city several years after the duke, observed that the *anciennes* were "mild, an amiable people with less energy and less irascibility than the emigrants from the other states." He was quick to add that they were also "generally more sober and moral than the Americans."[11]

The commercial, political, and cultural competition between the two groups in southeastern Louisiana was intense. Commercially, the *anciennes*' limited experience in the ways of finance and their narrow educational background put them at a disadvantage in their attempt to compete with the aggressiveness of the Americans. Thus, by the time young Duncan Kenner returned to America from his studies in Europe, the Americans in New Orleans had succeeded in gaining financial ascendancy over their more conservative neighbors. Politically, however, the *anciennes* held numerical superiority over the Americans for some time and were able to influence the political events of the period. While their political power remained strong in the rural sections of South Louisiana, the *anciennes* steadily lost ground in New Orleans, where the number of immigrants continued to swell throughout the antebellum era.[12]

Culturally, the *anciennes* considered themselves superior to the newcomers, they were averse to making changes, and they were content with their individualistic way of life. To limit the American influence upon their culture, the *anciennes* established broad social barriers designed to limit contact between the two cultures. Even intermarriage with the Americans was frowned upon by the old families of the state.[13]

The passage of time and the onset of the Civil War eventually reduced the tension between the two groups. However, during most of the antebellum period, the Americans and *anciennes* rarely shared common interests. Accommodations between the groups were usually made by individuals rather than by large-scale cooperation between the cultures. On occasion the more diplomatic among the young Americans of the time mastered French and some of the colloquial customs of the *anciennes* and began to court and marry their daughters.[14]

One such young American who was able to transcend the cultural barriers between the rival groups was twenty-six-year-old Duncan Kenner. With his father having been among the first Americans to establish himself in New Orleans and his mother being a member of one of the leading families of the Natchez region, Kenner was looked upon with less suspicion by the *anciennes* than many of his American peers. Kenner's father had established close business and personal ties with many of the leading *ancienne* families of the area. When William Kenner died, many of the old families assisted the Kenner children in getting established on their own. Among this group was the prominent Bringier family.

The Bringiers resided on some of the most elegant estates in the region. Emmanuel Marius Pons Bringier, the first member of the family to settle in Louisiana, had established White Hall Plantation in St. James Parish on which was situated one of the grandest homes in Louisiana. His son, Michel Doradou Bringier, owned the nearly-as-impressive Hermitage Plantation in Ascension Parish. This estate had been a wedding gift to Doradou and his bride, Elizabeth Aglae DuBourg, from his father. With the death of his father, Doradou acquired the former's holdings at White Hall and thus became one of the most powerful planters in the region. It was during his patriarchy that the great influx of Americans into the region occurred and the rift between the two cultures developed.[15]

Despite his position as the head of one of the wealthiest and most respected of the *ancienne* families, Bringier apparently was not as suspicious of the Americans as were many of his *ancienne* neighbors. For example, of his six daughters, five married Americans and only one married a member of one of Louisiana's *ancienne* families. Marie Elizabeth Aglaé Bringier, the fourth of Doradou's daughters, married her cousin Benjamin Tureaud, a member of one of the oldest and most opulent of South Louisiana's *ancienne* families. The Tureauds resided at Tezcuco Plantation. The rest of Doradou's daughters married prominent Americans. Among these was his eldest daughter, Rosella, who married Hore Browse Trist, the brother of Nicholas P. Trist, who negotiated the Treaty of Guadalupe Hidalgo. The two brothers had been wards of Thomas Jefferson and were reared at Monticello in Virginia. Rosella and her husband lived on Bowden Plantation in Ascension Parish, and he served as the first American Collector of the Port of New Orleans. Louise Françoise Bringier, the second eldest of Bringier's daughters, married Martin Gordon, Jr., the son of Martin Gordon, Sr., one of Andrew Jackson's closest friends. Louise's husband was one of the area's leading commercial factors and served in that capacity for Duncan Kenner. The youngest Bringier girl, Anne Octavie, married Allen Thomas of the New Dalton and New Hope plantations. A lawyer, Thomas rose to the rank of brigadier general in the Confederate army during the Civil War and after the conflict was active in Democratic politics, eventually being appointed United States minister to Venezuela.[16]

Although the sons-in-law discussed above represented an impressive cross section of the elite of the American community in Louisiana, it was Doradou Bringier's other two daughters, Myrthé and Nanine, whose husbands were most in the public eye. Louise Marie Myrthé married Richard "Dick" Taylor. The Louisiana-born and only son of President Zachary Taylor and his wife lived on Fashion Plantation in St. Charles Parish. During the war he proved himself to be a capable commander by defeating the superior Union forces of General Nathaniel P. Banks at the Battles of Sabine Crossroads, which turned back the North's ambitious Red River Campaign of 1864. Gradually rising in rank, he eventually ended up as commander of the Confederacy's Department of Alabama, Mississippi, and East Louisiana.[17]

The fourth of the Bringier children and the third eldest daughter, Anne Guillelmine, would fall in love and marry a young planter and politician named Duncan Kenner. Probably named after her great uncle and godfather, the Catholic apostolic administrator for New Orleans, Bishop Louis Guillaume Dubourg, she was known all her life as Nanine. The courtship and marriage of Duncan and Nanine personified the social changes which were gradually affecting the way the American and *ancienne* cultures learned to live together in Louisiana.[18]

Although few details of the young couple's courtship are known, it is unlikely that it followed the *ancienne* custom in Louisiana of arranged marriages. Nanine's mother had been a fourteen-year-old bride of convenience in a matrimonial alliance between her family and the Bringiers. Arranged by her uncle and her future father-in-law, she only saw her groom once before the marriage ceremony. On the other hand, it is likely that the courtship of Nanine and Duncan followed more closely the American custom of courting. They probably knew each other for some time before they became engaged. Despite the suspicions that the *anciennes* held toward the Americans, the Bringiers continually came in contact with them and probably were quite familiar with the members of the Kenner family. William Kenner and the Bringiers did business together. Furthermore, the Bringiers' city homes on the Esplanade and later on Canal Street in New Orleans brought the two families into proximity with one another. While staying at their city residences, it is likely that both families on occasion frequented some of the same social events. Likewise, it is possible that the families became close simply because their plantations were located in proximity to one another. The Bringiers had a reputation for being among the most extravagant entertainers who lived along the banks of the lower Mississippi. When they entertained, they doubtless invited their neighbors from the surrounding estates. To have done less would have been a breach of the area's custom of hospitality which included the tradition of opening one's home to any traveler, friend, or stranger, who might have been passing through the vicinity and, because of the lack of public inns, needed a place to stay for the night.[19]

Throughout the antebellum South, parents carefully supervised the social contacts that their daughters were allowed to make. While allowed to attend social events, they were constantly chaperoned. Often male suitors of eligible belles called at the girl's home in pairs so as to avoid neighborhood gossip. A single or frequent visitor to a belle's house could provoke speculation about his intentions. Unlike suitors in the North who were given the opportunity of private audiences with their sweethearts, Southern couples were not allowed to meet alone. The mother of the girl or some other family member usually was expected to be in the room with the young couple at all times. Furthermore, the New England custom of bundling (the practice of wrapping a courting couple in covers and allowing them to sleep in the same bed) was not practiced in the antebellum South and was looked upon as being odd and totally inappropriate.[20]

As a native Louisianian or "Creole," Duncan Kenner was afforded a greater degree of acceptance by the *anciennes* than some of the Americans who were just settling in the region. Having spent most of his life in Southeast Louisiana, he was familiar and comfortable with the *anciennes'* culture and also spoke fluent French. Thus when the courtship between Duncan and Nanine grew serious, her father and mother, along with the rest of the *ancienne* community, accepted the idea of marriage between the twenty-six-year-old American and his sixteen-year-old *ancienne* fiancée.[21]

Weddings were one of the most important social happenings during antebellum times in the South. Members of the planter class found such events to be of enormous interest. Friends and family members from far and near, from parents to distant cousins, were invited to attend the nuptials, which were usually elaborate ceremonies attended by large numbers of convivial guests.[22]

Except for the fact that it took place at the home of the bride's father, little is known of the details of the marriage ceremony between Duncan and his young bride; however, considering the status of the two families involved, it is probable that the wedding on June 1, 1839, followed the Southern antebellum tradition of extravagance. Among those who served as witnesses for the Catholic nuptials were the bride's parents, Duncan's older brother Minor, A. Christopher Colomb, a first cousin of the bride, and a family friend, P.W. Nicholls.[23]

Following the wedding the young couple set up housekeeping on Duncan's property in Ascension Parish, where they moved into a small dwelling while their grand home was under construction. Completed within a few years, the beautiful Ashland plantation house remained the family's home throughout most of Duncan's life. Set back from the river and backdropped with live oak, magnolia, pecan, and other trees, the large square-shaped house possessed a monumental quality. The interior of the house was nearly as impressive as the outside. It was furnished with magnificent pieces of furniture, some made by the area's leading craftsmen and others painstakingly crafted by slave artisans who lived on the estate. The house was tastefully adorned with many engravings, prints, and oil paintings, most of which were other keepsakes from Kenner's horse-racing competitions also decorated the home's interior. As the Kenners were connoisseurs of both mind and palate, the house was also equipped with one of the most splendid private libraries in the region.[24]

The young couple adjusted well to married life at Ashland. Kenner remained busy overseeing the construction of the new house and the growing of the estate's crops, as well as with his business interests in New Orleans and a budding political career. Nanine occupied her time buying furniture for the new house and visiting her relatives who lived near Ashland. Fortunately for Nanine, her marriage to Kenner did not take her very far from her family and the area in which she had grown up. Thus, during Kenner's frequent trips away from Ashland, Nanine did not have to suffer the hours of loneliness that many other antebellum wives had to endure while their husbands were away on business. Her family and their Hermitage Plantation were only a few miles and a short buggy ride downriver from her home at Ashland.

Taught from birth to devote themselves to their blood relatives, antebellum women sometimes experienced difficulties when they married and were required to shift loyalties to their husbands. This does not seem to have been a problem for Nanine for, although relationships with in-laws were crucial to family harmony in the antebellum household, the Kenners and the Bringiers apparently had no major difficulties in their relations with one another. It was not uncommon for Southerners to become embroiled in squabbles with their children and their children's spouses. Among the most common causes of such intra-family quarreling were financial matters. At times, planters openly meddled in their married children's business affairs. However, despite being involved together in several financial undertakings, theses two families avoided the squabbling which often affected other antebellum families. One reason for the congenial relations between the Bringiers and Kenner was that the financial dealings between them were not one-sided. It was not just a case of well-to-do in-laws lending the struggling young couple money and giving advice on how to get started. Although Kenner borrowed a great deal of money–at least $150,000–from Nanine's father during the first few years of his marriage, surviving records from both Kenner and the Bringiers reveal that, as his prosperity increased and theirs declined, Kenner loaned members of Nanine's family amounts of money running into six figures during the final years of the antebellum period.[25]

Despite the differences which sometimes erupted among family members, closeness between children and in-laws was the rule in the South during antebellum times. Although Kenner's support of his wife's family members might have been unusually strong, support by planters of their in-laws was commonplace. As long as an individual had any blood or marriage claim, custom held that the planter possessed an obligation to support them. One such family encumbrance which cost Kenner a sizeable amount of money involved Nanine's brother Martin. The youngest of the nine Bringier children, Martin had a great fondness for drink and good times. A true example of the rich and reckless spendthrift, Martin was nevertheless jealously safeguarded by his mother. With the death of his father in 1847 and the accompanying decline of the Bringier fortune, Martin's devil-may-care ways led him to exhaust his resources, thus forcing him to turn to Kenner for assistance. Not wanting to let down a member of the family, Kenner provided him with a monthly allowance which remained his primary source of income for several years.[26]

The home of the antebellum planter in Southeast Louisiana was frequently a busy and crowded place. As a consequence of the code of hospitality which encouraged visits from relatives and friends, the plantation home was usually filled with children of both sexes, all sizes, and many colors—for it was not uncommon for the children of the slave house servants to have the run of the house. Although women in the Old South felt an obligation to have a child during their first year of marriage, the Kenners did not have their first child for nearly two years after their marriage. Named for his father, baby Duncan was born in 1841.[27]

Kenner and Nanine did not have their second child until five years after the birth of young Duncan. The birth of a child was usually a joyous occasion for the antebellum family. However, the birthday of Martha Blanche Kenner on May 2, 1846, was a day of tragic irony for the Kenners and their relatives. For on the very day that the family was blessed with the birth of a healthy young daughter, the family was devastated by the death of five-year-old Duncan. Surviving data do not reveal the cause of death of the Kenners' first-born child.[28]

The death of a child was not an uncommon event for the antebellum family. Parents were usually careful to take extreme precautions to protect the precarious health of their infants. Despite these efforts, the South was plagued with an infant mortality rate higher than the rest of the nation. A comparative survey cited by Catherine Clinton in her study of the plantation mistress found that, while the infant mortality among Northern planters was 12 percent, the rate for the Southern planter class was 14 percent. According to the same source, a comparison of 1860 mortality rates revealed that where there were 7,267 deaths of children aged zero to five years in the North, there were 17,619 deaths in the same category in the South.[29]

Fortunately for the Kenner family, the rest of the children born to Nanine and Duncan were healthy and all lived to reach maturity. A second daughter, Frances Rosella Kenner, was born at Ashland on April 23, 1849. She eventually married on her twenty-first birthday the Confederate Civil War hero Joseph Lancaster Brent.[30] The Kenner's final child was a son. George Currie Duncan Kenner was born on the Ashland estate on February 11, 1853. Named for his father's beloved brother, George later moved to Nashville, Tennessee, where he died in January, 1881, thus being the only one of Nanine's and Duncan's adult children who did not outlive their father.[31]

Despite the joy relatives felt over the survival of childbirth by both mother and child, society placed a priority on dynastic survival. Female babies sometimes suffered from the preference shown to male offspring. Historian Clinton, in her work *The Plantation Mistress*, maintains that the Southern preference for male progenies went deeper than just the belief that Southerners without sons were faced with genealogical extinction. According to Clinton, it was part of a larger ideological structure that held that men were superior and women were inferior. Not only were gender roles rigidly applied to the societal status of individuals in the Old South, they also permeated the antebellum family. For the family was not only a microcosm of Southern society as a whole, but it was also an instrument of implementation. The home, according to Clinton, served as training ground for the cultural gender roles of the era, with the preferred status of males being generated as well as reinforced by family roles. Whatever pampering a daughter might receive from her parents, she was never accorded the options that her brother was given. Instead, she was usually given the power only to influence children in such a way as to maintain the societal status quo.[32]

Despite their close association with their husbands who were the movers and shakers of the political and social events in the antebellum South, Nanine and other aristocratic white women of the region had relatively little input into the outcome of the major events of the time. The inferior status of the antebellum female was largely the result of the romantic attitude toward women which dominated the culture of the Old South. Chivalry, as practiced during the antebellum period in the South, dictated a code of gracious manners which determined that a woman was to behave always in a highly feminine way and that it was her place to look up to the male as the protector and augur of wordly wisdom. It was her duty to marry early, stay within the sphere of the home, bear and raise numerous children, and uphold the traditions of the South, which included the defining of gender roles. With only a few exceptions, such as the famous feminists and abolitionists Sarah and Angelina Grimké of South Carolina, most women of the period accepted without public protest the status of their sex.[33]

Though theoretically placed on a pedestal by society, the majority of Southern women spent many laborious hours carrying out important responsibilities. Despite the presence of many servants, Nanine and the wives of most other planters were in charge not merely of the everyday events in the mansion but of the entire range of domestic operations across the plantation, from food and clothing to the spiritual and physical care of both their white and black families. The domain of the plantation mistress often extended from the locked pantry in the Big House to the slave hospital to the estate's slaughtering pen for livestock. Few events on the plantation escaped the attention of the mistress, unless they were crop-related, in which case they were considered the responsibility of the overseer. On occasion, she was even called upon to serve as an intermediary between slave and master, thus circumventing the authority of the overseer and making her role pivotal in the effective operation of the plantation.[34]

Most mistresses of estates the size of Ashland used house servants to mitigate the burdens associated with the rearing of their children. However, despite the presence of these slave assistants, most of the tiresome details of child care remained the responsibility of the planter's wife. Even the task of administering daily discipline to the planter's children was assigned to their mother. Southerners believed that the delinquency of a child was usually the result of negligence by the youth's mother, for only diligent efforts on the mother's part would prevent children from wandering astray.[35]

Despite such parental concern for their behavior, the life of a child on the sugar estate was a happy one. European visitors to the region sometimes took note of the Americans' indulgence of their children. A French nobleman who visited Louisiana during the antebellum period observed that the children of the region were "absolute masters of their fate [with] the authority of the parents [being] no restraint at all." One despairing plantation mistress commented that "our children are spoiled by our institution. It is very difficult to educate them; they never exert themselves in any way; they always depend on the slaves."[36]

In addition to being responsible for her children's discipline and physical well-being, the antebellum Southern female played a pivotal role in the spiritual realm of her family. Throughout the South religious affiliation varied from region to region. Episcopalianism dominated the planter class in the upper and coastal regions, whereas Catholicism prevailed in Maryland and the sugar regions of Louisiana. The major non-Anglican Protestant sects, including the Baptists, Methodists, and Presbyterians, were sprinkled across the rest of the plantation South. In Southeast Louisiana most of the *ancienne* planters were Roman Catholic, with the Methodist faith being the most common Protestant sect among the non-*ancienne* population. There were also sizable numbers of Episcopalians and Presbyterians in the region.[37]

Kenner was reared as an Episcopalian and Nanine as a Roman Catholic. However, denominational affiliation, though hotly contested by some individuals, was not emphasized by many of the planters in the sugar parishes of Louisiana. In some families and communities, individuals who belonged to one church occasionally attended services of another denomination. It was also common for individuals to switch churches. Among these was Duncan Kenner. The exact date of his conversion to Roman Catholicism is not known; however, since he and Nanine were married in a Catholic ceremony it is possible that Kenner's change of religion came early in his adulthood.[38]

The educational facilities in Louisiana had changed little in the years since Kenner's childhood. The state still lacked an effective educational system and suffered from a high rate of illiteracy. It was not until the state adopted a new constitution in 1845 that the legislature was directed to establish free schools throughout the state. Despite this and other efforts, results were mixed. There was little support among the people for public education. Most individuals gave little thought to the advantages of an education. Children were needed at home to assist their parents in working the family's farm or business. Likewise, few wealthy families availed themselves of the opportunity to place their children in the state's schools because of the belief held by most Southerners that attendance in the public primary and secondary schools carried with it the stigma of accepting charity. Most planters in rural Louisiana generally preferred to provide their children with tutors and private schooling.[39]

In spite of the existence of what at that time was considered a fairly effective public school in the town of Donaldsonville just a short distance from their plantation, Duncan and Nanine, like most members of their class, chose not to send their children to the state-supported schools. Instead, they followed the practice of hiring a tutor to educate their children. Most families of means used tutors to prepare their children for future entry into private schools located nearby, or into prestigious institutions in the East or in Europe. The services of a tutor varied in cost. Some lived in the homes of their students and were paid as little as $15.00 a month, while others, such as the teacher who worked for Kenner's uncle, William J. Minor, were paid as much as $1,500 a year. The spending of such funds did not always insure a quality education for a planter's children. So disappointed was Nanine with the quality of training her children were receiving at their home in Ascension Parish that she spent most of her time during the winter months in New Orleans with her children so that they could be schooled by the "good teachers."[40]

The education received by the Kenner children was not very different from the classical curriculum followed by their father as a young student. The entire educational system of the antebellum South from the elementary level through college was based on the classical tradition. Though this was also true for education in the North, the Southern devotion to the traditional values of the classics was greater. "Gentlemen" of the Old South were expected to have a classical education. Curriculums often included studies in Greek, Latin, French, reading, writing, calculation, orthography, geography, design, and music. Female students were given courses designed to prepare them to be good wives and mothers. Subjects covered included manners, morals, modern language, piano playing, singing, drawing, painting, and fancy needlework.[41]

The tastes and habits acquired during their years of formal education were not forgotten by Southerners after that schooling was completed. Many sugar planters devoted much of their time to reading and to study. Kenner was said to have possessed at Ashland and in his New Orleans town mansion one of the finest private libraries in the state. Each day he attempted to devote several hours to literary pursuits. A person of enterprise and inquisitiveness, he read for both pleasure and business. From his readings he often acquired new ideas which he applied to his agricultural and business ventures. Kenner's love of reading was not an isolated occurrence in the Old South. For although there was widespread illiteracy among Southerners, many others read and owned considerable numbers of publications. For example, the libraries of Daniel Clark and of D. Rouquette included over 700 and 1,300 volumes respectively. The region also boasted of several community libraries such as those found in New Orleans, St. Francisville, and Alexandria.[42]

The material that the planters read varied greatly and lacked a concentration in any special area. Reading for both enjoyment and information, they exhibited broad literary interests which were indicative of the cosmopolitan nature of planter society. Though Southerners read the works of such earlier writers as William Shakespeare, John Milton, John Bunyan, Oliver Goldsmith, and Miguel de Cervantes, they preferred the works of the nineteenth-century school of romantic authors. Among the most popular of these were Lord Byron, Thomas Moore, James Fenimore Cooper, Alexandre Dumas, Southern author William Gilmore Simms, and the very popular Sir Walter Scott, whose *Ivanhoe* had great influence upon the South's romanticism. Besides their love of romantic fiction and poetry, Southerners also enjoyed many nonfictional works, including the histories of W. H. Prescott, George Bancroft, and Edward Gibbon. Theological works, scientific works, travel accounts, and gift books also were popular reading materials on the plantations. Finally, Southerners read a great deal of periodical literature, ranging from such contemporary newspapers as *Le Vigilant*, which was published in Donaldsonville just a few miles from

Ashland, to the periodicals *De Bow's Review*, *Harper's Magazine*, and *The Southern Literary Messenger*. Included among Kenner's favorite reading materials was the popular horse racing periodical *Spirit of the Times*, to which he subscribed for many years both before and after the Civil War.[43]

In addition to their reading, planters, like most other Southerners, enjoyed outdoor activities. Hunting was the most popular of these activities in the sugar region of Louisiana. The area's many bayous and lakes abounded with ducks and other wildlife. Wild deer, bears, rabbits, and quail were found in great numbers in the swamps and forests of South Louisiana. Both day- and week-long hunting trips were common events during the antebellum era. Similarly, with the area's many waterways—most notably Lake Pontchartrain and the Gulf of Mexico—providing some of the most productive opportunities, fishing was a popular sport among the people of Southeast Louisiana.[44]

Such outdoor diversions were important, for they helped break up the tedium which sometimes occurred during the uneventful periods on the sugar estate. Although located in an area where some of the South's wealthiest residents lived, Ashland, like most other plantations, sometimes suffered from a dull and monotonous routine. Except for the frequent visits by friends and relatives and the occasional stopover by flatboats which floated by the Kenner estate on their passage down the Mississippi River to New Orleans, life at Ashland, though sometimes adorned with luxurious trappings, was largely a solitary and simple existence.[45]

Though the Kenners knew and corresponded with their counterparts throughout the state, their actual contacts with them were mostly limited to occasional meetings when the planters and their families were visiting in New Orleans. Each area in the sugar region did, however, have its own self-contained social orbit. Within each neighborhood, including the lands bordering the Mississippi, Bayou Lafourche, Bayou Teche, and the Attakapas region of Louisiana, there were often close associations among friends and relatives. In Ascension Parish the Kenners, Bringiers, Trists, Tureauds, McCalls, Prestons, Mannings, Minors, Doyals, and Landrys, all enjoyed neighborly contacts.[46]

The rural nature of Louisiana made it difficult for a planter to find alternatives to the routine of the plantation. Though the population of the state had increased rapidly during the antebellum period, showing a 55 percent increase during the first forty years of the nineteenth century, few urban areas developed. In 1860 there were just a handful of urban communities in the state. Excluding New Orleans and its surrounding faubourgs, the only urban communities were Baton Rouge, Shreveport, Plaquemine, Donaldsonville, Homer, Alexandria, Thibodaux, and Minden. Of these, only Baton Rouge had a population in excess of 5,000, with the others having fewer than 2,500 each.[47]

Located a short distance across the river from Ashland was the town of Donaldsonville. With nearly 1500 inhabitants in 1860, the little community had limited offerings for the region's planters in the areas of culture and entertainment. Described by the British traveler William Russell in 1861 as a place of "odd, little, retiring, modest houses," the only structures of note in the town were the elegant Ascension Catholic Church and the Ascension Parish Court House and jail. Besides being the location where Kenner usually attended church services and handled much of his legal business, the town of Donaldsonville also served as a commercial center where Kenner and the other planters of the region were able to make supplementary purchases of items needed on their estates. The town also offered the inhabitants of the region some simple diversions from their day-to-day routines. Included among the town's offerings were weekend horse races; frequent military parades, reviews, and balls sponsored by the local militia units; several restaurants; and an assortment of other merchandise outlets, including the shop of "the Parisian Rougeau" where books were bound and popular novels and nonfiction works were rented for $3.00 per year.[48]

Despite its rural location and relatively small size, the Donaldsonville community manifested a keen interest in the arts. Not only were theatrical events in New Orleans closely covered in the local press, but the town boasted of its own active theater. "Le Théâtre des Variétés" featured both locally produced productions and the works of traveling groups, with offerings in 1850 alone ranging from the internationally popular *Le Barbier de Seville* to the not-so-famous *The Wife Won a Lottery Prize*. The local newspaper, *Le Vigilant*, also did its part to preserve and promote the area's culture. By waging a tireless campaign for a national literature in French, the small town paper gave the sugar region of Southeast Louisiana an extraordinary impetus in literary production. Publishing both local, national, and international authors, the paper included in its column many different types of works including poetry, fables, ballads, short stories, novels, and novelettes which had Louisiana as a background.[49]

In addition to their frequent visits to the town of Donaldsonville, the Kenners and their planter neighbors in the river parishes also spent considerable time in New Orleans. Whether for reasons of business, shopping, schooling for the children, or the desire for the entertainment of the city, the Kenners sometimes spent weeks in the Crescent City. Though it was common practice for planters and their families to stay in one of the city's more lavish hotels while visiting New Orleans, some of the more prosperous planters, including the Kenners and the Bringiers, maintained townhouses. With extensive real estate holdings in the city, over the years Kenner used several different properties as his townhouse. However, Kenner's favorite and the one he and Nanine lived in until his death was an impressive mansion located at 257 Carondelet Street in the American sector of the city. When Kenner was away on business or remained at the plantation and Nanine and the children stayed in the city they sometimes stayed at "Melpomene," the magnificent townhouse of her parents.[50]

Regarded by many as the Paris of America, antebellum New Orleans offered its visitors a welcome relief from the tiresome routine of life on the plantation. One of the nation's leading commercial centers, the Crescent City during the period leading up to the Civil War was also considered to be one of America's cultural centers. Though the American influx during the first decades of the nineteenth century had altered the commercial character of the community, culturally the city continued to possess an air which was thoroughly French. As was the case in the Kenner household, many inhabitants of the area often used French instead English to communicate with one another at home and while visiting others. Besides the continued widespread use of the language, the French influence permeated many of the means of entertainment and relaxation in the city. Like few other places in the nation at the time, in New Orleans there existed a passionate love of the good life.[51]

The theater was one of the main forms of entertainment in New Orleans. It was enjoyed by both residents and visitors. With tickets usually costing between $1.00 and $1.50, the theater was popular entertainment for the common people of the city as well as for the more affluent residents. Of the city's theaters, the American generally offered performances for the lower classes. The upper classes usually attended either the Théâtre d'Orléans, where the works were usually performed in French, or the lavish St. Charles Theater, with its four tiers of boxes, magnificent chandelier, and finely appointed private rooms, where the offerings were in English. Among the more successful productions performed in the city during this period were the plays *King Lear*, *Richard the Third*, *Regulus*, *Marie Stewart*, and *William Tell*. The classic works of Corneille, Racine, and Voltaire were particularly popular with the patrons of the Théâtre d'Orléans.[52]

The opera was also a very popular entertainment for both the rich and poor. The city boasted of one of the oldest resident opera companies in the country. However, despite its popularity among city dwellers, seemingly Kenner was not attracted to the opera. As a leading member of the prestigious Boston Club, he is listed in the organization's records as having donated money to several fund-raising drives for needy causes, but his name is conspicuously absent from the list of contributors to the French Opera House.[53]

Along with the Pelican and Pickwick clubs, the Boston Club was one of the leading gentlemen's clubs in New Orleans. Active even today, the club is the oldest social club in the Crescent City. Founded by a group of affluent gentlemen for the purpose of playing the card game of "Boston," membership in the club was restricted, normally taking years of being on a waiting list before an individual could obtain entry into the club. Usually restricted to approximately 150, the membership consisted of men who could not only mix a good drink or play a good hand of cards but also were the moving forces behind the political and commercial destinies of the state. Among its more prominent members were the so-called "big four" of antebellum Louisiana politics—Judah Benjamin, John Slidell, Pierre Soulé, and Randall Hunt.[54]

Despite its social trappings and political status, the Boston Club remained largely a place of relaxation and gambling. At times quite large sums were bet at the club's gaming tables. Playing a card game similar to poker known as "brag," John R. Grymes was said to have lost many thousands of dollars. However, the distinction of perhaps the largest loss at a single sitting of cardplaying at the club during the antebellum years belongs to Duncan Kenner. It was reported by a club member that in just one sitting of "Boston" Kenner lost $20,000, and this was said not to have been an unusually large sum for him to lose! A person who loved to gamble, Kenner spent large sums of money to support his gambling habits, which involved both card playing and horse racing. An individual of lesser resources could hardly have supported such an extravagant hobby.[55]

New Orleans also offered planters and their families many fine shops which catered to the tastes of the wealthy with the latest styles and products from the North and from Europe. Families were also able to enjoy the city's fine restaurants and public squares. Another popular entertainment was a visit to the various circuses which frequented the city in the winter months because of its mild climate.[56]

The residents and visitors to the city also enjoyed celebrating national and religious holidays. Among the most important celebrations were the anniversary of the Battle of New Orleans, Washington's Birthday, and the Fourth of July. These occasions were observed with a great deal of patriotic fervor with parades by the local militia units, fireworks, and special religious services. Like today, the most significant of the religious holidays observed by the city's inhabitants was Christmas. A day primarily reserved for religious observance, it was not celebrated except by the children who received a visit from Papa Noël. Adults exchanged gifts a week later on New Years, which was celebrated as a day of gaiety and rejoicing.[57]

The most famous of New Orleans' pastimes was its annual Mardi Gras. During the antebellum period this pre-Lenten event gradually evolved from being observed with balls to the form for which it has become so widely known today with parades and street parties. An event celebrated by all segments of the community, Mardi Gras soon became a major social event eagerly participated in by members of the community's upper class — including Duncan Kenner, whose participation is noted in the court journal of Rex, the king of carnival.[58]

Private balls and dinner parties were also favorite pastimes of the social elite in Louisiana. Just as popular on the plantation as they were when the family stayed at their townhome in the city, these events of formal entertainment were usually extravagant and grand. Because of the Southern tradition of hospitality, the planter and his family often had guests for meals. By contrast, the ball was special; it was usually an infrequent celebration, often seasonal in nature, in which the host planter used the opportunity to showcase his wealth and liberality.[59]

Like most individuals who enjoyed the social status that they held, the Kenners from time to time held their share of elaborate and fanciful balls. Little is known of the details of these special events; however, it is unlikely that they varied much from those described by the writer Louise Butler when she wrote of the typical planter ball as having

> beautiful women, gorgeous costumes in real lace, real silk or hand embroidered lavishness, jewels, plumes, made the scene . . . delightsome music filled the air. Then the staircase was garlanded

in roses all the way up its three-storied extent, vases on mantels and brackets filled with flowers .... About midnight supper was announced and the hostess led the way to the dining room. Of the menu, the cold meats, salads, salamis, galantines quaking in jellied seclusion, ... were served from side tables leaving the huge expanse of carved oak, be-silvered, be-linened and be-laced, for flowers trailing from the tall silver epergne in the center ... fruits, cakes in pyramids or layers ... , iced and ornamented; custards, pies, jellies, creams, Charlotte Russes of home-concocted sponge cake spread with raspberry jam encircling a veritable Mont Blanc of whipped cream dotted with cherry stars; towers of nougat or caramel, sorbets and ice creams served in little baskets woven of candied orange peel and topped with sugared rose leaves or violets.

Various wines in cut glass decanters, each with its name carved in silver grapeleaf suspended from its neck, champagne frappeed, were deftly poured by the waiters into gold traced or Bohemian glasses.

Illuminating the whole were wax candles in crystal or bronze chandeliers, and, on the table, in silver or delicate Dresden candelabra.

More dancing followed supper and just at dawn when the guests were leaving . . . a plate of hot gumbo, a cup of black coffee and enchanting memories sustained them on the long drive to their abodes.[60]

In addition to their extravagant social events and their frequent visits to the city, the Kenners and most other successful planters also varied their life style with occasional travel. Though Kenner himself made frequent trips for business and political reasons, the other members of the family also were able to travel. Among the family's most common destinations were the homes of Duncan's relatives in Natchez. Like many other sugar planters, they also enjoyed vacationing with the Bringiers in Newport, Rhode Island, and at the popular While Sulphur Springs in Virginia where there were comfortable accommodations in a large hotel and numerous cottages. However, since these resorts were so far from home and required such an effort to get the family there, most planters preferred to vacation at the various resort cities along the Mississippi Gulf Coast. Because of the poor health conditions which usually prevailed in sub-tropical New Orleans during the summer months and because of the lack of intensive planting activity at this time on the area's plantations, most of the region's well-to-do families chose the summer months to visit the coast where the gulf breeze and the high ground and pine forest offered a welcome change from the uncomfortable conditions found back home. With the humidity of summer beginning to settle on New Orleans, Martin Gordon, Kenner's factor and brother-in-law, wrote in early June 1855 to his friend Benjamin Tureaud, who was vacationing at Bay St. Louis: "Doctor Campbell and his gang take their departure today for the Bay of St. Louis; On Friday next, Kenner and his troupe will go over; You will soon have a devil of a Crowd at the Bay." Gordon ended his letter with the comment, "I wish to God I could leave the City," a sigh of regret and envy probably voiced by many an individual whom circumstances required to remain in the city through the summer months.[61]

Though the numerous diversions listed above amused large segments of the populations of antebellum Louisiana, it was also during this period that interest developed in organized sporting events. Clubs were started to help finance and encourage many different types of sporting activities. Interest in these activities grew quickly. In the space of roughly five decades, organized sports rose from a relatively insignificant place in the region's leisure habits to a leading role. By the end of the century sporting events had become the major source of amusement in New Orleans, a city renowned for its variety of entertainments and pleasures.[62]

The earliest organized sporting activity to take hold in the area was that of thoroughbred horse racing. The sport in America traced its roots to the colonial period in New York and the Southern colonies. However, with the rise of strong anti-gambling feelings in these areas during the latter decades of the eighteenth century, enthusiasm for the sport declined sharply along the East Coast. Just as the interest in turf sports began to wane in the East, it began to increase in the lower South. Many prosperous planters in the latter region, like Kenner, were either migrants or the sons of migrants from the East where horseracing was an established pastime of the gentry. Hence, as they accumulated wealth, they also adopted some of the trappings that they had associated with the well-to-do from their past experiences.[63]

Corresponding to the rapid expansion and success of the sugar and cotton interests in the lower South, the popularity of horse racing soared markedly during the 1830s and 1840s. During this period, local and out-of-town turfmen founded three jockey clubs and several racetracks in the New Orleans area alone. These included the Louisiana Course, located slightly to the southeast of the city; the Eclipse Course, near present-day Audubon Park; and the area's leading track, the Metairie Course, which was located on the Metairie Ridge in Jefferson Parish. During most of the antebellum period, racing in the New Orleans area was supported primarily by the region's well-to-do citizens. Although Sunday scrub races often attracted large crowds, most regular meetings catered to the affluent and were scheduled on weekday afternoons; this effectively limited the attendance of most working-class citizens. Furthermore, seating arrangements separated the various spectators at the races. Women, who came by invitation, occupied the ladies' stand, jockey club members and their guests the members' stand, and everyone else the public stand. The admission price of one dollar, the figure charged at most tracks, also discouraged working-class attendance, for that sum represented a day's wage or more for many of the region's laborers.[64]

Though patronized primarily by individuals of high social ranking, the sport was not universally popular among persons of that class. Despite their love of good times, most of the *anciennes* preferred the pleasures of masked balls, concerts, the theater, and games of chance and seldom shared the Anglo-American love for the turf. One such American who, despite close ties to the *anciennes* community, loved the sport of horse racing nearly as much as his prized plantation was Duncan Kenner.[65]

Kenner's enthusiasm for the sport came to him naturally. As a migrant from Virginia, where the sport was extremely popular for some time, it is probable that William Kenner introduced his sons to horse racing. Though the connection between William Kenner and his eastern relatives is unclear, it is known that many of the Kenners who resided in Virginia loved and participated in horse racing, especially Captain Rodham Kenner, a Revolutionary War hero who was considered one of the greatest racers of the colonial period. Furthermore, Duncan's older brother Minor was among the earliest individuals in Louisiana to promote horse racing as a sport. Along with several other leading citizens, including John Slidell—the individual who helped train Duncan in the law—Minor was among the first to become a member of the New Orleans Jockey Club in 1837.[66]

Having been interested in racing from his youth, Duncan, while continuing his education in Europe in the 1830s, studied the sport as it existed in England and on the Continent. When he returned to Louisiana he concentrated his efforts on his Ashland estate. There he indulged his taste and started to build a stable of the finest horses he could find. Not just content with the locally available stock of horses, Kenner looked to both the Eastern Seaboard and Europe for prized animals to improve his own stables. Because the subtropical climate of southern Louisiana did not promote proper growth in racing horses, Kenner and other planters of the region with racing stables seldom bred their animals in the Deep South itself. Instead, they bred their mares with Northern sires and foaled them in Virginia, Carolina, Kentucky, or Tennessee.[67]

At Ashland Kenner constructed a full-size racetrack and employed a full-time trainer to run his stables. George Washington Graves, a long-time companion, was the individual who assisted him the most in building a successful racing stable. Originally from Virginia, Graves' friendship with Kenner extended back to the time when Duncan and his brother George had lived together and shared ownership of Ashland. It was also during that period, before Duncan's marriage to Nanine, that Kenner acquired his first racehorses. From that time on Graves remained employed as Kenner's trainer. So close was the relationship between the two that Kenner constructed for Graves a small one-story cottage just to the rear of the Great House. The trainer was also afforded the privilege of taking both his breakfast and dinner with the family at the main house, and his supper was brought out to him at his residence. The Kenner children looked upon him almost as a member of the family. As soon as he was heard moving in the morning they would run out to meet him. They also loved to sit and talk with him for hours as he sat in one of two large-bottom armchairs which stood on each side of his front door. When the children were not in the chairs listening to his stories, Kenner and Graves often would sit and leisurely discuss their horses.[68]

Few individuals were as successful as Kenner at being a breeder, and racer of thoroughbred horses. From the time he became interested in horse racing until many years later when he retired from active participation in the sport, Kenner continually worked toward improving the sport. One example of his successful efforts to improve the quality of racing in the South was Kenner's use of professional jockeys. Through much of the antebellum period, little regard was accorded jockeys, many of whom were slaves. Most turfmen of the period placed their confidence in their horses, believing that well-qualified riders contributed little to a race's outcome. Kenner, on the other hand, gave nearly as much attention to the training of his young Negro riders as he did to his steeds. The success of his efforts was demonstrated when one visitor to the estate wrote about the jockeys: "These little fellows sat their horses so well, one might have thought till the turn in the course displayed their black faces and grinning mouths, he was looking at a set of . . . young gentlemen out training."[69] Only a few jockeys ever became widely known for their riding ability. Among these was one of

Kenner's slaves, Abe Hawkins. Known familiarly just as "Abe," during his career he rode many of the antebellum South's champion mounts. Another of Kenner's riders was Henry Hammond. A light-skinned mulatto slave who had originally come from Virginia, Hammond's work with Kenner's horses so impressed his owner that when he grew too heavy for racing he was made the family's coachman and eventually became the favorite slave of the Kenners and was able to advance to the favored slave roles of family cook and butler.[70]

Kenner was not alone in his efforts to improve the caliber of antebellum horse racing in Louisiana. Joining with Kenner to spearhead the effort were three other planters—Thomas Jefferson Wells, whose brother James Madison Wells would become a Reconstruction governor of the state; Adam L. Bingaman, a Mississippian; and William J. Minor. The single-minded devotion and intense competitiveness of these four enthusiasts did more to improve the quality of the Southern thoroughbred than the efforts of any others in the Deep South. They gained little financially, for, when compared to current standards, the purses which they won were not very large. Raised primarily by entry fees and contributions from local hotels, social clubs, and newspapers, the money won in competition mostly went for the payment of salaries for trainers, transportation costs, stabling fees, and other miscellaneous expenses.[71]

If it was not for pecuniary gain, why then did business-wise individuals such as Kenner spend so much of their personal fortunes and dedicate so much of their energy to the sport of thoroughbred racing? The answer was that the sport by its expensive nature and tradition was identified with the upper classes of Europe and colonial America. It was a badge of aristocracy which relatively few of the South's many planters had the money and expertise to excel in. Those who did were truly in a class by themselves, admired by their peers and by the many popular spectators of the sport. Added to this avidity for recognition was the Southerner's sense of individualism, which, according to historian W. J. Cash, was "far too much concerned with bald, immediate, unsupported assertion of the ego . . . placed too great stress on the inviolability of personal whim, and . . . was full of the chip-on-shoulder swagger and brag of a boy." This attitude was translated into the satisfaction which flowed to Kenner and his fellow racers when one of their favorite thoroughbreds demolished the opposition on the turf.[72]

The grandiloquence which colored the gentlemanly racing competition of the antebellum period was demonstrated in the sometimes heated rivalry between Kenner and Thomas Jefferson Wells. The most famous incident in the competition between these two leading racers occurred at the fashionable Metairie racecourse sometime before the war. After one of Kenner's horses had beaten one of Wells' animals, Wells loudly proclaimed that if he and not his jockey had ridden his steed the race would have been won. Hearing the boast, Kenner impetuously challenged Wells to enter the same two horses in a $1,000 sweepstakes with the two planters themselves as the jockeys. Not only did Wells eagerly accept the proposition but an Englishman known as Mr. Holland requested and was given permission to ride his horse in the race and to add another $1,000 to the stake.[73]

On the day of the race dozens of friends of each of the three riders gathered to witness the event. Racing during the antebellum period differed from the modern sport in several ways. Rather than the single dash of today, most races consisted of heats at distances of one to four miles each. This practice was designed to test an animal's endurance as well as its speed. Since the usual practice was for a winning horse to have to capture two or three heats, depending on the distance, some contests required as many as eight heats for a winner to be named. As was the case with Kenner and Wells, most wagers were made on a personal basis, for there were no bookmakers or parimutuel machines at the tracks.[74]

A great deal of high priced betting along with much teasing and fun at the expense of the riders took place during the moments leading up to the start of the contest. During the first heat the Englishman's stirrup broke, causing him to fall off of his horse while making the first turn on the track. Kenner and Wells continued to race at full gallop to the finish line with Wells taking the heat.[75]

Physically used up after the taxing race, both middle-aged gentlemen retired to the weighing room to rest. While stretched out on a bench, Kenner was upbraided by his trainer and close friend, George Graves, for not riding with more skill, and Graves suggested that he ride the next heat. On the other side of the room, Wells' trainer congratulated him for winning the heat and assured him that he had no worry about winning the next heat. Wells, still puffing and blowing from his ride, curtly responded to his trainer, "Don't bother me . . . I wouldn't ride another heat for $10,000." No less fatigued, Kenner, upon overhearing Wells' comments, thought this an excellent opportunity to bluff his opponent. Hoping to get a walkover win,

Kenner nimbly sprang to his feet and exclaimed that he was ready to start the next heat. Wells, with his honor on the line, rose and started toward the track. Realizing that a continuation of the contest could have dangerous consequences for the two riders, friends convinced them to postpone the race until a future day. When the race was finally run professional jockeys were used, and Kenner's rider, wearing the "red and red" (cap and jacket of the same shade) colors of his stables and riding his Richard of York, won the contest and collected the winnings.[76]

In addition to his competition with Wells, Kenner also had a long-standing, spirited—though friendly—rivalry with his uncle William Minor, which centered around two of their favorite horses. In the 1840s hundreds of dollars passed between the two racing enthusiasts at the various competitions between Kenner's Verifier and Minor's Voucher. That Kenner took his racing seriously was again demonstrated in the spring of 1853 at the Metairie Course when, after the completion of a two-mile race in which his fine three-year-old Arrow was beaten by Sallie Waters of Mobile, Kenner offered to put up an additional $20,000 for a purse for another race between the two horses. To Kenner's chagrin the offer was declined.[77]

Obviously, winning meant much to Kenner. But on at least one occasion, losing was preferred by him or someone else involved with the Kenner stables. Sometime after the Metairie Jockey Club adopted rules to insure honest racing, track stewards expelled Kenner's leading jockey, Abe Hawkins, "for plain, positive, and palpable dishonesty—in plain terms, 'throwing off' a race which he had already won by sawing his horse around."[78]

Among the planter turf enthusiasts of Southeast Louisiana, Kenner maintained one of the largest stables of thoroughbreds. For example, Alexander Porter, the leading turfman of the Teche region, usually maintained around a dozen horses in his stable, and William J. Minor maintained twenty animals; in comparison Kenner kept stabled about thirty thoroughbreds. Included among his horses were such animals as Grey Medoc, who won eighteen of his first twenty-three races; Minnehaha, who held for several years the record for running the mile; Kendall, whom Kenner named for his friend, George W. Kendall, founder of the New Orleans *Picayune*; Louis d'Or, Panic, Luda, Rupee, Grey Fannie, and Pat Golray. To acquire such quality stock Kenner readily paid premium prices. For instance, in 1859 when the average price for a good thoroughbred horse was about $1200, Kenner willingly paid the top price of over $1800 for his new animals.[79]

Kenner's interest in the sport went deeper than just the breeding and racing of his horses. He was among the leading turfmen who actively worked to improve the sport by increasing its acceptance by the public, particularly the social elites of the community. For example, when the racing enthusiast Richard Ten Broeck established a joint-stock company called the Metairie Association and purchased full control of the fashionable Metairie Course in 1851, Kenner was among the fourteen additional stockholders of the association. Only 300 shares of stock were issued at $100 each. Of these, Ten Broeck held 145 shares and Kenner and William J. Minor each owned twenty-five. The association completely renovated the track's facilities by erecting new stables, enlarging and beautifying the grandstand, and by furnishing the ladies' stand with parlors and retiring rooms.[80]

Though the changes brought by the association were successful in upgrading the track, policy differences between Ten Broeck and Kenner, Minor, and Thomas Jefferson Wells led to considerable feuding among the stockholders. The quarreling finally resulted in the reorganization of the Metairie Association in 1857 with the purchase of Ten Broeck's interest in the Metairie Course by Kenner, Minor, and Wells. At that time the new majority stockholders added additional improvements to the racing facility, including the first brick-and-iron grandstand in the United States.[81]

The efforts of Kenner and his cohorts met with great success. Attendance at the local tracks swelled. Largely because of the endeavors of the region's planters, by the eve of the Civil War New Orleans was recognized as the center of thoroughbred racing in America. No track in the country could consistently duplicate the races sponsored by the Metairie Association. Regardless of any shortcomings possessed by the region's planter class, the quality and success of their thoroughbreds were beyond dispute. Their wealth, leisure, and land made it possible for them to develop fully the Southern gentry's commitment to a sport long identified with the aristocratic classes of Europe and America.[82]

V

THE POLITICAL ARENA

Despite a preference for the pursuit of culture and leisure, an antebellum gentleman was also expected to give of himself to his community. Among the more common social duties performed by the planters were careers in the military or politics. With its high-sounding titles and musters and with the existence of slavery involving latent fears of insurrection, the military tradition in the South was such that a larger proportion of Southern men entered the army as a profession than did their Northern counterparts. As was common among the feudal noble classes in Europe, sons of impoverished planter families often chose careers in the military. Among those individuals who fell into this category were many of the Confederacy's most prominent military leaders, including Robert E. Lee.[1]

Many other Southerners participated in the political activities of the day. However, in spite of widespread political activism, politics rarely dominated the life of the antebellum sugar planter. As with many of the other activities in his life, politics was but one of a planter's many interests. Planting, family life, and recreation, such as Kenner's horse racing, each claimed more of the planter's time than did his political activities. "Professional" politicians were rarely found in the Old South. Though there were exceptions, the political leaders of the antebellum South were usually important planters with large estates who seldom looked upon themselves as having a "political career." Instead, they simply considered their political activities as a duty and an obvious right of their class.[2]

In the practical sense, the South of the antebellum period was no democratic society. Governed by members of the planter class who for the most part were intelligent, shrewd, benevolent, and tolerantly paternalistic, the Old South was ruled by an oligarchy. The average white resident rarely was able to rise to the level of political prominence. Those who did usually accomplished their goal by first climbing the economic and social ladder; in essence, they became part of the ruling class.[3]

As a young man, who in his teens owned several hundred acres of some of the most productive agricultural lands along the lower Mississippi River, Duncan Kenner never had to worry about having to climb the economic or social ladders. From early adulthood, Kenner had easy entry into the arena of political prominence. Although his grandfather, Stephen Minor, was a distinguished military professional, neither Duncan nor his brothers ever showed any interest in following a military career. With their father having served as a justice of the peace in Mississippi and as a member of the Orleans Territory's legislative body, the Legislative Council, Duncan and his brothers were no strangers to the world of nineteenth-century Southern politics. As was typical in the homes of most Southern aristocrats, whenever their father got together with other men, politics ranked with crops, the weather, and slaves as a staple of conversation.[4]

With the death of Duncan's father, his political tutorship did not come to an end. Because of their young age, William Kenner's children were given a great deal of assistance by their father's friends. Among those who helped were some of the state's most prominent political leaders, for example the eccentric Etienne Mazureau, a state senator and attorney general (1820-1823), who was one of the leading political orators of his day. Following his return from a tour of Europe, young Duncan was able to sharpen further his political acumen during the years that he studied the law in the office of John Slidell. One of the consummate political minds in antebellum Louisiana, Slidell was a member of the Democratic party and a supporter of Andrew Jackson. During the years that Kenner worked in his office, the strong-willed and politically ruthless Slidell advanced politically to a point where he was appointed by Jackson as the United States attorney for New Orleans. It was also during the period of Kenner's tutorship that Slidell made his first attempts at elective office. Though initially unsuccessful, Slidell remained active in politics and gradually emerged during the early 1840s as the dominant Democratic leader in the state. In 1853 he was elected to the United States Senate.[5]

The time he spent working with Slidell stirred Kenner's political interest to a point that, within a few months after he left the New Orleans law firm, Kenner was seriously considering entering politics. His interest in elective office was further aroused in the spring of 1835 when Duncan's older brother Minor was elected to the Jefferson Parish Police Jury (the parish governing authority similar in nature to a county commission). The following summer, having moved his primary residence to his property upriver from New Orleans, Kenner ran for and was elected to the lower house of the state legislature as a representative from Ascension Parish.[6]

At the time he entered the political arena, Kenner aligned himself with the Democratic party. At first glance this would seem to have been an odd choice for the novice politician to have made. Considering his background as the owner of a large and expanding sugar estate, it would have seemed likely for Kenner, as was the case with most of the state's sugar planters, to have joined the Whig political party. The fact that sugar could not be produced profitably in Louisiana without protection by the national government led the sugar growers of Louisiana, almost without exception, to follow the Whig party and its platform supporting internal improvements, the tariff, and the United States Bank. What then did the Democratic party have to offer that enticed Kenner into its fold?[7]

The answer was less one of platforms and policies than of personalities and traditions. At the time that Kenner first ran for office, Louisiana was just beginning to venture into the realm of party politics as conducted in other parts of the nation. During the years of Louisiana's territorial status and the first decades of its statehood, its people were not particularly interested in national politics. Political events far away in the nation's capital were foreign to most native Louisianians, and most of the newly arrived American settlers in the area were too busy securing an economic base to put much energy into national politics. Political issues, when discussed, usually centered around the bitter ethnic controversy which raged between the *ancienne* residents of the state and the "American newcomers." It was not until the 1820s, with the appearance of Andrew Jackson and his detractors on the national scene, that Louisianians began to take an interest in national politics; and it was not until several years later that party politics began to dominate local political campaigns.[8]

With political ideologies and parties just beginning to take form in Louisiana, Kenner seems to have made his political alliance with the Democrats based as much on personal traditions as on political issues. A personal admiration for Andrew Jackson, the hero who had saved New Orleans from the British in 1815, and his months of work with John Slidell both contributed to Kenner's decision to join the Democrats. It is also possible that his dealings with his future inlaws affected his choice of political parties, for the Bringiers had close contacts to leading Democrats. One of Nanine's sisters, Rosella, was married to Hore Browse Trist, a kinsman and ward of Thomas Jefferson, who was regarded as the founder of the Democratic party. Another of Nanine's sisters, Louise, was married to the son of Martin Gordon, Sr., collector of the port of New Orleans and a bosom friend of Andrew Jackson. So close was the relationship between the Bringiers and Jackson that, when the general and his wife visited the New Orleans area after the war with Britain, they paid a long visit to the family at their White Hall plantation.[9]

Kenner's first term in the Louisiana legislature was largely uneventful. As a freshman legislator the young representative from Ascension Parish spent most of his time learning the idiosyncrasies of the legislative process and performing the routine duties expected of a legislator by his constituents. Much of the routine involved the handling of special petitions for relief. They included such requests as one from the Volunteer Company of Cannoneers of Donaldson "praying for some field pieces," and another to assist in the establishment of a college for Ascension Parish. Kenner also served on several special legislative committees which usually handled relatively minor issues. Among these were a special committee to oversee the celebration of Andrew Jackson's victory at New Orleans and a committee to examine the New Orleans Catholic Asylum for the relief of male orphans.[10]

His work on the more important legislative standing committees was not much more impressive than were his assignments on the special committees. For example, as a member of the standing Committee on Agriculture, Manufacture, and Commerce, he made reports on the harbor master, port wardens, and river pilots of the port of New Orleans and investigated the state's model farm. Probably his most memorable action as a member of a legislative committee came as a member of the Committee of Enrollment when he proposed the act which created Caldwell Parish. A similar list of mundane legislative actions is reflected in the various resolutions and bills that Kenner supported during his first term in office. Though most dealt with parochial issues which concerned his home district, Kenner did take the unusual position, considering his strong personal feelings on the subject, of supporting legislation to limit both gambling and the use of lottery tickets in Louisiana.[11]

The most important position obtained by Kenner during his first term of office was his election by his legislative colleagues to the board of directors of the Citizens Bank in 1839. His selection was quite an honor for the twenty-six-year-old representative and showed the degree of respect that the freshman legislator had earned from his fellow lawmakers during his first months of political office. His appointment to the directorship was a significant honor, for at the time the state's banks were entering a period of crisis, and the legislature was looking for individuals to stem the deteriorating situation.

For years, because of its growing agricultural and commercial economy, Louisiana had maintained a strong banking system. Up until the 1820s the banks of the state had been characterized by sound conservative banking practices. However, with the boom period of rapid plantation and business expansion which started in the late 1820s, the banks of Louisiana became more speculative in their operations, with New Orleans becoming one of the most speculative banking communities in the country. However, the good financial times in Louisiana gradually ebbed with the onset of the national financial panic of 1837. That economic crisis evaporated the profits of the state's largest banks, including the Citizens Bank of Louisiana which for years had done more to facilitate commerce in the Mississippi Valley than any other bank in the state. Banking difficulties continued to plague Louisiana for years to come.[12]

Though he had earned the respect of his colleagues during his first term, Kenner's tenure in the legislature was short. Despite the opinion of Mrs. George Currie Duncan, a family friend who wrote sometime following Kenner's first legislative session that he had "acquitted himself . . . to the entire satisfaction of his constituents," he failed to win re-election to the legislature. Much had happened to change the political environment in Louisiana. The economic crisis of 1837 caused such financial problems in the once-prosperous state that it stigmatized the Democratic party and led to the defeat of many of its candidates, including Kenner. First signs of the changing political attitudes of the state's voters appeared in the gubernatorial election of 1838 when the party polled only 47.2 percent of the vote for its nominee. The Democratic decline continued in the election of 1840 when the Democrats not only lost legislative seats, including Kenner's, but, with only 40.3 percent of the votes, the party for the first time in its history failed to win the state's electoral votes for the Democratic nominee for president. In Kenner's home district of Ascension Parish, the party's presidential vote during the four years of his term declined from 76.1 percent of the vote in 1836 to only 50.0 per cent of the vote in 1840. Such a precipitous decrease in the Democratic presidential nominee's ability to draw voters in his district demonstrated the difficult task the young freshman legislator faced in his unsuccessful effort to remain in office.[13]

During the early 1840s Kenner devoted most of his time to his family, his private business dealings, and the construction of his grand manor house at Ashland Plantation. As suggested by the naming of his estate after Henry

Clay's home in Kentucky, during the period of his hiatus from elective office Kenner's political views and party allegiance changed. Though Kenner did not actively participate in Whig affairs until he re-entered the political arena, his shift in political philosophy began sometime before he officially made the switch in parties. As a freshman legislator, he pursued an independent course and did not always vote with the members of his party. Elected to office at a very young age, Kenner matured politically during his first term, changing from a young man whose political alliances were greatly influenced by the opinions of friends and acquaintances to a more determined and wiser individual whose political decisions were based more upon his personal feelings than those of his peers.[14]

Kenner's re-entry into the hustings of Louisiana politics began when the legislature, in 1844, called for a constitutional convention to rewrite the state's thirty-year-old charter. Running as a Whig, Kenner was elected to the convention as the senatorial delegate from the district of Acadia (the parishes of Ascension and St. James). Ironically, this event, which brought him back into public service and marked Kenner's official transition from Democrat to Whig, also was the instrument which insured the permanent declivity of Whig political power in the state.[15]

Louisiana's original organic law had been written at a time when the makeup of the state's population was considerably different than that which existed in the 1830s and 1840s. Drafted at a time when the state was just beginning to experience the rapid influx of new inhabitants, the early constitution was written hurriedly by a convention dominated by conservatives and well-to-do *anciennes* from the southeastern sector of Louisiana. The document limited both suffrage and representation to such a degree that the majority of the state's people, white and black, were excluded from effective control of their government. The franchise was limited to white males who had purchased public land or paid state taxes. This single stipulation kept as many as two-thirds of the state's adult freemen from the polls. Furthermore, voters were restricted in their choice of elected legislative and executive officials to candidates who possessed landed estates which ranged in value from $500 to $5,000. Consequently, the Louisiana legislature soon became dominated by the landed aristocracy.[16]

Louisiana, like many other states in the Deep South, experienced a dramatic population increase during the first half of the nineteenth century. Doubling between 1810 and 1820, and again by 1840, much of the increase in the state's population resulted from the migration of individuals from states to the east and north of Louisiana. A large percentage of these new residents settled in the northern parishes of the state with many of them becoming cotton farmers. Politically, the majority of the migrants were infused with the rural populism of Jacksonian Democracy and its ideology of unlimited opportunity in a landed society.[17]

As the small-farmer class increased in size, so did the pressure to change the state's organic law. Their Jacksonian doctrines led them to insist that Louisiana's existing constitution be revised in order to drive aristocracy and privilege from state government by providing manhood suffrage and equal representation. Opposition to the move for constitutional revision was led by the Whigs. Many of them feared that such radical changes as those proposed by the Democrats would result in disaster, perhaps even revolution. They favored a government run by gentlemen of principle and property who best knew the needs of the less educated and less capable masses.[18]

Despite determined efforts by the Democrats to instigate constitutional reform in the state, for years their attempts only met with limited success. However, the Panic of 1837 dramatically changed the situation. The financial depression which followed the panic had a paralyzing effect on the banking and business interests in the state and spread so much consternation among the state's planters and commercial interests that many of them began to look favorably on constitutional reform. They hoped for some sort of constitutional guarantee which would protect commercial credits in the future. This new support for constitutional change so reinforced the increasing Democratic push for reform that the legislature called for a convention to meet in 1844 at the village of Jackson in Feliciana Parish.[19]

The delegates to the convention were chosen in an election in July, 1844. In that contest the voters of the state were nearly equally divided in their choice of party members, electing thirty-six Whigs, thirty-nine Democrats, one non-partisan, and one "probable" Democrat. Among the seventy-seven delegates were some of the state's leading political minds. Chief among these were the Whig sugar planter and jurist from New Orleans, Judah P. Benjamin, who would later serve as U.S. senator and as a member of Jefferson Davis' cabinet; and Pierre Soulé, one of the most influential Democratic political leaders in Louisiana, who would also later serve as a U.S. senator and as minister to Spain. Other notables chosen as delegates to the meeting were Isaac T. Preston, a future state supreme court judge; Solomon Downs, a leading Democratic official who had been a prime mover in the efforts to modify the 1812 constitution and who would later be elected to Congress; George Eustis, a future chief justice of Louisiana; and Charles M. Conrad, who later served as ad interim secretary of state and as secretary of war in the cabinet of President Millard Fillmore. Hence, the time that Kenner spent at the convention working alongside of and sometimes matching wits with the state's most prominent political personages did much to sharpen his political acumen, enabled him to make valuable political contacts, and solidified his position in the Whig party.[20]

As provided for in the legislative call for a constitutional convention, the delegates assembled in the small town of Jackson on August 5, 1844. Though the delegates were fêted with balls and banquets, little was accomplished during the first days of the meeting. Except for some routine organizational matters, the only major issue discussed while the delegates sat in Jackson was the suitability of the town as a site for the convention. Kenner was among the first to voice his dissatisfaction with the inadequate facilities and to recommend that the meeting be moved to a more suitable environment in New Orleans. Despite heated opposition to the idea by some delegates, a majority of the members agreed to relocate and to postpone further deliberations on revising the state's constitution until after the presidential election in November. Thus after less than three weeks of meetings, the convention adjourned on August 24, 1844, and agreed to reconvene in New Orleans on January 14, 1845.[21]

Kenner had recommended to the convention that the state legislature's Hall of the Representatives be used as the new meeting place for the convention. However, when the group reconvened in New Orleans the legislature was in session, so they met instead in the ballroom of the St. Louis Exchange; when the legislature adjourned they moved to the capitol. Although the convention's progress was often slow and tedious, leading one local newspaper to describe it as a "snail pace gait," Kenner opposed efforts to limit the time of debates. He also took a conservative position by opposing efforts to broaden the scope of authority granted to the assembly by the legislative act which called for constitutional reorganization.[22]

The deliberations of the convention were often marked by sharp disagreements among its members. One area of wide disagreement concerned Article Three of the new constitution which dealt with the executive branch. When the committee appointed to study the subject, of which Kenner was a member, recommended that only a native citizen of the United States, or an inhabitant of the Louisiana Territory at the time of cession, should be eligible to become governor or lieutenant governor, a heated debate occurred. It soon developed into a defense of the French heritage of many of the state's inhabitants. So telling were the arguments of such delegates as Soulé and Bernard Marigny that the convention as a whole rejected the committee's proposal by a vote of forty-one to twenty-seven. The convention also turned back efforts to establish a $5,000 property qualification for the state's chief executive. Qualifications for governor which were approved by the convention provided that he had to be at least thirty-five years old and a citizen of the United States and of Louisiana for at least fifteen years. Elected by direct vote of the people, he was ineligible for reelection for at least four years following the end of his term.[23]

The convention further liberalized the new constitution by eliminating property qualifications for legislators and by extending suffrage to all white males who were twenty-one years old and citizens of the United States and Louisiana for two years preceding the election. Though many in his party opposed the general move of the convention to make state government less restrictive, on many issues Kenner followed an independent course. Although he did not support some of the efforts to liberalize the executive branch, he supported the move to deprive the governor of some of his appointive powers by making most parochial offices elective. Kenner also favored making changes in the state's judiciary; however, with the exception of making their terms of office six years instead of life, the new organic law remained conservative on the question of the judiciary. State judges were still appointed by the governor with the approval of the senate.[24]

Kenner's experience as a member of the board of directors of the Citizens Bank served him well as a convention delegate. The financial hardships which had afflicted the state and its citizens as a result of the Panic of 1837 were still fresh in the minds of many Louisianians while the convention was in session. To prevent a repetition of the financial crisis, Kenner and a majority of the delegates took a sound money approach to the banking question. The state was forbidden from entering into partnership with private corporations, and the legislative power to grant charters was restricted. Kenner favored going even further by making it illegal for individuals to circulate paper money by any corporation or person from other states; however, a majority of the delegates failed to support Kenner's position.[25]

Kenner met with greater success in his efforts to improve the system of public education in the state. There had been few improvements in Louisiana's educational system since the German traveler Karl Postl had visited New Orleans in 1826 and noted that the educational facilities were "inferior to those of any city of equal extent and less wealth" in the nation. Though various legislatures had periodically reserved some funds for schools, the public for the most part continued to stigmatize public education as being only for indigent children. So fruitless had been the state's efforts to promote public education in Louisiana that in 1836 the legislative committee on education reported that the existing system was utterly useless. Yet, despite such dire reports, it was not until the constitutional convention met nearly a decade later that the issue of adequate public education for Louisiana was addressed.[26]

At the convention no delegate was more active in promoting public education than Kenner. His efforts, along with those of G. Mayo, the delegate from Catahoula Parish and chairman of the convention's committee on education, were not without opposition. Opponents complained that in the past the legislature, on various occasions, had wasted large sums of money which were supposed to benefit education, and they expressed concern that the body might do the same thing in the future. Kenner responded by asserting that "the proceeds . . . donated for the purpose of education, should be religiously appropriated to that object." Kenner steadfastly opposed any attempts to dilute efforts to get a meaningful educational program through the convention. For example, an effort to place in the constitution merely the phrase that the legislature "shall encourage the institution of common schools" was opposed by Kenner as inadequate. "To 'encourage' is not the proper word," declared Kenner. "I would make the requisition imperative. Not that the legislature shall 'encourage' the institution of common schools, but that the legislature shall establish throughout the State a system of free schools, for the education of all the people of the State." He observed that "to accomplish this desirable result, I would make it imperative upon the legislature to raise the means for the maintenance and support of free schools." He concluded his remarks with a statement which, for the most part, would become the guiding principle of public education in Louisiana. Kenner called on his fellow delegates to make it "our first duty, to establish the system of free schools, accessible to all, to the rich and to the poor indiscriminately, and to provide adequate means to keep up that system, and to maintain its usefulness."[27]

Kenner's call for equal education of both the rich and poor would in the long run be a major factor in establishing a viable system of public education in Louisiana, for it addressed an underlying cause for the failure of public education in the state throughout most of the first half of the nineteenth century. This was the belief that state-supported public schools were for the poor and that attendance at such institutions stigmatized those individuals who fancied themselves to be members of the social elite. Although this wall of prejudice concerning public education never totally disappeared from the psyche of many Louisianians, particularly in the southern part of the state, efforts by Kenner and other supporters of public education at the time did go a long way toward opening the schools to all of the "free" youth of the state, and eventually removing much of the stigma formerly attached to "gratuitous instruction."[28]

Despite their differences, members of the convention ultimately gave overwhelming support to the concept promoted by Kenner of free education for the people. The delegates placed into the new constitution a section which, for the first time in the state's history, required that the legislature establish free public schools throughout Louisiana and which directed the state to provide some means of support "by taxation on property or other-wise" for the continued upkeep of the new schools. The widespread support for this measure evolved from the growing temper of Jacksonian Democracy, which served as a catalyst for many other changes made by the convention.

Other significant reforms included a broadening of the suffrage and reapportionment of the legislature to give increased representation to the northern parishes of the state where the preponderance of the small Jacksonian farmers resided. The realization that the aristocratic power-brokers who had previously controlled political affairs in Louisiana were now going to have to share power with the common man led many in the convention to look more positively toward upgrading the state's educational system. Kenner summarized the feelings of many of the delegates when he stated that he "considered that the superstructure for universal suffrage was free common schools" and that in taking steps to establish a public school system the delegates had "done what was indispensable."[29]

An issue on which the delegates demonstrated far less unanimity than on the education question was that of reapportionment. Much heated debate occurred as the delegates attempted to address the important issue of legislative representation. The 1812 constitution had stipulated that representation was to be "equal and uniform" according to the number of electors. Though over the years the legislature had acted to meet the legal demand for periodic reapportionment, it had failed to make the changes either equal or uniform. Consequently, both the house and senate were grossly unrepresentative of the state's population. New Orleans, for example, with a quarter of the state's population, had only two seats in the senate; by contrast, several black belt or sugar districts with an equal proportion of the state's population claimed seven senators—or half of the entire upper chamber of the legislature.[30]

Three major positions on apportionment were presented at the convention by delegates from various sections of the state. The planter parishes preferred that representation be based on total population (each slave would count as three-fifths of a free person), while the farm areas favored apportionment based solely on the state's white population. The third position was that of the delegates from New Orleans, who felt that the other proposals were unfair to the city. Since the city paid about two-thirds of the state's taxes, they wanted taxable property to be used as a basis for representation. After considerable deliberation, the convention delegates decided on a compromise solution which satisfied planters by apportioning senatorial representation on the basis of total population and other white voters by apportioning the lower chamber of the legislature on the basis of qualified electors.[31]

Although the arrangement approved by the convention gave New Orleans the balance of power in the house, many delegates from the state's largest city resented what they considered to be an unjust arrangement for the city. Bernard Marigny, a delegate from New Orleans, went so far as to suggest that the city refuse to pay taxes or even separate from the rest of the state. Adding to feelings of resentment of the New Orleans delegation was the convention's decision to remove the capital from the city.[32]

In the protracted debate over apportionment, Kenner sided with the planter delegates from the black belt on most issues, including their endeavor to obtain additional seats in the legislature. So successful were his efforts that his own senatorial district of Acadia was awarded an additional seat in the senate. Despite his close ties to the city and many of its delegates, Kenner worked to limit the centralization of power in New Orleans. To dilute the city's power he favored a plan to divide New Orleans into several electoral districts which possessed dissimilar political interests. It was thought that such a division would limit the ability of the city's political leaders to unite and to concentrate their political power. Though resisted by members of the city's delegation, the convention eventually approved a plan which divided New Orleans into eight electoral districts. Kenner also sided against the New Orleans delegation on the issue of locating the capital outside of the city. Castigating opponents for having what he labeled "pitiful local feelings and prejudices" and for demonstrating a "dog-in-the-manger" attitude, Kenner called on the delegates to support the new constitution "on the higher and nobler ground of its extending and securing greater civil and political rights to the great body of our citizens."[33]

As illustrated by his comment above, Kenner's speeches during the convention on occasion had the ring of a Jacksonian Democrat. Despite his political affiliation with the Whigs, obviously some of Kenner's feelings remained true to the beliefs he had developed during the early period of his political career when he was a Democrat. Also evident in his comments concerning the need for free public schools "for all the people of the state," Kenner's sympathies for the common man were never more obvious than when he defended the right of the people to be able to vote on the ratification of the new constitution. Somewhat surprisingly, the delegate with whom Kenner debated the issue was Solomon Downs of Ouachita Parish, one of the most influential Democrats in the state and, before the convention, one of the most important proponents for constitutional reform. Downs claimed that he was against letting the people vote on ratification because he was afraid of the influence that local officials would exert on the outcome of the plebiscite. Kenner countered Downs' argument in a speech in which he not only demonstrated his feelings for the people of Louisiana but also his ability as a debater and public speaker. Kenner observed "that it stuck a plain man like [himself], with some surprise, that such a proposition should have come from [Downs]. It seemed to [Kenner] a strange situation in man's ingenious work, that one who has stood in the foremost ranks could have by any legerdemain so suddenly have changed his position." Kenner went on to point out that

> the delegate (Downs) in all that he has been pleased to tell us, gives us but a single reason why the constitution should not be submitted to the people. And that is, that he fears it will be rejected. Now I would ask the delegate from Ouachita, for whom are we making this constitution? Is it for the convention, or is it for the people? If we are making it for the people, then I consider it our duty to lay it before them. We ought not to lose sight of the responsibility we owe to the people, nor attempt to hedge ourselves behind the doctrine that it is unsafe to commit the result of our labors to the judgement of the people.[34]

As with most other major issues he chose to support, Kenner had the support of a majority of convention delegates who chose to have the new constitution put to a vote of the people. With the major issues of the convention addressed, the new constitution was accepted by the delegates on a vote of fifty-one to fifteen. When the issue was put before the people, the delegates were not disappointed with their decision to let the voters of the state decide on the new organic law. Although many citizens were not pleased with every section of the newly drafted constitution, few preferred to retain that of 1812. Despite a large number of people who simply chose not to vote, the new charter was overwhelmingly accepted by the voters. Of the less than fourteen thousand votes which were cast, the supporters of the new constitution captured the lopsided total of 12,277 as compared to only 1,395 votes for the opposition. Forty-four of Louisiana's forty-five parishes reported election results. Of these, only one—the sugar parish of St. John the Baptist—voted by a forty-eight to thirty-eight margin to reject the new document.[35]

Despite the fact that both the Whigs and Democrats claimed credit for the success of the charter with the state's voters, the new constitution proved to be a pivotal event in the history of political parties in Louisiana. For, although the convention was a personal success for Kenner because the issues he had most cared about were all adopted, the new constitution would be one of the major tools in the hands of the Democrats in wresting political power away from his own political party. To be sure, gentleman rule was maintained, but the new constitution was in fact a concession by the elite to the common man. The new charter reflected the Jacksonian mistrust of banks and monopolies. This budding Jacksonian Democracy would quickly grow into the dominant political movement in the state.[36]

In the months leading up to the convention the Whig party had suffered some major reverses in Louisiana, losing both the 1842 gubernatorial and 1844 presidential elections. However, it was the adoption of the 1845 constitution which sealed the fate of the Whigs in Louisiana. The new instrument of government enfranchised the poorer classes who were moving into the state in ever-increasing numbers and who, when settled, usually became Democrats. From the time of the new constitution onward, the Whigs became a minority party which only occasionally could arouse the support of the people of Louisiana.[37]

VI

WHIG LEADER

Within weeks of the popular vote on the adoption of the state's new constitution in 1845, campaigning began for the legislature and other state offices. Among the many candidates for elected office was Duncan Kenner, who entered the race for the state senate seat for Ascension Parish. Kenner actually was the incumbent. In 1844, when everyone's interest was focused upon the effort to bring about constitutional reform and the selection of representatives for the convention, Kenner had not only won a seat at the convention but also to the legislature as a senator. Because the latter met concurrently with the constitutional convention, only passing interest was given to the legislative assemblage by either its members or the people of the state.[1]

Because the new legislature would have much to say about the implementation of the new constitution, Louisianians viewed the 1846 elections with more seriousness and interest than usual. As with most campaigns for political office in antebellum Louisiana, the election was hard fought. Candidates attracted much public attention as they stumped their districts speaking either to large audiences at mass meetings or talking individually with residents with whom they came in contact. Office seekers either traveled alone or in groups; on occasion candidates for the same office journeyed together and took turns in speaking to their constituents. At times campaigns even took on the look of a traveling minstrel show as the candidates joked, played pranks on each other, told stories, and sang songs to their audiences.[2]

In the campaign the Democrats were determined to build on the Jacksonian theme of the needs of the common man versus the wants of the privileged, whereas the Whigs endorsed the undistinguished motto of "principles and not men" as their campaign theme. To get their point across the Democrats attacked the Whigs for supporting the tariff, which, they claimed, led to the accumulation of vast wealth for the few. To the voters the election became a struggle between "monopoly and privilege and money on the one hand, and justice, common sense, and the rights of the masses on the other."[3] The Democrats' efforts succeeded in putting the Whigs on the defensive and forced them to center their campaign efforts around defending the tariff and limply denouncing their opponents as anti-tariff politicians.

The Democratic strategy worked. Isaac Johnson, the Democratic gubernatorial candidate, defeated his Whig opponent in thirty of Louisiana's forty-five parishes. Even in Kenner's home parish of Ascension, where the tariff was looked upon favorably because of the area's sugar economy, the Democrats made a strong showing. In a letter to William Minor in Natchez a short time after the vote and before he knew all of the statewide results, Kenner glumly wrote: "the elections have been very animated, but I have carried my election by eight votes—two democratic representatives were elected from our parish—one by two and one by four votes—the parish went democratic for governor and lieutenant governor—by thirty for the first and sixty for the second." He concluded with the lament that "our defeat throughout the state will be overwhelming." Fortunately for his party, things did not turn out quite as badly as Kenner predicted. Though they lost the executive office and the Democrats held a two-vote majority in the senate, the Whigs were able to win a majority of three seats in the house of representatives. Furthermore, the new Democratic governor was a member of the predominantly Anglo-American West Feliciana aristocracy who did not act as a strict party man. Hence, over the period of his administration there were relatively few changes between the new Democrats and the old Whigs.[4]

The new legislature met in early February, 1846, and began the process of activating the new constitution. Though much of the work dealt with routine and uncontroversial issues, one of the most hotly debated subjects at the session was the constitutional provision which required the removal of the state capital from New Orleans. Those who supported the effort criticized the length of the legislative sessions held in the Crescent City. They speculated that the many distractions found in the city kept the lawmakers from concentrating on their legislative duties. Adding to the heat of the debate was the fact that nearly every city in the state had supporters in the legislature seeking the new capital. Of the various communities mentioned as an alternative location for the capital, Baton Rouge, St. Francisville, and Donaldsonville were the leading contenders. Kenner pushed hard for Donaldsonville, the parish seat of his home parish of Ascension. He pointed out to his colleagues that Donaldsonville was conveniently located and was accessible from nearly every section of the state. In spite of his efforts, Kenner's arguments in favor of Donaldsonville went unheeded by the legislature. Once before, in 1830, the capital had briefly been moved from the Crescent City to Donaldsonville. That experience had been such a fiasco that Kenner's appeal for the establishment of the capital in his home district stood little chance for success. After much debate, Baton Rouge was selected as the new capital.[5]

In the spring, constitutional reform and state politics were overshadowed by national events. Paramount among these national issues was the war with Mexico. Fueled by the expansionist mood of the country and by President James K. Polk's assertions that the Mexicans had invaded our territory and had "shed American blood upon . . . American soil," Congress declared war against Mexico on May 13, 1846. With the outbreak of hostilities between the two nations, war fever spread quickly throughout Louisiana. Even before the president sent his war message to Congress, Kenner and his colleagues in the legislature appropriated $100,000 for the purpose of equipping regiments of volunteers from Louisiana to be placed at the call of General Zachary Taylor at the war front. In addition to sponsoring the funding for what he called the "Louisiana Legion," Kenner later proposed to tender General Taylor a sword in recognition of his valiant service in the Mexican conflict. His motion was unanimously adopted.[6]

The war with Mexico was not the only national issue to receive the attention of state legislators. The American effort to expand its territorial holdings into the Southwest was but one goal of the proponents of Manifest Destiny. From the beginning of his administration, President Polk had pressed the American claim to all of Oregon. Though the president received strong support for his position from the states of the old Northwest, the great majority of the members of Congress, both Democrats and Whigs, favored a settlement of the Oregon dispute with Britain on the basis of a partition of the territory at the forty-ninth parallel. Southerners in particular were not interested in vast territorial additions to the Pacific Northwest, and they feared taking any action which might endanger British markets for their agricultural surplus. However, as in the case of his support for the war with Mexico, Kenner demonstrated the depth of his nationalistic feelings and his independent political thought by strongly supporting the doctrine of Manifest Destiny–a stand which was in support of a Democratic president and in opposition to the majority of his fellow Whigs around the country. In an address to the legislature he embraced Polk's efforts to secure the whole of Oregon. On the basis of priority of exploration, Kenner declared that the claim of the United States to the boundary 54' 40" was unquestionable.[7]

It did not take long, however, for the novelty of the international situation to wear off and for the legislature to return its attention to implementing the terms of the new constitution. In early 1847 the question of education and the new constitution came before the state lawmakers. Louisiana Secretary of State Charles Gayarré reported to the legislature on the "precarious existence" of the state's educational system. He warned that its "days [were] numbered" and that quick action was needed by the legislature. As was the case at the recent constitutional convention, Kenner was in the forefront of the drive to bring about the needed educational reforms. His effort to improve the system by introducing a bill to "establish free schools throughout the state" won Kenner the praise of a New Orleans paper, which expressed pleasure that at least one legislator was making an effort to put into effect the educational reforms mandated by the constitution.[8]

Sometimes referred to by the press as the "Kenner Bill," the proposal for free schools throughout Louisiana was eventually passed during the session. Though the issue was not a partisan one, the debate on education was sometimes punctuated with long-winded discussions of parochial issues. One such discussion involved Kenner and concerned the choice of a location for a state university. As he had at the constitutional convention when he resisted the efforts to keep the capital in the Crescent City, Kenner also thought that the state's largest city was not a good choice for the location of a university. He claimed that locating a university in New Orleans would expose its young students to the varied diversions of urban life which would negatively affect their concentration and possibly undermine the desire of some for an education. Kenner's rather provincial argument against the establishment of a university in the state's largest city did not go unanswered. One of the more effective replies came from the *Daily Delta*, a newspaper which on occasion had positive things to say about Kenner. It stated that "we regret to see so intelligent and patriotic a gentleman, and legislator as Mr. Kenner . . . discouraging a university in New Orleans." The paper went on to point out that the most prestigious and flourishing colleges in the world were to be found in the largest cities. The paper argued that a large city offered the added security of a large police force which might be needed to control unruly students. Finally, the *Delta* ended its remarks on the subject by making the point that New Orleans had had a medical school for some time without any of Kenner's predicted consequences having taken place.[9]

Kenner's colleagues in the legislature failed to agree with him on this issue. As authorized by the constitution, the state appropriated revenues for the establishment in New Orleans of the University of Louisiana, which it was hoped would have colleges of medicine, law, natural sciences, and literature. Though the new university's schools of medicine and law were successful, those of literature and natural sciences never developed because of insufficient operating funds. The university remained in existence until the outbreak of the Civil War. Despite his unhappiness over the location of the university, Kenner continued his activism for years as one of the chief supporters of a free public school system for Louisiana.[10]

Throughout his legislative career, Kenner applied himself to the task at hand. Whether it was a major issue such as constitutional reform or simple petitions of relief from his constituents, he diligently sought to have his position on an issue accepted by his colleagues. His skill on the floor of the legislature, along with his ability as a speaker, his good judgment, and his thorough knowledge and mastery of the workings of the legislative committee system, all brought Kenner recognition not only from his fellow lawmakers but also from people and politicians throughout the state. Among the honors bestowed upon the legislator was his selection in 1847 as vice-president of the Bar Association of New Orleans.[11]

The most significant acknowledgement of Kenner's rising political stature came in 1848 when the Whig party turned to him as its nominee for one of the most important political offices in the state. The tenure of United States Senator Henry Johnson was drawing to a close, and both the Whigs and Democrats hoped to replace the senator with one of their own.

Since the state legislature then chose United States senators, it appeared that, because the Whigs now held a narrow majority of two votes on a joint legislative ballot, they had the advantage. However, because of the lack of party unity which Louisiana's Whigs sometimes displayed on crucial votes, there was much public interest and political concern over the outcome of the contest. The New Orleans *Daily Delta* reported that "the town is agog about the election," while the Whig paper, the *Baton Rouge Gazette*, publicly voiced concern over the lack of party unity.[12] The paper commented that:

> On former occasions, we have seen the mortifying spectacle of a legislature of Louisiana, with a Whig majority, electing a Democratic Senator, in consequence of local feeling or personal preference. It is time that the Whig party of Louisiana should adopt a system of [more] rigid discipline, than heretofore [has] been practiced in the ranks, and we are glad to perceive a growing disposition to do so.[13]

Unfortunately for Kenner and the Whigs, when the legislature met in late January to choose Louisiana's new United States senator, the worst fears of the *Gazette*'s editor and the party faithful were realized. In an effort to keep their party members in line, the Whigs used the Democrats' custom of the caucus to choose a single nominee to support for the office. When they met on January 20 there were several individuals interested in the Senate seat. On the first ballot Judah P. Benjamin received 25 votes; Kenner, 24; Randall Hunt, 9; Henry Johnson, 2; and candidate James Elam received no votes. On the second ballot only the top two vote-getters remained in the race. Kenner picked up most of the votes of the first ballot's losing candidates and thus captured the nomination with 36 votes to Benjamin's 26. Meanwhile, the Democrats selected Kenner's acquaintance and former employer John Slidell as their nominee. They also agreed, however, to turn to Pierre Soulé after the second ballot by the legislature if Slidell was unable to win the nomination at the outset.[14]

There was an interval of several days between the time of Kenner's selection as the Whig nominee and the actual election by the legislature. This time was a period of considerable speculation and anxiety over the outcome of this major political contest between the two parties. Public interest in the race was intense. Though there was much interest over who would be the Democratic nominee, for that party did not caucus until the very night before the election, there also continued to be considerable speculation among state political leaders and the public over the question of whether the Whigs could hold their members in line to vote for their nominee.[15]

The issue was finally resolved when, at 12:20 p.m. on January 24, 1848, the legislature met in the hall of the state house of representatives to choose a new United States senator. Tension was great. The reporter for the *Daily Delta* noted the mood when he wrote: "The house hall was densely crowded, many . . . distinguished citizens were in attendance, and the important event was about to transpire. Anxiety and painful suspense were depicted on many countenances."[16]

As soon as the assembly was called to order, Kenner and his Whig allies realized that they were going to have problems. As the house clerk called the roll of the members present, all but one responded. Isaac A. Myles, a Whig from Washington Parish, failed to answer the call. His absence caused a great sensation, for without Myles' presence the joint assembly consisted of 129 members, with 65 votes needed to win. Realizing that their prospect for victory was substantially lessened without Myles, the Whigs attempted to strengthen their position with a parliamentary procedure. They protested the right of Senator John Bell of Orleans Parish to vote in the election because the senate at that time was investigating his right to sit in the senate. However, after only limited debate, the Democrat president of the senate dismissed the Whig protest, claiming that it violated the rules of the meeting.[17]

When the assembly returned to the matter at hand, the nomination process for the senate race was completed. John Bell, having successfully avoided the Whig challenge, was given the honor of nominating the Democratic nominee, John Slidell. Kenner's name was placed into consideration by his friend and political ally, Christopher Adams of Iberville Parish. When the balloting started, Kenner attempted to break some of the tension in the hall by playfully hesitating to cast his own ballot for himself as if he had second thoughts. The mood in the room, however, quickly became more serious when Maunsel White, Democratic senator from Plaquemines, threw his vote away by casting it for an un-nominated individual. Unfortunately for Kenner and the Whigs, White's defection from Slidell did not help them, for Representative Baldwin of Sabine Parish, who had been considered a member of the Whig camp, cast his vote for Slidell. Hence the first ballot ended with Kenner receiving a total of 64 votes (15 in the senate and 49 in the house) and his opponent earning an equal number (one more than Kenner in the senate and one less in the house).[18]

A second vote was taken with the same results. With an obvious deadlock in place, the Whigs attempted to break off the contest by moving to discontinue the joint session. After heated debate, the senate withdrew to its chamber where the Whigs again renewed their efforts to challenge Bell's right to take part in the election. When their efforts proved futile and motions to adjourn the senate and the house also failed, the two legislative houses reassembled together.[19]

Considerable behind-the-scenes maneuvering had taken place while the two houses caucused. The Democrats now moved to break the impasse. Senator Bell, who had been in the center of so much of the day's events, rose and nominated Pierre Soulé for the office in question. Events moved quickly. Slidell, who was not pleased with the move to replace him with Soulé and who would from that time on be a bitter political enemy of the new Democratic nominee, nevertheless remained a loyal party man and threw his support behind Soulé. With the political momentum now in their favor, the Democrats pushed for a new vote. There was little that Kenner and his supporters could do. Five individuals who had cast their votes against Slidell in the first round of voting now shifted their support to Soulé. They included the Democrat Maunsel White and four Whigs, Senators Felix Garcia and William Parham and house members Bienvenue and Watkins. Only one Slidell voter named Baldwin switched his support to Kenner. Thus, the final vote for the United States Senate seat was 68 votes (19 in the Senate and 49 in the House) for Soulé to 61 for Kenner (13 in the upper house and 48 in the lower).[20]

The vote of the legislature ended Kenner's chance for a seat in Congress; however, it did not stop the controversy and speculation which had engulfed the campaign from its start. Not unexpectedly, the surprise election of Soulé caused much consternation throughout the state, with the Whigs denouncing and the Democrats lauding the results. The Whig press in particular was not pleased. One Whig editor commented that "it would require a more astute Oedipus than him of old to account for the means by which the Democrats have elected a U.S. Senator . . . with a clear Whig majority of two."[21] The most bitter comments concerning the Whig disaster were reserved for those Whigs who had not supported their party's nominee. The New Orleans *Bulletin* bitterly attacked the party traitors and concluded that, "As for Isaac A. Myles . . . we think it will be fortunate for his fame, if some accident has removed him from this to a better world, as no less excuse will be satisfaction for his mysterious absence." The paper went on to castigate the other turncoats with the comment that "Baldwin's voting for Slidell and not for Soulé showed his illegal bargain ended with the former."[22] The *Baton Rouge Gazette* expressed a similar view with the comment that, "If he [Kenner] is not a U.S. Senator now in the stead of Pierre Soulé, it is because he was incapable of doing what he considered wrong in consequence of the treachery of William S. Parham."[23]

While the Whig press viciously assailed its opponents and those individuals responsible for their party's defeat, the Democratic press reveled in its victory by lauding Soulé's success. In caustic language typical of the political papers of the time, the *Democratic Advocate* of Baton Rouge even belittled the defeated candidate's vote for himself by commenting that

"Kenner was driven to the alternative of voting for himself, a rather delicate matter, and in pressure he did it as timidly as a Miss, the first time she whispered yes."[24]

Many Whigs considered the election to have been stolen from them. As noted earlier, there was much conjecture in the period leading up to the vote that something was going to happen which would give the election to the Democrats. The *Daily Picayune* even published before the election an anonymous letter in which the author reported that he had heard two Democrats, one of whom was a legislator, "say very confidentially that the Democrats would elect a United States Senator." The unnamed writer went on to question whether any Whig legislators would publicly vote for a Democrat or if "any of them [would] be sick . . . and not attend." Observing "that in times past money has effected wonders," the *Picayune*'s anonymous correspondent concluded, somewhat expectantly, that the Whigs would simply have to wait to see "who are the Judases."[25]

With so many in the state holding a similar belief to that of the *Picayune*'s writer and with the furor over the Whig setback growing, several legislators who had unexpectedly voted for the Democratic nominee instead of Kenner scrambled to explain their position to their colleagues and constituents. On the day following the election, Senator Parham addressed the senate and defended his vote by claiming that he had determined that a victory by Kenner was impossible because of Whig dissension. Originally he had expected Kenner to win, as every Whig at their party caucus promised to stand by the nominee. However, when it was rumored about an hour before the vote that Myles was absent, he concluded that something would happen to deny the Whigs their one-vote majority. During the actual voting, when the Whig Baldwin voted for Slidell and Kenner was unable to gather enough votes for victory on two ballots, he decided that something had to be done to deny the race to Slidell. After unsuccessfully trying to get another Whig candidate into the race, he informed one of the Democratic leaders that he would vote for Soulé. He then approached Kenner, telling him that the only way to keep Slidell from winning would be to divide the Democrats. Kenner replied that "perhaps it was a trick on the part of the opposite party" to get Soulé elected. Parham claimed that at that time he did not know of anyone else who would vote for Soulé, and in any case he preferred the election of Soulé, whom he considered a man of ability and a true patriot, by Slidell's defeat rather than Slidell's victory by Kenner's defeat.[26]

After explaining his own actions, Parham then concluded his remarks by commenting on the motives of two other legislators who had crossed party lines in the election. Echoing the popular sentiment of the day, Parham declared that he, along with many others, "believed that improper means had been used, both in procuring the absence of Mr. Myles and getting Mr. Baldwin to vote against Mr. Kenner," and he hoped that through a proper investigation the truth of the matter would be revealed.[27]

Parham's defense was followed by similar ones by Garcia in the senate and Watkins in the house. Both claimed that they had switched their vote from Kenner to Soulé only because they believed that the former had lost his chance of winning and they wanted to take steps to prevent Slidell from being elected. However, despite their pleas for understanding from their colleagues, bad feelings remained. Many of Kenner's supporters did not accept their explanations and did not mind letting them know of their unhappiness. For example, when Parham was challenged on his vote by Senator Martin, the discussion between the two legislators on the floor of the senate became so heated that the exchange of coarse and vulgar epithets soon led to the trading of physical blows between the two lawmakers.[28]

The question of what really led to the Whigs' unexpected loss in the senate race became even more clouded when Representative Jones of Jefferson Parish openly accused the absent Isaac A. Myles of Washington Parish of fraud. In a written statement to the house, he claimed that Myles had told him on the Saturday before the Monday election that he had been offered four Negroes not to vote for a Whig for United States senator. Jones urged that a committee be appointed to investigate the alleged corruption. Disclaiming any knowledge of the affair, Democrats seconded the motion and voted with the Whigs to form an investigative committee.[29]

When the "Myles Committee" began to gather its evidence it quickly became evident that it would be difficult to discern what had really happened in the election. Each of the legislators whose votes for U.S. senator had seemed questionable was called to explain his action. Most explained away their actions with vague political excuses. However, testimony was given which tended to exonerate Myles of the charges that he had accepted a bribe not to be present when the vote was taken. An individual identified only as Colonel Staples reported to the committee that he had introduced Myles to Slidell and that afterwards he had heard him express great satisfaction for Slidell. He also testified that after the election he spoke with Myles and asked him if the rumors about his taking a bribe were based upon fact. Myles replied that he had not been bribed. The only thing offered him, he explained to Staples, was a promise by the speaker of the house to place him on any committee he might select. The speaker later denied any ulterior motive in making the offer.[30]

Some of the most unexpected testimony before the committee occurred when Jones was called before the group to repeat his accusation about Myles. After hearing his comments and those of others who had knowledge of the events leading up to the vote for U.S. senator, the committee reached the following conclusion:

> A few days before the election, Jones went to the gentleman who was considered the choice of the democratic party, and told him he was no great shakes of a whig anyhow–he was too liberal for his party-that his parish, he believed, was democratic–that he would not on any terms vote for . . . the probable candidates of the whigs–that he was poor and sickly, and his health would be benefitted and his life prolonged by a visit to Cuba.[31]

With the accuser thus becoming the accused and with additional testimony from other witnesses which revealed that legislators other than just Jones and Myles were involved in making deals during the senate election, the "Myles Committee" was unable or unwilling to give a definitive report of wrongdoing in the election. Instead, it reported on March 7 that, from the evidence reviewed, the committee did not "feel authorized to report any breach of privilege [had] been committed." According to the committee, offers of the same type had been made to others in the house, as well as to Myles, and in their judgement the offers were considered to be "perfectly in accordance with parliamentary usage." They did, however, believe that part of the evidence was of such a nature that a written report was needed. The committee's report was quickly adopted by the legislature, and, with public interest waning, the issue was allowed to die without any real penalties being assessed against those individuals involved in the scandal.[32]

Despite their disappointing defeat in the senatorial race, Kenner and his Whig colleagues were able to come away from the election with the satisfaction of knowing that the Democrats' victory was not won without cost. For although they had entered the election as allies, Slidell and Soulé, the two most important leaders in the Louisiana Democratic Party, became bitter political rivals as a result of the contest. The surprising turn of events which denied victory to Slidell so affected him that he became the determined and implacable foe of Soulé for political control of Louisiana.

The rivalry between the two Democrats remained a central theme in the state's politics up to the eve of the Civil War.[33]

Louisiana's Whigs quickly put the senatorial election behind them and began to look forward to the next political contest, the presidential race in the fall of the year. Both state and national Whig leaders' hopes ran high for victory. Borrowing from the Democratic tradition which had given the country the Jackson presidency, the Whigs turned to a public hero, General Zachary Taylor, who could exploit his military fame to obtain the presidency. A Mexican War hero, Taylor was a Louisiana planter who owned more than one hundred slaves and had never been a member of the Whig party nor had ever voted in a presidential election. His Democratic opponent, Lewis Cass of Michigan, was also a general in the war with Mexico and was a politician who had always tried to placate the South. Whereas the Whigs did not bother with a platform, the Democrats supported the American involvement in Mexico and declared that the federal government had no right to meddle with slavery. The campaign was largely one of ambiguities and personalities and ended with Taylor narrowly winning in both Louisiana and the nation. The Democratic defeat nationally was the result of a strong third party showing in New York by the Free Soil ticket headed by former president Martin Van Buren. In Louisiana, Taylor carried the state with 54.6 percent of the vote by doing extremely well in the planter areas of both cotton and sugar country.[34]

Their victory in the presidential election gave the Whigs in Louisiana high hopes for success in the next state election contest with the Democrats. Within a few weeks, the enthusiasm and confidence of the Whigs was reinforced when the party won a smashing victory in the New Orleans municipal elections. In light of these successes, Louisiana's Whigs began to set their sights on the state's upcoming gubernatorial campaign. Confident of their chances for victory, the Whigs began to review carefully their prospective candidates for the state's highest office. Among those prominently mentioned were Bannon Thibodaux, the only Louisiana Whig in Congress; Judah P. Benjamin; Alexander Bullitt, editor of the *Daily Picayune*; and Kenner, who was now looked upon as a spokesman for the state's country Whigs.[35]

Although on the surface things looked promising for the party, beneath the public image party unity was beginning to show some strain. Many of the old "setfast" Whigs, as distinguished from the younger and more liberal members, were disgruntled with President Taylor's failure to reward supporters from his home state with appointments to federal office. But the dissatisfaction of the "setfasts" went beyond that which they directed towards the president. They also found it increasingly difficult to agree with the younger and newer members of the party, who were more practical, vigorous, energetic, and adaptable to change. In spite of their success in recent elections, the lack of agreement between the old and new factions of the party did not bode well for the Whigs.[36]

When the state nominating convention met in Baton Rouge, more than three hundred delegates took part. Though several other individuals had been mentioned as likely candidates, the delegates, after only two ballots, nominated Alexander Declouet for governor. The convention then selected Kenner as its nominee for the office of lieutenant governor. Despite its consensus on a choice of nominees, the convention reflected the developing factionalism which was beginning to afflict the party. When the young Whigs sponsored a resolution calling for the election of the state judiciary and denouncing the Democrats for appointing corrupt judges, the older "setfast" party members opposed any such change in the system. Though he personally liked the system of election, Kenner sided with the conservatives and opposed the proposal for political reasons because he thought it was unwise to antagonize the politically powerful state judiciary. Joining with Kenner and the conservatives, the majority of the delegates voted down the measure. Despite the convention's vote on the issue, the question of electing judges became an important issue during the ensuing campaign, with both parties, ironically, supporting and claiming it as their own.[37]

Opposing Declouet and Kenner were the Democratic nominees, Joseph Walker for governor and John B. Plauché for lieutenant governor. Like the Whigs, the Democrats also had problems between the older and young members of the party. Both groups agreed upon Walker as their nominee, but only after he agreed to be true to the principles of the party. This unusual requirement was added because it was well known that Walker had many friends who were Whigs, and the Democrats wanted to avoid a repetition of the behavior of the previous Democratic governor, Isaac Johnson, who had irritated many of his party's faithful by appointing Whigs to office.[38]

The campaign itself was distinguished by a lack of major issues between the two parties. For the most part, the Democrats attempted to make the point that their party represented progress and that the Whigs favored holding on to the current evils rather than entertaining measures of reform and experimentation. In the rural sections of the state the Democrats depicted their party as seeking to protect the people against the encroachment of the moneyed interests, whereas the Whig party's chief goal and purpose was to acquire wealth. On the other hand, the Whigs continually alluded to their ties with President Taylor. They also attempted to use the issue of naturalization of foreigners as a point against the Democrats by showing that Declouet had opposed making the naturalization laws more restrictive while a member of the senate. During most of the campaign, however, the issues raised in the respective party platforms were subordinated to bitter personal attacks by the candidates against each other. Kenner, for example, on several occasions attacked his Democratic counterpart for having only a limited knowledge of English which he claimed would limit the French-speaking Plauché from working effectively with the members of the senate.[39]

As the campaign continued and the parties and nominees exchanged charges and countercharges, both political camps were criticized by the press and by other observers for conducting a campaign devoid of principles and apparently aimed only at acquiring power and the taste of victory. The absence of clearly defined issues caused much public interest to be directed to the peripheries of the campaign, such as the public meetings, parades, club organizations, and songs, all of which were designed to enliven the campaign as election day neared. Clubs such as the Kenner Guards and Declouet Rangers and their Democrat counterparts played important roles in stirring up public support for their favorite candidates.[40]

In the antebellum South there were generally two types of successful politicians—the aristocratic type represented by Kenner and the folksy, demagogic type who duped unsophisticated rural voters by imitating the language and manners of the common man and by telling jokes. Among those who appealed to the feelings of the common man was Kenner's running mate. At rallies he would frequently belittle Joseph Walker, his Democratic opponent, by singing the familiar tune "The Ranger's Lament for Poor Old Joe," the chorus of which ran:

> Take off the saddle from his back,
> Pull down the fodder from his rack;
> There is no more run in poor old Joe--
> Turn him out to grass and let him go.[41]

Possessing a keen sense of humor, Kenner was not above poking a little fun at his political opponents during his campaign speeches, as demonstrated by his comments during the 1849 race about his opponent's poor mastery of English. For the most part, however, Kenner's reserved and undemonstrative temperament and his refined manners kept him from adopting many of the garish campaign techniques of some of the South's more flamboyant politicians. Despite his intelligence and sense of humor, his speech-making ability never matched the level of talent he demonstrated in mastering the intricacies of the legislative process. Though usually well received by his audience, Kenner's speeches were not equal to those of Louisiana's most brilliant politicians—for example, the Kenner's family's friend Etienne Mazureau, who reportedly gave speeches which ran up to six hours in length.[42]

Of the many political gatherings that occurred during the campaign, one of the largest and most elaborate took place in New Orleans on the eve of the election. The Whigs of the city hosted a barbecue at the plantation home of Judge Joachim Bermudez on Gentilly Road. Six thousand persons attended and took part in the festivities. The Declouet and Kenner Guards were present along with many of the area's most prominent Whigs. Tables overflowed with roasted meats, and caskets of claret and ale were consumed while several bands played lively music under hundreds of political banners and symbols. Handbills were distributed to remind everyone present to vote for the party ticket on election day. Several of the notable Whigs who were present gave speeches; however, it was Kenner's oration which most affected the crowd. The press reported that upon his appearance there was a burst of enthusiasm, for Kenner was highly esteemed by his political friends and was a warm favorite of the party's supporters. In his address to the crowd Kenner gave his standard campaign speech. He reviewed the work of the campaign and mentioned the success of the Whigs in electing Taylor. He warned about the possibility of a let-down after such a great victory but added that, judging from the enthusiasm of the people present, the upcoming vote held great promise for the Whig nominees. Before ending his remarks, Kenner commented briefly on the controversy which had arisen over his comments concerning his opponent's poor command of English. To those in the opposition party who took exception to his observations, Kenner stated he had been guided in his comments by earlier remarks on the subject by none other than General Joseph Walker, the Democratic gubernatorial nominee.[43]

The large and raucous campaign rallies, which were by then a mainstay of Louisiana elections, continued up until the very eve of the vote. The balloting took place on Monday, November 5, 1849, and was one of the most active ever to take place in the state during the antebellum period. The results of the election took some time to tally, but when all the votes were counted, the Democrats had won victories in the races for the state's two highest offices. With 51.4 percent of the vote, Walker had narrowly defeated Declouet by a little more than a thousand votes, 18,566 for the Democrat to 17,553 for the Whig. Kenner did a little better than his running mate by losing the lieutenant governorship to Plauché by a vote of 18,200 to 17,385, or a margin of 815 votes. The greatest support for the Democrats came from the interior sections of the state, where the small farmers dominated, and from Orleans Parish. The Whig candidates not only did well in their traditional strongholds, such as Lafourche and the sugar lands along the Mississippi, but they also carried many of the cotton plantation parishes in the northern part of the state. The unity between the two planter groups in support of Whiggery was such that the election nearly turned in favor of Declouet and Kenner. The salient factor in the results was the vote in Orleans Parish, where many of the Democrats who had deserted their party in the recent presidential race to vote for Taylor returned to support their party's choices in the 1849 gubernatorial contest.[44]

In spite of the disappointing loss, Kenner continued to play a central role in the course of Whig politics in Louisiana. Within months of the end of the gubernatorial election, the voters of the southeastern portion of the state were faced with a special election to fill the vacancy left in the Second Congressional District when Charles Conrad resigned his seat in Congress to accept an appointment to the president's cabinet as secretary of war. At first Kenner was mentioned in the Whig press as the logical candidate for the party's nomination. But he let it be known that he did not want the nomination, although he was concerned about who would receive it.[45]

The contest for the nomination was between the "Country" and "City" factions of the Louisiana Whig Party. Though the larger geographical portion of the district was rural and allied with the "Country Whigs," the populated areas of Jefferson Parish—Algiers, which was located directly across the Mississippi River from the Vieux Carré section of New Orleans, and the city's Second Municipality—were centers of strength for the "City Whigs." Before the Whigs met in convention to choose their nominee for the race, the "City Whigs" united behind the candidacy of Theodore Hunt. They also were able to get assurances of support for their man from several of the country delegates to the convention. With this extra help, the New Orleans area delegates were primed for victory.[46]

Not wanting to see the urban Whigs acquire additional influence at the expense of their own power base, Kenner and several of his "Country Whig" colleagues moved to deny the "City Whigs" their expected victory.

The key to victory centered on what technique would be used in counting the votes in the convention. The urban Whigs expected to use the ratio which had been used at the last Whig gubernatorial convention. Known as the "numerical basis," the plan called for votes to be allotted according to the number of Whig voters in each parish. With the population concentrated in their area, the advantage of this plan for the "City Whigs" was obvious. Kenner maneuvered to undercut the plan of the city delegates by substituting a plan of his own. Labeled the "legislative basis," Kenner's plan called for convention votes to be based upon an area's legislative representation. For example, under the "numerical basis," Jefferson Parish with the town of Lafayette would have received seven votes in the convention; by contrast, under Kenner's "legislative basis," this parish adjacent to New Orleans and a "City Whig" stronghold would get only three votes.[47]

Caught off guard by the surprise move by Kenner and the country delegates to undermine their alliance, the city delegates reacted with outrage and claimed that the country delegates were going back on an agreement which had been reached between the two groups at the gubernatorial convention of 1849. Kenner and other opponents of the numerical plan responded with a plea designed to win back the votes of those country delegates who had earlier promised to support the city plan. They contended that the basic issue was simply a struggle for power between the city and country and that the country delegates needed to unite in order to protect their minority rights in the party. The conflict was finally resolved when the city representatives were assured that the country group only wanted to make the point of their minority rights and that they held no animosity towards the city's candidate for the nomination, Theodore Hunt. The question was called and voted upon, and Kenner's proposal was accepted.[48]

The convention then turned its attention to the selection of a nominee. Since the rural Whigs had gotten their way on the representation issue, the party's "City Whigs" expected their candidate to be selected. The "Country Whigs," however, having gained additional strength from their victory on the representation issue, were unwilling to concede the nomination to their urban opponents. Instead of uniting behind Theodore Hunt, the city's candidate, the convention permitted the names of several individuals to be placed before the group for consideration. This effectively diluted the strength of the "City Whig" faction. Realizing that they were about to lose their chance to have their candidate chosen, the "City Whigs" called a brief recess and appealed directly to the various country delegates who had earlier promised support for the city candidate to redeem their pledge. With control of the nomination in their grasp, the rural Whigs ignored the pleas of the New Orleans area delegates and supported the "Country" candidate, Henry A. Bullard. When the convention reconvened, Bullard was awarded the nomination on the second ballot. Stunned by their defeat, the city delegates fiercely denounced the "Country Whigs" for their political subterfuge and legerdemain. Kenner's plan had worked. He had not only successfully denied the "City" faction of the party the congressional nomination that they at one time had in their pocket, but in one brief encounter he had also managed to undercut his opponents' base of support and had made them, as one New Orleans paper reported, "as weak and impotent as Sampson was after he had lost his locks."[49]

In spite of their anger over being "chiselled" by the "Country Whigs" on the nomination, the "City Whigs" pledged their support for the convention's nominee. Although hard feelings between the two Whig factions continued, their efforts in support of Bullard proved successful and he was able to defeat the Democratic nominee, Henry Johnson, in the congressional election. Unfortunately for the "Country Whigs," their victory was short-lived, for Bullard did not live long after winning election to Congress. With his death, affairs returned to their status before the Bullard nominating convention. With the memory of their defeat in the previous convention and how it was orchestrated fresh in their minds, the urban Whigs were determined to regain some of the ground they had lost to their country opponents. Because of the announced defection of several delegates who had supported his position at the previous convention, Kenner realized that the odds were against his being able to repeat his control of events at the new meeting.[50]

When the convention met, the "City Whigs" had on their agenda a re-examination of the controversy over the "numerical" and "legislative" allotment of delegates. When the "Country Whigs" approached the issue with an open mind and amicably agreed to accept the "numerical" basis, much of the tension between the two factions of the party evaporated. The new harmonious relations between the state's Whigs carried over to the selection of the nominee. For, although the "City Whigs" had a preferred candidate for the nomination, they went along with the choice of the rural delegates, and J. Aristide Landry of Ascension Parish was nominated by acclamation. Hence, despite the reversal on the issue of the allotment of delegates, Kenner's sagacity in both conventions strengthened his position in the power structure of the Louisiana Whig Party and placed him in the forefront of the "Country" faction of the party.[51]

Kenner's leadership position in the party placed him at the top of the list of possible candidates for important upcoming elections. When the Whigs turned their attention to the selection of a nominee for the impending United States Senate race in which the incumbent was a Democrat, Kenner was among those individuals most frequently named by the Whig press as a possible party nominee. However, his lack of support among the urban Whigs caused him to be passed over for the nomination. An unexpectedly strong showing by the Whigs in the 1851 general election in New Orleans gave the "City Whigs" an edge in party strength and threw the nomination to one of Kenner's opponents. At the party caucus in which the senate nominee was chosen, there were three major candidates—Kenner, Judah P. Benjamin, and Randall Hunt. Benjamin was selected on the second ballot, receiving thirty-seven votes to Kenner's nineteen and eleven for Hunt. The Whig's recent gain in strength in local elections also added to their power in the legislature. Thus, when the senatorial election took place in the lawmaking body, Benjamin defeated the Democratic incumbent, Solomon Downs, by twelve votes.[52]

Thus, despite his rise to the pinnacle of power and respect among the wealthy agrarian faction of the Louisiana Whig Party, Kenner was unable to marshal behind him the support of a majority of his party. Because of this failure to unite his party behind him, Kenner never achieved his goal of a statewide political office for which he labored so long.

VII

A DECADE OF CHALLENGE AND CHANGE

Mid-century was a period of major changes in the political affairs of the people of antebellum Louisiana. By the end of the 1850s, parochial issues which had dominated the political scene in Louisiana during the first half of the nineteenth century were overshadowed by the more pressing issue of the continued survival of the Union. With few exceptions, such as the enthusiastic support given to the American war with Mexico by both Whigs and Democrats in the state, political parties in Louisiana tended to observe how national issues were received in other states before they focused upon them at home. Such had been the case in the 1849 general election when Kenner ran for the lieutenant governorship. National issues were seldom mentioned in the political oratory of that contest. The 1849 race, however, marked the last time for many years that national issues would play only a minor role in the politics of Louisiana.[1]

The issue which ended the political isolation of Louisiana's political parties was slavery. By the end of the 1840s, the issue of slavery was the paramount concern in the state and throughout the nation. The slavery question rose in importance with the end of the Mexican War and the introduction in Congress in 1846 by a northern Democrat of the Wilmot Proviso, which declared that slavery could not exist in any new territory obtained from Mexico. Although it never passed, the proviso helped to arouse intense sectional animosity in Louisiana and the rest of the South. Southerners looked upon the legislation as a potential lethal assault on their political power, their safety, and their honor. Both Whigs and Democrats in the region denounced the proposal, and each quickly tried to place the responsibility for it on the other.[2]

The Wilmot Proviso and its possible consequences for Louisiana and the rest of the South remained a topic of discussion. For example, following the largely parochial gubernatorial campaign and election of 1849, Joseph Walker in his inaugural address not only discussed the need for an elective judiciary and improvements to the public school system but also denounced the abolitionists. Moreover, the new governor asked that Louisiana join the other slaveholding states in sending delegates to the Nashville Convention, which was scheduled to convene in June, 1850. This conference had been requested by the participants of a Mississippi convention in the fall of 1849. The stated purposes of the meeting were to advance unity among the Southern states and to "adopt some mode of resistance" to Northern "aggressions," particularly the efforts to keep slavery from the lands obtained during the Mexican War.[3]

Despite the unpopularity of the Wilmot Proviso and its advocates, there was a divergence of opinion in Louisiana over the advisability of participating in the Nashville conference. With the support of both the former and current governors of the state, the Nashville project enjoyed enough public support, particularly among Democrats, to make it a formidable political issue. In late February, when the issue finally reached the floor of the legislature, the Louisiana senate voted twenty-six to one to adopt the so-called "Slavery Resolutions," which recommended that each parish send a representative to the Nashville conference. The senators also resolved that, "should Congress inhibit slavery in the territories, abolish it in the District of Columbia, or restrict intercourse between the states, Louisiana would resist it to the last extremity."[4] Following this action by the senate, opposition to the plan became more vocal with some of the state's leading publications objecting to the proposal because sectional agitators would control the meeting, thereby compounding the worsening antagonism between North and South. By contrast, other publications which also opposed the sectional antagonists argued that Louisiana should be represented at the meeting so that its weight could, if necessary, be thrown on the side of the Union. Still other opposition papers declared that it was obvious that the real purpose of the convention was disunion. Such disputations proved effective in slowing the momentum of the convention movement in Louisiana. Eventually, interest in the issue waned to such a degree that the Louisiana house never voted on the senate resolutions that favored sending delegates to Nashville. Thus, when the convention met, the only Southern states which failed to take part were Louisiana and North Carolina.[5]

Other factors which had their roots in the nation's capital also influenced the state's political leaders to back away from the Nashville Convention. Some support that the Nashville Convention had first received in the state was a consequence of the growing feeling of frustration felt by many Louisiana Whigs towards the administration of President Taylor. They had worked hard for his election, and, though he had never openly condemned the Wilmot Proviso, Southern Whigs counted on Taylor's Southern background and their own campaign rhetoric to win him to their side of the debate on the issue of slavery in the new territories. However, much to the dismay of his Whig supporters in the South, Taylor moved quickly to shut slavery out of the Mexican cession. So upsetting was Taylor's position that the young Louisiana Whig diarist, Samuel J. Peters, Jr., a former supporter, wrote just five short months after the presidential inauguration: "The whole United States was never in a worse condition than they are in the present moment. President Taylor is detested by all."[6] Hence, when the resolution for support of the Nashville Convention came before the state senate, many Whig legislators, attempting to stake out a position in contrast to Taylor's on the slavery issue, voted for it.[7]

In Washington, D.C., the debate over the future of slavery in the territories had escalated sectional tensions and recriminations into a raging invective which racked the already-exposed nerves of both Northerners and Southerners. The heightened stridency and bitterness of the opposing groups resulted in an ever-increasing number of angry resolutions by legislators in which some even dared to speak of disunion. With the political cauldron of the nation boiling furiously, the aging Henry Clay proposed to quench the sectional fires by attempting to placate both sides in the controversy. His compromising effort provided for several reforms including the admission of California as a free state; the organization of two large territories, Utah and New Mexico, under the principle of popular sovereignty; the termination of the slave trade, but not slavery, in the District of Columbia; a new and stringent fugitive slave law; a resolution that Congress did not have the right to interfere with the domestic slave trade; and reimbursement to Texas for territory added to New Mexico.[8]

The introduction of Clay's compromise measures in January precipitated one of the great debates in American political history. For the next six months Congress deliberated the merits of the proposal. It was during the height of the debate in Congress that the issue of the state's participation in the Nashville Convention was debated in Louisiana. Both Democrats and Whigs in Louisiana closely followed the congressional debates. The failure of the state house of representatives to pass the senate resolution supporting the Nashville Convention was largely due to the Compromise debates, particularly Daniel Webster's dramatic Seventh of March Speech in support of the compromise. The latter's remarks were warmly received by many in Louisiana. Great praise was heaped on the senator from Massachusetts for being a true statesman. This was not the case when John C. Calhoun, the leader of the Southern Democrats, supported the extreme Southern position which called for constitutional guarantees of the South's equality of rights with the North and demanded that the North stop its agitation on the divisive slave question. Several newspapers in the state condemned Calhoun's speech, and at least one labeled it "a manifesto tending to the dissolution of the Union."[9]

Public opinion in Louisiana on the issue was not well defined. The reports of the state's newspapers on public attitudes towards the compromise tended to be shaded by each paper's political leanings. For example, the *Bulletin* stated its belief that not three hundred persons in the entire state were opposed to the compromise; by contrast, a survey taken by the *Delta* showed that a majority of the country people opposed the proposal. Differences of opinion on the merits of the 1850 compromise also existed among the state's congressional delegates in Washington, with the majority being opposed to the bill. However, the most significant differences were between the state's two Democratic senators. Pierre Soulé, who favored the extension of the Missouri Compromise line to the Pacific Coast, helped to lead the opposition to Clay's proposals, while Solomon Downs supported the measure and was given the honor of being the first senator to speak in favor of it. Of the major political factions in Louisiana at the time, the majority of the Whigs, including Duncan Kenner, looked upon the Compromise of 1850 primarily as a Whig program; therefore, they supported Clay's efforts and censured Soulé for his opposition. The state's Democrats were divided into two hostile factions. On one side were the ultra Democrats who supported Soulé's position in opposition to the com-promise. The second faction of Democrats consisted mostly of conservatives who supported Downs' position. They condemned Soulé for what they considered to be his inflammatory disunion addresses. However, despite the growing awareness and concern in Louisiana over the slavery issue, the Louisianians did not totally abandon the introspective nature of their political concerns.[10]

Louisiana's voter emphasis on local issues was demonstrated in the statewide elections held in the fall of 1851. The Whigs and Democrats were about equal in strength going into the elections. Because of dis-agreements among party members, particularly over the congressional debate on the Compromise of 1850, the Democrats cautiously put together a platform lacking in issues and strong positions so as not to weaken party unity any further by a public debate on the slavery issue. The Whigs, on the other hand, entered the race with a considerable degree of unity and harmony among their members. Many parish-wide meetings had been held in the weeks preceding the campaign. From these gatherings there emerged a general consensus among the Whigs in support of Clay's compromise as well as for the new president, Millard Fillmore, who had acceded to the presidency in July following the death of President Taylor.[11]

Of the various questions addressed by the two major parties, the drive for constitutional reform developed as the most effective and popular issue of the campaign. For some time there had been a growing feeling among Democrats and Whigs that the Louisiana Constitution of 1845 needed reforming. The Jacksonians disliked the long term of office enjoyed by the governor, the limited extent of his appointive power, and the restrictive suffrage requirements of the 1845 document. Similarly, businessmen in the state, particularly in New Orleans, were dissatisfied with the document because it restricted the right of the legislature to borrow money, banned charter banks, prohibited loans to internal improvement companies such as those which constructed Louisiana's much needed levees, and placed restrictions on the life of corporations.[12]

Though there was much agreement in the state for constitutional reform, there was less consensus on how these reforms should be achieved. The Democrats, still partially disarrayed as a result of their disagreements on the Compromise issue, did not put forth a clear plan for constitutional reform. The popular conception was that they favored such reforms as could be accomplished within the framework of the old constitution. By contrast, the Whigs, fully aware of the unpopularity of the 1845 document, proposed a full convention with the authority to remodel the entire instrument. The election results proved the wisdom of the Whig strategy. They swept to victory throughout the state, with their most impressive gains coming in New Orleans. The vote gave the Whigs a majority in both houses of the legislature, with seventeen members in the senate and fifty-six in the house as opposed to the Democrats' fifteen senators and forty representatives.[13]

Among the Whig victors on election day was Duncan Kenner, who won his race for re-election to the senate from Ascension, St. John the Baptist, and St. James parishes. Taking his seat in January, 1852, he was appointed to the committee of public education, finance, banks and banking, federal relations, and internal improvements. During the first days of the new session, Kenner was preoccupied with an unsuccessful effort to become the Whig nominee for the upcoming U.S. Senate race. After losing out to Judah Benjamin in his quest for the Whig senatorial nomination because of his lack of support among the large number of "City Whigs" in the legislature, Kenner turned his attention to legislative matters. The dominant issue in the session concerned the need for a new state constitution. Despite a determined effort by the Democrats to prevent a convention, the Whig majority in the legislature passed a bill which called for a referendum to be held in April to allow the people of the state to vote on the fate of the proposed convention. On election day the voters of the state, Whigs and Democrats, voted in large numbers in favor of the proposed convention. For example, in New Orleans alone the question passed by a margin of 5,490 to 171. Only in some country areas, where there was concern over the possibility of the capital being moved back to New Orleans and fear that unwarranted concessions would be granted to banks and monopolies, did any opposition to reform efforts materialize.[14]

The people of Louisiana still had one more vote to cast before the constitutional convention could get underway. This was the important vote to select the delegates who would serve at the convention which was scheduled to meet in Baton Rouge in early July. The delegate election followed a pattern different from most others experienced in antebellum Louisiana. Having been rebuffed by the voters in earlier contests on the constitutional question, many of the state's Democratic leaders decided upon an unusual campaign tactic for the delegate-selection process. Instead of actively confronting the Whigs over the choice of convention delegates, Democratic chieftains chose to allow the Whigs to make the constitution and consequently did not field a major effort against their political opponents. According to the Democratic plan, they would permit the Whigs to more or less have their way on the new constitution. Thus, when the people grew dissatisfied with the outcome of the convention, the Whigs would reap the criticism and the Democrats would be in a position to make impressive gains in the upcoming November elections—the year's most important political prize. Despite grumblings over the tactic by the party's rank and file, the Democrats stuck to their plan and lost overwhelmingly. Out of the twenty-eight delegates sent to the convention from New Orleans only one was a Democrat. Statewide, the results were only slightly better. Out of the 126 delegates who assembled on July 5, 1852, eighty-five were Whigs and forty-five were Democrats.[15]

Most of the state's Whig leaders, including Kenner, Benjamin, Conrad, and Declouet, were selected as delegates to the meeting. When the conference convened, one of the first items of business was the selection of the con-vention's officers. Possibly as an honor to one of their party's most faithful warriors who had failed to find success in previous political battles, the Whigs displayed their political control of the meeting by honoring Kenner with the presidency of the convention. Judah Benjamin was chosen as the leader of the Whig majority.[16]

Upon taking his seat as presiding officer, Kenner made a brief address to the assembled delegates. In it, he promised zeal, fidelity, and strict impartiality in the discharge of his duties. He concluded with the promise to run a tight convention in which parliamentary rules would be rigidly enforced because, as he explained, his legislative experience had taught him the advantage of moving with dispatch.[17]

Kenner was a man of his word. Despite the difficulty of the task of re-writing the state's 1845 organic law, all convention business was completed before the end of the month. Besides keeping things moving along by employing strict parliamentary procedure, as president Kenner possessed the power to appoint the members to most of the delegate committees. His authority to decide on the makeup of the committees enabled him to exert considerable influence over nearly all of the business which transpired at the meeting.[18]

An example of Kenner's insistence on an orderly convention was reported by the *Baton Rouge Gazette* during the convention's waning days. Delegates were tired after a long hot day of debate and were anxious to leave for the day. A motion was made to adjourn but could not be approved because of parliamentary technicalities. These were quickly cleared up, and the motion to adjourn was approved overwhelmingly. As soon as the vote was taken, members headed for the chamber's exits, canes and hats in hand. Kenner slammed his gavel to the podium and sternly ordered the departing delegates to return to their places; the convention had not been formally dismissed.

Hats were taken off and the embarrassed members sheepishly returned to their seats. As soon as everyone was seated and there was silence in the room, Kenner announced that the meeting was adjourned for the day.[19]

The convention made slightly more than a dozen major changes in the old constitution. Many of the articles of the 1845 document were re-adopted without change. This enabled Kenner to move things along at a rapid pace. Speeches were limited to thirty minutes—a restriction of which apparently many delegates took full advantage. The local press on at least one occasion complained of the lengthy speeches of the delegates. With the membership so decidedly Whig in its make-up, Judah Benjamin, the convention's majority leader, was able to block successfully the submission of most hostile amendments which might have caused any kind of serious debate. As a result of such maneuvering there was little rancor during the convention.[20]

Although there was little public debate during the convention, more attention was devoted to the troublesome question of representation than to any other subject. The decade-old argument over the degree to which the city of New Orleans deserved to be represented and the question of how to count slaves and free Negroes in other sections of the state for purposes of representation were two of the most controversial issues. These issues were resolved when Kenner and other large slaveholding planters pushed through a plan which called for the total population of an area, black and white, slave or free, to be counted equally. Such a provision limited the power of such areas as the Florida Parishes and the northwestern portion of the state but was a source of strength to the eastern and southern plantation parishes. In essence, under the plan, the 3,000 whites of West Feliciana Parish and their 10,000 slaves were politically equal to the 13,000 whites who lived in the First Ward of the city of New Orleans.[21]

As in the past when the issue had been publicly debated, the city press and many of the state's urban politicians spoke out strongly against the measure. Despite the outcry, the Whig leadership at the convention was determined to have the policy of equal representation included in the new organic law of the state. With such an advantage given to the planter population, some Whigs optimistically predicted that the party would be in a position to retain control of Louisiana for the next thirty years. So tempting was this plum of political power that several prominent Whigs were willing to reverse long-standing personal positions in opposition to equal representation in order to build support for the party. Kenner was not one of these, for he usually supported the idea of enhancing the power of the socially elite planter class. However, his friend Judah Benjamin did have to adopt quite a different position from that which he had previously espoused. In the 1845 constitutional convention he had strongly opposed the idea of slave representation in any form as being "unjust and iniquitous." According to his biographer, Benjamin radically changed his position on the issue out of party loyalty. He was deeply concerned over the weakening of the Whig party nationally and thought that strengthening the party in Louisiana by unifying it on the issue of slavery would infuse new life into the national Whig body.[22]

There was little controversy over other proposed changes in the constitution. Kenner and Benjamin methodically moved the meeting along, quickly addressing issues, adopting parts of the old constitution, revising and discarding others, and adding completely new sections. When completed, the document was fairly well received, because the Whig leadership had, for the most part, stayed in line with the public demand for reform. The new document was more liberal and democratic, and in some cases more radical, than its predecessor. Suffrage was extended to all white males twenty-one years of age or older who were citizens of the United States and who had been residents of Louisiana for one year and of the parish for six months. The old constitution required a residency in the state of two years and one in the parish. Additionally, the new document eliminated distinctions between naturalized and native citizens. The only restriction on age and residence in the new organic law applied to the governor, whose age requirement was dropped from thirty-five to twenty-eight. The period of citizenship required of the state's chief executive was shortened from fifteen years to four years.[23]

The new document called for the legislature to be elected biennially and to hold annual sessions. One of the most striking differences between the old and new constitutions was a provision which required the popular election of judges. However, despite the popularity of this move to democratize the judiciary, the delegates did receive some criticism for their efforts—not for what they had written into the new law, but because of what they had failed to put into it. In their rush to liberalize the choice of judges, the convention had failed to specify qualifications for the state's supreme court justices.[24]

In addition to the state's judges, the convention made the offices of attorney general, secretary of state, secretary of the treasury, and district attorney elective. The delegates also liberalized the means of amending the constitution. Under the old document, amendment was a tedious process which required approximately five years and the consent of the governor to complete. The new organic law could be amended by an affirmative vote of two-thirds of the legislature and the approval of the voters at the next general election.[25]

Financial and commercial considerations also played a significant role in the drafting of the new constitution. Ever since the adoption of the old constitution in 1845 commercial groups in the state had pushed for constitutional changes designed to benefit Louisiana's business interests. The 1845 constitution had so severely restricted the banking industry in Louisiana that by 1850 there were only five commercial banks operating in New Orleans. This was an insufficient number to afford adequate banking services to the area's agricultural and business community. Hence, when the opportunity presented itself in the popular ground swell for constitutional reform, the Whigs moved to include in the new constitution various pro-business changes that the commercial interests wanted. Most important among these economic reforms was a liberalization of the state's banking laws. Changes in the banking laws included: an increase in the state's capacity to borrow money; the empowering of the General Assembly to charter conservative specie-paying banks; and repeal, by omission, of the old constitutional restrictions prohibiting monopolies and limiting the life of corporations to only twenty-five years.[26]

The decade of the 1850s was a period of great interest in the expansion of railroads throughout most of the nation. Louisiana Whigs favored internal improvements on both the national and local levels. They actively promoted New Orleans as the ideal eastern terminus of the first transcontinental railroad. They also favored state aid in order to expand Louisiana's budding rail industry. So successful were the railroad promoters in the constitutional convention that the delegates voted to permit the state to subscribe one-fifth of the stock of railroad and other internal improvement companies.[27]

With the goals of the convention achieved, the meeting was adjourned on July 31, 1852. Before officially ending the convention, Kenner briefly addressed the assemblage. In his concluding remarks, he reviewed his pledge of zeal, fidelity, and impartiality and praised the delegates' diligence which had enabled them to complete their work in less than twenty-five days. He hoped that the new law would bestow honor and prosperity upon the people and predicted that the new constitution would prove satisfactory to many, but would not be approved by the people without criticism.[28]

Plans called for the new constitution to be submitted to the electorate at the time of the presidential election in November. The Whigs were determined to have the new organic law for which they had worked so hard approved by the people. Consequently, they mounted a protracted campaign in support of the new constitution. As it turned out, opposition to the convention's work was rather limited. The influential parishes on the Red River and along the Mississippi, where the state's planter population was concentrated, received too many benefits from the new law to object to its adoption. Similarly, the country parishes of the north and northwest did not oppose the work of the convention, for they liked the expansion of the number of elective officials.[29]

The principal opposition developed over the same issue which had caused the most conflict during the convention—the question of using the total population as the basis of representation. Meetings were organized in several North Louisiana towns to denounce this part of the document, and at least one New Orleans paper attacked the document as being the "negro-good-as-a-white-man Constitution." Supporters of the constitution characterized the arguments against adoption as "utter nonsense." According to the document's defenders, the only effect of the total population basis would be to give parishes with slaves more influence than they would otherwise have. This would help to protect long-cherished Southern institutions by giving planters the power to protect their own rights. Whig supporters of the new constitution in New Orleans argued that it was to the city's benefit to accept the document, for, if it were to be done over, the country delegates would be far less likely to be as liberal as they had been at the most recent constitutional convention.[30]

On election day the voters of the state ratified the new constitution. However, the margin of victory was not as large as many had hoped, nor was it as one-sided as the ratification vote for the 1845 constitution had been. Ratification won 19,383 votes, and 14,989 ballots were cast against ratification. Returns showed majorities in favor of adoption in twenty-six parishes. Somewhat surprisingly, the largest vote for the constitution was given by parishes where the slave population was relatively small. For example, Orleans, Jefferson, and Lafourche parishes, with large white populations, gave a majority of 2,000 votes for adoption; whereas, Tensas, Pointe Coupée, Iberville, and West Feliciana parishes, with large slave populations, voted overwhelmingly against ratification. The reduction in voting residence to one year and the promise of increased prosperity from the promotion of banks and railroads seems to have done more than any other issue to convert the urban voters to support the ratification effort. Roger Shugg in his work *Origins of Class Struggle in Louisiana* explains the negative vote in some of the black-belt parishes simply as being a result of "traditionally Democratic" elements who opposed the constitution because it was a child of the Whig party.[31]

Despite the closeness of the vote in some areas of the state, the successful ratification of the 1852 constitution was interpreted as a major victory for Louisiana's Whigs. However, the more important consequences of Benjamin's and Kenner's efforts to bring about a new constitution were to be found in the lasting nature of the ideas and provisions which had been established during the brief convention at Baton Rouge in the summer of 1852. So significant was the document produced by the meeting under Kenner's tutorship that even though the Constitution of 1852 was to last only sixteen years before it was revised, a staff report by the Louisiana Legislative Council in 1964 commented that the 1852 document constituted the real basis of each of the constitutions since adopted for the state, with the exception of that adopted in 1868 during the Reconstruction era.[32]

In addition to serving as a basis for Louisiana's constitutional development for over a century, the 1852 constitution also proved to be beneficial for the state's economy. Under the new constitution with its favorable business provisions, state banks witnessed an increase in capitalization from $20,000,000 with deposits totaling over $11,500,000 in 1855 to nearly $25,000,000 and deposits of almost $20,000,000 just five years later. The period following the adoption of the new constitution was also an auspicious time for the state's railroad industry. Many groups took advantage of Louisiana's liberalized attitude towards the railroads. Abetted by a generous allocation of lands for all rail expansion by the federal government, railroad building in Louisiana made great strides during the remainder of the 1850s.[33]

Among those who attempted to make money from the railroad fever which swept the state during this period were Kenner's brothers, William Butler and Minor. They hoped to take advantage of the plan by the New Orleans, Jackson and Great Northern Railroad to run track through their plantations in Jefferson Parish. The two brothers hoped that the new railroad would facilitate their plan to start a residential community at Minor's Belle

Grove and Pasture plantations. With antebellum New Orleans being one of the dirtiest and consequently one of the unhealthiest cities in the country, the Kenners reasoned that with so many seeking refuge from the disease-ridden city, a settlement that was far enough away to avoid the filth and disease but still close enough for easy transport back and forth to the city was bound to be a financial success. Unfortunately, their plan did not meet with the quick success that the Kenners had expected. When William Butler died after being stricken during one of the worst yellow-fever epidemics in New Orleans history, Minor continued the project and succeeded in establishing the little community of Kennerville. Never the commercial success the two Kenner brothers had hoped for, the settlement remained small until the 1950s when the post-World War II migration to suburbia occurred. Today the city of Kenner with a population in excess of 70,000 is one of Louisiana's largest municipalities.[34]

Even as the state was going through the process of rewriting its constitution, the major political parties in Louisiana were laying the groundwork for the 1852 presidential campaign. Though there existed considerable support for such individuals as Stephen Douglas, James Buchanan, and Franklin Pierce, the Democrats of the state met in convention and decided to support Lewis Cass' bid for their party's presidential nomination. In opposition to the Democrats' choice, the Whigs supported the candidacy of Millard Fillmore. From the time he had assumed the presidency following the death of President Taylor, Fillmore had remained popular with the Whigs in the state because of his support for the Constitution and the 1850 compromise. The president's popularity was demonstrated at the Whig state convention in Baton Rouge in mid-March. With Kenner and many other leaders of the party participating, and despite a limited effort by some of the delegates to win support for the candidacy of the Mexican War hero Winfield Scott, the delegates unanimously selected Fillmore as their choice for president. As expected, they also endorsed a platform supporting the state's upcoming constitutional convention and the Compromise of 1850.[35]

Although the Louisiana Whig party favored the nomination of the incumbent president, the Whig National Convention, which met in Baltimore, chose Winfield Scott instead as their presidential nominee. The military hero of the war with Mexico received the support of Northern Whigs, who, unlike the Southern faction of the party, wanted a candidate who had no connection with the compromise and especially with the enforcement of the Fugitive Slave Act. Although disappointed in not having their candidate chosen by the national convention, Kenner and other Louisiana Whigs accepted the choice of the convention, for the latter also accepted as the cardinal platform declaration the finality of the 1850 compromise.[36]

In their efforts to carry the state in the November presidential election, Kenner and the Louisiana Whigs emphasized the importance of maintaining the compromise, and they castigated Franklin Pierce, the Democratic nominee, for being opposed to the Fugitive Slave Law. Moreover, they alleged that the Democrats were attempting to involve the United States in European politics by their efforts in support of the Hungarian patriot, Louis Kossuth. Pierce was attacked as a person who was unsympathetic to the South, and in the southern portion of the state he was denounced as being anti-Catholic. The Democrats countered in similar fashion, accusing Scott of being an abolitionist and characterizing Whigs in general as being secretive, rich, and living in "palaces."[37]

Having Scott at the head of their ticket did not build confidence among the Whig faithful in Louisiana. However, having the ratification vote on the new constitution occurring at the same time as the presidential vote was thought to be an asset for the Whigs since they had been instrumental in creating the new organic law. Additional optimism arose from the warm reception that Scott's proxies received in rallies around the state. At one rally in Baton Rouge in August in which Kenner was one of the principal speakers in support of the Whig presidential nominee, a crowd estimated at from four to five thousand people attended and cheered the ticket.[38]

Shortly after Kenner addressed the Baton Rouge rally, he and five others were chosen by the Whig Central Committee to serve as presidential electors. To the disappointment of Kenner and his electoral colleagues, they were not given the opportunity to cast their ballots for their party's nominee. For, in spite of the voters of the state approving the new Whig-promulgated constitution, the states' voters preferred the Democratic nominee for president by a vote of 17,426 to 15,967. Nationwide the results were much the same, as Scott carried a total of only four states.[39]

Though frustrated in their efforts to carry the state in the presidential election, Kenner and other Louisiana Whigs took solace from the fact that the voters had approved the constitutional reforms that they had worked so long and hard to achieve. Indeed, it was noted by the *New Orleans Weekly Delta* that "the Whigs, in the late Presidential contest, manifested a decidedly greater interest in the Constitutional question than in that of the Presidency." However, with the ratification of the new constitution, both parties had to begin immediately to prepare for another election to choose officials who would inaugurate the new charter of government. As in the past, Kenner was prominently mentioned as a possible candidate for governor. Among those listing Kenner as a possible gubernatorial choice was the *Daily Delta*, which described Kenner as being sagacious, popular, and active. The paper predicted that, if chosen by the Whigs, the president of the recently ended constitutional convention would prove to be a troublesome opponent for the Democrats. However, these conjectures were only a recurrence of the frequent mentioning of Kenner's name as a possible candidate for high state office. When the Whig convention met to choose its candidates, Kenner did not even have his name placed in nomination. The Whigs turned instead to Louis Bordelon, the state auditor, as their candidate for governor, while the Democrats picked Paul Hebert.[40]

This final campaign in a year marked by an almost continual series of campaigns and elections was one of indifference and listlessness. Many of the issues discussed were simply repeated from the earlier elections of 1852. When the votes were counted on election day, the Whigs suffered an even greater defeat than they had in the presidential race in November. The returns not only showed a victory for the Democrats in the governor's race but also in a majority of the legislative races around the state. So successful were the Democrats' efforts that they won control of both houses of the legislature.[41]

Thus, as the year 1852 faded into history so too did the power of the Louisiana Whigs. After the disastrous defeats of November and December the Whigs never recovered the stature they had held for so many years. Within a few months in 1852 the Whigs experienced, on one hand the exhilaration which came from shepherding through the re-writing and adoption of a new state constitution with the expectation of years of Whig control and, on the other, the bitter and costly defeats in the presidential and general elections at the end of the year. Among the reasons for this rapid change in political fate was the simple fact that support for the new constitution did not necessarily reflect adherence to the principles of the party which had crafted it. Those Democrats who supported the new organic law did so because they felt that it contained provisions which would be beneficial to Louisiana, not because they accepted the political doctrines of the Whigs. This fact was not recognized by the party's leaders, including

Kenner. In addition to the party's inability to retain the support of those Democrats who had voted for the constitution, the Whigs also managed to lose the loyalty of many of their own supporters during the fall's presidential campaign. Millard Fillmore's failure to win the nomination of the national party disappointed many Louisiana Whigs, who found themselves unable to support the candidacy of Winfield Scott. Added to this disillusionment was the presence of third-party movements which tended to provide disenchanted Whigs with an outlet for their frustrations without having to turn to the arms of the much-disliked Democrats.[42]

Therefore, failure in both the national and state elections in the fall and winter of 1852 shattered the Whig party in Louisiana. Although the party had suffered similar defeats in earlier years and managed to recover, this time things were different. Much had changed on the national level. In the past when the state party had suffered political setbacks, the feeling of unity which came from having a strong and united national organization permitted the state's Whigs to pull together and recover from their wounds. This was not the case following the 1852 defeats. By then, the intense sectional dispute which had erupted over the Compromise of 1850 and the later introduction by Stephen A. Douglas of the Kansas-Nebraska Act had so polarized the various sectional components of the national party that the Whigs would soon vanish as a major political force from both the national and state political scenes. The extent of the disintegration of the party as a political power was demonstrated by the results of elections in other Southern states during the months following the debacle in Louisiana. In political contests for eleven governorships, and twenty-two legislative chambers, the Whigs managed to capture only two of the possible thirty-three. Furthermore, in the congressional elections for the Thirty-third Congress, Southern voters selected sixty-five representatives; of these, only fourteen were Whigs.[43]

Despite the increasing number of defections from the Louisiana Whig party to other political organizations, Kenner attempted to remain active in the politics of his dying party. By mid-1853 the party in Louisiana was barely able to mount an effort in the congressional elections of that year. When the Whigs met in convention at Donaldsonville in August to select their nominees for the Second Congressional District, the once-gala event hardly had enough representatives present to call itself a convention. Only seven parishes were represented at the one-day meeting. Even with such a limited number of delegates present, the group had a difficult time agreeing on their nominee. Three names were placed in nomination, with Kenner supporting the candidacy of the incumbent, J. Aristide Landry of Ascension Parish. However, Landry lost the nomination by more than a two-to-one margin to the candidate of the city delegation, Theodore G. Hunt of New Orleans. The party also selected candidates to run for state treasurer, auditor, and superintendent of public schools. Although Hunt went on to win the election to Congress, it was of little consequence to the party, for the Democrats won sweeping victories in most of the other races which took place throughout the state, including the contests for Louisiana's three other congressional seats.[44]

The Whig election effort of 1853 marked the dying gasp of the once-proud and powerful political party in Louisiana. So complete and sudden was the disappearing act of the Whigs that one of the party's journals asked a few months after the election, "Will any person skilled in finding clues to mysterious disappearances tell us what has become of the whig party?"[45] The national party managed to hold a nominating convention for president in 1856, but their nominee and effort were largely overlooked in the struggle between the Democratic party and the new and growing Republican party.

With the collapse of their party, Kenner and other long-time members of the Whig party felt politically stranded. After having bitterly contested the Democratic party for decades for political control of Louisiana and the nation, the majority of Whigs refused to join the Democrats. Hundreds of politicians and thousands of voters across the South looked for a new political home, a new party that would honor Southern rights and offer them sustenance and reward. The answer to the problem facing the former Whigs appeared in the form of the Know-Nothing or American party. So successful were the Know-Nothings in attracting the politically homeless Whigs that by mid-decade the new party appeared to be practically fully matured as a political organization. Buttressed by the infusion of many former Whigs who brought along their organizations and newspapers, the new party in 1855 was able to mount campaigns against the Democrats in every Southern state.[46]

The Know-Nothing party had started as a nativist movement to halt immigration, suppress Catholics, and save America from the menace of "Popery." In the North the party had expanded rapidly by broadening its appeal to attract anti-Nebraska men and abolitionists alike. Though opposition to foreigners and Catholics existed in the South throughout the nineteenth century, the ostensible targets of the party, Catholics and immigrants, were not numerous in most of the antebellum South. At the mid-century point the population of the fifteen slave states was over ninety-five per cent Protestant and native-born. In Louisiana, with its large number of Roman Catholics, there was little inclination to condemn the church. Many of the old-line Whigs in the state, however, did resent the influx of foreigners into the area, for they believed that Democratic success had been built upon the votes of the New Orleans Irish and other foreign elements. Despite the acceptance of the party's basic tenets by many of the state's former Whigs—by some, vociferously and wholeheartedly—orthodox Know-Nothing doctrine was distinctly secondary in importance to most members of the party in Louisiana. The real attraction of the young party for the old-line Whigs, such as Kenner, was that it provided a convenient political base outside of the Democratic party.[47]

Large-scale defections of Southern politicians from the Whig party started sometime before the disastrous electoral defeats of 1852 and 1853. Although such eminent former members of the party as Robert A. Toombs and Alexander H. Stephens transferred their allegiance to the Democratic party, a far greater number of Whig leaders did as Kenner and joined the Know-Nothings. So pronounced was this shift that the top echelons of the new party consisted overwhelmingly of former Whigs. Among the prominent Whigs who joined Kenner in his switch to the Know-Nothings were Senators John J. Crittenden and T. G. Pratt, Governor Charles S. Morehead of Kentucky, and gubernatorial nominee Pierre Derbigny in Louisiana.[48]

Kenner probably made his switch to the Know-Nothings sometime in the latter part of 1854. It was at this period that the national Whig party largely collapsed over sectional differences brought about by the congressional debate on the Kansas-Nebraska bill. Introduced by Stephen Douglas, the bill inflamed the nation's passions on the slavery issue. The act threatened to repeal the Missouri Compromise and, by implication, the Compromise of 1850 through the use of "squatter sovereignty." Settlers or "squatters" who moved to territories were to decide for themselves by popular vote whether slaves would be permitted in the area or not. Northern Whigs castigated the bill and called on Southerners in the party to join them in defeating this effort to repeal the Missouri Compromise and to weaken the Compromise of 1850. The Southern faction of the party, however, was split over the issue. Among the bill's opponents were some of the Whig's most influential papers. For example, the *New Orleans Bee* claimed that the South gained nothing because Nebraska and Kansas would never recognize slavery, nor would any area where slavery was unproductive ever be converted into a slave state by such a principle. On the other hand, there were many Southern Whigs who favored the bill because they thought that the South would regain rights unwisely surrendered in earlier congressional actions on the slavery issue. Included among the Southern Whig camp which supported passage of the bill was Kenner. Although he had supported the Compromise of 1850 as a final settlement of the slavery issue, he sided with those who looked upon the issue as being a case of Southern honor and equality and who considered the Kansas-Nebraska bill to be a real benefit because it perpetuated the principle of non-intervention regarding the institution of slavery.[49]

Though the bill eventually passed Congress and was signed into law by President Pierce, the results of its passage were very different from what Kenner and most of its supporters expected. Instead of bringing an equilibrium to the political tug-of-war over the slavery issue, passage of the Kansas-Nebraska bill ushered in a series of events which would eventually have tragic consequences. Among the immediate effects of the new law was the final demise of the weakened Whig party. Unable to unite on a common position on the bill, the Northern and Southern factions of the party went their separate ways. Many of the Southern Whigs, including Kenner, joined the Know-Nothings, while others from the party's Northern faction linked up with the emerging antislavery Republican party. The Democrats likewise suffered a loss of unity as a consequence of the bitter debate over the bill. In addition to the ominous realignment of the nation's political parties, passage of the act initiated a period of turmoil and violence in the Kansas Territory when proslavery and antislavery settlers fought for control of the region. Hence, whereas the Compromise of 1850 had been hailed as the final settlement of the slavery question, the Kansas-Nebraska bill reopened the issue and was accompanied by a great deal of violence and sectional rancor.[50]

The first known public pronouncement by Kenner of his allegiance to the Know-Nothings occurred when he actively supported several of the party's candidates in the state elections of 1855. In this campaign the party mounted a strong and popular ticket headed by their gubernatorial candidate, Charles Derbigny of Jefferson Parish, one of the earliest members of the Louisiana Know-Nothing Party. The platform adopted for the campaign was similar in substance to that of the national party, with a major reservation against the anti-Catholic positions of the national organization. The Louisiana Know-Nothings also attached to their platform planks which they hoped would prove popular to the residents of the state. Among these were the retrenchment of state expenditures, greater support for public education, a constitutional reform of the state land commissioners to improve property rights, and a more effective operation of the Department of Internal Improvement with a view toward improving inland navigation. The local party also denounced the Pierce administration for appointing foreigners as ministers and for retaining Free Soilers in federal offices. On the important question of where the party stood on the slavery issue, the national organization attempted to straddle the issue by simply ignoring it. By contrast, the Louisiana party showed by its oral expressions as well as by its membership among the wealthy planters who had recently abandoned the Whigs that the state party was indeed Southern in its position on slavery.[51]

The Democrats countered the nomination of the popular Know-Nothing candidate by picking Robert C. Wickliffe as their choice for governor. A member of one of the state's aristocratic families, he had distinguished himself as a state legislator and was a strong supporter of Douglas and the Kansas-Nebraska Act. Like most Louisiana elections of the time, the campaign had its share of political hyperbole. Unfortunately, the last days of the race were marred by an unusual amount of political violence. Gradually escalating during the campaign and centering in New Orleans, the violence reached its peak on the eve of the election when supporters of the Know-Nothings attacked Democratic marchers in the streets of the Crescent City. So upsetting was the situation that it was reported that on election day a majority of the voters went to the polls armed with pistols and bowie knives.[52]

Although many of the contests were close, the Democrats captured a majority of the races across the state. The Know-Nothings won only one of the state's four congressional seats and eight of the eighteen vacancies in the state senate. Thus, the Democrats had an eighteen to thirteen edge in the state's upper house. In the lower house, the two parties were almost equally represented, with the Know-Nothings holding two fewer seats than their rivals. Similar results occurred in the governor's race, with the Democrat Wickliffe getting over 3,000 votes more than his Know-Nothing opponent.[53]

So confusing and controversial were the events surrounding the voting that immediately after the election the Democrats filed lawsuits across the state wherever there was suspicion of Know-Nothing election corruption. The frauds and riots in New Orleans, in which they themselves had played a leading part, gave the Democrats an opening to attack the Know-Nothings. The victories of three Know-Nothing candidates for the state senate, Leon Burthe, J. J. Michel, and Glendy Burke, were challenged by their Democratic opponents. The issue was referred to a special committee on contested elections. The committee's meetings were nearly as controversial as the election that it had been established to investigate. The majority Democrats summoned witnesses but denied the same privilege to minority members on the committee. Kenner and other Know-Nothing members of the legislature bitterly complained of such unfair treatment. Despite determined efforts to counter the moves of the committee's majority by Kenner and the other Know-Nothings, the committee decided by a vote of sixteen to ten to vacate the seats of the three Know-Nothing candidates.[54]

The partisan press in the state had a field day with the accusations by each party against the other. The pro-Know-Nothing *Daily Comet* in Baton Rouge stated that Kenner's eloquent remarks in behalf of the members of his party were delivered in his capacity as a senator and a citizen and in behalf of the freemen in Louisiana. In a later article, the paper added that "it would have done you good to listen to the able and logical arguments of that gifted Senator of Ascension who was listened to with the most profound attention." The writer concluded that Kenner's review of the facts in the case "was truthful, plain, and convincing to an unprejudiced mind."[55]

The Democratic press could hardly have disagreed more with the above assessment. The *Weekly Advocate* considered Kenner's defense of the Know-Nothings to be his political death warrant. Kenner's defense of discredited Know-Nothing behavior was likened to a receiver of stolen goods, for "those who are willing to accept a badge of wrong from evil doers, shall pay the penalty for such dereliction."[56]

Despite the predictions of the Democratic press that Kenner would be harmed by his defense of the Know-Nothings, he continued to be a major influence on the political affairs of the state. For their part, the Democrats in Louisiana and elsewhere in the South became less concerned with carrying out their threats to destroy the political careers of the Know-Nothings who had opposed them in the recent elections and instead became more interested in winning over to their side their former adversaries. Instead of concentrating on local issues as they had done so many times in the past, the Democrats turned their attention to slavery. They charged that the Know-Nothings were in alliance with the hated abolitionists. Across the South, Democratic newspapers deluged their readers with evidence designed to show the relationship which they claimed existed between Northern Know-Nothings, Free Soilers, and abolitionists. Any article from Northern papers that revealed a connection between the Know-Nothings and Free Soilers was inserted in the columns of Southern Democratic papers. Repeatedly, the papers pushed the argument that in the North, Know-Nothingism was indistinguishable from abolitionism. As their efforts to hang the political albatross of abolitionism around the necks of the Know-Nothings began to bear fruit, the Southern Democrats worked diligently to win political converts to their crusade to preserve the South and its cherished institutions. Specifically, the Democrats contended that despite the popularity in the South of the probable Know-Nothing presidential nominee, Millard Fillmore, he had little chance to win the 1856 presidential election. Thus, the best interests of the South required that all Southerners unite behind the Democratic party in order to stop the rise of the Republican party and its presidential nominee, John C. Frémont.[57]

As in other sections of the South, the Louisiana Democratic Party's attempt to weaken the Know-Nothings and draw defectors into its ranks paid off. Many of the "old Whigs" in the state went over to the Democrats. Most prominent among the crossovers to the Democratic party was Judah Benjamin, who announced his intention shortly before the national nominating convention met. With Benjamin and several of his friends and colleagues having switched political allegiances, speculation soon developed in the press and political circles over Kenner's position.[58]

In early June, Kenner attended a Know-Nothing meeting in Thibodaux in which he was unanimously chosen by those present to represent the Third District in the upcoming state Know-Nothing convention. However, shortly after the Know-Nothing press listed Kenner as an "elector" to the state convention and as a member of the "Fillmore Rangers," the papers without any explanation began to list another individual as the elector from the Third District. There was no indication of why Kenner's name was removed from the list of electors. Immediately, the rival press and political pundits began to conjecture about what was taking place. Did the party initiate the change or did Kenner decline? With so many recent crossovers to the Democratic party having taken place, it was only natural that much of the speculation centered on the possibility of Kenner following it. Instead of squelching the speculation by making a public statement on his future, the normally open Kenner dropped from the public scene.[59]

During this period when Kenner was obviously mulling over his political future, charges and countercharges over what his decision would be continued to be exchanged between the two parties. Statements by individuals who claimed that they had official word that Kenner would or would not join the Democrats were contradicted almost immediately by others who claimed the opposite. So ridiculous did the situation become that the Donaldsonville *Vigilant* offered to wager fifty dollars that Kenner would support the Democratic presidential nominee in the upcoming election.[60]

During the period that Kenner remained out of the public eye, the state's Democrats continued their campaign to downgrade the efforts of the Know-Nothings by labeling them as being violent ruffians and anti-Catholic. At the same time, they worked diligently to protect their own desired image of being the South's main hope against Northern political incursions. Among the individuals pushing the Democratic line was the newly converted United States Senator Judah Benjamin. In late September, at a time when speculation was beginning to mount over Kenner's political future, Benjamin gave several powerful speeches which did much to buttress the Democratic position in the state. In his comments he repeatedly stressed three ideas: first, that the effort by the abolitionists to repeal the Missouri Compromise showed a lack of national faith on their part; second, that the Know-Nothing party was a "delusion" and that its presidential nominee, Fillmore, did not deserve the support of Southerners; and third, that members of the Democratic party alone stood by the Constitution in defense of the South's institutions.[61]

The Democrats' efforts did not fall on deaf ears. For among those who were paying attention to their arguments was Duncan Kenner. After weeks of self-imposed exile from the public scene and just days before the presidential election, Kenner broke his silence on his political allegiance. In a statement to the press he announced officially that he had decided to discard all political prejudices and old party associations to return to the party of his youth. In explaining his decision to abandon the Know-Nothing cause, Kenner listed some of the same arguments expounded by the Democrats. Thus, he saw recent Democratic election victories in the North as undermining Fillmore's chances for success in the approaching election. He concluded that continued support for the Know-Nothing candidates would only further divide the South and probably would throw the election into the House of Representatives. In short, a vote for Fillmore would only be a vote for the much disliked Republican nominee, John C. Frémont.[62]

Kenner wanted Louisiana and the rest of the South to support James Buchanan's effort to win the presidency. He feared that if the election were indecisive and Congress had the opportunity to select the next president, there would be much political wheeling and dealing among those groups and individuals vying for the office. Specifically, he feared that Fillmore might succeed by compromising and trafficking with the Free Soilers. Everything possible had to be done to prevent the North from obtaining a large portion of the patronage in the new administration, for Kenner believed that if you "give them the federal blood to suck for the next four years . . . they will be upon us in 1860 like a strong man refreshed by sleep."[63]

Kenner's fear that Frémont and the Republicans might capture the presidency was based upon his belief that, unless the South solidly supported the Democrat Buchanan, the contest would eventually be decided by the Congress. In that situation he speculated that Frémont might obtain enough support in certain areas such as Iowa and Delaware, despite the existence of Democratic strength in these states, to award the presidential prize to the Republican nominee. Primarily for this reason, he concluded that "the South has too much at stake to run any unnecessary risks in this election. Better by far, it seems . . . to vote for Buchanan and decide the contest by the people . . . [for] after careful investigation of the whole matter I cannot see any other plan that will lead us out of [our] present difficulties."[64]

Results of the bitterly fought 1856 presidential election showed that Kenner's assessment of the situation was not far off the mark. Though out of the running itself, the Know-Nothing ticket could have easily denied victory to the Democrats. In spite of the fact that Buchanan won the contest with a 500,000-vote plurality over his nearest opponent, Fillmore's strong showing nearly cost the Democrats the election. In Louisiana Fillmore polled 48.3 percent of the vote and in Kentucky and Tennessee 47.3 percent. A shift of a little less than 8,000 votes would have given these three states to the Know-Nothings, leaving Buchanan with only 144 electoral votes, four short of victory. The selection of the president would then have become the responsibility of the House of Representatives, where the Republicans controlled a majority of the votes and might well have been able to put together enough support to elect Frémont or someone other than Buchanan.[65]

Though pleased with the election of Buchanan, Southerners, nevertheless, were dismayed by the great gains made by the Republicans in contests across the North. The party had definitely established itself as a powerful and permanent force in the North. The South was facing much more than a temporary political phenomenon. The South was now confronting a moral crusade bent on putting an end to slavery extension, if not the institution itself, and one also determined to weaken the South's political influence in Washington. With precious little room left for compromise, a power struggle between national factions unlike any ever experienced by the nation was now well under way. Prophetically, just a few days after the vote, the New Orleans *Crescent* correctly discerned the seriousness of the situation by asserting that "the free soil war against the South is to be continued unto the bitter end."[66]

The 1856 election would also mark, for all practical purposes, the end of the Know-Nothing party as a viable political entity. With a few exceptions, such as in New Orleans where the party controlled the city politics until the Civil War, the Know-Nothings ceased to function within months of the vote. Like a meteor—initially a bright flame, then rapidly burning out—the Know-Nothing party in the South had developed quickly because it was at the right spot at the right time in the political evolution of the region. The demise of Southern Whiggery gave the Know-Nothings the opportunity to draw members to their ranks by concentrating their attention on narrow and popular issues. However, for a party to prosper and remain strong in the antebellum South, more substance was needed. To remain viable during this period a party had to present itself as a champion of Southern honor and a protector of Southern interests. Among the most important of these interests was the institution of slavery. To flourish over an extended period of time, a political party had to convince Southerners that it could protect slavery; this the Know-Nothings failed to achieve.[67]

As if attempting to find his niche in his new political affiliation, Kenner continued for several months to keep a low political profile and largely to remain out of the public limelight. As a new Democrat, he did not find a settled situation in his new party. For despite its success at the polls and its vanquishing of its Know-Nothing opponents, the Democratic party in Louisiana was beset by much internal conflict. For some time the Democrats had suffered internal difficulties because of a dramatic clash of personalities between the party's two leading figures in Louisiana, Pierre Soulé and John Slidell. At odds since 1848 when Soulé was chosen over Slidell (and Kenner) for the U.S. Senate seat, the two men waged a frequently bitter political contest for control of the state party and its patronage powers throughout the 1850s. Unfortunately for the Soulé faction, the contest was unequal. Soulé was no match for the politically astute Slidell. Hailed in Louisiana as "King John" and the "autocrat," Slidell, by shrewd manipulation of both convention and causes and painstaking attention to the distribution of patronage, was able to control Democratic activities throughout the state during most of the decade leading up to the Civil War.[68]

The influence of Soulé on Louisiana Democrats had antedated that of Slidell. However, when President Pierce honored Soulé with an appointment as minister to Spain, the way was opened for Slidell to expand his political base at Soulé's expense, both on the state and national levels. In the election of 1856 Slidell, by helping to hold the South for the Democrats, was instrumental in getting his friend Buchanan elected to the presidency. His closeness to the president greatly enhanced his political fortunes in the state. At the same time that Slidell's influence was reaching its zenith, Soulé returned to Louisiana from his overseas assignment and immediately re-organized the opposition against Slidell and his political organization.[69]

The split in the Louisiana Democratic Party between the two factions paralleled that which divided the national organization, with Slidell's supporters being pro-administration and Soulé's backers being pro-Douglas. During the decade preceding the outbreak of hostilities between the North and South, the political positions of the state's two Democratic factions underwent a metamorphosis. At the beginning of the decade and as late as 1856, Slidell was an avowed Unionist who continued to align himself with the conservative policies of Buchanan. Soulé and his supporters, on the other hand, were more sectional in their feelings and backed Douglas and his plan of popular sovereignty. However, by the end of the decade the positions of the two factions had changed. Though the situation on the national level remained the same, the positions of factions within the state were completely reversed. Soulé, who remained a strong supporter of Douglas, had become a nationalist like his mentor. Slidell, on the other hand, with the end of the Buchanan presidency, hardened his opposition to the policies of Douglas and became a sectionalist.[70]

Though they had often been on opposing sides during their careers in the legislature, including opposing one another in the 1848 senatorial race, Kenner sided with the Slidell faction of the party in the debate over national issues. A believer in the rights of the state and of the South, Kenner had looked on with disquietude at the rapidly unfolding events of the decade in which Southerners and their institutions increasingly came under attack from their critics. With each new national issue debated between Northerners and Southerners, the once-strong Unionist feelings of Kenner and most other Louisianians gradually weakened. This pressure to change grew in intensity as the great Whig Compromise of 1850 dissolved in the heat of the debates of the times. Among the other events of the decade which influenced the metamorphosis of opinion in Louisiana were the hated personal liberty laws of the Northern states, Harriet Beecher Stowe's bitter antislavery novel *Uncle Tom's Cabin*, the antislavery activities in Kansas, and the Northern apotheosis of John Brown following his unsuccessful raid on Harper's Ferry. These events, which many Southerners viewed as aggressive acts against them, clearly eroded the Unionist sentiments which had dominated the state in 1850. Looking ahead to the upcoming presidential election in 1860, many in the state viewed the aggressive actions of the North as an unhappy foreboding of what was to come.[71]

The schism within the ranks of the Democratic party in Louisiana continued into the critical election year of 1860. The gubernatorial contest was for the most part a partisan battle between Slidell and Soulé for control of the party. Slidell's firmly entrenched political machine was able to secure nomination of its candidate, Thomas O. Moore. In a desperate move of opposition, Soulé put together a coalition of anti-Slidell Democrats and the remnants of the Know-Nothing party to nominate Thomas J. Wells to oppose Moore. Their efforts proved futile. As expected, the Slidell organization was able to fend off the criticisms of its detractors and to win a majority of votes in all but two of the state's parishes. Such results gave Slidell and his fellow state and Southern rights advocates a commanding position in determining the course Louisiana would follow during the politically stormy months which lay directly ahead.[72]

William Kenner (1776-1824)
Courtesy of Kenner Historical Museum

Mary Minor Kenner (1787-1814)
Courtesy of Kenner Historical Museum

Lithographic portrait of Duncan at age thirty-three made by Jules Lion in New Orleans in 1846.
Courtesy of The Historic New Orleans Collection

Late nineteenth-century photograph of the Ashland manor house.
Courtesy of Mrs. Joan McKee

Undated photograph of the Ashland sugar house in operation at the height of the cane season.
Courtesy of Mrs. Joan McKee

December 1882 photograph taken in front of the Bowden plantation sugar house shed of Duncan (seated on left) and several acquaintances including his son-in-law, Joseph L. Brent (standing next to Kenner). Courtesy of Mrs. Joan McKee

The only known photograph of Kenner at his Ashland estate shows an elderly Duncan standing in front of the mansion holding the hand of his granddaughter, Nanine Brent, while accompanied by an overseer named Eastwick and the family dog, Medor.

Courtesy of The Historic New Orleans Collection

Nanine Bringier Kenner (1823-1911) in her later years.
Courtesy of Mrs. Joan McKee

Author's photo of the once grand Bringier family tomb, as it exists today, located in the Catholic cemetery at Donaldsonville across the Mississippi River from Ashland. Duncan's grave is the second from the left on the bottom row.

Author's photos of front (from the Mississippi River levee) and side views of Ashland-Belle Helene as the majestic structure appears today.

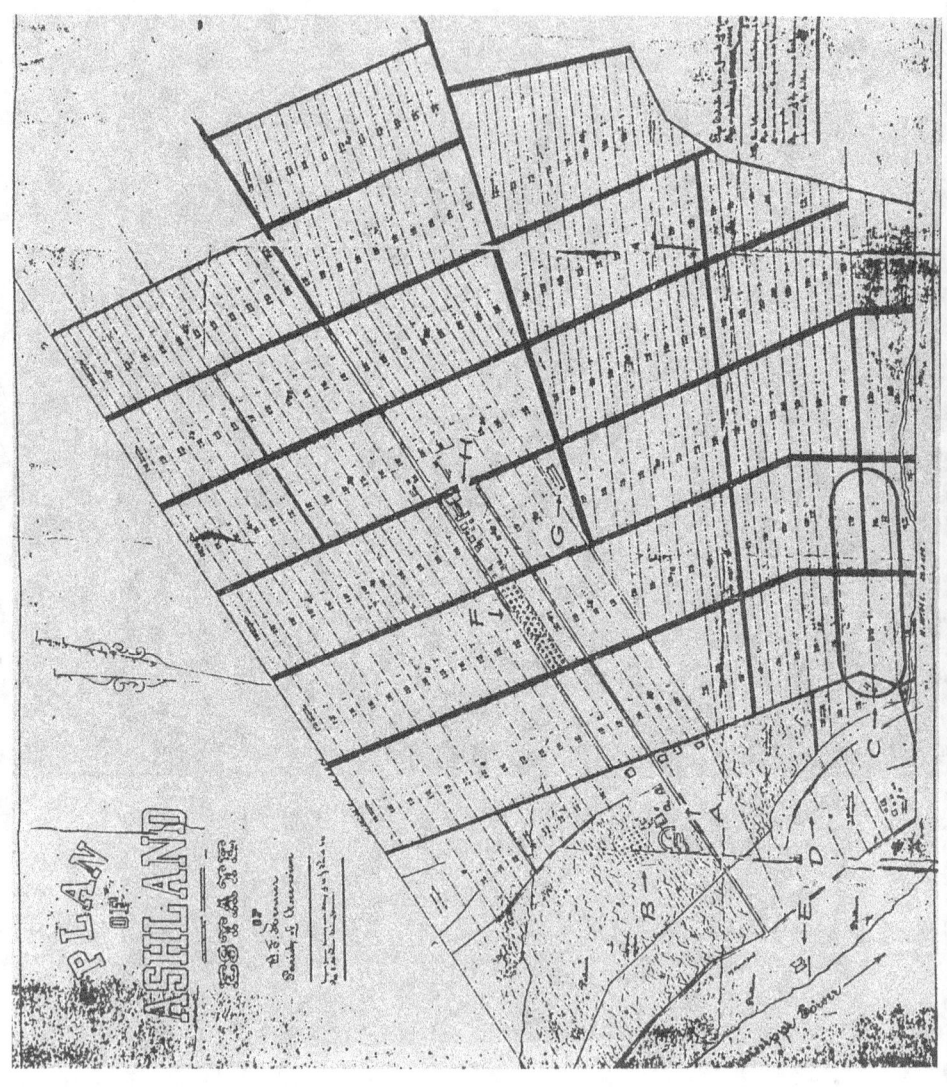

Photocopy of a survey of Ashland made during the mid-to-second half of the nineteenth century showing (A) manor house with smaller kitchen and outbuildings, (B) orchard and garden, (C) race course, (D) lagoon, (E) warehouse, (F) slave cabins, (G) stable, (H) sugar house.
Courtesy of Mrs. Joan McKee

VIII

SERVICE TO THE CAUSE

In his final message to the Louisiana legislature on January 17, 1860, Governor Robert Wickliffe reviewed the relationship between the federal government and state over the preceding years and concluded that the history was one of a "quarter-century of sectional warfare waged by the North against the South." According to the retiring governor, the cloud which was "once a mere speck upon the horizon, has attained such dimensions that it blackens the skies." Such aggression by fanatics in the North against "our Constitutional rights," he concluded, had to be "confronted and beaten back" by the people of Louisiana and the other Southern states.[1] Though the remarks of the outgoing governor were perhaps stated somewhat more stridently than most Louisianians at the time would have phrased them, Wickliffe's speech did serve to highlight the degree to which the state of relations between the North and the state had deteriorated over the preceding decade. Louisiana, a state with two strong, viable political parties and clearly Unionist in its sentiments at the start of the decade, had assumed a far different status by the spring of 1860.

Less than a week after Wickliffe delivered his speech, Louisiana's new chief executive, in his inaugural address, reviewed the sentiments of the people of his state and region. Thomas Overton Moore spoke of the loyalty of the people of the state for the Union. Reminding his listeners that "Louisiana has always been moderate and conservative in her sentiments," the new governor pointed out that "events seem to be hastening to a crisis in the relation which these states bear to the Union in which her duty to herself and to her sister states may be brought into painful conflict with her devotion to the Union." His most serious concerns centered upon "the condition to which the Southern States will be reduced if a political party, organized in only one section of the country and with followers or sympathizers in the others should obtain possession of the government, when the only foundation on which the party rests is detestation of slavery, and when the minority slave section will be without the power to protect itself through the instrumentality of Federal authority." He maintained that "every state must be permitted to determine her own social institutions, and left to enjoyment of them in peace." Moore then closed his brief but significant speech with the hope and belief that "there will yet be allowed to all the states independence and equality, and that harmony and peace will be restored to our people without a sacrifice of interest or loss of honor."[2]

As the people of the state became increasingly aroused over the national political controversy, they began to pay more and more attention to the approaching national political conventions. With the Republicans scorned across the South, the political interest of Louisianians centered on the Democratic party. In March, the state party held its meeting in Baton Rouge to choose delegates to the Democratic national convention. The factionalism between the supporters of John Slidell and Pierre Soulé which had dominated Democratic politics in Louisiana during the previous decade was carried over into the convention. Soulé's supporters looked with favor on the candidacy of Stephen Douglas and derided the Slidell backers for being mere political puppets. Slidell opposed the Douglas candidacy and did not want to chance the inclusion of Soulé supporters in the state's national delegation for fear that their presence would result in a divided delegation. In the end, Slidell's control of federal patronage in Louisiana and recent victories by his followers in state politics provided him and his backers with enough control to rebuff the efforts of his opponents to win places in the delegation.[3]

The 1860 national convention of the Democrats met on April 23 at Charleston, South Carolina. The very citadel of Southern radicals, Charleston was perhaps the worst place that could have been chosen for a convention which hoped to make moderate decisions. Despite the location of the meeting and the influences of the locals on its participants, the followers of Stephen Douglas gained control of the convention. The Southern delegates were determined, whatever the cost, not to accept either Douglas as the party nominee or his platform on the territorial issue. Nevertheless, a majority of the delegates voted to adopt the Douglas plank which evaded the issue of the positive maintenance of slavery in the territories and only vaguely declared that the party would abide by Supreme Court decisions such as Dred Scott. Angry at the rejection of their position, which was more assertive on the slavery issue, the Southern delegations, led by the Alabama contingent, walked out of the convention and decided to reassemble at Richmond. The remaining delegates were unable to nominate a candidate and shortly thereafter adjourned to meet later in June at Baltimore.[4]

Whatever chance the national party had to reunite for the upcoming presidential race was lost when the Douglas-controlled Baltimore convention chose to readmit some of the old bolting delegations from Charleston but refused to seat the original Alabama and Louisiana delegates. Instead of readmitting the delegation headed by Slidell, the convention instead selected a challenging group from Louisiana which was led by the pro-Douglas Pierre Soulé. This action by the convention led to another bolt of delegates from the nominating convention. The Baltimore delegates, thereupon, proceeded to pick their hero, Douglas, as the nominee of the national Democratic party. The bolters, reconvening in a meeting of their own, formed the Southern Constitutional Democratic Party and nominated John C. Breckinridge of Kentucky as their candidate. Breckinridge, who had been vice-president in the Buchanan administration, was a staunch supporter of slavery and believed in the theoretical right of secession.[5]

With the Democrats split, a third group of Southerners who distrusted both Douglas and Breckinridge organized still another political effort to capture the presidency. Forming the Constitutional Union Party, they supported a platform with only a single plank in it—the preservation of the Union, the Constitution, and the enforcement of laws. Meeting in Baltimore, they selected John Bell of Tennessee as their nominee. Composed chiefly of former Whigs, the platform of this party appealed especially to the border states of the South. The party realized that it had a difficult task in its quest for the presidency. However, Bell's supporters believed that he would have a good chance to be elected if the electoral college failed to return a majority for any other candidate and the presidential selection process shifted into the House of Representatives.[6]

The division of the Democrats into three opposing groups presented the Republican party with a golden opportunity to win the election of 1860. Selecting Abraham Lincoln of Illinois, a lawyer whose debates two years earlier with Stephen Douglas had crystallized the party's identity, the Republicans put together a strong platform which appealed to the material interests of the East by its advocacy of a protective tariff, to the workers of the North and European immigrants by a homestead plank, and to the moral ardor aroused by the growing antislavery movement.[7]

The presidential campaign in Louisiana was primarily a contest between Bell and Breckinridge, although Douglas did have a large following in New Orleans. Attempts were made by the Bell supporters to show that Breckinridge's position on the territorial question was identical with that of Douglas. They also contended that their candidate was the only hope that the South had to defeat Lincoln. This was a throwback tactic by which the Democrats had carried the state for Buchanan in the 1856 election. Breckinridge's people countered with the cry that Bell was not suited for a stormy presidential administration, and they labeled the candidate as being simply a "quaint, homely, sleepy old gentleman." Of the other two candidates, Douglas was depicted as an "abolition traitor" who wanted to rule or ruin the South, and the hated Republican, Lincoln, was dismissed as the "dirtiest and meanest abolitionist alive."[8]

In the election, Kenner continued the practice of keeping a low political profile that he had instituted when he switched his political affiliation to the Democratic party. Perhaps his reticence was encouraged by the fact that Kenner's home region of Ascension, Assumption, and Lafourche parishes was a Soulé stronghold and one of the few Douglas areas in Louisiana. Considering the depth of secessionist feelings he expressed in the period following the election, it is probable that Kenner supported the efforts of Breckinridge and that he opposed those of his neighbors in their support of Douglas in the 1860 presidential contest.[9]

The consequences that Duncan Kenner and nearly all other Southerners had dreaded for so long occurred on election day, November 6, 1861. Winning with a plurality popular vote of 39.2 percent, Lincoln captured the requisite number of electoral votes. However, in Louisiana, as in most other Southern states, he did not receive a single popular vote. Of the other candidates in the race, Breckinridge carried the state with a vote of 22,681, to Bell's 20,204, and Douglas's 7,625. The fact that the winning candidate in Louisiana received less than 45 percent of the vote demonstrated the existence of a strong conservative element in the state. The Bell-Douglas votes came principally from the southeastern portion of the state, the site of many of the area's great plantations, and from the industrial and commercial center of New Orleans.[10]

Breckinridge carried a total of thirty-six parishes statewide, Bell nine, and Douglas only three. Regardless of his poor showing across the state,

Douglas did well in Kenner's political back yard, carrying the three parishes of Ascension, Assumption, and Lafourche. In contrast to the Unionist feelings of most of his constituents and fellow planters, Kenner assumed an ardent states' rights stance—a position that did not always make him popular with his neighbors and friends. Even his relative William J. Minor, as early as 1856, had labeled the talk of secession as "perfect madness," and thought that Kenner was "making a fool of himself" because of his public pronouncements on the issue.[11]

As in the rest of the South, the election of Lincoln marked in the eyes of the people of Louisiana the culmination of a political process long watched with mounting apprehension. It placed in the executive office of the national government a man and party who represented the interest of the areas of the country outside of the South, and who were acknowledged enemies of the state's most sacrosanct social and economic institution. Though everyone in Louisiana agreed on the seriousness of the situation, there was some disagreement as to what would be the appropriate action for the state to take. Many hoped for a compromise solution to the crisis. One group in the state favored waiting until after the inauguration of Lincoln to see what he would do as president before taking any drastic action. Others wanted a convention of all Southern states to be called to plan some united action. However, the dominant political group in the state, of which Kenner was a member, considered the Republican victory in the election sufficiently dangerous to justify the immediate secession of Louisiana and the entire South.[12]

State elections during the year had reinforced Slidell's position as Louisiana's dominant political figure. The crushing defeat of the Soulé faction afforded Slidell the power to direct the actions of the state during the post-election crisis. Seeing no alternative to secession, the one-time moderate, who for years had thought that the South would be able to rule within the Union, moved Louisiana toward the fateful decision to depart the Union. The newly elected governor, Thomas Overton Moore, who had been handpicked by the Slidell machine, reversed his position in opposition to secession, called a special session of the legislature, and recommended that a state convention be called for the express purpose of taking the state out of the Union. Meeting in early December, the legislature agreed to the governor's request and set January 7, 1861, for the election of the delegates.[13]

During the three weeks that preceded the vote for the delegates to the convention, a vigorous campaign was waged between two sets of candidates. The Secessionists were mostly extreme Democrats who had supported Breckinridge in the presidential race and favored emulating the fire-eaters of South Carolina in immediately and unconditionally seceding. The Cooperationists, on the other hand, included the followers of Bell and Douglas who preferred to postpone secession so that the slaveholding states could take some form of united action which might win concessions from the North. Kenner entered the race for the delegate seat from Ascension Parish as a Secessionist.[14]

As word of secessionist activities in other Southern states reached Louisiana during the campaign, the Secessionists gradually gained strength. Despite the fact that many in the state thought that secession was decidedly against the economic interests of Louisiana because of the area's extensive financial connections with the Midwest and because of the tariff protection afforded to its planters, the voters of the state went to the polls and selected nearly two Secessionists for every Cooperationist chosen. Even New Orleans, whose merchants and immigrants were expected to oppose leaving the Union, went Secessionist. Statewide the Secessionists gathered 20,448 votes to the Cooperationists' total of 17,296. Of the candidates chosen, eighty were Secessionists, forty-four were Cooperationists, and six were labeled as being "doubtful" delegates. Only nineteen of the state's forty-eight parishes went for Cooperationist candidates.[15]

Unfortunately for Kenner, the voters in his district did not share the opinion held by the majority of those who cast ballots across the state. For one of the few times in his political career of twenty-four years, Kenner was rejected at the polls by his constituents in Ascension Parish. Of the eight candidates who ran for seats in the Secession Convention from Ascension Parish, Kenner finished a disappointing seventh.[16] His surprisingly poor showing in the contest was probably due to Kenner's strong position in favor of immediate secession. Of the areas in Louisiana that voted against immediate secession, none had stronger Unionist sentiments than did the sugar planters and other voters of Ascension. Of the 2,525 votes cast in the election in Ascension, 1,598 or more than 63 percent of the votes went to candidates who were not in favor of immediate secession.[17]

The convention met at Baton Rouge on Wednesday, January 23, 1861, with 127 delegates present. The meeting was dominated by members of the state's planter class, with twenty-five sugar planters and forty-one cotton growers in attendance. On the second day of the session, Governor Moore addressed the meeting and informed the members that in the week following the election he had seized from federal authorities most of the major military properties in the state, including Forts Jackson and St. Philip which controlled access from the Gulf of Mexico to New Orleans by way of the Mississippi River. The convention quickly approved the governor's actions and proceeded to debate the pros and cons of joining the growing movement of seceding slave states. The prevailing mood of those in attendance was aptly summarized by a secession delegate who told the convention that "the time for argument has passed. . . . We were sent here to act. We are in times of revolution."[18] After a couple of days of discussion and despite the impassioned pleas of several Cooperationists to take some action other than an immediate withdrawal from the Union, the delegates on January 26 voted 113 to 17 to adopt an Ordinance of Secession.[19]

Despite the fact that the action of the convention was decidedly against the economic interests of Louisiana, the majority of the people of the state received the news of secession with enthusiasm. At the time the action was taken by the convention, the state—and New Orleans in particular—was enjoying great prosperity, with nearly half of the nation's exports passing through that port. The fact that secession would very probably threaten the region's commercial success by restricting the area's prosperous trade with the East and Midwest and would jeopardize the much-cherished tariff protection enjoyed by the sugar planters was considered to be less important by Louisiana's powerful planter aristocracy than preserving its most cherished institution. Regardless of other financial consequences which might result from their actions, the state's planters and great slave owners were willing to lead the movement that carried the state into secession in order to protect a more important interest—their slaveholdings.[20]

Subsequent events would prove the folly of the decision of the planters to risk all in a challenge with the North. In the early days of 1861, however, few in the South were fully cognizant of the enormity of the task which lay before them. Aristocratic planters, yeoman farmers, and city dwellers of the South held an unquenchable faith in the military prowess of their fellow Southerners and in the political acumen of their leaders. Additionally, the sugar planters of Louisiana were not overly concerned about their economic future. The British journalist William Howard Russell found the belief of the planters in the Southern cause "indomitable." They believed that the ability of their slaves to grow corn, sugar, and cotton along with the region's martial tradition made the South invincible. Popular opinion at the time held that the economy of the North would collapse without cotton and other Southern agricultural products. Russell wrote that, "with France and England to pour gold into their lap with which to purchase all they need in the contest . . . [Southerners] believe they can beat all powers of the Northern world in arms." The British journalist reported that cotton and sugar planters alike boasted that "Cotton was King" and that the nations of Europe and their industries would be prostrate without the staple. Such need would insure the support of the European powers for the Southern Cause.[21]

After adopting the Ordinance of Secession, the convention in Baton Rouge adjourned to make room for the regular session of the legislature. Reconvening in New Orleans on January 29, the convention agreed to send six delegates to the convention of all seceding states which was to meet in Montgomery, Alabama, on February 4, 1861. The delegates were directed to assist in forming a provisional government modeled on the United States Constitution. Although opposed by D. W. Adams, W. R. Adams, and his wife's brother-in-law Richard Taylor for the honor, Kenner was chosen to represent the Second Congressional District at the Montgomery meeting. Also chosen from their respective congressional districts were Charles M. Conrad, Edward Sparrow, and Henry Marshall. John Perkins, Jr., and Alexander Declouet were picked as Louisiana's two delegates at large to the meeting. With the spirit of secessionism rampant across the state, the choice of the six delegates was widely acclaimed. The *Picayune* praised the selection, asserting that "the choice . . . is eminently judicious, and one that will give general satisfaction." According to the paper, the six were among the most eminent citizens of Louisiana and were men of high character who were deeply interested in the state's prosperity.[22]

On the designated date, Kenner and the other members of the Louisiana delegation, along with delegates from South Carolina, Georgia, Florida, Mississippi, and Alabama, assembled in the chamber of the Alabama senate in Montgomery (the Texas delegation arrived later). The fifty members of the group were among the most outstanding citizens and political leaders of the South. Forty were lawyers and seventeen were planters. The remaining members included physicians, businessmen, teachers, college presidents, editors, and church ministers. Nearly half of the group had previously served in the United States Congress, and two had been cabinet members for United States presidents.[23]

An optimistic and patriotic harmony prevailed among the delegates. Though they all realized that their reason for assembling was a result of the radical act of secession of their respective states, most of the individuals present were basically conservative in outlook. Like Kenner, the great majority had supported the actions of their state governments in withdrawing from the Union and were now ready to create a new nation in which the Southern status quo would be protected from encroachment. They knew that events were moving quickly and that the need for action was urgent. Most pressing was the need to form a provisional government, for it would give immediate unity to the seceded states during the risky period while a permanent constitution was being written. The document was quickly prepared and was unanimously adopted by the delegates on only the fourth day of the convention.[24]

The provisional constitution was designed to speed the creation of an interim government and to give direction to the writing of a permanent constitution. It retained the basic elements of the United States Constitution with various changes dictated by the wish to protect the institution of slavery and the rights of the individual states. Among the few innovations included in the document were the election of the president for a single six-year term, the right of the president to veto items in appropriation bills, the establishment of a budget system, and amendment of the constitution by a two-thirds vote of the states instead of the three-fourths vote stipulated in the United States Constitution.[25]

After approving the provisional constitution the delegates turned their attention to the selection of a provisional president and vice-president. The South's rich political tradition provided the delegates with a plethora of claimants to the new nation's highest office. Because of the desire to present to the outside world a picture of harmony and unanimity at the meeting, the customary political maneuvering and posturing usually associated with the election of the South's leaders was largely avoided. Among those who sought the position of provisional president were Robert Toombs and Howell Cobb of Georgia. However, their personal rivalries, ambitions, and animosities operated to cancel one another's chances. This opened the way for the selection of Jefferson Davis of Mississippi as provisional president. Though many delegates at the convention preferred other individuals as their first choice for the presidency, Davis was a popular second choice. His conservative position on secession caused many of the moderates present to support him with the hope that his selection would be viewed favorably by Virginia, which remained undecided on secession.[26]

Kenner, a strong supporter of Davis, did not have much difficulty in convincing his colleagues to support his candidate. As he later explained, support for Davis was based on the simple belief that "we were seeking the best man to fill the position, and the conviction at the time, in the minds of a large majority of delegates, that Mr. Davis was the best qualified, from both his civil and military knowledge and experience, induced many to look upon Mr. Davis as the best selection that could be made." According to Kenner, "there was not the slightest opposition to Mr. Davis on the part of any of our delegation . . . all appeared enthusiastic in his favor."[27]

In addition to choosing Davis to lead the new Confederate government, the convention picked Alexander Stephens of Georgia as vice-president. On February 9, both men were elected unanimously on the first ballot to their respective offices of Confederate president and vice-president. The choice of the two men was viewed by Kenner and many other delegates as evidence of the strength of the moderate faction at the convention.[28]

The moderates hoped that the election of Davis, instead of one of the Southern extremists such as Robert Barnwell Rhett of South Carolina or William Lowndes Yancey of Alabama, would be looked upon favorably by the border states and that this would result in a workable and close union of all the Southern states. Ironically, at the same time that they were working and hoping for a peaceful solution to the secession crisis, Kenner and the other delegates did not forget the possibly dangerous consequences of their actions. In a letter to his friend and former Louisiana governor, A. B. Roman, written on the same day that Davis was chosen by the convention, Kenner admitted that it was the Mississippian's military reputation as much as his moderation which brought him the Confederate presidency. According to Kenner, "the election of Davis and Stephens is regarded here as an evidence of the strength of the moderate party–and but for the convictions of Davis' qualities as a military leader, in view of war–the position of the naming might have been reversed."[29]

Immediately after choosing the leaders of their new government, the members of the Montgomery Congress turned to the creation of a permanent constitution. Drafted by a committee composed of two members from each state, the Constitution of the Confederate States of America was unanimously adopted by the convention on March 11, 1861. As with the Provisional Constitution, the Confederate organic law largely followed that of the United States. The new document differed from the old national model primarily in its emphasis on states' rights and its specific guarantee of slavery. Additionally, the delegates included some reforms which had little to do with Southern rights and were only designed to make a government that would be better than the old constitution. Despite the opposition of Kenner and the other sugar planters present, the delegates outlawed the protective tariff. They also barred Congress from appropriating money for internal improvements and gave the president of the Confederacy powers which in some ways exceeded those of the United States president. For example, he was given the line item veto on appropriations bills. Furthermore, except on those occasions when the president made a specific request for an appropriation, a two-thirds majority vote of the Congress was required to approve appropriation. The new document retained the restriction of the Provisional Constitution which limited the chief executive to a single six-year term of office. Thus, somewhat ironically, in spite of its Southern orientation in several places, the permanent Constitution prescribed for the new Confederate government much the same kind of union that the Southerners had just dissolved.[30]

The continuity between the old and new constitutions was not unexpected. Southerners had always revered the original document and maintained that they had the Constitution on their side in their philosophical dispute with the North. Additionally, the delegates to the convention were for the most part members of the conservative planter aristocracy of the South, and as such they were comfortable with most of the provisions of the old document. Kenner also maintained that, as in the case of their choice for president and vice-president, the delegates were attuned to the political needs of the time. In his letter to A. B. Roman, Kenner commented, "I hope and think there will be found nothing in the constitution . . . which will in the least degree have a tendency to prevent a cordial union of all the Southern states—such is the earnest wish of all the Louisiana delegates."[31]

Kenner's prediction that the new organic law would be well received proved to be accurate when it was referred to the seceded states for ratification. In Louisiana the document was laid before the state secession convention. After some debate, mostly involving the issue of whether the new constitution should be submitted to the people for ratification, the Louisiana convention on March 21, 1861, ratified the document by the lopsided vote of 101 to 7. The constitution received similar receptions in the other Southern states. Even though only five states were needed for ratification, by April 22 the new national charter had been ratified by all seven of the states which had sent representatives to the Montgomery Convention.[32]

With a bewildering array of problems facing the new government, the Montgomery Convention did not wait for the constitution to become final and definitive through the ratification process before it launched a full-fledged government. Legislative functions were handled by the convention, which constituted itself as the unicameral provisional legislature of the Confederate States.[33]

In addition to the problems of state that they had to confront, the members of the Montgomery Convention also faced problems of lodging. The people of Montgomery were eager to please their honored visitors and made every effort to offset the deficiencies of their small city. In spite of the endeavors of the residents to accommodate the needs of their guests, the Alabama capital city could never compensate for the paucity of its accommodations and overflowed with the crush of government officials, their families, and the hordes of lobbyists who populate all governmental centers. In late April, following the secession of Virginia, Congress accepted the invitation of the Virginia legislature to make Richmond the new seat of government. The comfort of the government officials was by no means the only reason for the switch. The large and wealthy state of Virginia was a vital component of the fledgling Confederacy, and moving the national capital to Richmond was looked upon as an appropriate way to both solidify and celebrate the Old Dominion's ties to the new nation. The new capital location also moved the Confederacy's governmental and military command closer to the region where the approaching conflict with the North would most likely be decided. In Richmond the Congress used the Virginia State House as its meeting place.[34]

Lodging was much easier to obtain in the new Confederate capital than in Montgomery. As the South possessed few railroads, travel over long distances was no easy task. For this reason, as well as the many political and military uncertainties of the time, Kenner chose not to have his family accompany him while he was performing his congressional duties in Richmond. To see after his personal needs, Kenner brought with him his most trusted servant, Henry Hammond. Hammond was a mulatto slave who was originally from Virginia. While in Richmond, Hammond served Kenner as his housekeeper, caterer, and general servant. Each time Kenner made the long and sometimes perilous trip back to Louisiana, Hammond traveled with him.[35]

Kenner and Hammond did not reside alone while in the Confederate capital. They shared lodgings with several other congressmen from Louisiana including Charles Conrad. Also residing in the house was Kenner's longtime personal and political acquaintance Judah P. Benjamin and his servant, Henri. Benjamin was a member of the president's cabinet. Chosen at first to serve in the relatively minor position of Confederate attorney general, the Louisiana barrister and plantation owner quickly rose in stature to become a major figure in the administration of Jefferson Davis.[36]

Though not comparable to their lavish plantation residences back in Louisiana, the Richmond dwelling of Kenner and his roommates, at Number Nine West Main Street, was comfortable. An unimposing two-story brick house, the building rented for the relatively high price of $250 per month, with the lease stipulating that there were to be "no ladies nor children . . . in the house, and the bed linen [had] to be returned."[37] Fortunately, the personal fortunes of Kenner and the other residents permitted them to live in any type and style of housing they desired, for their government salaries alone would have required them to choose cheaper quarters. As a member of the cabinet Benjamin earned $6,000 a year; at first, Kenner and the other members of Congress earned only $8 each day that Congress was in session and an additional ten cents a mile for the distance traveled to and from the capitol. Later, because of the rapid inflation which afflicted the South during the life of the Confederacy, congressional salaries were raised and even doubled several times before the end of the war.[38]

Kenner's personal feeling was that service in the Congress was a patriotic duty and responsibility and that the salary received was only incidental. So strongly were his feelings on this issue that in March, 1862, he supported the unsuccessful effort of a political adversary, Henry Stuart Foote of Tennessee, to abolish all salary and mileage payments for the members of Congress during the war or to reduce their pay to that of privates in the army. The motion lost by a vote of thirty-one in favor to fifty-five against.[39]

Kenner's legislative experience served him well during his time in Congress. In the Provisional Congress he was in the forefront of those members who sought a sound economic program for the new government. He strongly supported the need for a protective tariff and endorsed governmental aid to address the South's dreadful lack of railroads. Kenner took a pragmatic approach to the needs of the Confederacy. He maintained that necessity rather than public approval should be the guiding principle of the Congress. Hence, he favored stringent confiscation and sequestration laws and higher taxes. During the five sessions that the Provisional Congress met, Kenner served on the committees of Finance and Patents.[40]

In May, 1861, the Provisional Congress, with its members all having been appointed by state secession conventions, decided to hold a popular election for its members and chose the first Wednesday in November for the vote. The original spirit of harmony which had predominated during the early days of the new nation and the Provisional Congress soon gave way to campaigning and political maneuvering.[41]

The new congress, which was officially to be called the First Congress, was to be bicameral with a senate and a house of representatives. There was much debate concerning the best candidates for the new senate seats. Among those mentioned for the Louisiana senate seats were Kenner and his housemate, Judah Benjamin. However, neither was successful. William J. Minor, though pleased that the "Jew Benjamin" did not capture the seat, was disappointed that his nephew Kenner was not chosen by the legislature for the job. According to Minor, who had campaigned actively against Benjamin, the northern portion of the state was entitled to one of the seats, which the cotton interest demanded, and the second seat was to go to the sugar interest in the state's southern sector. In Minor's opinion, "Kenner was decidedly the best and ought to have been elected."[42] Instead, the legislature selected cotton planter Edward Sparrow and the respected New Orleans lawyer and state attorney general, Thomas J. Semmes, for the two open senate seats. Failing in his senate bid, Kenner was returned to the Confederate Congress by being elected to the house of representatives from the state's Third Congressional District.[43]

The so-called First Congress of the Confederacy convened in the Virginia State House in Richmond on February 18, 1862. Modeled after the organization of, and possessing similar authority to, the United States Congress, the house had an authorized membership of 102 and the senate had 26 members. However, the many problems associated with the war including the disruption of transportation facilities and the occupation of Confederate territory by enemy troops, limited the participation of many of the representatives who were elected to the body. Only eighty-five of the members were present for the opening session of the house. Quickly getting down to work, the assembly created twenty-two standing committees, with Kenner winning assignment to the prestigious and powerful Ways and Means Committee which handled most of the tax and financial issues of the Congress. His earlier efforts in the Provisional Congress, in which he had exhibited common sense and a no-nonsense approach to addressing problems, won him recognition among his congressional colleagues and his consequent appointment as chairman of the Ways and Means Committee, a position he held throughout most of the life of the Confederate Congress.[44]

In spite of the worsening military situation, the Confederacy went ahead with the regularly scheduled congressional election in November, 1863. By then much of Louisiana and Ascension Parish were under the control of United States military forces. With the situation in the state in such a dire predicament, political campaigns did not arouse much enthusiasm. Those congressmen, including Kenner, who sought re-election were returned by the voters to Richmond, where they continued to serve until the collapse of the government.[45]

As in all legislative bodies, much of the day-to-day work Kenner performed as a Confederate congressman dealt with mundane issues, such as the establishment of mail routes and the purchase of stationery for members of the House. However, as chairman of one of the most important committees of the Congress, Kenner remained busy and involved in most aspects of the Confederate government. For example, when General Harry T. Hays, a brigade commander of Louisiana soldiers in General D. H. Hill's division, despaired over the lack of supplies, he wrote to Kenner for assistance. Kenner took the general's complaints directly to General Abraham C. Myers, the Confederate quartermaster-general, and urged that the needs of the Louisiana unit be met.[46]

As a member of the Ways and Means Committee, Kenner was heavily involved in the efforts of the government to finance the needs of the Confederacy. With the nation involved in a life and death struggle with the armies of the Union, the military needs of the Confederacy obviously received top priority by the Congress. However, since the region was basically agricultural and without large amounts of specie or an adequate number of banks, the South faced monumental financial problems. Constantly under military pressure, the South never had the luxury of being able to work out a balanced and carefully constructed financial program.[47]

Kenner and his congressional committee had only three primary options in raising revenue to finance the war: taxation, loans, and treasury notes.

Although Kenner, for the most part, supported the efforts of Confederate Secretary of the Treasury Christopher G. Memminger to establish a financial support base for the government through a process of limited taxation, his colleagues in the Congress were reluctant to impose the types and amount of taxes which would have been required to put the budding nation on a firm financial footing. The few taxes passed proved to be unpopular with the people, and thus taxation never became a major resource for the Confederate treasury. Historian E. Merton Coulter concluded in his study of the subject that, throughout its entire existence, the Confederacy raised a mere one percent of its income by taxation.[48]

With taxation excluded as a major source of revenue, Secretary Memminger, with the support of Kenner and the other members of the Ways and Means Committee, endeavored to finance the Confederacy by loans and the issue of treasury notes. The government's attempts to obtain large loans were not much more successful than its efforts at taxation. During its existence, the Confederacy was able to procure several large loans with both domestic and foreign sources. Secured for the most part by the South's agricultural products, the various loans realized a little over $700,000,000 or approximately 39 percent of the financially starved government's total revenues. As with his support for Memminger's taxation proposals, Kenner worked closely with treasury officials to obtain the much-needed loans. In the latter stages of the war, Kenner even agreed to make the perilous trip to Europe himself to assist in procuring a loan.[49]

With neither loans nor taxes supplying the government with sufficient revenues, the Confederacy inevitably turned to the issue of paper money in order to pay its expenses. Kenner and every other responsible leader in the government realized the perils of fiat money. Memminger himself labeled the process "the most dangerous of all methods of raising money."[50] However, the need of the nation's business community for currency, the inadequacy of other fiscal measures, and the desire of most members of Congress to avoid taking the tough steps needed to keep the nation's currency sound led the Confederacy to issue immense qualities of treasury notes during the course of the war. The flooding of the country with Confederate paper notes caused a rapid increase in prices and all the financial ills of an hyperinflated economy.[51]

Failure of the Confederate Congress to take effective action to address many of the troubled nation's problems resulted in the body being disparaged by many as being weak and inadequate. Commenting on the nation's financial problems in February, 1863, the spirited Edmund Ruffin wrote in his diary:

> Our congress is discussing the subject of finance... It is of vital importance that something effective shall be done to guard & pressure public credit, & to properly direct the actual means of our people for the defence of the country. But little has yet been done by this weak body, which does not approach what is needed for the crisis, & does not truly represent either the spirit, the intellect, or the self-sacrificing patriotism of the people of the C.S.[52]

In addition to criticisms of the floundering economic policies of the legislative body, the propensity of the Congress to hold many of its sessions in secret also caused a great deal of concern and a growing lack of confidence among the public. Belittling the custom of doing its work behind closed doors, one newspaper editor in Georgia maintained that "nothing but motions to adjourn, tinker the currency, or appoint days of fasting and prayer, is done in open session."[53] Though there were occasions when he supported secret sessions of the Congress, such as when the body was discussing sensitive financial or military matters, Kenner for the most part opposed the custom of secret meetings. In an address to the assemblage in early March, 1862, Kenner publicly decried the policy by declaring that "the government could not stand if [the] mysterious policy was persevered in."[54] Kenner was by no means the only government official to complain about the legislature's frequent secret sessions. Though Kenner was joined in his complaint by such renowned critics of Congress as the fire-eater William Lowndes Yancey and the irascible and unpredictable Henry Stuart Foote, perhaps the most devastating comment on the practice came from the nation's vice-president. In commenting on the secretive nature of the First Congress, Stephens proclaimed that the Confederacy's lawmaking body had "sat with closed doors [and] it was well they did, and so kept from the public some of the most disgraceful scenes ever enacted by a legislative body."[55]

Despite the urgency of many of the issues before Congress, bills requiring expeditious action often moved slowly through the legislative process. Even perfunctory activities of the legislature often were delayed because of excessive parliamentary manuevers and long-winded speeches of the members. The languorous character of the Congress did not promote a feeling of cooperation between the executive and legislative branches of the government. With so many of his recommendations and suggestions meeting with legislative inaction, President Davis did not take the Congress into his confidence or go to any pains to explain his plans or ideas to it. The aloof manner in which he treated the Congress sometimes led to a strained relationship between the two branches of government.[56]

Throughout the life of the Confederate Congress, there existed a hostile and vociferous minority which criticized nearly every action taken by Davis. A warm personal friend of the president, Kenner usually supported the requests and recommendations of the chief executive. Among his votes in support of Davis were his support of a bill permitting the limited suspension of the writ of habeas corpus and his vote upholding the veto of a bill designed to increase the strength of heavy artillery for seacoast defense. The Confederate president deemed the latter to be an intrusion by the legislature on the executive department. The president's influence upon the legislative branch is demonstrated by the fact that of the thirty-nine bills vetoed by Davis, Congress voted to override only one. However, Kenner's support for Davis was not automatic. He often voted for resolutions questioning presidential actions or requesting official reports from the administration on military actions. The efforts of Congress to learn more about the military situation were common and not unexpected. There were even some attempts by the body to exercise some direction over the military affairs of the nation. Though these actions sometimes proved to be a nuisance to the administration, they never approached the degree of annoyance and interference that Lincoln and his military commanders faced from the United States Congress and its Committee on the Conduct of the War. The president's relations with the Confederate Congress often varied with the stresses of the times. Hence, as the military situation worsened towards the end, his influence on the Congress nearly evaporated. Despite the Confederacy's growing feeling of despair, Kenner was among those congressmen who, for the most part, remained loyal and supportive of Davis until the end.[57]

As illustrated earlier by Edmund Ruffin's view of the lawmaking body, the Confederate Congress was a disappointment to even some of the most patriotic of Southerners. There were numerous reasons for this widespread dissatisfaction. As the body met day after day with few tangible results being demonstrated, the Congress was almost continuously charged with doing nothing but wasting time on trivialities. So common were delays over minor items—for example, hours-long debates over a time to adjourn–that one of the members commented that "if the house would adjourn and not meet anymore, it would benefit the country."[58] Additionally, the Congress suffered from poor attendance and displayed a peevish, fault-finding temper. Though many of the South's leading politicians were participants in the Congress, its actions and debates lacked much of the aura and spirit that the United States Congress had exhibited in the tempestuous years leading up to the war, when such great orators as Calhoun, Clay, Adams, and Webster had participated in the debates of the nation's legislature. The Confederate Congress lacked leadership, and it failed to address the most sensitive issues, especially the levying of proper taxes and the fair and impartial conscription of men and supplies. The over-cautious nature of the Confederate congressmen was reinforced by the lack of a viable two-party political system. Thus, there was no institutionalized way to influence policy from outside the government. Finally, even before the outbreak of hostilities between the North and the South, Southerners regarded service in the military as more dignified than any but the highest political service. Thus, with the coming of the war, the new nation's most capable men flocked to take the field in defense of the South's honor. For the duration of the conflict, Davis, his principal cabinet members, and military officers of the country's armies and fledgling navy captured the imagination of the country rather than the nation's congressmen.[59]

However, despite the legitimacy of much of the criticism directed at it, the Confederate Congress was better than many of its critics contended. According to historian E. Merton Coulter, the Congress during its lifetime showed a boldness of imagination as it faced unprecedented difficulties. Despite some shortcomings in the law, Coulter saw the Confederacy's system of conscription, with exemptions for occupational reasons, as a more logical and just system than the one later established by the United States. Other successes of the South's national legislature included a tax-in-kind, unheard of in American law, which provided for the impressment of farm products by the government at fixed prices, and several constitutional reforms, including the single-term presidency.[60]

During the life of the Confederacy, 267 men served at some time in the Congress. Of those, almost one third had at one time or another been members of the United States Congress, while others, like Kenner, had gained experience in their state legislatures. The vast majority of the members, 213 of the 267, were either practicing attorneys or, like Kenner, had studied the law but had not actively pursued the profession. Of this number, 108 of the lawyers were also engaged in farming and planting.

Forty-one other members pursued agriculture to the exclusion of other occupations. Five others were journalists, two were doctors, one was a clergyman, and one other was an educator.[61]

Though the group was dominated by lawyers, the monetary worth of the various participants in the congresses varied greatly. The wealthiest member of the body was Kenner's colleague from Louisiana, Senator Edward Sparrow, whose worth was estimated to be over $1,000,000. On the other end of the financial spectrum was Robert B. Hilton of Florida, who reported on the 1860 census that his total worth was a mere $50. The median estate of all the Confederate congressmen was $48,000. The wide disparity in the worth of the members of Congress was repeated in the size of their slaveholdings. Twenty-one congressmen owned no slaves and more than forty others owned five or fewer. Most members, 122, possessed between six and fifty Negroes. Only seven of all the men who served in the Confederate Congress owned vast holdings of slaves. Of this number, five were sugar planters from Louisiana, with Kenner having the largest slave force of 473. Of the 167 individuals in the nation in 1860 who owned as many as 300 slaves, three served in the Confederate Congress. Besides Kenner, Edward Sparrow of Louisiana owned 460 slaves and John Perkins, Jr., of Louisiana possessed 340 Negroes.[62]

During the life of the Confederacy there were three separate congresses. The first was the Provisional Congress, which held five sessions between February 4, 1861, and February 17, 1862. The next congress and the first to be elected by the people was named the First Congress. It held four sessions between its beginning date of February 18, 1862, and its adjournment on February 17, 1864. The last or Second Congress existed long enough to hold two sessions between May 2, 1864, and its final adjournment on March 18, 1865, shortly before Richmond was evacuated by Confederate forces. Though Congress continued to meet and function up until the very collapse of the Confederacy, attendance by its members was often lax. During its four-year life span there was a frequent turnover in membership. So great was the change in membership that, during its period of existence, only Kenner and twenty-six others served continuously from the beginning to the end of the Confederate Congress.[63]

IX

THE HOME FRONT

Although his congressional duties kept him in the Confederate capital a large part of the time, Kenner took advantage of every possible opportunity to return to his family and home in Louisiana. His absence from Ashland for lengthy periods was not a serious burden on the smooth operation of the estate, for his pre-war business and political activities had frequently absented him from the plantation. Because of the amount of time he was away from the plantation, Kenner had long before established an effective management system for the estate so that it functioned smoothly in his absence. Ashland's pre-war system of absentee management, which included Mrs. Kenner; his devoted companion and thoroughbred trainer, George Washington Graves, and the estate's overseers, proved to be a key factor in Kenner's ability to maintain his holdings during the turmoil of the war years.

In the early days of his service in the Confederate Congress, Kenner found on his visits home that the day-to-day events of the sugar region had undergone no abrupt changes. To be sure, there was some anxiety among the planters over the tightening of financial credit and the resulting decline in land values. Additionally, there was concern over the region's Negroes and how they might take advantage of the departure of so many able-bodied white men from the area to serve the cause. Still, the familiar routine of plantation life and the production of the sugar crop continued through the tense months of 1861.[1]

Despite the escalating military conflict, the sugar crop of 1861 was one of the largest ever produced. However, the strain placed upon the local transportation facilities made shipment of the crop difficult and caused a sharp decline in the price. Though irritating to the planters in 1861, such obstacles were minor when compared to the difficulties the region was to experience before the conflict would come to an end.[2]

Another change noticed by Kenner during his home visits was a subtle shift in the region's political attitudes. Whereas in the months leading up to the secession of Louisiana the overwhelming majority of the state's sugar planters had been opposed to secession, actual secession and the outbreak of hostilities led many sugar planters to re-think the "indomitable" attitude noted by William Howard Russell in his visit to the area during the early months of the war.[3]

Sugar planters put considerable effort and resources into their endeavors to enlist troops for the cause. Dozens of local military units were raised and armed by the planters and their local governing bodies. Among the many young men from the region who took up arms in defense of the Confederacy were members of Kenner's family including his nephew, Philip Minor Kenner, who served as third corporal in the Orleans Light Horse Company, and his cousin Duncan Minor. The son of William J. Minor, the latter served in the Natchez Light Infantry against the wishes of his Unionist father. Tragically, like many thousands of other Southerners, young Minor did not survive the conflict, dying of typhoid fever just a few months after enlisting.[4]

In addition to the growing size of the military casualty list, the financial cost of war became increasingly burdensome to the people of southeastern Louisiana during the fall of 1861. The Federal navy was gradually tightening its control of the Gulf of Mexico and its blockade of the region's most important trade artery—the Mississippi River. Consequently, the price of sugar continued to fall at the same time that the cost of corn, pork, and most other plantation necessities were increasing. The shortage of such staples to feed the slaves at home and the troops at the front led many of the area's planters, including Kenner, to shift a portion of their acreage from the production of sugar to that of corn.[5]

Visits home were a great source of enjoyment for Kenner. Not only did he relish the time he was able to spend with Nanine and the children, but Kenner also enjoyed the social life he got to share with his friends and neighbors. Despite the changes introduced by the outbreak of hostilities, the planters continued to entertain during the early months of the war. Most social events, including dances, bazaars, and even weddings, took on patriotic and military trappings. Although fewer extravagant events occurred, many smaller social activities continued undisturbed. Dinner parties remained perhaps the most popular form of polite intercourse among the planters. An example of one such gathering was reported by Russell on his visit to the region. Attending the sumptuous supper with the English journalist were Kenner, his brother-in-law, M. S. Bringier, and their neighbor, John Burnside.[6]

Also, during the early months of the secession crisis, the region's planters refused to let the worsening political and military situation dampen their love of good horseflesh. As late as January 1861, the New Orleans *Daily Delta* was headlining "First day of winter racing, Mr. Duncan F. Kenner's *Sid Story* won mile sweepstake . . . , purse $500." Even with Federal troops moving towards his estate in Terrebonne Parish in November of the same year, William J. Minor ended a letter concerned mainly with political matters with a discussion of how well the training of his thoroughbred was proceeding.[7]

Though the life, labor, and diversions of the sugar planters outwardly remained very much the same as before the South seceded, everyone realized that things were indeed very different. Much of the social gaiety of the antebellum period was now replaced with the sobering knowledge that they were indeed at war and that the conflict was coming nearer. Because they were separated from their Northern adversaries by a tier of states which spread from Virginia to Arkansas, Louisianians felt relatively secure from invasion by land. However, as the war intensified and rumors increased about the impending arrival of a Federal fleet off the mouth of the Mississippi River, anxiety increased among the people.[8]

Official word of the enemy's proximity reached the Crescent City in late December of 1861, when it was reported that a large Federal naval force had anchored off Ship Island in the Mississipi Sound. However, even with this increased threat to the area, the Kenners and their neighbors went about living their lives as normally as they could. As was the family custom, Mrs. Kenner decided to go ahead with her plans to spend the winter months in New Orleans so that the children could be educated by better instructors than were available in Ascension Parish.[9]

The determined efforts of the Kenners to maintain their normal routine came to a shattering end in late April, 1862. In a matter of just a few short days, the lifestyles which many Louisianians and their ancestors had known for generations were unalterably changed.

Kenner was away in Richmond attending a session of Congress. Nanine and the children remained in the city on their winter visit. With so many of the family's males away serving the Confederacy, several of its young and female members extended visits to Melpomene, the New Orleans residence of Nanine's mother, Mrs. M. D. Bringier. Anxiety in the queen city of the South had greatly increased during the warm sunny days of early spring. It was at that time of the year, when the Mississippi River was at its highest, that the Federal naval squadron from Ship Island sailed up the mouth of the river to begin an attack on Forts St. Philip and Jackson. These two formidable structures, located on the Mississippi approximately seventy-five miles below New Orleans, were the city's only real defense against the enemy fleet. Everyone realized that if the Union fleet passed the forts, the city was doomed. In the event of such an emergency all residents were advised to listen for the warning signal of the city's bells being rung twelve times, three times in succession.[10]

On the morning of April 24, the Kenners and the rest of the city's inhabitants were shocked to hear the ringing of the alarm. The Kenner children were in their schoolroom on their grandmother's estate, where their teacher, an Englishman and Southern sympathizer named Professor Melhado, slowly counted aloud the tolling of the alarm bells. Once the fatal number had rung, the old gentleman took up his hat, bade the children a good morning, and hurried away to ascertain what was about to happen to the city and its residents.[11]

The Union fleet under the command of David G. Farragut had successfully fought its way past the forts on the Mississippi and had rapidly proceeded up the river to a point where the fleet's guns were in a position to destroy the city. Large fires were set by retreating Confederate troops in an effort to destroy anything that the Federals might be able to use for military purposes. Great confusion and fear spread throughout New Orleans. At the Melpomene estate, the Kenners and their relatives quickly made ready to leave the city. Relatives and friends from around the city were gathered, including Mrs. Kenner's sister Myrthe Taylor, the wife of Confederate General Richard Taylor. The family party eventually numbered about twenty, not including the indispensable servants who accompanied their masters on their flight from the doomed city.[12]

With all the transportation arteries leaving the city clogged with military troops and supplies, obtaining passage for such a large party would ordinarily have been an almost impossible task. But the Bringier-Kenner party was by no means an ordinary one. Nanine's brother-in-law, Major (later General) Allen Thomas, was able to arrange passage for the group on a steamboat specifically assigned to evacuate the families of Confederate officers from New Orleans. Among those who joined the Kenners on the trip on the overcrowded vessel were the wife and children of General Mansfield Lovell, the Confederate commander of the city.[13]

Although most of the passengers on the steamboat were heading further up the river to places still under the firm control of the Confederacy, the members of the Bringier-Kenner party decided to disembark at Amedee Bringier's Hermitage Plantation, across the river from Donaldsonville and a short distance down the Mississippi from Ashland. Upon their return to Ashland, the family was advised by friends to move to safer quarters at the summer resort at the Belle Cheney Springs in the pine woods of the Opelousas country. Despite this advice, the family decided to remain at Ashland.[14]

Kenner returned home a few days later. By coincidence, the First Session of the First Confederate Congress had adjourned in Richmond just a few days after the Federal forces had commenced their bombardment of the forts below New Orleans. As he did whenever Congress was not in session, Kenner obtained the necessary travel passes from the office of the secretary of war and immediately headed home. Back on the plantation and in spite of the frequent presence of Union naval vessels passing on the river, Kenner and his neighbors were determined to keep things on their estates as normal as the times would permit. During the next few weeks the biggest worry for Kenner was not the Federals but the high level of the river. Not only did the high water permit the oceangoing Federal warships to make their way far up the Mississippi, it also threatened the entire levee system which protected the sugar estates along the river. To keep general order and to restrain the slave population, the area's planters and managers organized a patrol corps.[15]

The Federal force that occupied New Orleans was under the command of the much-disliked General Benjamin Butler. Because the newly arrived Federal troops spent most of their first weeks in Louisiana consolidating their holdings in and around New Orleans and in advancing up the river to capture the important cities of Baton Rouge and Natchez, the plantations along the river were not seriously bothered by the enemy troops in the area. So commonplace did the presence of Federal vessels passing on the river become that the region's residents hardly took notice of them. The fact that the Federals had not yet made any landings in the area only added to the residents' complacence. However, this complacency nearly cost Kenner his freedom.[16]

On the afternoon of July 27, 1862, Kenner and his children took their usual horseback ride along the road which paralleled the levee. Upon their return the young girls joined their mother on the front upstairs gallery which overlooked the levee road and the river. Kenner continued to ride through and inspect his fields and was joined by his friend and trainer, Graves, and a neighbor, Henry Doyal. As they rode the three men could hear the repeated whistles of a river steamer which seemed to be landing at the Ashland warehouse. Thinking that the vessel was making a delivery of supplies he had ordered, Kenner headed for the dock in the fading light of the day. Nearing the road which led to the landing, Kenner came upon one of his old field hands who informed him that, instead of carrying the expected shipment, the boat was filled with Federal soldiers.[17]

Fortunately for Kenner, the schedule of the soldiers on the vessel did not go according to plan. They had hoped to capture Kenner by docking silently after dark. However, the pilot of the vessel was an acquaintance of Kenner. Instead of waiting until dark, he made the landing at sundown, and it was he who had sounded the whistle which alerted Kenner to the presence of the vessel.[18]

The sudden arrival of the Federal troops at Ashland was not totally unexpected. With the presence of Union vessels on the river, Kenner had made preparations for a speedy escape in case such a plan were ever needed. He had selected one of his favorite and fastest thoroughbreds, Sid Story, to be kept ready for him. Kenner was confident that the speed of his fine race horse together with his knowledge of the area would enable him to elude capture with only the briefest of warnings. Thus, on that July evening when his field hand informed him of the approach of Federal troops from the newly arrived steamboat, Kenner immediately attempted to flee. To his astonishment his especially chosen escape horse balked and refused to budge. Fortunately for Kenner, his friend Doyal offered the Confederate congressman his horse to make good his escape. Making the exchange, Kenner quickly headed away from the landing area.[19]

Stopping by his overseer's house, Kenner gave his manager parting instructions. Explaining that he thought the soldiers would remain only a short time, perhaps only overnight, Kenner instructed Mr. Brag to keep all of the hands together while the Union troops remained at Ashland. Kenner hoped that, by keeping the slaves together and under the watchful eye of

Brag, he would be able to control their behavior and limit any problems that might arise.[20]

Departing the overseer's house and using back roads, Kenner next headed up the river to William J. Minor's Waterloo Plantation. There Kenner's cousin Stephen, the son of the owner, provided him with a carriage and trusted driver who took him further upriver to another friend's estate, where Kenner was again provided with a fresh carriage and coachman. Eventually he was taken across the river in a small skiff. Since the western side of the river was still controlled by the Confederates, Kenner reversed his direction and headed down river to the vicinity of Donaldsonville where he could safely remain close to Ashland and his family.[21]

While Kenner was making good his escape, Nanine and the three children remained at Ashland. As was the family custom, they were spending the cool hours at sunset sitting on the upstairs gallery enjoying the breezes which blew off of the river. Shortly after hearing the whistle of the approaching steamboat, they noticed a rider galloping at full speed past the manor house towards the rear of the property. None recognized that the rider was Kenner. A few moments later, Mr. Graves breathlessly rushed up the houses's winding staircase to announce, "Mrs. Kenner, the Yankees have come and Mr. Kenner has gone away." Relieved to know that her husband was safe, Nanine quickly began to gather the silver from the dining area. Before she could finish her task, the sounds of approaching soldiers were heard. Mrs. Kenner directed that Graves receive their uninvited guests, and she returned upstairs to gather together the three children, a boy of nine and two girls of thirteen and sixteen.[22]

Once upstairs in her bedroom with the children, Nanine placed the silver in her wardrobe, locked it, and then calmly sat down to await further events. A short time later, Graves and several Federal officers appeared at the door of the bedroom. Colonel John A. Keith of the 21st Indiana Infantry introduced himself as the commander of the expedition and explained that he had orders to arrest Duncan Kenner and to take whatever of his property he deemed to be of use to the United States government. His authority to seize Kenner's property was based on two acts passed by the Federal Congress in August, 1861, and on July 12, 1862, just a few days before the Ashland raid. These acts authorized the confiscation of property employed in aid of the rebellion. The effectiveness of these statutes depended upon their implementation by the local military commander. In Louisiana the Federal commander, the despised Benjamin Butler, enthusiastically enforced the confiscation acts, asking "is it not the well-settled law of war to-day [*sic*] that the whole property of alien enemies belonged to the conqueror, and that it is at his mercy and his clemency what should be done with it?"[23]

Mrs. Kenner received the Federal soldiers coldly but not uncivilly. Colonel Keith inquired about the whereabouts of Duncan Kenner. Nanine explained that she had not seen him since he left the house shortly after the family had dined at approximately three o'clock. Not satisfied with Mrs. Kenner's response, Colonel Keith explained that he would have to search the property and seize whatever he deemed necessary. To that Mrs. Kenner answered simply, "I am powerless to prevent you from taking what you please." She then asked Graves to lead the soldiers on a thorough search of the house. Finding no one hiding in the house, Colonel Keith assured Mrs. Kenner that she and her family would not be mistreated.[24]

The 300 soldiers of the Federal force continued to search the property until late into the night and resumed their hunt at first light the next morning. No effort was spared in their attempt to find the fugitive Confederate congressman. Every structure, no matter how small or broken down, was carefully checked by the soldiers. Neighboring plantations, including Waterloo, were also searched. Fortunately for Stephen Minor, the servants who had assisted Kenner in his escape the night before remained silent about the event.[25]

Back at the Ashland manor house, Colonel Keith showed that he was a man of his word in more than one way. When one of his troopers made his way to the second floor of the large house and began to annoy members of the family, the incident was reported to Keith. The latter immediately had a guard placed at the bottom of the staircase to see that no one would be allowed on the second floor without permission and that nothing in the house would be taken away or destroyed without orders. However, the Union officer was equally exacting in enforcing his orders to seize items he deemed useful to the government. His soldiers were permitted to roam over the grounds and to take or destroy whatever they wanted.[26]

Realizing that Ashland's location close to the river made it vulnerable to the enemy, Kenner had taken steps to prepare for the possibility that the estate would be visited by Federal troops. Unfortunately, he miscalculated. The house was protected, but the rest of the estate's buildings were fair game for the visiting troops. Expecting Ashland to be the focal point of any Union presence on the plantation, Kenner had removed many items from the big house and dispersed them around the estate. His large stock of wine, for example, was removed from the house and placed under the flooring of one of the large brick pigeon houses which stood a short distance from the kitchen. However, some of the slaves who knew where the wine was hidden informed the soldiers and assisted them in getting it out of the floor and in drinking it. Most of the consumers complained that the contraband was too weak and sour for their taste. The lack of enjoyable taste, however, did not seem to stop the soldiers from consuming large quantities of the spirits. Local tradition has it that drunken soldiers scattered along all the roads in the vicinity of the plantation and that the jails of the parish were filled to overflowing with the imbibers of the Ashland liquor stock.[27]

Similarly, Kenner had removed his paintings, most of which were of family members and his prized thoroughbreds, and had them stored in the home of George Graves, his horse trainer and friend. But since Graves' small house was included in the area where the Federal troops had free rein, everything in the place, including the paintings, was broken and destroyed. In her reminiscences, Kenner's daughter, Rosella, remembered how she had peered under curtains that shaded and screened the upper gallery to witness a soldier with his penknife cut an oil painting of a racehorse from its frame.[28]

Most of his family's silver suffered a similar fate. When Kenner decided to hide his valuables, he had all of the silver in the house, with the exception of the forks and spoons, packed in a trunk and sent several miles away from Ashland to the home of Jerry Segoud. The latter was a family friend who lived at New River in an isolated location. He had lost a leg and thus would not be expected to serve in the military during the war. However, the slave who had driven the cart which had carried the silver to Segoud's place informed the Federal soldiers at Ashland of the shipment. Segoud was later arrested by the troops and, according to an account written by Rosella Kenner, was maltreated and beaten until he told where the trunk was hidden.[29]

The Union occupation of the Kenner estate lasted for three days. By the time the Northern troops boarded their ships and steamed away, Kenner's once plush estate was greatly plundered. Before the raid the plantation had been fully stocked. In the pasture were herds of cattle and sheep to provide fresh meat for the family and work force. The storehouses were full of salted meat and the corn cribs were filled. The sugar houses were loaded with about 300 hogsheads of sugar. All of this and everything else they could carry was hauled away by the Federals.[30]

Though the items listed above were of great value to the family, the greatest loss to the Kenners was the confiscation of their beloved horses. At the time of the raid, Kenner had over sixty horses at the plantation. Except for a few old mares which were hidden by the stable boys in the woods, all of the carriage, work, and racing horses—even the children's ponies—were led, as Rosella Kenner recalled, in a long funeral procession down the road to the Union steamboats. Only one racehorse named Whale was not taken because he would not allow anyone except his grooms to ride him, and they refused to cooperate with the frustrated soldiers who tried to mount him. The only other animal intentionally left behind by the Yankee troops was the personal pony of Kenner's son, George. Observing how upset the little boy was with the pending loss of his pony, Colonel Keith ordered that the pony be returned to the boy.[31]

The compassion that Colonel Keith showed to little George Kenner was not typical of the attitude exhibited by the Northern troops that occupied Ashland. For example, despite the presence of a large slave force numbering in the hundreds, all of the food supplies at Ashland were hauled away by the soldiers. Also, all the white men on the plantation, including Graves and the three overseers employed by Kenner, and those on neighboring estates were arrested by the Yankees and brought to Ashland for questioning.[32]

While at the Kenner plantation the men were held in the center hall of the ground floor of the big house. Mrs. Kenner had mattresses brought down to the men, and she directed her servants to provide comfortable bedding and plenty of good food for the prisoners. Among those held were two neighboring planters—Henry Doyal, who had changed horses and made Duncan's escape possible; and Stephen Minor, who was allowed to visit the family on the second floor of the building. Both men had been arrested by the Federals when they visited Ashland to see how Nanine and her children were being treated by the soldiers. Ironically, though the two men were placed under arrest, they were not searched. Both carried pistols which the Union guards never discovered. Consequently, they were able to slip the weapons to one of the trusted female house servants who wrapped the guns in her apron and brought them up to Mrs. Kenner on the second floor of the mansion.[33]

When the Federal troops were ordered to leave Ashland and move up to Baton Rouge where an engagement with Confederate forces seemed likely, they not only took along as many supplies as they could but also many of the plantation's slaves and all the white men whom they had arrested. This meant that for miles around there were no white men remaining. Such an occurrence was a truly frightening experience for Mrs. Kenner and her children. In the past every effort had been made to provide the white population of the neighborhood with adequate protection from their large slave population.[34]

Fortunately for the family, Henry Hammond, Kenner's personal servant, remained at the estate and saw to it that Mrs. Kenner and her family were kept safe. So confident was Mrs. Kenner of Hammond's trustworthiness that she gave him one of the pistols which had been hidden from the Yankees. The foreman of the field hands was also called, and he and several of the estate's most trusted slaves were placed by Hammond as guards around the house while he sat all night with gun in hand at the door of the upper hall. The night passed without incident.[35]

The next day, the plantation was visited by Mrs. Kenner's mother who insisted that the family leave with her for safer ground. With the Federals gone, other friends also visited Ashland to offer their assistance, for rumors had spread that the house had been burned and that Mrs. Kenner had been arrested and taken away. Duncan also sent word to his family that he was safe and waiting for them not very far away at a friend's estate on Bayou Lafourche. Mrs. Kenner allowed the house servants to decide for themselves whether they wished to accompany the family into exile. All but one of the five house servants chose to join the family. Before crossing the river on the Donaldsonville ferry, the little expedition stopped at Hermitage Plantation where Mrs. Kenner's mother packed her things and joined the caravan heading for the Confederate lines on Bayou Lafourche.[36]

With the family reunited, the Kenners traveled deeper behind Confederate lines to the town of Houma where they were met by William Minor, Jr., who was then living at his Southdown Plantation. Since Minor had recently completed a large new plantation house, the Kenners remained there comfortably for nearly three months. During most of the time the family stayed at Southdown, Kenner was not present because he and Henry Hammond had to return to the Congress in Richmond. When he returned to the region at the end of October, the area around Houma was threatened by a new Federal offensive into the Lafourche country. Packing their things, the little expedition again set out ahead of the advancing Yankees. Traveling through the Teche country of southern Louisiana, the family eventually made their way to Opelousas where they found several of their friends and relatives living. Feeling that the area was safe, Kenner and Benjamin

Tureaud, Mrs. Kenner's brother-in-law, rented a large house and a parcel of land at Moundville, near the town of Washington and a short distance from Opelousas.[37]

Though the new residence met the needs of the family, the Kenners were eventually forced to leave it just as they had Ashland. Not only had the Opelousas area become a popular place of exile for planters such as the Kenners who had been forced out of their homes along the Mississippi, but the little town also became the Confederate state capital when Baton Rouge was captured by the Federals. As the state capital, the little town naturally became an important military objective for the Northern forces in Louisiana. With the area becoming increasingly contested by the military units in the area, the Kenners decided in late 1863 to relocate to safer and more comfortable ground farther north in the town of Natchitoches. Located on the Cane River in the northwestern section of the state, the town was one of the most secure sites in Louisiana. Natchitoches had long been a center of commerce for the cotton planters who dominated the area.[38] Many planters of the region owned elegant town homes in Natchitoches, making it, as one visitor during the war described it, "a well built and picturesque village pleasantly situated on the Cane River and decidedly the most elegant inland town which I have yet seen in Louisiana."[39]

The exodus of the Kenner family from the threat of Federal invaders was not an isolated occurrence. As soon as the Union forces at New Orleans began to extend their control up the river, scores of sugar planters hurriedly left their estates for safer locales. However, unlike the Kenners, many planters attempted to take their Negroes and other movables with them. Large numbers of planters and slaves made their way to Texas or, like the Kenners, to North Louisiana.[40]

Ironically, as historian Charles Roland observed in his book *Louisiana Sugar Plantations During the American Civil War*, it is probable that if the planters had remained on their estates and swallowed their pride, their property would have fared far better than it did by their abandoning it. Many Union soldiers concurred in this belief. One Federal officer wrote that if the planters had remained in their homes they would have been provided military guards against the most flagrant vandalism. "The blacks," he recalled, "[had] the credit of doing most of the looting, and they in turn [were] looted by the *mauvais sujets* of the rank and file."[41] Though this was not the case at Ashland where the Federals were searching for a known leader of the Confederate Congress, the policy of protecting inhabitants from vandalism was demonstrated in the town of Kennerville, which had recently been started by Duncan's brothers as a real estate venture. Learning of the foraging and plundering of a Wisconsin regiment in the town, General Butler became outraged and ordered guards posted to protect the town's inhabitants from any further disturbances. He also ordered that a board of inquiry be convened to investigate fully the complaints of the townspeople against his soldiers.[42]

Matters remained unsettled in Ascension Parish. Federal troops frequently passed through the area but seldom stayed long. The Mississippi River was a convenient channel for the Northerners to transfer their men and supplies, and thus they chose not to deploy large numbers of troops to protect their interior lines of communications. Not until late in the war was land seized by the Union soldiers except in cases where an area was needed as a base for an advance into the Confederate-held inland areas of the state. There was relatively little major fighting in the area around Ashland. However, there were quite a few minor skirmishes, most of them near the town of Donaldsonville. Throughout the war, the little river community was regularly occupied by either Union or Rebel forces. With the river and major bayous under the control of powerful Federal gunboats, most Confederate forces in the immediate area of Ascension were organized into small guerrilla bands who were content to harass the Yankee soldiers. One Confederate partisan group which had its camp on the west side of the Amite River was headed by Captain Henry Doyal, the same gentleman who had assisted Kenner in his narrow escape and who had been held briefly as a prisoner at Ashland. Sniping attacks by the Rebels against the gunboats plying the river often resulted in the powerful vessels blasting away with their canons against the homes and towns along the banks of the area's waterways. Both the town of Donaldsonville and Hermitage Plantation were on the receiving end of gunboat fire during the war.[43]

To the devastation of the war in Southeast Louisiana was added the confiscation policy of the United States government. Anyone who had not sworn allegiance to the United States was subject to having his property seized. Despite the fact that nearly 70,000 persons took the oath in little more than a month after the policy was implemented in Louisiana in September, 1862, many others, including the Kenners, ignored the order and suffered the consequences.[44]

Kenner's holdings, including sixteen valuable real estate plots in New Orleans and his Ashland and Bowden plantations, were among the very first properties seized under Butler's confiscation order. Much of the confiscated property was sold at auction by Federal agents. Reportedly some of the prized thoroughbreds from Ashland were sold for as much as $20,000 apiece. Although an exact tabulation of the amount of goods seized from the estates of Confederate sympathizers in Southeast Louisiana is unknown, the total disposed of during Butler's tenure as military commander was probably in excess of $1,000,000.[45]

To the disappointment of few, General Butler retained his command in Louisiana for only two months after he issued his sequestration order. He was replaced by General Nathaniel Banks, who took a more conciliatory approach to the area's inhabitants. The number of formal confiscations was reduced and could be carried out only upon specific orders. Nevertheless, Banks' relative leniency did not halt the considerable destruction, looting, and neglect of property which accompanies any invading army. The losses caused by the war to the sugar industry in Louisiana were staggering, with the total capital investment in the sugar industry dropping from $194,000,000 in 1861 to no more than $25,000,000 or $30,000,000 at the end of the conflict.[46]

Federal officials did not wish to see the vast agricultural lands in their occupied area remain unproductive. Therefore, they made elaborate efforts to keep the many blacks of the region actively engaged in agricultural activities. From the earliest days of the Union occupation of Louisiana territory, long before Lincoln's Emancipation Proclamation, Federal authorities in the state were plagued with the problem of large numbers of field hands from the plantations flooding their lines and having no means nor great desire to support themselves. The obvious solution to the problem was to keep the Negroes working, preferably on the very agricultural estates most of them had recently abandoned. Since most of the owners of the area's plantations had fled, there was a need to find able managers for the abandoned properties. This was accomplished by offering the vacant estates for lease and the multitude of unemployed blacks as cheap, albeit paid, work force.[47]

Although the Federal policy of confiscating and leasing the land of Confederate sympathizers proved to be costly to the original owners of some properties, it proved to be a godsend for Kenner. In many cases, with the owner of the property gone, the place simply fell into disrepair. At Ashland, Kenner's absence was filled by George W. Graves, an individual who knew nearly as much about the operation of the plantation as did

Kenner himself. With the area crowded with Northerners who had hurried south to take advantage of what they expected to be a financial bonanza, Kenner was fortunate that his lifelong friend Graves was able to obtain the valuable and much desired lease on Ashland. Surviving records do not shed much light on the leasing of Kenner's Ascension Parish holdings. However, it is possible that the friendship and business relationship that Kenner's brother-in-law, Martin Gordon, Jr., had with General Banks proved beneficial for Kenner and Graves. So close was his association with the Federal commander that the ubiquitous Gordon was free to move unhindered across the military lines. Indeed, he was widely suspected of being involved in illegal cotton trafficking, particularly during the general's ill-fated Red River Campaign of 1864.[48]

Under Graves' management the Ashland estate did not suffer many of the problems that numerous neighboring properties experienced. However, despite the presence of Graves, Ashland's productivity during the war was only a shadow of what it had been in the antebellum era. Managing a sugar estate during the war was very different from what it had been. The most important difference was the replacement of the slave labor system by a cash-wage labor force. Not unexpectedly, this transition from slave to wage labor was not a smooth one. The old discipline of the sugar estate was gone; tact and a threat of docking wages had to replace the whip and stocks as the motivating factor in getting the field hands to work. Few planters found the new system to be satisfactory. They complained that their former slaves were now "going, coming, and working when they please and as they please."[49] So poor did the relations between the workers and managers on Kenner's estate become that on at least one occasion Federal troops had to be called in to help discipline unruly Negroes for stealing fifteen barrels of sugar and hiding it in their quarters.[50]

In order to lease Kenner's Ascension Parish properties, Graves and an individual named W. P. Russell[51] had to post large bonds and agree to substantial rents for both the 2,500-acre Ashland estate and the 1,100-acre Bowden property.[52] The increased cost of growing cane during the war because of the excessive expense of provisions and the extreme unreliability of the labor force led many planters in the sugar region to abandon the cultivation of the staple crop. Everywhere in the region, on both sides of the military lines, planters sought to diversify their agricultural production. Many turned to an increased production of vegetables to meet the growing demand for food caused by the war. Others were encouraged by the high price of cotton to turn to the production of that staple despite the unsuitability of southern Louisiana for the crop.[53]

The situation on the Kenner estates in Ascension Parish was much the same as on the neighboring properties. The slave force of 473 which had existed on the estates in 1860 was reduced by more than half. Those workers who did remain could not always be counted on to be present when they were needed. For example, an April, 1865, report of the Treasury Department's Plantation Bureau noted that the Bowden property was being operated by four whites and 87 "employees"; whereas, Ashland was being maintained by seven whites, 143 "employees" and 40 helpers. A follow-up survey by the same agency less than sixty days later showed the unstable nature of the post-emancipation labor force. The Bowden laborers had increased to 93 but the Ashland force had shrunk to just 125 workers.[54]

As with other planters in the region, the loss of nearly half of their pre-war work force and the high demand for cotton during the war led the managers of the two Kenner plantations to cut back on their sugar acreage and to diversify their crop production. When the war ended, 1,034 acres were under cultivation on Ashland, including 225 in cotton, 600 in corn, 129 in stubble corn, and only 80 acres in cane. At Bowden, 905 acres were divided among 640 acres of corn, 150 of stubble corn, and 115 of cane. Unfortunately for the managers of the Kenner estates, their efforts to diversify yielded no greater economic returns than those reaped by their neighbors. Though many of the growers in the area attributed their difficulties in some degree to their problems with the new system of wage labor, government inspectors emphasized in their reports that the area's crop failures were not a consequence of the demise of slavery. For example, Plantation Bureau agent Joseph Diggs, writing in his monthly report in October, 1864, about the estates in Ascension Parish, concluded that the crops on the area's plantations were generally poor. According to the agent, "[the] cotton crop is a total failure . . . [and] the corn crop is nearly the same." He added, "there is but very few plantations that had made enough to carry them through . . . the season." Even the traditional sugar crop was not benefiting the planters because it was "all so [sic] unusually small." It was so poor in fact that the agent worried that, "if seed is taken, little will be left for sugar." Agent Diggs concluded that the crop failure "wasn't the fault of the present system of labor"; rather, it was caused by "the severity of last winter and a long drought in the spring."[55]

Ironically, the same agent several months before had taken the opposite point of view and blamed the crop problems on "successive showers" which had made "it impossible to plow." However, after briefly noting that "the bottom of the cotton looks very poor" at both Ashland and Bowden, Diggs concentrated on the new labor system. He observed that, "of the working hands, there has been considerable disputing on nearly every plantation, on . . . pay days between the overseers and employees about the time and labor performed." According to Diggs, the worker contended, "in most cases, that he worked the full time and the overseer . . . 'visa versa' [sic]." The agent ended his report with the observation that, although it was "impossible to decide which is right or which is wrong," he believed that the system was workable.[56]

Hence, the transition from slave to free labor was accomplished on the Kenner estates in much the same way as on most other large sugar estates in southern Louisiana. Much confusion and many problems accompanied the switch, with the three major groups involved each viewing the situation quite differently. The planters firmly believed that without the system of slave labor their investments in their sugar estates would soon be worthless. On the other hand, the Federal authorities were determined to prove their preconceptions about the evils of the peculiar institution and minimized the problems of the new wage labor system. Finally, the blacks themselves were not completely satisfied with the new arrangement. Many of them considered that they were emancipated not only from slavery but also from the status of manual laborers. Thus, when the Federal officials, in an attempt to provide a workable means of support for the hordes of free Negroes who were wandering about the region, herded the former slaves back upon the very plantations from which they had recently fled, a more acrimonious relationship than previously existed soon evolved. Consequently, the inefficiencies of the trial stage of the system of free Negro labor nearly destroyed the sugar industry on Ashland, Bowden, and most other plantations in Southeast Louisiana.[57]

Though it is unlikely that Kenner played a major role in the management of affairs on his plantations during the wartime occupation of the area by the Federals, it is probable that he was in contact with Graves and kept abreast of events on his estates. With his brother-in-law, Martin Gordon, Jr., having easy passage through the Federal lines, it was relatively easy for Kenner to communicate with Graves.

With the bulk of his resources tied up in his estates in Ascension Parish, it was natural for Kenner to be concerned about their preservation. Not unexpectedly, however, Kenner's main interest was in the well-being of his family. Because of his responsibilities as a leading member of the Confederate Congress, Kenner was obligated to spend a large portion of his time in Richmond away from his wife and children. Despite the long distances and inconveniences involved in traveling across nearly the entire breadth of the Confederacy, Kenner took advantage of every opportunity to return to Louisiana. The primitive nature of most of the South's transportation facilities made cross-country travel laborious. Because of the Federal occupation of the area, the most difficult and dangerous part of the trip occurred as Kenner neared home and it became necessary to cross the Mississippi River.

Until Union forces laid siege to Vicksburg, Kenner was able to cross the river without undue risk. However, with the arrival of Federal forces at Vicksburg, the passage across the river became far more hazardous and difficult. Kenner and his servant Henry Hammond, who always made the trip back to Louisiana with his master, shared the perils and hardships of the trips. As the Federal forces tightened their control of the region and increased their gunboat patrols along the river, it became almost impossible for Kenner and his servant to find ferry boats to take them across. Often the two men had to resort to crossing the turbulent river in a small skiff, while swimming their horses alongside the little boat.[58]

The visits to Louisiana by Kenner had more purpose than just a family reunion. The trips gave Kenner valuable first-hand knowledge of conditions in the South, particularly in the Trans-Mississippi Department of the Confederacy. On most trips the Confederate congressman found deteriorating military and social institution. Using his influence in Richmond to do what he could to assist the people and Rebel forces in the region, his efforts sometimes proved to be more prophetic than beneficial to the cause.

Among his efforts was a desperate appeal to President Davis for reinforcements for Vicksburg. On a trip home to Louisiana in early June, 1863, Kenner, while passing through Jackson, joined Governor John J. Pettus and several Mississippi congressmen in requesting that the Confederate president immediately send 30,000 troops to break the siege of Vicksburg. In their letter, Kenner and the Mississippians acknowledged that fulfilling their request would "possibly involve the surrender of all Middle Tennessee to the enemy." Regardless of the risk, Kenner and the authors of the letter maintained prophetically that, "the failure to re-enforce to this extent certainly involves the loss of the entire Mississippi Valley."[59]

Unfortunately for the cause of the South, the Confederate president rejected the request for massive troop reinforcements for the besieged rebel fortress. As Davis saw the issue, if he reinforced Vicksburg at the expense of Middle Tennessee, the cost might be the "dismemberment, through the center, of the Confederacy." Though the president's fears were not without justification, it is not likely that the consequences of pulling Confederate forces out of Tennessee to maintain a Rebel stronghold on the Mississippi would have equaled the disastrous consequences that the fall of Vicksburg had on the Southern Cause.[60]

Although future events proved the validity of Kenner's fears with respect to Vicksburg, not all of his observations concerning contemporary events were as accurate. In September, 1864, in a letter to Governor Thomas Moore of Louisiana, Kenner completely misjudged the significance of the recent capture of Atlanta by General William T. Sherman. He dismissed the defeats of Confederate Generals Joseph Johnston and John Hood by Sherman as simply a case of too few resources against overwhelming enemy forces. Despite the loss of one of the South's major cities, which also served as a vital railroad hub and supply depot, Kenner naively considered Sherman's campaign to be "a complete failure." As he saw the situation, the Southern forces in the areas were not defeated, for Hood's army was "intact [and] in good spirits." On the other hand, because of the approaching winter, he looked upon Sherman's position as being a weak one. He did not see any way for Sherman to feed his large army bivouacked at Atlanta. Kenner predicted that Sherman would hold the city for political reasons until the presidential election in November and then he would have to "fall back." Kenner concluded his note to the Louisiana governor with the hopeful comment that he was "sanguine of [George] McClellan's election and with it a change of policy."[61]

Unfortunately for the Confederacy, neither of Kenner's optimistic predictions proved accurate. In the first week of November, Lincoln won re-election by defeating McClellan. An even more disappointing event for the South than the presidential election results occurred later in the month when Sherman, instead of retreating north as Kenner thought he would, advanced south from Atlanta on his famous and devastatingly effective March to the Sea.[62]

Kenner's most controversial involvement in military affairs concerned his role in the bitter dispute between Edmund Kirby Smith, commander of the Confederacy's Department of the Trans-Mississippi, and the militarily brilliant brother-in-law of Kenner, Richard Taylor. The controversy between the two Rebel generals centered around events following the Southern victories at Mansfield and Pleasant Hill in April, 1864. In the two battles, which took place in Northwest Louisiana not far from where the Kenners were in residence, the outnumbered Confederate forces under the direct command of Taylor defeated a large Federal invasion force under the command of General Nathaniel Banks. So effective was Taylor's strategy that Banks' entire Red River Campaign was aborted.[63]

The dispute between the generals erupted even before the defeated Yankee force had made good its escape. With Taylor's forces maneuvering to engage Banks' invasion force before the battles, Congressman Kenner urged General Kirby Smith to send Taylor desperately needed reinforcements. Unable to convince the overly cautious department commander to send help to Taylor, Kenner contacted his brother-in-law by letter and reported that, "I called General Smith's attention to the great importance of sending you re-enforcements [sic] immediately. What was my astonishment when he replied that you did not desire any reinforcements." Kenner concluded his account of the discussion with Kirby Smith with the forceful exclamation that the general's presumption that additional troops were not desired was simply "impossible."[64]

The lack of reinforcements prevented Taylor from pressing his victory and permitted Banks to escape with both his army and his gunboat fleet, which almost certainly could have been bottled up and destroyed on the shallow Red River. After seeing the battered enemy slip away from his grasp, Taylor angrily informed Kirby Smith of Kenner's note and remarked sarcastically that he "certainly would have been the first commander possessing ordinary sense who voluntarily declined reinforcements [sic] while retreating before a superior force."[65]

So upset was Taylor over Smith's bungling of the opportunity to crush Banks' force of 30,000 troops and their fleet that he asked successfully to be relieved from further duty under Kirby Smith. Taylor's departure did not end the controversy, for Kenner was as upset with Kirby Smith as had been Taylor. Additionally, Kenner's role as a civilian and as an important congressional leader gave him recourse that the frustrated General Taylor did not have. As he had frequently done during his trips home, Kenner reported his observations concerning the Mansfield and Pleasant Hill operations to his housemate, Judah Benjamin, back in the Confederate capital.⁶⁶

In a letter to the Confederate secretary of state, Kenner wrote at length about General Kirby Smith's failure to take advantage of the opportunity gained by Taylor's forces at Mansfield and Pleasant Hill. Requesting that the president be informed of his comments, Kenner condemned Kirby Smith for his inactivity and his failure to move against Banks. According to Kenner, not only did Kirby Smith's hesitation permit the escape of a large Federal force, but it also permitted Banks to send those same troops to reinforce other Federal units. As Kenner viewed the situation, when Kirby Smith relieved Taylor of his command, the Confederate Department Commander went into the interior of Texas at the encouragement of his wife and remained for some six weeks. "In the meantime," Kenner sardonically observed, "Walker's [Taylor's replacement] troops some 15,000 strong . . . under their new leader who was without instructions or order from the head of the Department, have passed eight or ten weeks in an inglorious idleness almost in sight of Banks army–allowing that army to be sent off . . . to reinforce Sherman, Grant . . . and Canby . . . ." Most irritating of all to Kenner was the fact that upon returning from his stay in Texas, Kirby Smith countermanded the plans of his staff to threaten the Federals in lower Louisiana because, "the troops should be made comfortable in camp [because] . . . the weather was too hot [and] . . . it was so late that nothing could be done which could compensate for the loss of our men by sickness." To Kirby Smith's excuses Kenner sarcastically responded, "Northern Yankees can raid and destroy our country in summer, but Creoles and Texans cannot be allowed to defend it–for fear of the bad effects of their own climate." Kenner ended his letter to Benjamin with the conclusion that, although the Confederate forces in his home state were not adequate to dislodge the Yankees from their stronghold in New Orleans, they were "sufficient in number to have compelled Banks to have kept his entire army sweltering in the sun in the vicinity of New Orleans."⁶⁷

Though Kenner's observations concerning Kirby Smith's hesitation for battle and the lost opportunities for the Confederates in Louisiana were not without merit, it is doubtful that a more assertive policy would have had any real effect on the outcome of the war. It is unclear just what effect, if any, Kenner's scathing criticism of Kirby Smith had on the general. He remained in command of the Trans-Mississippi Department until the end of the war. On the other hand, Kenner's praise of General Taylor and his reports on the situation in Louisiana during and after the Red River Campaign did not harm the cause of the flamboyant Taylor in his dispute with the powerful Kirby Smith. Though Taylor was relieved of his command by Kirby Smith as he had requested, President Davis and the Confederate Congress were not willing to lose the services of such a valuable and capable military commander. After being honored by a joint congressional resolution which thanked Taylor and his men for their victories, he was appointed commander of the Department of Alabama, Mississippi, and East Louisiana. On May 8, 1865, Taylor surrendered the last army of the Confederacy east of the Mississippi River.[68]

X

THE MISSION

The success achieved by the Confederates in Louisiana in stopping General Banks' Red River Campaign was not repeated in other theaters of the great war between North and South. In spite of the defeat of Banks by Taylor, the Southern cause had suffered many setbacks during the year 1864. Particularly in the all-important region around the young nation's capital at Richmond was the war going poorly. General Ulysses S. Grant had assumed command of all Union forces in early March and had almost immediately advanced to the vicinity of the South's capital city. Despite valiant efforts by General Robert E. Lee and his haggard army to repulse the Yankee threat to Richmond, the momentous struggle between the two armies turned into a more-or-less stationary conflict of trench warfare centering around the community of Petersburg, about twenty miles to the south of the capital.

After spending much of the summer at home in Louisiana observing the military and political situation and visiting with family and friends, Kenner returned to Richmond in the fall of 1864. He found the city bracing for its fourth and possibly final winter as the seat of government for the battered Confederate States of America. With an enemy army camped only a few miles away, the melancholic realization of the deteriorating military situation increased the apprehension of the populace concerning what the coming months would bring.[1]

With its armies in retreat on almost every front, the Confederacy by the end of 1864 was also experiencing serious political difficulties. In the fall elections of that year, Abraham Lincoln had been re-elected to the presidency, thereby destroying any hope of a negotiated end to the hostilities without the surrender of the South. Furthermore, the recent military setbacks experienced by the armies of the South provoked new recriminations in the Confederate government. Vice-President Alexander H. Stephens even went so far as to arraign openly the government for incompetence and despotism. Some Southern states refused to obey the Richmond authorities and even threatened to make peace with the United States on their own. Soldiers and clerks complained of special treatment given to rich propertyholders. Most incredible of all, there was talk among members of the Confederate Congress and in the hostile press of deposing Jefferson Davis and replacing him with Robert E. Lee.[2]

With hostility towards the administration reaching the flash point, Davis and his secretary of state and confidant, Judah P. Benjamin, realized that any chance of a military victory by the South was quickly evaporating. If the Confederacy were to be saved, the two men concluded that some type of immediate assistance from foreign powers had to be obtained. Previous attempts to secure recognition or other assistance from the powers of Europe through offers of commercial advantages, military alliance, or by international complications had failed. The "King Cotton Diplomacy" of the Confederacy had been effectively countered by the policies of the United States.[3]

Of the various issues which contributed to the failure of Confederate diplomatic efforts, slavery was one of the most significant. Historians today still disagree as to what extent the slavery question damaged the chances of the South in gaining assistance from England and France. But, at the time, it was widely accepted by many American and Confederate officials that the issue was of considerable importance.[4]

During the early months of the war, for purely domestic reasons, the American secretary of state, William Henry Seward, chose not to present the American conflict abroad as a struggle over the peculiar institution. This decision limited the ability of United States diplomats to exploit the evident antislavery sympathies of the European public. From the outset of the war, Confederate diplomats had discerned that antislavery sentiment was general throughout the Continent. In their first dispatch home after reaching Europe in the spring of 1861, Confederate emissaries William Yancey, Pierre Rost, and A. Dudley Mann wrote that "the public mind here is entirely opposed to the Government of the Confederate States of America on the question of slavery, and that the sincerity and universality of this feeling embarrasses the Government in dealing with the question of our recognition."[5] Their observations were strongly supported by Confederate propagandist Edwin DeLeon. Having been sent abroad by Benjamin to "enlighten" the European press, he reported in September, 1862, that slavery was "the great bugbear in France, and those who professed to be our advocates were pleading pitifully an extenuation of our sins in this respect and shuddering at the epithet *esclavagiste* with which the paid partisans of the North are pelting them."[6]

Similar perceptions of the widespread and unrelenting hostility to slavery held by the majority of Europeans were reflected by all of the Southern agents who served on the Continent. John Slidell, who arrived in early 1862 to head the Confederate diplomatic effort in France, confirmed in his first dispatch to Richmond the universality of antislavery sentiment in Europe. In a letter dated February 11, 1862, to Robert M. T. Hunter, then the Confederate secretary of state, Slidell spoke of the widespread sympathy he found among many in Europe for the South. However, he went on to emphasize that this support was undermined by a "regret that slavery exists amongst us." Many Confederate sympathizers expressed the "hope that some steps may be taken for its [slavery's] ultimate but gradual extinction."[7]

Despite the official silence on the slavery question by the American secretary of state, United States diplomats abroad were quick to comprehend its importance as a valuable diplomatic weapon. As popular sympathy for the Confederacy increased in both France and England, representatives of the United States in Europe warned Secretary Seward of the need for a clarified and strengthened policy on the slave issue. In early 1862, Seward's trusted advisor Thurlow Weed reported from Paris that a commitment to destroy slavery would gain much support for the Northern cause in the French government. Henry Adams, the son and secretary of the American minister to England, Charles Francis Adams, wrote Frederick W. Seward, the son of the secretary of state, "If some real emancipation step could be taken, it would be the next best thing to taking Richmond for us here [in London]."[8] In August, 1862, as rumors of possible European intervention spread across the Continent, John Lothrop Motley, the American minister to Austria, reported in a letter to his mother that "the only thing that saves us yet from a war with the slave holders, allied with both France and England is the antislavery feeling of a very considerable portion of the British public."[9]

Despite a desperate need to gain recognition from the European powers, Davis and other Southern leaders refused to make any concessions on slavery. Instead, the Confederate government's reaction to European public condemnation of slavery was always one of resentment. The Confederacy had long been sensitive and suspicious of any discussion on the subject by outsiders and was unwilling to debate its merits or demerits. Southern perturbation over the European criticism simmered throughout the first two years of the conflict until January, 1863, when Benjamin instructed his agents in Europe to decline any negotiations which in any way related to slavery.[10]

By the time Kenner returned to the Confederate capital in the chilly waning days of 1864, it was evident to the nation's leaders that if the South were to survive, more men and supplies had to be acquired immediately. The question was how to obtain these desperately needed items? The only possible solutions seemed to lie in European recognition of the Southern cause or an expanded, though extremely controversial, use of the slave force in the nation's military struggle.

Secretary of State Benjamin realized even more fully than did President Davis that desperate measures were needed to forestall the collapse of the Confederacy. He proposed to Davis that future negotiations with the Europeans be on the basis of emancipation of the slaves and the government seizure of cotton in order to purchase ships to break the blockade. Although Benjamin's suggestion was a radical departure from the previous policy of the Confederate government, it was not an entirely new concept.[11]

Following his visit to Louisiana in the summer of 1862, when Federal forces were expanding their territorial holdings along the Mississippi and throughout Southeast Louisiana, Duncan Kenner had become very pessimistic over the outlook for the Confederacy. Having to abandon his lands and evacuate his family for their safety convinced Kenner that the South could not succeed if it adhered to its present slave policy and as a consequence failed to secure the assistance of France and England. Kenner informed his friends Davis and Benjamin of his then-radical conclusions during the first weeks of 1863. He also notified the two government leaders that he intended to move in Congress that a commission be sent to France and England to propose that if the two European powers would acknowledge the Confederate States of America, it would abolish the institution of slavery. Davis and Benjamin strongly opposed Kenner's plan. At the time, they were not as alarmed as Kenner over the Confederacy's chances for success. However, in spite of his lack of enthusiasm for the plan, President Davis permitted Kenner to present his idea to his key advisors at a secret cabinet meeting. Like Davis and Benjamin, the Rebel cabinet rigorously opposed Kenner's plan and urged him not to press his initiative. Meeting with such determined opposition from the government's leaders, Kenner decided that the time had not yet arrived to make such a drastic proposal public.[12]

Though he refrained from pushing openly for his plan of emancipation, Kenner was convinced that it was the only way to save the Confederacy. He continued to discuss the proposal in private conversations with friends and associates, particularly Judah Benjamin. Few in Richmond, if any, were closer to the controversial cabinet officer than his fellow Louisianian. As old friends boarding together in the same house in Richmond, the two men often talked confidentially about the problems of the nation.[13]

Gradually, as the plight of the Confederacy worsened, Kenner's arguments for emancipation led Benjamin to warm to the plan. Davis moved more slowly. He contended that the plan of emancipation was clearly unconstitutional. Article I, Section 9 of the Confederate Constitution explicitly prohibited the Congress from passing any law "denying or impairing the right of property in negro slaves." Davis knew that because of the prolonged sectional controversy that had preceded secession, no other constitutional belief held greater sway in the South than the belief that the existence of slavery in a state was exclusively the affair of that state and not of the national government.[14]

Kenner and Benjamin countered the Confederate president's arguments with the claim that such a radical plan for ending slavery was justified because it was required for the survival of the nation. To buttress their position, the secretary of state and the congressman from Louisiana were able to present evidence to Davis that such action would receive the backing of at least a portion of the public. Though not as bold as Kenner, there were those in the South who wanted to address the Confederacy's worsening manpower crisis by an expanded use of slaves in its military conflict with the North. As early as the summer of 1863, the Jackson *Mississippian* had dared to proclaim that slavery should be sacrificed for the sake of the Confederacy's national independence. Perhaps the most surprising comments on the subject of Southern emancipation were made by the highly respected Richmond *Enquirer* on October 6, 1864. The Richmond paper stated:

> We should be glad to see the Confederate Congress provide for the purchase of two hundred and fifty thousand negroes, present them with their freedom and the privilege of remaining in the States, and arm, equip, drill and fight them . . . . This war is for national independence on our side, and for the subjugation of white[s] and the emancipation of

negroes on the side of the enemy. If we fail the negroes are nominally free
and their masters really slaves. We must, therefore, succeed.

Though the *Enquirer* was heavily criticized for its position, it received support from several other Southern papers, including the Lynchburg *Virginian* and the Mobile *Register*.[15]

Davis gradually tempered his staunch opposition to any tampering with the institution of slavery. In the summer of 1864, the Confederate president cautiously began to recede from his earlier position. In an interview with a Northern journalist, Davis emphasized that the South, contrary to the many speeches Southern politicians had given on the subject, wanted first and foremost not slavery but national independence. However, Davis' most surprising change of position on the question of emancipation occurred when he sent his annual message to Congress on November 7, 1864. In that message he called for the employment of slaves in such government occupations as cooks, teamsters, and hospital attendants. In itself the proposal was not very radical, for Congress had authorized such action several months before. The shock came when the Confederate president called for the government to purchase slaves rather than impressing them into service and to "liberate the negro on his discharge after service faithfully rendered."[16]

Response to Davis' November proposal to free a limited number of slaves to perform service to the Confederacy was for the most part highly critical. Notwithstanding this criticism, Davis, desperate for a means to reverse the worsening military situation, turned to Kenner's proposal as a possible answer to the South's dilemma. In late December, 1864, when he finally gave Benjamin permission to proceed with the ambitious plan of offering total emancipation in return for recognition by the European powers, the Confederate president decided that because of the many political and legal consequences of his decision it was necessary to guard against exposure until after the mission had succeeded. He expected that success would reconcile the people to the means used to obtain the end.[17]

With the decision having been made to proceed with the daring operation, the mission had to be planned. After discussing the issue with his cabinet in late December, 1864, Davis decided that only one man would be sent to carry out the delicate assignment. James Mason and John Slidell, the Confederate representatives in Britain and France respectively, could not be relied upon because it was feared that they would not be enthusiastic about the new policy. Thus, it would be better to send a new agent who supported the plan wholeheartedly. Time was of the utmost importance. Sherman was continuing his advance through the heartland of the Confederacy virtually unopposed, much of the South's transportation system was in a state of collapse, and the army was staggering from massive desertions and poor morale. With the situation worsening daily, there would be no time for communication and consultation with officials in Richmond. Therefore, the mission had to be entrusted to a man of sound judgment who would be ready to meet all contingencies that might arise. Political considerations also necessitated that the diplomat chosen have a good and commanding influence in Congress so that a link could be established between that body and the executive authorities in regard to the emancipation proposal.[18]

The one person who seemed to have all the necessary qualifications for such a momentus and hazardous mission was the person who had originally advocated the plan—Duncan Kenner. The Louisiana congressman was informed of Davis' plan at a meeting in late December, 1864. Summoned to the Confederate president's private residence, Kenner was surprised to find a cabinet meeting in progress. Called into the meeting by Davis, he was informed by the president that he had been selected to perform a most delicate and important mission, one on which the fate of the Confederacy probably depended. Thus, nearly two years after Kenner had first broached the idea to Davis, the Confederate president was now officially authorizing Kenner to go immediately to Britain and France to bid for their recognition of the Confederacy in return for the emancipation of the slaves of the South. He was empowered to represent the Confederacy with full power to sign whatever he deemed necessary to succeed in his mission. The Louisiana congressman was also authorized to sell all of the South's cotton in order to obtain revenue with which to purchase war materials. These financial transactions were dependent upon the success of his delicate diplomatic negotiations.[19]

Though pleased that Davis had finally accepted the idea that drastic action was needed to win assistance for the South from the European powers, Kenner took a day or two to consider the ramifications of accepting the mission. After consulting with Judah Benjamin, he met with Davis and told him that he would undertake the mission only if certain conditions were met. Kenner explained to the president that he knew the Confederate diplomats, James Mason, Dudley Mann, and especially John Slidell, very well. He doubted that they would cooperate fully in helping him to carry out his assignment. To avoid any problems with the three diplomats, Kenner requested broad powers. Specifically, he asked for the power to "make or unmake ministers abroad and that . . . [he] be given written authority to and full powers to remove ministers and agents, financial or political, of the Confederacy who should oppose [him]." Though his request in essence granted him absolute authority while in Europe, Davis at once agreed to all of Kenner's demands and ordered Secretary of State Benjamin to prepare the necessary papers.[20]

Even though he had originated the idea of offering emancipation for recognition, Kenner intended that congressional approval be obtained before the drastic act was undertaken. He pressed the president and secretary of state to confer with the members of Congress on the issue. Benjamin did not think such action was needed because the instructions for the mission were based on the principle that the Confederacy was a *de facto* government and could adopt extra-constitutional powers if necessary for its preservation. Kenner did not accept Benjamin's argument and continued to press for congressional consultation on the mission.[21]

Finally heeding Kenner's advice, Davis and Benjamin arranged for a meeting with several of the leading members of Congress. If either of the two Confederate leaders had any doubts about their choice of Kenner, they were dispelled at this meeting. The majority of the congressional leaders present strongly opposed the plan and protested that emancipation of the slaves would financially ruin them. Kenner quickly rose to the defense of the mission. He explained to his congressional colleagues the need for such drastic action. Boasting that he and his family probably owned more slaves than all of the other members of Congress combined, he emphasized that he was not asking anyone to make a sacrifice that he himself was not ready to make. Kenner's staunch defense of the plan relieved many of the doubts of the congressmen at the meeting. Davis and Benjamin were certain that they had found the right man for the job.[22]

On December 27, 1864, Benjamin wrote dispatches to Mason and Slidell in Europe to advise them of the Kenner mission. In the messages the usually optimistic secretary of state showed signs of despair and desperation. He stated that during its four-year struggle for independence the South really had been fighting the battles of Britain and France. If the war had only been against the North it would have long been over; but the Confederacy had not expected Europe to assist the United States by abandoning the rights of neutrals, by closing ports to Southern prizes, and by confiscating vessels being constructed for the Confederacy. "No people," continued the secretary, "have ever poured out their blood more freely in defense of their liberties and independence nor have endured sacrifice with greater cheerfulness than have the men and women of these Confederate States. They have accepted the issue which was forced on them by an arrogant and domineering race, vengeful, grasping, and ambitious. They have asked for nothing, fought for nothing but for the right of self-government, for independence."[23]

After cautioning the nations of Europe against future aggression by the North, Benjamin warned that, unless the Confederacy received aid from Europe, it would be forced to "consider the terms, if any, upon which we can secure peace." Finally, towards the end of the dispatch, the secretary of state approached the main point of his note to the Confederate diplomats in Europe. Were there no terms upon which the South could gain recognition? "Are they [Britain and France] determined never to recognize the Southern Confederacy until the United States assent to such action on their part?" Or did they wish to recognize the South but were held back by some unknown objection to the cause? If such obstacles did exist, then "justice equally demands that an opportunity be afforded us for meeting and overcoming those objections, if in our power to do so."[24]

Benjamin concluded the long dispatch with a brief introduction of Kenner. He hinted at the broad powers that Kenner was to possess in the upcoming negotiations. "I . . . authorize you officially," wrote the secretary, "to consider any communication that he may make to you verbally on the subject embraced in this dispatch as emanating from this Department under the instruction of the President."[25]

In addition to the diplomatic duties assigned to him by the president and the secretary of state, Kenner received instructions from Treasury Secretary George A. Trenholm on the secondary objectives of his mission. As on the military front, the Confederacy was near economic ruin. Trenholm, one of the wealthiest men in the South, had served as secretary of the treasury only since July, 1864. As treasury secretary he had striven, without much success, to improve the Confederacy's desperate financial situation. One of his plans to bring economic relief to the faltering South called for the procurement of a large loan from European sources. The plan required the establishment by several interested European financiers of a bank in Europe, to be called the Franco-Confederate Bank, with a branch in the Confederacy.

The solvency of the bank was to rest on cotton, which was to be shipped to Europe and sold at fifty cents per pound.[26]

Preliminary negotiations for the loan had taken place before the Kenner mission was authorized. The secretary had used his background and connections in the import-export firm of Frazier and Trenholm to open negotiations for the European loan. By December, 1864, these negotiations had reached a critical stage. B. S. Baruc, an agent for several French bankers, had arranged for the Confederacy, using cotton as security, to receive a loan of fifteen million pounds sterling. All that was needed was for the Confederate government to give its approval and for the final terms of the loan to be arranged.[27]

On January 4, 1865, the Confederate Congress passed legislation authorizing the secretary of the treasury, under the direction of the president, to solicit the much-needed loan. The president was also given permission to appoint an agent of his choosing to make the final negotiations for the loan. Since Kenner was preparing to leave on his diplomatic mission and since he also served as chairman of the House Ways and Means Committee, he was the obvious choice for the job. As part of his instructions in arranging the final terms of the loan, Kenner was to see that the money was placed to the credit of the Frazier and Trenholm Company, which served as a depository for the Confederate States. Thus, the money would be in the treasury and would be immediately available for use by the Confederacy.[28]

Such were the responsibilities entrusted to Duncan Kenner by the leaders of his beleaguered government. With the belief that the future of the Confederacy depended upon the success of his assignment, Kenner prepared for his fateful mission. He was given letters of introduction to the various people he would have to work and negotiate with, and he was also provided with a voucher for the payment of his expenses while on the mission. The expense money was to be handled by the Frazier and Trenholm Company in Liverpool and was not to exceed two thousand pounds.[29]

As soon as all preparations were complete, Kenner embarked on his mission. He originally planned to sail on a blockade-runner from a Southern port to Nassau and from there on to Europe. Sometime around January 12, 1865, Kenner left Richmond on a special train and headed for the South's only open port on the east coast—Wilmington, North Carolina. Reaching the port after a couple of days of travel, Kenner was disappointed to learn that he would not be able to sail immediately for the Bahamas because of the presence of a large Federal fleet bombarding Fort Fisher, the Confederate fortress protecting Wilmington. Although he wanted to attempt to sneak past the blockading fleet on a night when there would be little moonlight, circumstances did not prove propitious for such an attempt. Before all the necessary arrangements could be completed for the run past the Federal warships, disaster struck. On January 15, after suffering a severe bombardment and ground assault, Fort Fisher fell to attacking Union forces. It was now impossible for Kenner to escape the blockade from the Wilmington area.[30]

Though there was still a possibility that he could get out through Charleston, Kenner decided that he could reach Europe at least a month sooner by way of the Potomac River and New York City. Having made his decision to sail from an enemy port, Kenner returned to Richmond to inform President Davis and Secretary Benjamin of his new plans. He met first with his friend Benjamin. Surprised by the boldness of his plan, the Confederate leader told Kenner that he considered it madness for the Confederate congressman to attempt to travel such a long distance through enemy territory. The secretary was sure that he would be captured and shot. Despite this warning, Kenner refused to change his daring plan and insisted that Benjamin inform the president of the new turn of events.[31]

Because of the secrecy surrounding the mission, Kenner remained concealed in the house that he shared with Benjamin while the secretary consulted with President Davis on Kenner's new plan. Like Benjamin, the Confederate chief executive objected strongly to Kenner's plan to sail from New York. He thought the plan far too risky. Davis told Benjamin that he would not have Kenner's death on his hands and that the Confederate congressman had to find a safer way to get to Europe. However, after some discussion and Benjamin's explanation of Kenner's determination to make the dangerous journey, the president reluctantly consented.[32]

To assist the diplomat on his perilous trip through the very heart of enemy territory, Davis detailed two young signal officers named Howell and Merrick to accompany Kenner. The two officers were natives of Maryland and were familiar with the terrain along both sides of the Potomac River. The two men were not acquainted with Kenner and were told that his name was A. B. Kinglake and that he was a Confederate officer trying to get to Canada in order to aid some Southerners who had been arrested for operations on the Great Lakes. Since he had the distinguishable physical trait of being nearly bald, Kenner provided himself with a brown wig as a disguise.[33]

On the night of January 18, 1865, Kenner and his two companions set out—he for the second time that week—for Europe. The journey northward was made under the most severe conditions. The winter weather in January, 1865, was unusually cold. The little party suffered greatly from the frigid temperature and freezing wind. Cautiously moving along, the three men soon passed through the lines of the warring armies and entered enemy-controlled territory. After four or five days the small party reached the west bank of the Potomac River at a point about fifteen miles from Fort Johnson, a prison on the Maryland side of the river.[34]

Upon seeing the river, the three men realized that crossing it would be a hazardous undertaking. The Potomac was swollen and full of large pieces of heavy floating ice. Nevertheless, Kenner decided the urgency of his mission required that they immediately attempt a crossing. The little party of Confederates was able to make contact with a group of Southern sympathizers who were willing to help them cross the river. A large boat was obtained for the hazardous river passage. In addition to the dangers of wind, current, and ice, Kenner and his companions also had to be careful not to be spotted by one of the Union gunboats that constantly patrolled the river. Because of the frequency of the patrols, the group did not attempt the crossing until late in the night. However, after struggling for half an hour to break through the ice to the other side, the boatmen told Kenner that it was hopeless to continue and that if they did not get back to the southern shore they would likely be captured by the gunboat patrol. Having failed on their first attempt to cross the Potomac, the little group of Rebel agents made several other unsuccessful attempts during the next few days to cross. Kenner had no choice but to wait for the dreadful weather to moderate.[35]

It took an entire week for the weather to clear sufficiently to permit a river crossing. Although the Potomac was several miles wide at the point of passage, Kenner and his aides crossed to the Maryland side without mishap. Landing on the northern bank about 11:00 p.m., Kenner and his men immediately made their way to the closest safe house, which was located six miles inland from the landing.[36]

The next day Kenner and his two aides continued their journey northward. The weather had again turned foul. Unable to find horses, the three men were forced to walk through the ever-deepening snow. They forged ahead for several hours. By noon the group had reached the vicinity of the town of Port Tobacco. The difficult conditions exhausted Kenner to such an extent that the small party was forced to seek shelter. Fortunately,

Howell, the aide who was most familiar with the area, was able to locate a friendly plantation. Kenner and his two companions were given food and were driven by members of the family to a nearby village where the group paid $80 in gold for an old dilapidated carriage. Also obtaining horses, the party continued north. After traveling until dark, Kenner decided that the services of Merrick were no longer needed. Kenner thanked him and ordered him to return to Virginia.[37]

Kenner and Howell continued to head north. When they neared Washington they stopped at another house chosen by Howell because he knew it to be a safe haven for Confederate agents. Upon entering the dwelling, Howell asked Kenner to turn over all his papers and money to the woman who lived in the house. Though he did what he was asked, for the rest of the night he slept little because his orders and the $18,000 in cash he was carrying were in the possession of a young woman whom he had never met before that night. His anxiety was heightened by the absence of Howell, whose lodgings were in another part of the residence. The next morning Kenner realized that his fears had been groundless. As soon as he and Howell had eaten their breakfast, the woman, without saying a word, returned to Kenner his papers and money. Once on their way again, Howell explained to Kenner that the reason for the strange exchange of his papers was simply to protect their security. The house in which they had stayed was suspected by the authorities of being a Confederate safe house. As such, it was frequently searched in the middle of the night by Federal troops. Consequently, if a raid had taken place during the night, they would have probably searched the men and not the woman.[38]

Discarding the old carriage that they had previously acquired, the two Rebel agents moved cautiously through the Maryland countryside around Washington, D. C. Except for the times they could get a ride on passing wagons, most travel was done on foot. So close did they come to the enemy capital that on one occasion they could see the nearly completed dome of the Capitol. Fearing that they were getting uncomfortably close to the Union stronghold, Kenner and Howell headed in a northeasterly direction for the little community of Bladensburg.[39]

When the two agents reached Bladensburg they boarded the first train going to Baltimore. Both men realized that because Kenner was so well known to many people in the Washington and Baltimore areas, they were taking a great chance of being recognized and captured. To minimize the risk, they rode in the no-smoking car because it was customary for this car to be occupied mostly with "country people" and thus there would be less chance that one of them would recognize either of the two Confederates. They also chose to sit on opposite ends of the car to insure that in case of difficulty one or the other would be able to escape. Both agreed that if the other were recognized and arrested nothing would be done by the person who remained free to aid his troubled comrade.[40]

Fortunately for the two Southerners, the train trip to Baltimore was uneventful. However, when they reached the city, they were displeased to discover that there would be an hour's wait before the train for Philadelphia departed. Because he and his family knew so many people who lived in the Baltimore area, Kenner felt certain that if he remained in the depot until it was time to board the train he would be recognized. To pass the time, Kenner and Howell hailed a carriage and had the driver take them from one cheap clothing store to another under the guise that they could not find what they wanted. After purchasing a few items to allay the suspicion of the carriage driver, the two men returned to the depot. It was dark and the two agents had little difficulty in boarding the train to continue their journey northward.[41]

The trip to Philadelphia was also made without incident. However, on the train between that city and New York the two Confederates narrowly escaped detection. Having made train connections in Philadelphia early in the morning, Kenner and Howell found the train more crowded than the late night one from Baltimore. The two agents were unable to get separate seats, as they had done earlier, and were forced to sit together. Kenner sat in the corner of the seat with his hat pulled over his face pretending to sleep. Opposite to Kenner and his aide sat two suspicious-looking men who continually eyed the two Southerners. As the train continued on, the tension increased. Howell decided to test the situation. He rose in an unconcerned manner and approached one of the "detective looking" men and asked for the time. When they replied, Howell began a discussion with them over whether it was permissible to smoke in the car. Determining that it was, Howell gave them both cigars. The friendly gesture relieved the tension which had been building, and shortly afterwards the two men got up and left the car. Howell's directness had obviously removed any suspicions they had about the two Southerners. Both Confederate agents were convinced that the two men were detectives and that they had come close to being discovered.[42]

The train arrived in New York City early in the morning of February 6, 1865. Kenner and Howell immediately went to the Metropolitan Hotel. However, when they requested a room, seeing no baggage and the ragged condition of their clothing, the clerk told them that all of the rooms in the place were taken. They would have to wait for someone to check out. Frustrated, the two agents decided that it was better for them to wait for a room than to travel around New York looking for another place to stay. Thus, they sat and warmed themselves by the hotel's fire and waited until late in the evening for the clerk to find a room for them.[43]

It was obvious that the clerk had waited until he had just the right room for the two slovenly attired travelers. It was at the very top of the hotel and was later described by Kenner as being "the dirtiest room" in New York City. Kenner immediately sat down and penned a note to Mr. D. M. Hildreth. The latter was an old friend of Kenner's, who had been a fellow member of the exclusive Boston Club in New Orleans before the war. Hildreth had left the Southern city shortly after it was occupied to become one of the proprietors of the New York Hotel. Because Kenner had frequently stayed at the New York Hotel during the times he had visited the city before the war, he was afraid that if he went in person he would be recognized. Instead, he sent his trusted aide Howell to deliver the letter.[44]

Knowing that Hildreth would not recognize the name Kinglake and because security reasons made it impossible for him to use his real name, Kenner decided to use the name of a mutual friend in New Orleans to win Hildreth's cooperation. The letter read:

New York, February 6, 1865

My Dear Sir,

I am requested by . . . R. C. Camp, your old friend to deliver to you a package of great value for M.O.H. Norton, now in Liverpool. I am requested to deliver this package to you and to no one else.

A.B. Kinglake,

P.S. You will not at first probably recognize this signature but I suspect that when you see me you will instantly recognize me.

A.B.K.[45]

Kenner had Howell deliver the note to Hildreth. Though the former New Orleanian was puzzled by the note, he agreed to meet at once with the author of the message. Arrangements were made for the two men to meet in a room that was connected with, but outside of, Hildreth's hotel. Entrance into the room was through a door which opened onto an adjoining city street. Upon arriving at the designated meeting place, Kenner decided that only he and Hildreth should meet. Therefore, he told Howell that he realized that the latter undoubtedly knew by this time that Kenner was not who he had claimed to be. Nevertheless, Kenner explained that he was unable, because of security reasons, to identify himself. Hence, Howell would not be permitted to attend the meeting. Kenner gave his aide $20 and told him to "go out and see the sights" and to return for him in two hours.[46]

Shortly after Howell left, a brawny Irish porter entered the room and started to make a fire. While he was still kneeling at the fireplace, Kenner heard Hildreth approaching the room. He moved quickly to a position in the center of the room behind the porter. When Hildreth entered, he immediately recognized his old friend from the Boston Club. However, before he spoke, Kenner put his finger to his lips and pointed to the porter. To present an appearance of normality in the meeting so as not to raise the suspicion of the porter, Kenner spoke up and said, "I got back sooner than expected." Hildreth, who had turned "as pale as his shirt" and was in a state of momentary shock, meekly replied "yes" to Kenner's comment. The porter was told that the fire he had burning was sufficient and that he should leave the room.[47]

As soon as the porter retired, Hildreth locked the door, turned to Kenner, and said, "Great God Kenner! Where are you from? How did you get here and where are you going? Don't you know that your life is in danger?"[48]

Kenner answered that there were only two people in the entire world who knew that he was in New York—"You and I." He further explained that not even Howell, the individual who had safely led him all the way to New York from Virginia and who had brought Hildreth the letter, knew his true identity. "You and I have the secret," Kenner said, and "I certainly won't tell. You can if you like as you have me in your power."[49]

Kenner's directness calmed Hildreth. He became very cordial and the two men renewed their friendship. During their conversation, Kenner explained to Hildreth that he was on his way to London for commercial reasons. He asked his friend for help in purchasing a ticket for him on "any good liner." If possible, however, he preferred to travel on either the Cunard or a German line. Hildreth agreed to help. As the conversation ended, Kenner reminded the hotel proprietor that he could not mention to anyone that the Confederate congressman was in New York. Though he appreciated Kenner's concern, Hildreth explained that he had to tell his partner, Mr. Cranston, that he was going to permit Kenner to use a room in their hotel. Kenner agreed that Cranston might be told of his identity and added that, if the latter objected to his presence in the hotel, he would find other lodging.[50]

Cranston did not object to Kenner's presence, and he was allowed to remain at the hotel until he was able to sail for Europe. Kenner discussed with his New York hosts the best ship on which to book passage. The choice was between the Cunard and the Bremen lines. Cunard had a ship sailing for Europe three days earlier than did the German company. However, because there would be fewer Americans on the latter vessel and thus less risk of discovery, it was decided that it would be wiser for Kenner to wait the extra days and sail on the German ship.[51]

Accordingly, Hildreth went to purchase the ticket for Kenner's trip. When he returned with it he reported to Kenner that his luck was holding. For, if he had sailed on the Cunard ship as he had wanted to do, he would have encountered the irascible Henry S. Foote. As a member of the Confederate House of Representatives from Tennessee, Foote had frequently tangled with Kenner over political issues. While Kenner often supported Jefferson Davis, Foote opposed almost every plan proposed by the Confederate president. In January, just as Kenner was preparing to leave on his mission, Foote was arrested by Confederate authorities while trying to reach the North. When released he immediately headed North again with a plan of his own to bring about peace. Coolly received by Federal authorities, Foote left for Europe. Kenner was certain that if he had met his old political foe, he would have been turned over to the Yankee authorities.[52]

From the time he moved into Hildreth's and Cranston's hotel, Kenner did not leave his room until he left for his ship. Even his meals were served in his room by Cranston's personal attendant. The two hotel proprietors also assisted Kenner in his trip preparations. They acquired for him a trunk which had only recently come off a European voyage and was covered with advertisements and posters of foreign hotels to make it appear that the owner had lately been abroad.[53]

As the time for his departure drew near, Kenner thanked Howell for his faithful and extremely valuable service. He then gave the young Rebel two hundred dollars and ordered him to return home. They never saw each other again.[54]

On Saturday morning, February 11, 1865, Kenner left the hotel to board the Bremen steamship *America*. Arriving at the pier, Kenner was shocked to see several United States government officials standing near the gangplank of the steamer. As the Confederate approached the ship he noticed one of the government agents eyeing him. Kenner thereupon purchased a copy of the *New York Tribune* and nonchalantly began reading it. As he joined the other passengers waiting to board the vessel, he began to make small conversation in his fluent French with several of the foreigners who were also boarding. His casual manner apparently eased the officers' suspicions, and the Rebel agent was able to board the German ship without incident.[55]

The trip across the Atlantic was not a very comfortable one for Kenner. While on the *America* he continued to use his code name of A.B. Kinglake of Philadelphia. Most of the 254 passengers on the vessel were German traders returning to Europe. However, included among the passengers were two brothers from New Orleans and the United States consul to Stuttgart and his daughter. Though the possibility was slight, Kenner was afraid that he might be recognized by one of the Americans; therefore, he did not mix much with the other passengers on the ship. In addition to experiencing the discomfort of a rough voyage because of poor weather conditions, Kenner also had to tolerate in silence the many verbal attacks some of the pro-Union passengers heaped upon the Confederacy.[56]

After ten days in the rough and bitterly cold North Atlantic, the *America* docked at Southampton. As was the custom, Kenner and the other new arrivals went to the nearby coffee house of a local hotel. As the former passengers discussed the voyage and said their goodbyes to each other, some of the local residents, on learning that they were fresh from America, inquired about the latest war news. As had occurred frequently on the voyage, a few of the pro-Union passengers began to malign the South and its war effort. At first the reserved and undemonstrative Kenner held his temper, but the Unionists continued to heap scorn on the Confederacy. Having heard enough, Kenner rose to his feet and walked over to the table where the degraders were seated. In a loud clear voice which could be understood by everyone in the room, Kenner identified himself as a Confederate and added that "I have had to listen to your abuse during the voyage over, but I want you to understand that if I hear another word of it

The Mission

I will cut out your throats." With that, he returned to his table and finished his coffee. For the rest of the time he remained in the room, not a word was spoken.[57]

From Southampton Kenner proceeded to London, where he expected to find Mason. However, when he got to the office of the Confederate minister, he discovered that Mason had gone to Paris to meet Slidell. Kenner immediately sent telegrams to the two ministers and to Dudley Mann in Brussels informing them of his arrival in Europe. He also requested that the three diplomats meet with him in Paris.[58]

Long before Kenner arrived in the French capital, Mason and Slidell had discussed the question of emancipation and its possible influence on recognition of the South by the major powers of Europe. They had practically made up their minds that offering emancipation for recognition was futile. There seemed little chance for any such proposal to meet with success. This belief had been strengthened in mid-February when Lord Russell, the British foreign minister, had sent Mason and Slidell a joint letter in which he accused the Confederacy in harsh and threatening tones of alleged violations of British neutrality.[59]

Kenner reached Paris on February 24, 1865. When he arrived at Slidell's office in the Grand Hotel, he found Slidell, Mason, and an assistant, W. W. Corcoran, drafting a reply to Russell's harsh note. Dudley Mann had not arrived in time for the start of the meeting. Kenner explained to the men that he was directed to show his orders only to Mason and Slidell. The two men explained that Corcoran was their confidential advisor and that Kenner could discuss the reason for his mission in his presence. Kenner proceeded to explain the purpose of his mission and the intentions of President Davis and his cabinet regarding the institution of slavery. The diplomats were astonished and amazed at the scope of the plan. Noting an air of reluctance in their attitudes, Kenner handed them his written orders. As the ciphered instructions were decoded by Slidell's assistant, the three men continued to discuss the plan and its chances for success.[60]

While the conference was still in its early stages, the small group of Confederate diplomats was joined by Dudley Mann. As he had done for Slidell and Mason, Kenner briefly outlined the purpose of his mission to the newly arrived diplomat. In contrast to the lukewarm reception accorded the proposal by Slidell and Mason, Mann thought the plan feasible. Despite the favorable response, Slidell and Mason continued to express doubts about it. So upset did Mason become with the discussion that at one point he exclaimed that he would simply not obey the instructions. Slidell, exhibiting signs of hurt pride, also continued to oppose the plan and bluntly stated several times that he could not see any reason for Kenner's mission to Europe. He believed that the diplomats already stationed there were fully capable of carrying out any mission that President Davis might order.[61]

Having previously suspected that he might not receive the full cooperation of the three Confederate diplomats, Kenner had been careful to have deciphered first his appointment papers, which authorized him to remove from power anyone who would not cooperate fully with the plan. This took some time. However, when the papers were decoded and the full extent of Kenner's authority was known to the diplomats, their attitudes changed. Realizing that Kenner was determined to carry out his mission and that he had power to supersede or even remove them, Slidell and Mason offered their cooperation to Kenner.[62]

The conference between Kenner and the diplomats continued for several days. Before the meeting ended, Kenner advised the diplomats that, since they would shortly have to approach the British and French governments in an attempt to win their recognition, it would be prudent to delay any response to Lord Russell's criticisms.[63]

Though the precise objectives of Kenner's mission were kept secret, word of the Confederate congressman's arrival in Europe spread quickly throughout the Continent. Knowledge that some new Southern diplomatic effort was underway had an uplifting effect on the sagging morale of Confederate supporters in Europe. The *Index*, the chief Confederate propaganda publication on the Continent, contended that there would be "quite a turn to affairs in America" as a result of the secret negotiations. The London *Telegraph* of March 2, 1865, published a letter from Paris in which it was stated that "Mr. Kenner, a distinguished Confederate, has just arrived and brings what the Southerners evidently consider good news." So optimistic were some Confederate sympathizers that they confidently asserted that before the beginning of May there would be peace between the North and the South. Although their predictions would prove accurate, the "peace" they prophesied would be of a kind far different than they envisioned.[64]

At the Paris conference, the Confederate diplomats generally agreed that Great Britain was the key to European recognition of the Confederacy. Although at the time the French were playing for high stakes in their Mexican venture, they were not strong enough to embark on a policy that might bring them into a military conflict with the United States unless they had the backing of the British. Therefore, Kenner decided that the South's proposal to trade emancipation for recognition should first be made to the British. Accordingly, he directed Slidell not to broach the subject with the French until after Mason had discussed it with the British.[65]

Mason and Kenner arrived in Britain on March 3, 1865. Though Kenner was anxious to meet with the British authorities, Mason, having second thoughts concerning the merits of the plan, was very reluctant to begin the negotiations. He did not think the time was right for such a proposal. In support of his position, Mason cited Lord John Russell's curt note alleging violations of British neutrality, the recent defeats suffered by the South on the battlefield, and his belief that England was not willing to make any move towards recognition at any price. However, Kenner was determined to press forward, and he urged Mason to make contact with the British authorities. He believed that the British did not want to see a reconstruction of the Union and thus would be interested in the new Confederate proposal.[66]

Mason continued to hesitate. The latest dispatches from America had brought news of the burning of Columbia and the evacuation of Charleston. In a letter to Slidell, Mason expressed doubts covering the timing of new negotiations with the British. In his response, Slidell noted that he had "always thought that if the ministry feared reconstruction they would long since have recognized and perhaps gone further to prevent it. They may now feel that they have too deeply committed themselves to retrace their steps." He further advised that Mason and Kenner not make contact with the British until after Napoleon III had been consulted. Trusting in the wisdom and political acumen of the two veteran diplomats, Kenner changed his mind and consented to let Slidell meet with French officials before he and Mason made contact with the British.[67]

On the afternoon of March 4, the same day that he wrote Mason and Kenner suggesting that they delay making contact with the British—and presumably without waiting for Kenner's approval—Slidell met with the emperor. The meeting between the Confederate diplomat and the French leader did not accomplish much. As on previous occasions, Napoleon explained to Slidell that he was "willing and anxious" to act with England but that he would do nothing alone. Slidell then asked him to renew his overtures to the British for some kind of joint action on behalf of the Confederacy. The emperor immediately rejected this suggestion, explaining that his earlier proposals to the British "had been so decidedly rejected that he could not suppose that they would now be listened to with more fervor." Slidell continued to press for some kind of opening. He broached the question of emancipation. Napoleon III replied that, although the English might have been deterred by the question of slavery, that issue had never influenced his decisions concerning the Confederacy.[68]

Although Slidell's two colleagues in London were disappointed by his failure to win assistance from the French, the emperor's comment on English sensitivity over slavery seemed to offer a ray of hope for the South. For some unknown reason, however, Kenner and Mason delayed for nearly a week before approaching the British. Though it seems doubtful that Kenner would have delayed his efforts to achieve the primary goal of his mission in order to work on his secondary objective of arranging financial assistance for the Confederacy, the fact is that he initiated negotiations with several bankers for the sale of Southern cotton during this interim.[69]

Kenner's negotiations with the European financiers met with somewhat more success than Slidell's dealings with the French emperor. One reason for this was that, unlike his diplomatic effort in which there had been no preparatory discussions or contact, much preparation between the Confederate Treasury Department and European bankers had preceded Kenner's arrival on the continent. As noted earlier, Confederate Secretary of the Treasury Trenholm, for over six months, had been negotiating with an agent named B. S. Baruc for a loan of up to fifteen million pounds sterling.[70]

With news of the war growing increasingly dim for the Confederacy, Baruc's bankers, who included the directors of the Merchant's Bank and a Paris banker named Mr. E. Berlé (the Comte du Trembliem de Chauvigny), seemingly had second thoughts about committing such a large sum of money to the South. Through their agent, the financiers asked Kenner to approve an agreement in which the stated loan amount of fifteen million pounds would be transferred to the Confederacy through a series of smaller loans of three million pounds each. From his residence in the Burlington Hotel, Kenner took a tough position and immediately responded to Baruc that his new proposal was "entirely different from that submitted in Richmond" and would not be accepted. Although the introduction of new terms by the financiers did not scuttle Trenholm's loan plan, it did complicate the negotiations and slowed the influx of desperately needed monies into the treasury of the Confederacy. However, the hesitancy of the bankers demonstrated to Kenner the urgent need for progress in his diplomatic mission.[71]

Finally, on March 13, 1865, Mason addressed a note to Lord Henry John Palmerston, the British prime minister, requesting a private interview. The prime minister's private secretary replied the same day, appointing twelve noon of the following day as the time for the meeting. Because of Kenner's inexperience in international negotiations, the Louisianian decided that it would be better if Mason alone met with Palmerston.[72]

Late in the morning of March 14, Mason traveled alone to the Foreign Office for his fateful meeting with the prime minister. Though he realized that the destiny of the Confederacy probably depended on the outcome of his encounter with Palmerston, Mason still held reservations about the new Confederate offer of emancipation. He had never accepted the idea that the British had withheld recognition only because of their opposition to slavery. He believed the real reasons were twofold. First, there was a fear of war with the United States, and second, the British did not want to see the war end. The longer the conflict lasted in America the better off the British would be. As long as the hostilities continued, the economic and military competition of the Americans was reduced greatly. Hence, though Mason decided to follow his instructions and to present the Southern offer of emancipation, he also determined to play on the prime minister's fear of the consequences of a strong and united America.[73]

Mason started the interview by reading portions of the official instructions he had received from Benjamin and of Kenner's orders. He then discussed the recently completed Hampton Roads Conference between representatives of the Confederacy and the Union.[74] He denied the validity of then-current rumors which speculated that the conference had been part of a Southern plan for an aggressive alliance. Mason explained to the prime minister that a Northerner present at the Hampton Roads meeting had actually mentioned the possibility of an armistice between the belligerents in order to facilitate the dispatch of a joint American force against the French in Mexico. The Rebel diplomat attempted to exploit Palmerston's fear of the possibility of peace upon the basis of a military alliance between the North and South. Mason added that the Confederacy did not desire such an alliance but that there was no way to predict just how far necessity would drive the South to obtain peace.[75]

The Confederate diplomat also reviewed for the British official the past events of the war in which Southerners felt that they had not been treated fairly by the two principal European powers. At no time during the interview did he directly mention the abolition of slavery by name. He feared that if the issue were openly discussed it would have been found out by the enemy. Therefore, throughout the meeting, Mason repeatedly made oblique references to the South's willingness to abolish slavery.[76]

"I . . . impressively urged Lord P.," wrote Mason in his report on the meeting to the Confederate secretary of state, "that if the President [Davis] was right in his impression that there was some latent, undisclosed obstacle on the part of Great Britain to recognition, it should be frankly stated [so that the Confederacy] might . . . consent to remove it." He further explained to Benjamin that he had "returned again and again during the conversation to this point, and in language so direct that it was impossible to be misunderstood."[77]

Prime Minister Palmerston, an individual who personified John Bull in both appearance and overbearing manner, listened with interest and attention while Mason explained why he had requested the interview. When the British official finally spoke, he quickly denied that the slavery issue had ever been a barrier to recognition. Palmerston added that he now realized more than ever that the South was doomed. Each day reports were being received of new Northern victories. It was too late; nothing could be done to prevent the death of the Confederacy. All that England's recognition of the South would accomplish now was a probable war with the United States. It would not save the Confederacy. The old British gentleman, gracious, suave, and personally sympathetic to the Southern cause, simply assured Mason that his government's position on the Confederacy was not based on any "underlying" cause. As he had on previous occasions, Palmerston explained that on the question of recognition, the British government had not been satisfied at any time in the war that Southern independence could be achieved beyond doubt. After an hour of fruitless discussion, the interview ended; the last glimmer of hope for the Confederacy had faded.[78]

The failure of the Mason-Palmerston conference greatly disappointed Kenner and his diplomatic colleagues in Europe. However, Slidell did not fully accept the results of the session. Upon receiving word of the disappointing meeting, Slidell notified Kenner and Mason by mail that he did not think the old prime minister had been entirely frank about the slavery issue. He based this conclusion on his belief that British Foreign Minister John Russell was profoundly affected by the slavery question. This thought evidently disturbed Mason and made him think that perhaps he had not made himself sufficiently clear to the aging Palmerston.[79]

In order to remove any doubts that he and Kenner held on the subject, Mason sought out an old friend, the Earl of Donoughmore. He was a man of some influence in Britain. Mason hoped that he could help clarify the situation. The two men met on the evening of March 26, 1865. During the meeting, Mason frankly discussed the future of the Confederacy with his British friend. Donoughmore was greatly alarmed at what seemed to be the disintegration of the South's armies, as exhibited by Sherman's unimpeded march through Georgia and the Carolinas. The British nobleman concluded his comments about the South's military outlook with the remark "that but for slavery we [the Confederacy] should have been recognized two years ago."[80]

Mason was somewhat taken aback by Donoughmore's observation. In response Mason commented that in all his previous contacts with the British government, as well as among friends in and out of government, he had never heard it suggested that slavery had prevented recognition. Mason wondered why the consequences of the slave issue had not been discussed previously. Donoughmore answered that, "in his opinion it had always been in the way, and that after Lee's successes on the Rappahannock and march into Pennsylvania . . . and his army was at the very gates of Washington, he thought but for slavery [the Confederacy] should have been acknowledged."[81]

The British nobleman's remarks appeared to confirm Slidell's speculation on the subject and to offer a ray of hope for the Southern diplomat. Perhaps he had not been explicit enough in his interview with the British prime minister. To clarify the situation, Mason asked his British friend what effect an offer of emancipation would have at the present time on the relations between the Confederacy and Great Britain? Lord Donoughmore answered that, unfortunately for the South, the time had passed. It was too late for the Confederacy to secure assistance.[82]

Thus, Kenner's mission and the last diplomatic effort of the Confederacy ended as the Southern cause itself would end–in failure. A few days after Mason's meeting with the Earl of Donoughmore, Richmond was evacuated by the Confederacy. Seven days later, on Sunday, April 9, 1865, in the McLean house in the little village of Appomattox Courthouse, Virginia, the bloodiest conflict in America's history came to a close. The Confederate States of America were no more.

When news of the fall of the Confederate capital reached Europe, Kenner realized the hopelessness of the situation and began to make plans for his future. Would he remain in Europe or return to the uncertainty that awaited him and other Confederate officials in America? Though several of his acquaintances in the rebel government, including Slidell, Soulé, and Judah P. Benjamin, decided to take refuge abroad, Kenner elected to return to his family and home in Louisiana and to face whatever was in store. When the details of President Andrew Johnson's May, 1865, Proclamation of Amnesty became known to Kenner, he called at the United States Legation in Paris on June 20, 1865, and took the oath prescribed in the presidential amnesty decree.[83] However, as an official in the Confederate government and an individual whose taxable property exceeded $20,000, he was not covered by the general terms of the amnesty and had to petition for a special presidential pardon. Remaining in Europe for several more weeks until events in America became more predictable, Kenner sailed for the United States in late summer.[84]

The Kenner mission was the final diplomatic gasp of a desperate nation. There is little evidence that it had any possibility of achieving its primary goal of gaining recognition and thus saving the South from defeat. By early 1865 there was little anyone could have done to preserve the Southern cause. Even if Kenner had miraculously accomplished his mission and secured foreign recognition, it was too late. Richmond was doomed and Lee was trapped. Aid would have arrived too late to make any difference in the outcome of the war.

Whether the Confederacy could have achieved European recognition through abolition alone in the early stages of the war is also doubtful. Although the slave issue was a crucial factor in the Anglo-French failure to grant recognition to the South, it was by no means the only obstacle. The diplomatic tradition of the European powers cautioned against any recognition until the Confederacy had exhibited the power required to establish and maintain its independence. Without the certainty of a Confederate victory, European involvement would run the risk of either an eventual humiliating retreat from an established diplomatic objective or an open-ended military commitment to guarantee the South's independence. Furthermore, an end to the war in America would have terminated the lucrative war profits that the nations of Europe, particularly Great Britain, were reaping from a continuation of the conflict.[85]

Despite these contributing elements, the dominant factor in the failure of Confederate diplomacy was the military defeat of the South's armies, particularly at crucial times during the war. If in the early months of the conflict the leaders of the Confederacy had heeded Kenner's suggestion on emancipation and had coupled it with victories at such pivotal battles as Antietam and Gettysburg, might not the South have obtained recognition by the British and the French and hence victory? Even with the absence of timely victories on the battlefield, emancipation alone, if executed early enough in the war, could have been extremely beneficial to the Confederacy. Opposition to slavery was one of the major rallying cries for the Northern war party; without this issue it would have been much more difficult for the Lincoln government to sustain the popular support and morale which was critical to a Northern victory.[86]

XI

POSTWAR SURVIVAL

Duncan Kenner's decision to return to Louisiana from Europe at the end of the war was not made without some trepidation. The uncertainty, depression, and confusion felt by most Southerners following the collapse of the Confederacy and the assassination of Abraham Lincoln was intensified for Kenner and the other Rebel diplomats who found themselves many thousands of miles from where events were unfolding. News of the rapidly changing situation in the South which reached the Confederate colony on the Continent was usually dated and often offered contradictory indications of what the future held in store for the conquered rebels. Though the vanquished soldiers of the South were treated humanely, many of the defeated nation's ranking political leaders, including President Davis and Vice-President Stephens, were imprisoned. Many others, including Judah P. Benjamin and Governor Henry Watkins Allen of Louisiana, were in the process of fleeing the South to take up residence in foreign lands.[1]

Southerners were confused and uncertain as to what the official policy of the United States government would be on the question of reconstruction. Lincoln had developed a rather lenient plan for reconstructing the former Rebel states. However, with his death the reins of government passed into the hands of Andrew Johnson. A strong Unionist from Tennessee, the new president was not considered to be anti-Southern and even subscribed to the Southern tradition of states' rights. Yet, despite his Southern ties, Johnson strongly disliked the planter class in the South because he blamed them for pursuing reckless policies which culminated in secession and war. Many in the North looked favorably, at first, upon his ascendancy to the presidency, for they anticipated that he would support a firmer form of reconstruction than Lincoln had evinced. On the other hand, many Southerners, always ready to believe the worst of their Northern enemies, viewed the passing of Lincoln and the assumption of control by Johnson as an opening for the radicals and a mere preliminary to future blood-letting.[2]

During the first days of the new administration it appeared to many that the Northern radicals were going to get their wish for harsher treatment of the defeated South. Johnson's proclamation of amnesty seemed to imply that the planter class would be singled out for punishment. The plan, which in most aspects paralleled the Lincoln amnesty proposals, excepted from the general amnesty provisions anyone whose estimated value of taxable property was over $20,000. Persons belonging to the excepted classes were required to make special application to the president for their pardons. Despite the fear by Kenner and other Southerners that Johnson and the radical Northerners would use this provision of the amnesty plan to punish those who had held leadership roles in the antebellum and wartime South, it soon became evident that the president was more interested in humbling the leaders of the Confederacy by requiring them to make individual pleas for forgiveness than in exacting retribution. Johnson turned out to be remarkably generous in granting pardons to those individuals who petitioned for them.[3]

Kenner and other Southerners looked favorably upon Johnson's forgiving mood. The despair of the spring of 1865 gave way by summer to a feeling of optimism. It was this easing of anxiety among Southerners which convinced Kenner that he should return home and face whatever consequences lay in store for him. Unlike the hundreds of ex-Confederates—many of them personal friends and acquaintances—who fled to other countries, Kenner decided to join those Southerners who admitted defeat and urged cooperation between victor and vanquished in order to rebuild their shattered lives. Holding views similar to those of Kenner were such pivotal Southern leaders as former Confederate Vice-President Stephens, General Wade Hampton, the antebellum firebrand George Fitzhugh, and most important of all Robert E. Lee, who urged all to "unite in honest effort to obliterate the effects of war, and to restore the blessings of peace."[4]

On Monday, May 29, 1865, three days after General Kirby Smith had formally surrendered the last remaining military units of the Confederacy, Kenner visited the United States legation in Paris and took the prescribed oath of allegiance. Anxious to return home to his family and holdings, Kenner, in his interviews with John Bigelow, the United States minister, deliberately minimized his official role as a Confederate agent and masked the real reason he was in Europe. In a memorandum to Secretary of State William Seward concerning his talks with Kenner, Bigelow reported that the ex-Confederate congressman humbly asked to have his rights restored "as early as possible." Although "he [had] yielded to the pressure of public opinion about him so far as to cast his fortunes with the enemies of his country in the late rebellion he is now satisfied that the whole movement was a mistake." According to Bigelow, his interview with Kenner revealed that the latter had taken "no part in bringing about secession." Nor had he been "a member of any meeting or convention gotten up for the purpose of inducing the state to secede from the Union." With such statements, Kenner obviously "forgot" his efforts to win election as a secessionist to the Louisiana Secession Convention in 1861. Kenner also strayed from any embarrassment or other recriminations which could have arisen over disclosure of the plan to trade slavery for European recognition of the Confederacy, Kenner simply told American officials at the Paris legation that he had traveled to Europe "in the hope of being joined by his family."[5]

Kenner did not wait to find out if his pardon would be granted. A few weeks after submitting his request for amnesty, he sailed for the United States. Arriving in New York in late August, the ex-Confederate official discovered that his application for a pardon had not been properly executed and that he had to apply a second time. Disappointed at the delay, Kenner was nevertheless pleased to discover that there were ongoing efforts by at least one of his friends to obtain the presidential pardon he desired. Thomas Cottman, a long-time acquaintance of Kenner, and a one time secessionist, had managed to become close to the Federal authorities during the war. He had even served briefly in the United States Congress during the conflict as a representative from reconstructed Louisiana. Almost from the moment that Johnson announced his amnesty plan, Cottman had worked to obtain a pardon for his Confederate friend. Although his efforts were rebuffed by Secretary of State Seward because it was "indispensable that a person who desires the benefits of the amnesty proclamation should himself apply . . . to the president," Cottman and several other friends of Kenner did not give up.[6]

Among those who assisted Kenner in his efforts to win executive clemency was J. Madison Wells, the reconstruction governor of Louisiana. A native-born planter from Rapides Parish who had been a Whig during most of the antebellum era, Wells was an uncompromising Unionist who had known Kenner for years. Politically ambitious, Wells shrewdly calculated that the returning Confederates would in the future hold the balance of power in elections. Therefore, unlike his predecessor in the Louisiana governorship, Michael Hahn, Wells adopted a conciliatory attitude toward the former Rebels and gladly assisted the popular Kenner in his efforts to win a pardon.[7]

In spite of the assistance of influential friends and promises of quick action from Attorney General James Speed and even the president, no pardon was immediately forthcoming. With postwar political events in Louisiana moving rapidly and with his personal financial situation seriously weakened, it was imperative that Kenner obtain the pardon so that he could begin actively to rebuild his life and fortune. In mid-September when no pardon had been received, Kenner made another concerted effort to obtain amnesty. This time he turned to an old classmate from his days of study at Miami University of Ohio. Robert Schenck was an ex-Union general, and a current member of Congress and chairman of the Committee on Military Affairs, who had easy access to the president. On the suggestion of Cottman, Kenner wrote to his old friend and requested, "for someone who has 'entre' to the President, to take the trouble to bring the application to his notice, and request him to sign the pardon." Feeling obligated to elucidate why it was necessary for him to impose such a request on Schenck, Kenner explained that the issue was

> of the very greatest importance to me being no less than a question of bread and meat to my family. The possessor of quite a large fortune when the war commenced, I now find myself reduced to absolute poverty. And my only hope to begin life again with any prospect of success is to have restored to me the remnant that is left. To succeed in this, I must have the President's pardon. . . . With this I can begin, where I did 31 years ago, a wiser, if not a better man.[8]

The letter to Schenck seemed to have had the desired effect. Years later Kenner related to a friend that, armed with a letter of introduction from Governor Wells, he was able to obtain a brief meeting in Washington with President Johnson. The president told Kenner that if he wanted a pardon he would have to see a secretary named McCrary. According to Kenner, when he met the gentleman, who was a native of Kentucky, the ex-Confederate gave his name as "Kenner of Louisiana." The man replied: "I know you. I have been to your place. I went there on a flatboat." Kenner thought that "his cake was dough" because his plantation had often been visited by flatboats whose crews would trade supplies for chickens and other commodities. The business negotiations between the crews and Kenner were not always friendly, and Kenner feared for a moment that since he remembered the occasion so well, McCrary's visit to Ashland had not been pleasant. However, the official went on to say that he "remembered [Kenner] very well and very pleasantly" and that because both were very fond of horses Kenner had treated him to a tour of his stables. With that, the two men renewed their acquaintanceship and had a pleasant discussion of fine horses. Thus, the way was finally cleared for Kenner's pardon.[9]

Within days of his meeting with the president and his aide and before he even had a chance to return to Louisiana, Kenner was granted his pardon. Signed by President Johnson on October 4, 1865, and accepted by Kenner on the following day, the amnesty required Kenner to pay all costs associated with the proceedings and prohibited him from claiming any property which had been sold in accordance with the confiscation laws of the United States. Kenner also agreed that if he ever bought a slave or used slave labor the pardon would be voided.[10]

With his long-sought pardon finally in hand, Kenner returned to Louisiana, determined to rebuild the shattered lifestyle his family had lost as a result of the war. Not only did he find his personal finances and holdings wrecked, but he also found his state prostrate. Though much of Louisiana had escaped the large-scale military engagements that had wrought such great destruction in some areas of the state and across the South, Louisiana had paid dearly for its decision to join the Confederacy. Only three states, Virginia, South Carolina, and Georgia, paid a greater price in destruction and casualties than did Louisiana. Approximately one-fifth of the 56,000 men it enlisted in the Rebel cause died in battle or in hospitals. Additionally, emancipation of its slaves cost Louisiana one third of its economic wealth. Besides the loss in slaves, about one-half of all of the livestock in the state disappeared during the war years. Because of the size and complicated nature of their industry, the sugar planters of Louisiana suffered some of the greatest losses. Two-thirds of the farm equipment and machinery used in the production of sugar was destroyed or was rusted beyond repair. Of the 1,200 plantations involved in the production of sugar in 1861, less than 200 were still making sugar when Kenner returned home after the war. The Southern poet Sidney Lanier aptly summarized the lifestyle of many in Louisiana at the end of the war when he wrote that "pretty much the whole of life has been merely not dying."[11]

Many sugar planters, when faced with circumstances similar to those that confronted Kenner, could see little hope for a restoration of their fortunes. Accommodation to the new social order which demanded the abandonment of old beliefs, habits, and prejudices was too much for some Southerners to accept. Many an individual who in the ordered society of the antebellum era had served his family and community well experienced a gradual character disintegration during the months following the end of the war. With all kinds of work needing to be done, many who had never performed true physical labor simply could not bring themselves to undertake the tasks which had formerly been done by their slaves. The despair and frustration drove many to alcohol, gambling, family quarrels, and idle amusements. As summarized by historian J. Carlyle Sitterson, "The collapse of the economy left the majority of the people drifting without aim, without interest, without hope."[12]

Although many yielded to despair, Kenner grasped for opportunity. Like most other returning Confederates, Kenner turned to his agricultural holdings as a starting place from which to rebuild. The soil and its produce had afforded the good life before the war, and they would be the basis for a new start during the period of postwar difficulties. Though there was little hope that the sugar industry as a whole could be restored to its prewar level of prosperity, Kenner had more to be optimistic about than many of his planter colleagues. Unlike many of the region's sugar estates, Kenner's Ashland and Bowden plantations had remained in production throughout the war. Although seized early in the war and stripped by Union forces of much of their valuable livestock and equipment, to say nothing of losing a large portion of their labor force, the two Ascension Parish properties had remained in operation during most of the war through the Federal government's leasing program. The leasing of the Kenner estates during the war also provided those who continued to live there with early experience in dealing with a paid, rather than a slave, labor force. Finally, with his lifelong friend George Graves obtaining lease rights to the property, Kenner was fortunate that the management of his plantations remained in trusted hands during much of the time that the Kenner family was absent. Graves continued on at Ashland after Kenner's properties were returned to him. Therefore, his presence afforded valuable continuity in the management of the Kenner estates.

Also returning to assist the Kenners in their rebuilding efforts was Henry Hammond, Duncan's longtime servant who had continued to serve

Kenner during the time he lived in Richmond. When Kenner left on his secret mission to Europe and Richmond was abandoned by the Confederacy, Hammond had made his way back to Louisiana where he rejoined the Kenner family. Following his return to Ashland, he took charge of the garden which provided the family and overseers with food during the lean period immediately following the family's return after the war. The years that he spent with Kenner obviously whetted Hammond's appetite for the political arena, for the former slave eventually entered politics and won election to the Ascension Parish Police Jury.[13]

Upon his return to the area in late October, 1865, after receiving his pardon from the president, Kenner quickly regained possession of his properties. Although the latter were under the jurisdiction of the Freedmen's Bureau (officially the Bureau of Refugees, Freedmen, and Abandoned Lands) at the time, Kenner had surprisingly little trouble resuming control of his lands. Fortunately, President Johnson's pardons carried with them the restoration of any confiscated properties then held by the government. The only condition was a stipulation that Kenner honor the terms of the lease which was then in effect.[14]

Not surprisingly, sugar production immediately following the end of the war was low. Production which had peaked in 1861 at 264,000 tons dropped to only 9,950 tons in 1865—one of the smallest crops ever. The high cost of sugar machinery made the recovery of the industry painfully slow. Although vitality did gradually return to the cane industry as a whole, it was not until 1893 that sugar output reached the 1862 level. The situation was aggravated even further by low sugar prices. With only a few upward turns, the trend in prices for the product was almost continuously downward between the end of the war and the turn of the century. As reported by Professor Sitterson in *Sugar Country*, the price of sugar dropped from a peak of 18 cents in 1864 to 8.5 cents in 1874 and 6.5 cents in 1880.[15]

Though Kenner was fortunate to have had his land remain in production, many others, including relatives and friends, were not so fortunate. Most tried valiantly to combat the situation which resulted from the unsettled political and social conditions of the time. However, lacking the ability, flexibility, and resources of Kenner, they were not able to hold out until prosperity returned to the industry. Despairing of the situation faced by herself and the region's other planters, Kenner's sister-in-law commented in a letter to her son:

To carry on the place next year appears to be all that can be done; but where the money is to be gotten is more than I know.... Some say plantations in Louisiana will be a great deal more valuable soon. That may be, but I fear there will be a great deal of domestic trouble, politically, with the Negroes before things are settled.[16]

So destitute and desperate had become the plight of the family of Duncan's brother that in order to survive they were forced to sell some of their personal belongings, and they even discussed the possibility of selling the family's beloved Oakland Plantation at Kennerville where William Kenner had reared his family and had first become involved in the growing of sugar cane. Writing to her son Philip Minor Kenner in Natchez, Ruhamah Riske Kenner[17] described the depths to which she had been driven in order to survive: "I had to sell my diamond broach to Lathy for $300 to enable me to have any money at all. I never was so poor since I was married, and I feel it greatly."[18]

Duncan was not the type to overlook the needs of others. A man of generous feelings, Kenner often assisted less fortunate relatives and friends. Thus, in order to help his late brother's family, Kenner purchased a half-interest in Roseland Plantation at a sheriff's sale. In addition, for some months, he also provided his nephew Philip Minor Kenner and wife Ella an average of $300 a month in financial support and on at least one occasion in January, 1872, he made a loan of $2,600 to the couple. Kenner's assistance to his brother's family during their financial difficulties eventually amounted to over $12,000. This was a handsome sum for the time. With the sugar industry so depressed, once bountiful and proud sugar estates were being sold for as little as $10 to $30 an acre! Though humanitarian in nature, Kenner's generosity was at least partially directed at helping Philip Kenner to stabilize his own financial situation so that he would be better able to assist his mother in preserving the family's holdings at Oakland. Kenner obviously felt strongly about retaining the family homestead near the newly created town of Kenner (formerly Kennerville) in Jefferson Parish. He worked hard to have all members of the family aid in the effort to save the place and was not hesitant in applying pressure to win their participation. As one of his nephews noted, "Uncle Kenner put it to him [a relative named Harding], that as an heir, he ought to protect the property."[19]

Duncan and Nanine also assisted her family during the postwar period. Faced with the same difficulties as other large plantation owners of the region, the Bringiers found their once-prosperous holdings saddled with huge debts. So serious was the situation that the Hermitage, the family estate, had to be placed on the block at a sheriff's sale. As with Oakland, Duncan and Nanine were determined not to let the property slip out of the family's hands. At the sale in November, 1866, Nanine joined with two of her sisters, Louise (wife of Martin Gordon, Jr.), and Aglae (wife of Benjamin Tureaud of Tezcuco Plantation), to purchase the estate. A little over two years later, the three sisters turned the property over to their brother, Amédée, and his wife Stella, with the hope that they would be able to rejuvenate the plantation.[20]

Duncan and Nanine's charitable and caring nature was also demonstrated in the way they insulated Nanine's mother from the economic depredations faced by the postwar planter aristocracy. Because she spent most of her time at her splendid city estate of Melpomene in New Orleans, Mrs. Bringier did not fully appreciate the severity of the crisis which was destroying her family's once-numerous and grand holdings. Chief among the latter was the Hermitage, the Bringier country estate located a short distance from Donaldsonville. While her children struggled to maintain the family's lands, Mrs. Bringier knew little of the disaster at hand. Even when the situation worsened to meet her financial obligations, Duncan and Nanine protected Mrs. Bringier from the problem. They arranged to have her visit the resort of Bay St. Louis, Mississippi, on the days that the property at Melpomene was sold at a sheriff's sale. Kenner bought both the movables and the property.[21] A few days later when she returned from her visit to the coast, Mrs. Bringier resumed her life at Melpomene ignorant of how close she had come to losing everything. Kenner allowed her to continue to live at the mansion as if nothing had happened until her death in 1878. Kenner even saw to it that monthly allowances, which were to be paid by Mrs. Bringier to the family heirs for life, were made until her death.[22]

When Mrs. Bringier died, Duncan decided to recoup some of his expenses by tearing down the old mansion and dividing the grounds into building lots, which he subsequently sold. The Melpomene real estate project was only one of many that Kenner was involved in after the war. Though he had participated in the New Orleans real estate market during the antebellum period, Kenner was among the first to realize the business opportunities afforded by the postwar era. Either alone or in association with others, Kenner acquired numerous properties in New Orleans and in the plantation region. Many of his holdings in the city were located in some of New Orleans' most exclusive business and residential areas, including Canal Street and St. Charles Avenue. Unlike most of the major cities of the South, New Orleans had survived the Civil War without suffering major destruction. Ironically, because of the efforts by Federal officials to make the place a cleaner and more healthful community, the Crescent City in some ways was actually better off as a result of its occupation during most of the war. Undamaged by the war, postwar New Orleans experienced a substantial growth in population resulting from the return of old inhabitants as well as the influx of new ones trying to leave behind the destruction that the war had brought to their former homes. Thus, the increase in postwar population coupled with the fact that there had been no new construction in the city during the war made the New Orleans real estate market one of the few promising areas of investment in Louisiana. Rents more than doubled in 1865 alone, and the value of property in the Crescent City increased in value by as much as fifty percent. Determined to regain his fortune, Kenner quickly moved to take advantage of the real estate market and the financial opportunities it offered.[23]

Kenner's real estate ventures were not limited to his property acquisitions in New Orleans. Unlike many of his planter colleagues, Kenner continued to have faith in the future of the sugar industry. His interest in assisting his wife's family out of economic difficulties eventually led him to acquire the Bringier family's once-grand Hermitage and Houmas estates. Though he had worked to assist the Bringiers in saving their lands, prosperity never really returned. Consequently, Kenner became increasingly involved in the operation of the estates until he eventually obtained their ownership. In addition to the Bringier properties in Ascension Parish, Kenner also obtained Hollywood Plantation in East Baton Rouge Parish, and he continued to maintain a financial interest in his nephew's Roseland Plantation in St. Charles Parish.[24]

Kenner did not limit his postwar entrepreneurial efforts to real estate and agriculture. He realized that, despite the depressed economy which afflicted much of Reconstruction Louisiana, opportunity existed for profitable business ventures. One such enterprise involved Kenner's management of the Louisiana Levee Company. Among the most serious damages inflicted upon Louisiana during the war was the deterioration of the levees along its rivers, lakes, and bayous. Little maintenance had been performed on the levees during the war, and in the postwar years the economic recovery of the region was severely handicapped by frequent breaks in the levee system. Taking advantage of this business opportunity, Kenner purchased one thousand shares of stock in the Louisiana Levee Company, which constructed over 313 levees throughout the state. In addition, he became involved in the management of the company.[25]

Determined to diversify his financial holdings so that his and his family's future well-being would not be too closely tied to the capricious postwar sugar industry, Kenner often invested large amounts of money in businesses he thought possessed promising futures. Among his investments were sizeable holdings of stock in the New Orleans Pacific Railroad Company, the Southern Pacific Railroad, the Planters Fertilizer and Manufacturing Company, the Louisiana Sulphur Mining Company, the Canal Bank of New Orleans, the New Orleans Produce Exchange, and perhaps the Tehuantepec Inter-Ocean Railroad in Mexico. Additionally, Kenner was also interested in cotton, particularly the expanding use of some of the by-products of the industry. As markets in this area broadened, Kenner gradually increased his involvement until he eventually became the president of several companies specializing in the utilization of cotton products. Among these were the Union Cotton Tie and Compress Company of New York, the Louisiana Cotton Manufacturing Company (latter called the Crescent City Oil Company), and the Planter's Crescent Oil Company. The latter two companies concentrated on the use of the cotton seed in such products as cattle feed, fertilizer, soap, and chemical, mechanical, medicinal, and household oils.[26]

Kenner also profited financially from the many personal loans that he made to both relatives and acquaintances. Far from being a financial ogre who foreclosed quickly on defaulted payments, Kenner commonly charged 8 percent interest on the many loans he made. As demonstrated in his dealings with his mother-in-law and nephew, it was Kenner's generosity in providing financial support which enabled many of the once-prosperous members of the antebellum elite to survive the lean years of the Reconstruction era. So frequently did acquaintances turn to him when they needed cash that the list of promissory notes owed to Kenner at the time of his death took up more than ten pages of his succession document and ranged in value from a $20 loan to J. Ross Steward to two notes of $6,000 to Mrs. D. Ella Kenner of Roseland Plantation.[27]

Though many of his investment efforts proved lucrative, not all of his postwar business ventures were successful. One missed opportunity concerned Kenner's involvement in the gaslight business. A major stockholder and president for a time of the New Orleans Gaslight Company as well as a large stockholder in the Jefferson City Gaslight Company, both of which supplied fuel for many of the city's street lights, Kenner was always cognizant of his competition. Hence, when he heard of Thomas Edison's success with electricity and his development of the electric light bulb at his Menlo Park, New Jersey, laboratory, Kenner dispatched one of his assistants, S. H. Zilman, to investigate. Though electric arc lamps had been introduced a year or so earlier and Edison was in the process of establishing a factory to produce his newly invented light bulb, Zilman was not impressed. After visiting with the great inventor at his Menlo Park laboratory, Zilman wrote to Kenner that, although Edison had patiently explained to him both the scientific and commercial aspects of the future of electricity and the incandescent bulb, he was not persuaded. Accordingly, Zilman reported to Kenner that because of high costs and technical problems, "I think the gas companies have nothing to fear from electricity for general purposes." Kenner accepted the evaluation of his assistant and uncharacteristically failed to recognize the opportunities afforded by the new industry. Somewhat ironically, when electricity finally arrived in New Orleans under the auspices of New Orleans Public Service, the electric utility was housed ironically in the building formerly used by Kenner and the New Orleans Gaslight Company.[28]

Another business venture which failed to meet Kenner's expectations was his involvement with his brother-in-law and close friend Richard Taylor in the leasing and management of a commercial waterway in New Orleans called the New Basin Canal. Six miles long, sixty feet wide, and six feet deep, the canal had originally been constructed between 1831 and 1835 to give the American population of the city easy access to Lake Pontchartrain and the communities on the north shore of the lake. Largely neglected during the war, the Louisiana legislature authorized the leasing of the waterway in 1866 with the hope of having it revitalized. Taylor obtained a fifteen-year lease in March, 1866, and Kenner joined him as a full partner in January of the following year. Six months later they broadened the partnership to include James McCloskey. However, the partnership never worked out. Surviving documents suggest that Kenner and Taylor never fully informed McCloskey to what extent Kenner was involved in the ownership of the company. Despite the existence of a signed partnership agreement dated January 21, 1867, Kenner later denied during questioning related to a pending legal case concerning the canal that he was ever a partner of Taylor. Kenner claimed that his role was only that of agent "placed in charge of the Canal . . . by Richard Taylor." Kenner added that he had "no interest in the receipts of the Canal beyond what is owed me for services rendered as agent." This was obviously not the case and demonstrates a failure by Kenner to report the facts in order to protect either himself and/ or Richard Taylor from pending legal entanglements which were associated with the management of the New Basin Canal.[29]

Despite this later denial, Kenner shared equally in the profits from the operation of the canal, which amounted to approximately $29,000 for each of the three partners during the first two years of Taylor's lease. However, regardless of the profits derived from the canal, both the partnership and the business itself proved to be troublesome for Kenner. The business relationship between Kenner and McCloskey deteriorated when the two men disagreed over a $5,000 advance which Kenner had made to McCloskey. Kenner claimed that the money was a loan, but McCloskey stated that it was money owed to him from the business, and he refused to repay it. The dispute permanently soured the relationship between the two partners. McCloskey became so critical of Kenner's management of the company's books that Kenner demanded that Taylor take steps to put an end to the disagreements.[30]

The internal bickering only aggravated a deteriorating financial picture. Because of the increasingly large annual payments called for in the lease with the state, it became much more difficult for the company to show a profit. When the company failed to keep up with its lease payments the state opened an investigation. The situation continued to deteriorate until finally in August, 1873, the state annulled the lease and later obtained a judgement—which was never collected—against Richard Taylor.[31]

Though his business activities in New Orleans consumed much of his attention and time, Kenner's chief interest continued to be his agricultural holdings. The profits he earned from his non-agricultural businesses were often needed to support the operations on his sugar estates and frequently gave him leverage over his financially pressed competitors in the sugar industry in southern Louisiana. However, in addition to large sums of capital, the production of sugar also required an abundant supply of labor. Securing an adequate labor force remained perhaps the most difficult task for postwar sugar planters. Even though wage labor had been introduced on the Ashland and Bowden estates during the war, Kenner, like most of the other planters of the region, experienced labor shortages on his plantations during Reconstruction. The labor situation was aggravated by a reduction in Negro population in the sugar region following the war and by the postwar reluctance of former slaves who remained in the area to work with prewar efficiency.[32]

Various approaches were tried by the sugar planters to address the labor shortage. Among these were sharecropping, the subdivision of their estates, contracting with freedmen, and crop diversification. Kenner realized that for the sugar industry to survive in the postwar economy new ideas and efforts were needed. However, he refused to consider proposals which called for subdividing, in some fashion, his holdings. He desired more, not fewer acres. On the other hand, Kenner's natural inquisitiveness and love of scientific subjects led him to turn to some of the other options, chief among which was crop diversification. Of the crops considered for diversification, cotton and rice were the most popular among the many small farmers and planters of the region.[33]

The unsuccessful wartime attempt to grow cotton on his properties convinced Kenner and his managers that a repeat effort was unwise. Instead of cotton, Kenner looked to rice as the crop which offered the most promise as a supplement to the production of sugar. The level fields of his plantations along with the convenient and unlimited supply of fresh water in the nearby Mississippi River seemed ideal for the production of the grain. The war had so devastated the prewar rice-producing areas of the Carolina and Georgia coastlands that a successful Louisiana crop promised handsome profits. Furthermore, rice farming was a highly mechanized operation which attracted Kenner because of his lifelong propensity to keep pace with mechanical advancements in agriculture. The extensive use of machinery in the rice industry also offered the additional advantage of needing fewer workers than that of the production of sugar; thus, a conversion of his part of his land to the production of rice assisted Kenner in addressing the labor shortage which hampered agriculture in the postwar South. Choosing his Ashland estate as the center of his rice-growing effort, he became so involved with the new crop that he eventually expanded its production to his Houmas and Hollywood plantations. So successful were his efforts that by 1882 he totally ceased growing sugar as a commercial crop at Ashland. By 1886 Kenner was producing more rice on his Ashland and Houmas estates alone–13,782 barrels–than the 11,943 barrels that had been produced in the entire state in 1865. So prosperous was the new crop that Kenner constructed a steam-powered rice mill at Ashland to process the grain produced on his properties. Although rice culture made considerable inroads into the sugar region along the Mississippi, the area remained only a secondary center of the rice industry in the state. At approximately the same time that the sugar growers were discovering rice as a viable product, growers in the prairie section of southwestern Louisiana were expanding their cultivation of the grain even more rapidly.[34]

In spite of his interest in the cultivation of rice, Kenner remained a leader of the sugar industry in Louisiana throughout the postwar period. Kenner was among the first to examine the potential of labor-saving machinery as a possible means of alleviating the postwar labor shortage on the plantation. He had always been among the small circle of progressive sugar planters who applied scientific methods to the solution of their production problems. Among the technologies pioneered by Kenner was the introduction of the use of a portable railway with iron rails on his Ashland and Bowden estates. Probably the first planter to use this method, Kenner demonstrated to his colleagues the benefits of improved hauling methods. So impressive was the effort that by the end of the century, plantation railroads were commonplace throughout the sugar region.[35]

Kenner was also among the first to become involved in efforts to improve the industry's sugar mills. Because of dated machinery, the milling process was cumbersome and not very efficient. Hence, when a machinist named John McDonald failed to win financial backing for an improved milling process which used his new hydraulic pressure regulator, Kenner hired McDonald to build a hydraulic regulator for his mill at Ashland. After testing the device, Kenner found it to be an improvement which greatly reduced the amount of time the mill was down for repairs. Kenner's enthusiastic praise for the device led others to try the machinery, and it was rapidly adopted by the larger sugar mills throughout the South and Cuba.[36]

Not only was Kenner interested in increasing the efficiency of the industry by improving the milling process, but he also spent considerable time and effort in modernizing the various farm implements needed to raise a sugar crop. Among his endeavors was a promotional effort for the Bringier Pulverizing Cultivator developed by his wife's brother, Louis Bringier, who managed the Hermitage Plantation for Kenner. He also purchased the franchise rights for the states of Louisiana, Arkansas, and Mississippi for "the right to sell, use and manufacture the Eureka Decorticating Machines." However, the latter device must not have met all of Kenner's needs, for he worked with Michael Joseph Leruth and Leonard Sewell to design an improved decorticator. So successful were their efforts to improve the large roller device used in the crushing of cane that in May, 1887, they applied jointly for a patent for a decorticator of their own design. Unfortunately, Kenner did not live to see the patent issued on August 27, 1889.[37]

Of all his contributions, both before and after the war, to the sugar industry of Louisiana, Kenner's most important was his effort to awaken the planters of the state to the need to work together to improve their production techniques by forming professional organizations and agencies. During the decade of the 1870s the Louisiana sugar industry had regained some of its prewar vitality; yet, it was still handicapped by much inefficiency and many outdated practices. However, largely through the efforts of Kenner and a few other progressive-thinking sugar growers, the industry began a period of reorganization and revitalization which transformed the essentially outmoded antebellum industry into a modern productive one.[38]

The catalyst for this remarkable transformation of the sugar industry during the final decades of the nineteenth century was the formation of the Louisiana Sugar Planters' Association in 1877. Prior to the organization of this important group, several attempts had been made by the region's planters to work together to improve the industry. Probably the first of these efforts occurred in 1870 when Kenner and several other planters held an organizational meeting at the St. Charles Hotel in New Orleans. Despite an agreement to meet quarterly, no additional meetings ever took place. However, seven years later events took a different turn when a group of the region's leading planters and merchants met at Kenner's offices at the Crescent City Oil Company on Common Street in New Orleans. Though the purpose of the meeting was to discuss the need for tariff protection for the sugar industry, the group decided instead to form the Louisiana Sugar Planters' Association (LSPA). The new organization pledged to promote the culture of cane and the manufacture of sugar and to work for the passage of favorable federal legislation.[39]

There was some discussion as to who among the group would make the best president for the new organization. Although some support existed for John Dymond, Sr., a Canadian who had moved to Louisiana after the end of the war to take advantage of postwar economic opportunities, the group turned instead to Kenner. They thought that his close ties to Louisiana's antebellum aristocracy would provide the organization with leadership that would be socially and politically more acceptable to most of the region's planters than that of Dymond, who was regarded by many local planters as a carpetbagger. Under Kenner's stewardship, which lasted until his death, the association prospered. By 1883 the organization had approximately two hundred members, including most of the state's largest and wealthiest sugar manufacturers and landowners. Little time was lost by the association in implementing its many and varied goals. Association members tested and shared ideas for new techniques and machinery which held potential for improving production. The insistence by Kenner and other leaders of the organization on the importance of accurate statistics, scientific methods, and the testing of results made the Sugar Planters' Association a leading agency in the country for mechanical and general agricultural improvements.[40]

The emphasis by the association's leadership on collecting accurate scientific data, however, did not sufficiently address the needs of the sugar community. Most planters lacked the technical and scientific expertise needed to conduct adequately the systematic research required by the industry. The resulting scarcity of concrete data to support the various opinions expressed by members of the association at its meetings often resulted in heated debates and little agreement on which methods worked best. The long-windedness which characterized many of the association's meetings led one observer at the time to label the group as "that progressive body that does not progress."[41]

The unending disagreements over whose methods of sugar production were best convinced Kenner and the other leaders of the need for more scientific studies. Thus, when the United States Department of Agriculture, in February, 1885, manifested a willingness to sponsor the installation of an experimental diffusion battery on a Louisiana sugar plantation, considerable competition occurred among association members for the privilege of hosting the study. Eventually, the site for the experiment was narrowed to either former governor Henry Clay Warmoth's Magnolia Plantation or Kenner's Hermitage estate. Each man used his influence to win the placement of the experiment on his property. While Warmoth relied on his political contacts for help, Kenner argued that his Hermitage was more conveniently located than Warmoth's Plaquemines Parish estate, and he enlisted the support of his friends on the executive committee of the LSPA to influence the USDA to select the Hermitage. Kenner's strategy worked, and, by July, construction of the experimental device was underway at the Hermitage. Unfortunately, the Hermitage experiment never reached fruition because the foundry which had the responsibility for building much of the needed machinery failed to follow the design specifications. Without the proper equipment, the Hermitage study was canceled.[42]

The failure of the Hermitage diffusion experiment did not dampen Kenner's interest in either LSPA's dealing with the USDA, as urged by Congressman T. Floyd King from Vidalia, Louisiana, or the need for scientific study in the sugar industry. The failure of the USDA's Hermitage experiment convinced many in the LSPA that there existed a need for a planter-sponsored experiment station. By the fall of the year enough money was pledged by members of the association to establish the first agricultural experiment station in Louisiana. Originally located on land once owned by Duncan's father and brothers in the town of Kenner, the station was moved after four years to Audubon Park in New Orleans.[43]

Determined not to let the new experiment station falter, Kenner and his planter colleagues worked to create a separate, permanent governing body to manage the affairs of the facility. To meet this need, the planters organized on October 20, 1885, a nonprofit corporation called the Louisiana Scientific Agricultural Association (LSAA). Charged with the duty of developing and improving the agricultural resources of the state through scientific means, the LSAA was controlled by a forty-eight member board of directors elected by the membership. The board in turn chose the scientific association's officers, including a president, vice-president, and a six-man executive committee. Once again, as he had previously been honored with the presidency of the LSPA for his contributions to the sugar industry of Louisiana, the seventy-two-year-old Kenner was chosen as the first president of the LSAA. As with his presidency of the LSPA, Kenner continued unchallenged as president of the LSAA until his death.[44]

Although the LSPA's dedication and commitment to scientific study of the industry in Louisiana led to major improvements in the techniques used in the growing and production of sugar, the association's most pressing objective during its first years of existence was to counter those who were pressing Congress to reduce the import duties on sugar. From its beginning during the first decades of the nineteenth century the United States sugar industry has favored tariff protection by the national government to assure profitable prices for its produce. The postwar period saw a continued need for tariff protection by the sugar growers. With Congress controlled by the pro-tariff Republican party during most of the postwar years, there was never a serious threat to the sugar duty during the period from 1865 to 1880. However, even with protectionist Republicans in control of Congress, sugar planters remained alert to efforts to lower or remove duties. After all, the Republicans were not particularly interested in safeguarding the largely southern industry.[45]

During the late 1870s attitudes in Congress and elsewhere began to change on the issue of the sugar duty. The highly protectionist duties were considered by many to be an unfair means of taxing the common man while enriching the relatively small number of American sugar growers. Louisiana's sugar planters did not wait long before they moved to counter the budding campaign for lower sugar duties. At the very first official meeting of the Louisiana Planters' Association in January, 1878, Kenner announced that he and the other LSPA leaders had reached an agreement with the Cincinnati Grocers' Association by which the Midwest grocers would retreat from their demand for a lower sugar duty.[46]

With strong support from their membership, Kenner and several other LSPA leaders embarked on an effort to influence Congress on the tariff issue. On at least five occasions between the time that Kenner was first elected president of the LSPA and his death in 1887, the sugar industry sent delegations to Washington to resist efforts at reducing sugar duties. When he testified in Washington, Kenner usually emphasized the economic impact of the sugar industry upon Louisiana and the rest of the nation. He pointed out that about 350,000 persons were either directly or indirectly dependent on the industry and that $80,000,000 was invested in the state and another $44,000,000 in the form of supplies and machinery was purchased by the industry from other states. Kenner also maintained that whenever American duties had been decreased in the past, foreign producers such as Cuba had responded by raising their export rates. Thus, despite lower sugar duties, American consumers did not receive cheaper prices. Finally, Kenner and his colleagues argued that the protected sugar prices did not exceed 2.5 percent of the capital investment. Congress proved receptive to the arguments of the sugar delegations, for no changes were made in sugar duties during the first years of the existence of the LSPA.[47]

One result of the nation's high-tariff policy was the accumulation of large treasury surpluses. Through much of the postwar period, both major political parties mentioned the tariff issue in their political platforms; however, the parties usually addressed the issue only in general and non-specific terms with both taking for granted that some degree of protectionism was necessary to maintain employment. With both the surplus and protests over high tariffs growing, Congress in 1882 decided to establish a commission to report to it what changes were needed in the tariff in order to establish "a judicious tariff or a revision of the existing tariff upon a scale of justice to all interests."[48]

Because of the dependence of several industries besides that of sugar on the tariff, many in Congress as well as President Chester Arthur favored the creation of an expert commission which would study the national benefits derived from these industries and examine what proposed changes in the tariff would mean to the economy. Arthur spent a month selecting a nine-member commission. In choosing his nominees, the president sought to select individuals who represented major industries, were moderately protectionist, and commanded public confidence.[49]

When word of the creation of the tariff commission reached Louisiana, Kenner acted quickly to obtain a seat on the body for either himself or someone else from the sugar industry. Turning to his friend and fellow LSPA officer, John Dymond, Kenner explored the possibility of getting a Democrat appointed by the Republicans to the commission. Dymond, who had close ties to many of the leading Republican officials in the state, liked Kenner's plan and immediately asked Senator William Pitt Kellogg and United States Marshal Stephen B. Packard for assistance in obtaining Kenner's appointment. Their efforts proved to be successful. Among the nine members appointed to the board by President Arthur, two-thirds were representatives of protected industries, including Kenner for the sugar producers. Nominated by the president on May 15, 1882, Kenner was notified of his appointment a few weeks later and was asked by Secretary of the Treasury Charles Folger to come to Washington as soon as possible to begin work.[50]

Before departing for the nation's capital to assume his role as a tariff commissioner, Kenner received warm praise from the local press for his nomination to the commission. The press also extolled the beneficial healing effort that the rare bipartisan support which helped secure Kenner's appointment would bring to the politically fractured community. However, though there existed considerable support for Kenner's appointment, there was also substantial apprehension among the region's sugar producers because they were afraid that a revision of the nation's tariffs would greatly reduce the duties on foreign sugars. To counter these fears Kenner urged sugar planters to appear before the commission and explain how important it was for the country to protect the sugar industry, thereby enabling it to compete successfully with foreign sugar producers.[51]

Confirmed by the Senate without debate or any other discussion, Kenner was able to get down to work without delay. Traveling to twenty-nine cities around the nation between July 6 and October 16, the commission took testimony from 604 witnesses, including representatives of the Louisiana Sugar Planters' Association. After months of holding hearings and taking testimony, the commission released a report of 2,600 pages. In spite of an opening statement which called for a substantial reduction of the tariff, Kenner adeptly controlled all of the commission's discussions concerning the sugar tariff and in the end was able to get the commission to recommend only slightly reduced rates for imported sugar. Furthermore, the reductions generally applied only to low-grade sugar; the better grades, which for the most part were manufactured by the large producers of Louisiana, continued to be protected with high duties.[52]

Kenner accomplished his mission of protecting the large sugar producers of the state and the membership of the Louisiana Sugar Planters' Association from foreign competition by working out a compromise between the Louisiana growers and Eastern business interests. Acting as mediator between the two groups, Kenner forged an understanding in which the refiners' wishes were met by accepting their rates for the highest grades of sugar while the LSPA would determine the rates for the darker sugars. One LSPA member complimented Kenner on his success in the difficult negotiations by stating: "We have New York with us and Boston committed to the plan and now if you can carry the Tariff Commission I for one will appreciate the rare diplomatic power that gave us the victory."[53]

Fortunately for Kenner and the other protectionists on the Tariff Commission, the report of the group was not examined closely by Congress. When the Republican-controlled Congress began its review of the commission's report it acted with haste because the Democrats had won a majority in the House of Representatives in the recent fall elections and would take control of the lawmaking body in March, 1883. So many special interest groups, including the LSPA, had been involved in the commission's work that there was no clear understanding of just what would result from the group's report. Despite predictions at the time the group began its work that the commission's effort would eventually result in a tariff reduction of twenty percent, the actual decrease enacted by Congress in the Tariff Act of 1883 was only about 4 percent. Thus, Kenner and other protectionists achieved their objective of maintaining the bulwark of the protective tariff system while making concessions to the increasing public demand for a moderated duty system.⁵⁴

Kenner's success in opposing any changes which threatened Louisiana's sugar interests was a vital ingredient in the industry's postwar recovery and modernization. Although the 1882 Tariff Commission's work as a whole was labeled by some critics as being only a halfhearted attempt at national duty reform, Kenner's successful effort to preserve the protective status of legislation affecting sugar was a salient contribution to the industry to which he had contributed so much during his life. The security which the post-commission legislation provided Louisiana's sugar producers allowed planters in the state to turn their attention to improved marketing and, more importantly, to an increased emphasis on the role of science and new technology in solving the industry's problems. This process of modernization would not only lead the industry into the next century but would also form the base on which the nation's modern sugar industry continues to rest.⁵⁵

XII

RECONSTRUCTION AND REDEMPTION

Duncan Kenner's efforts during the postwar period to regain his finances and to rebuild his sugar holdings did not prevent him from becoming involved in the turbulent world of postwar politics in Louisiana. Despite his bitter disappointment over the defeat of the Confederacy and the great political, economic, and social changes it brought to the world he had cherished during the antebellum period, Kenner did not hesitate to remain in the political arena. So quick was his re-involvement that on the very day that a New Orleans paper reported his return to that city after receiving his presidential pardon in Washington, D.C., it also proclaimed Kenner's nomination by "friends" to represent the parishes of Ascension, Assumption, and Terrebonne in the Louisiana senate.[1]

Kenner was by no means the only ex-Confederate to re-enter the Louisiana political scene in the months immediately following the demise of the Confederacy. Returning home after the war, veterans of the conflict found the political situation in their state in a condition of flux. During the war, President Lincoln had promoted the establishment of a loyal government in the areas of the state controlled by Union troops. In February, 1864, voters in the federally controlled portions of Louisiana elected a state government, including a governor, seven other executive officials, and a legislature. Federal authorities also called a constitutional convention which drafted a new organic law in 1864. Dominated by members of the laboring class, the convention agreed upon a document which contained several major reforms, including a minimum-wage provision and the abolition of slavery. Yet the new constitution failed to grant suffrage to the former slaves.[2]

When the war ended, the ambitious and politically unscrupulous J. Madison Wells was governor of Federal Louisiana. Unlike his predecessor, who had wanted to punish the defeated Rebels, Wells, a long-time Unionist, assessed the changing political situation at war's end and realized that returning Confederate soldiers and their supporters greatly outnumbered those Louisianians who had remained loyal to the Union. Consequently, Wells took a conciliatory attitude towards the returning Confederate veterans by removing large numbers of Unionist officials and replacing them with former Rebels. Therefore, when Kenner returned to his home state he found a political atmosphere that was surprisingly congenial to former Confederates.[3]

Kenner, like most other returning Rebels, looked to the Democratic party as the vehicle for an attempted return to political dominance in the state. Preferring to call themselves Conservatives because of their opponents' efforts to label the Democrat party as the party of secession, the postwar party was more broadly based than it had been during the antebellum period. As the only conservative organization which still maintained its national scope, the party drew to its ranks many former Whigs and Know-Nothings of the prewar period. As the party quickly solidified its base, Governor Wells, in September, 1865, called for an election of state officials to be held in November. Thus, when he accepted the nomination of his neighbors for the state senate, Kenner became part of a movement which resulted not only in a near sweep by the Democratic candidates in the Louisiana election but also saw the election of ex-Confederates to political offices throughout the South, including the United States Congress.[4]

The victory of the Louisiana Democrats over their Republican opposition in the special election was complete. Though the result of the election was never really in doubt, the spectacular scope of the Democratic win shocked their opponents. So depressed was one Louisiana Republican that he complained to Nathaniel P. Banks that the newly chosen legislature should have been called the "second Secession legislature." Others predicted that the presence of so many former Confederates in the government would lead to dire consequences for both their party and the state.[5]

The predictions of legislative difficulties proved accurate. Meeting in the lecture room of the Mechanic's Institute on November 23, just a few days after the election, the legislature quickly got down to work. Difficulties soon arose when the governor and legislature split over the appropriate agenda for the session. Governor Wells put forth a program he somewhat naïvely hoped would appease the Democrats who had kept him in power. It included restrictions against anti-Democratic groups such as the nativist Know-Nothings, proposals to restore the parish judicial systems, plans to repair state credit and the damaged levee system, repeal of immigration restrictions, and a discriminatory tax on freedom to finance Negro schools. The legislators, however, instead of backing Wells, insisted on addressing means of overturning the existing government based on the Constitution of 1864 and on resolving the question of the role of the freedman in postwar Louisiana.[6]

Although he declined a proposal by fellow senators to nominate him for president pro tempore, Kenner played an active role during the session. Unlike the majority of his legislative colleagues, Kenner counseled a pragmatic policy of cooperation—rather than confrontation—with the national government. In particular, Kenner favored a more deliberate approach to the effort to throw out the 1864 constitution. In an address to his fellow senators, Kenner confessed that his personal feelings were with those members who favored calling a new constitutional convention. However, he went on to state forcefully that such a move would be detrimental to the best interests of Louisiana and the South. Since Louisiana was still ruled by military law, the state's hands were bound. Before attempting to revise the current constitution Kenner urged that a means be found to "get rid of military rule." To accomplish this goal, Kenner advised his fellow legislators to "look to the seat of government at Washington and harmonize our actions with national policy." As he pictured the situation, the 1864 constitution had been recognized by President Johnson, the one individual who could expedite the end of military rule in the state. Consequently, he suggested that the state's leaders demonstrate their confidence in and their desire to cooperate with the president's "patriotic endeavors to reconstruct the Southern states" by not overturning the much-disliked organic law. Though Kenner's efforts to defer any change in the constitution were not immediately accepted by his colleagues, his remarks did cause the legislators to reconsider their plans. After listening to Kenner's objections, the legislators eventually relented and dropped the issue when President Johnson let it be known that he found such talk of constitutional change to be unacceptable.[7]

Kenner's opposition to the will of the majority on the question of constitutional change was not typical of the position he took on most of the major issues handled by Louisiana's first postwar legislature. On the issue that probably most concerned the lawmakers in 1865, the question of how to handle the freedmen, Kenner led the way in formulating the legislature's position. Not only in Louisiana, but throughout the rest of the former Confederate states, the question of controlling the former slaves was a chief concern. White Southerners, who during the antebellum period had harbored deep fears of what would happen if Negroes were ever able to escape the controls of the plantation, now were obliged to deal with the problem they had dreaded for so long. Unhappy wartime experiences, such as the burning of Kenner's sister-in-law's barn on her Oakland Plantation by a Negro, reinforced the desire of many white Southerners to find a method of continuing to control their former wards. Additionally, Kenner and the other legislators were keenly aware of the labor crisis then being experienced on the state's large agricultural estates. Ignorant of Northern sentiment on the question of the role of the freedmen in the postwar South and overly confident of the ability of Andrew Johnson to control the radicals in Congress, most white Louisianians looked to the legislature for a solution to the problems resulting from emancipation.[8]

Kenner took the lead in preparing the necessary legislation which came to be known as the Black Code. Among the series of bills offered by him were acts designed to limit the influence of the Freedmen's Bureau, to punish persons who employed individuals who were already working on another plantation, to regulate labor contracts pertaining to agricultural pursuits, to prevent trespassing, to create a system of apprenticeships, and to define the civil rights of the state's freedmen. These and other acts passed by the legislature made up Louisiana's Black Code. Though it did not go as far as the codes of some other Southern states, the Louisiana legislation was designed to return the freedmen to the sugar and cotton fields in a condition that historian Roger Shugg labeled as being somewhere between peonage and serfdom.[9]

Few issues of the postwar period have provoked more controversy than the various Black Codes passed by Louisiana and other Southern states. Both contemporaries and historians have voiced widely differing views on the codes. Many Northerners, including the Radical members of the United States Congress, looked upon the Black Codes as an outrageous attempt by the South to cast the area's Negroes into a system of slavery only slightly modified from what had existed during the antebellum period. Southern whites, on the other hand, maintained that the intent of the laws were not to defy the North or to circumvent the results of the war. Southerners insisted that their laws represented a sincere effort to handle the urgent problems created by the abolition of slavery and that the Black Codes were simply modifications of laws already in force in the North. As with those who were contemporaries to the events, historians have espoused both sides of the argument. Some historians, such as Kenneth Stampp, have viewed the codes as an attempt by Southerners to "keep the Negro, as long as possible, exactly what he was: a propertyless rural laborer under strict controls, without political rights, and with inferior legal rights." Others, hostile to Radical Reconstruction, have defended the actions of the early postwar legislatures of the South as an expansion of the rights of blacks when compared to their rights during the antebellum era.[10]

Kenner certainly would have agreed with the latter group of historians. As if aware that future historians would examine postwar attitudes of the defeated Southerners, Kenner defined his position on the subject in a letter to a former classmate written shortly after his return to Louisiana. Countering the accusations of some Northerners that Southerners were attempting to undo the results of the war, Kenner responded:

> I see with great regret, that an impression prevails in certain quarters of the north, that the Southern people are not candid and earnest in their profession of a desire to return to the condition of loyal citizens of the United States. A more grievous error was never attempted to be propagated. Hypocrisy could never justly be classed among the vices and faults of character and education laid to the door of the Southern people. I have not yet met a man, who does not acknowledge and feel that the questions of secession and slavery are finally and irretrievably settled, and the feeling for a lasting piece and Union is general and genuine.

As to the question of what role the former slaves would play in the postwar South, Kenner stated that the South's feelings on the subject were similarly misunderstood by Congress and others in the North. Though his opinion of the character of the ex-slaves was not complimentary, Kenner maintained that, with the major exception of the vote, he and other white Southerners were willing to assist blacks in obtaining an expansion of their rights. According to Kenner,

> Every thinking man among us (and among these, I think, I can include 90 per cent of the former slave owners) desires to elevate the condition of the Negro–for intelligent and instructed labor has ever given better return than one that is not. We desire that the Negro should be given something to live and hope for beyond the mere gratification of his animal

passions and wants. He should be brought within the pale of the civil law—guaranteed all the rights of person and property, and consequently the incidental rights of easy access to our courts and of being heard therein as witnesses and parties to suits.[11]

It was the view of the white legislators that they were helping their former bondsmen by creating labor, social, and civil regulations which would assist the freedman in making his way in the new society created by the defeat of the South. Though blacks were to be given new privileges, the parameters of these freedoms were still to be defined by whites. Such theory was consistent with the paternalistic attitude toward blacks which had permeated relations between the two races during the antebellum period. As Kenner and other whites saw it, the new laws had the advantage of accommodating the social changes brought about by the loss of the war and the freeing of the slaves while restoring order to the economy and to what they viewed as being the proper social order in Louisiana. Such feelings did not contradict Kenner's position that the whites of the state had fully accepted the changes mandated by the war. The state's whites believed that the structure imposed by the postwar legislature was an honest effort in favor of all interests—planter and laborer, state and national governments, and black and white residents. All would benefit by the speedy recovery and establishment of order in Louisiana.[12]

Though willing to assist the state's freedmen to improve their social and civil status to some degree, Kenner and his colleagues had no intention of extending to their former slaves equal political standing. As they viewed the situation, granting the black man the right to vote would surely undo their efforts to improve the lot of all the state's people. In Louisiana and across the South whites contended that to admit ignorant blacks to political privileges would eventually lead to the existence of a massive pool of voters that could be easily controlled by others. Chief among these were their employers, who controlled their livelihood, and unscrupulous politicians, who would manipulate their votes. Whereas Kenner often spoke as a voice of moderation on some of the proposals made by his colleagues and other Southerners during the postwar period, he was adamant on the issue of granting suffrage to the freedmen. Even in a letter to his friend, United States General Robert Schenck, in which he sought assistance in obtaining a much desired presidential pardon, he did not soften his position on the subject.[13] Kenner explained:

> It is true we do not wish to clothe them [freedmen] with the political right of suffrage–not because we wish to oppress them, but because we know they are absolutely disqualified for its proper use. Two hundred years of ignorance and slavery is not the proper school to prepare the human mind to become the depository of the political power of the country. I would as soon think of holding up to our daughters as models of virtue the negroe [sic] women of the South, who from a life of long habit and teaching of their mothers and grandmothers have been led to look upon the marriage tie as an idle form–as to commit the future political destiny of our country to the lately freed black man. Demagogues and political tricksters would revel in the luxury of a negroe [sic] constituency.[14]

Kenner's feelings on the question of suffrage for the ex-slaves were not based solely upon race. As demonstrated years earlier during the constitutional convention of 1845 when he led the fight for the creation of a state-funded system of public schools, Kenner fervently believed that an educated electorate was essential for democracy to operate properly.[15]

Well intentioned or not, the efforts by Kenner and his legislative partners to pass the Black Code quickly resulted in a storm of protest from individuals in both the North and South. Among the first and most determined critics of Kenner and his opposed legislation was the Negro publication *The New Orleans Tribune*. Within hours of the introduction of Kenner's resolution, the newspaper condemned Kenner for his secessionist, lawless, and pro-slavery sentiments and deduced that Louisiana's freedmen could expect no justice from a legislature made up of individuals like Kenner. Seeing the issue as an effort by the state's planters to guarantee to themselves an adequate labor force, the journal concluded that Negroes in the state "would be very fortunate if the Legislature did not enact laws organizing a life-long apprenticeship." Contending that there existed sufficient legislation on the books to obtain the objectives of social order cited by Kenner, the publication proclaimed:

> Why then make new and special ones for freedmen only? . . . It is by disguising this instruction under the labor question that Mr. Kenner hopes to make different laws for the freedmen than anyone else. But Mr. Kenner wished to reach the labor question under a plea of pharisaical philanthropy. The poor freedman, how good a friend has he–a friend who is now busy in devising 'what laws are necessary to make his labor available to the agricultural interest of the State.'[16]

Concern over the Black Code legislation was by no means limited to the black press. Even the influential *Daily Picayune* voiced concern over the "tendency in the Legislature now in session, to launch out upon . . . general and experimental legislation" which it labeled "unwise, impolitic and premature." Prophetically, the paper cautioned the legislators to proceed with care because the unsettled national political situation might limit their application of "proper, wise, and efficacious remedies to the evils and disorders which, as great as they are, may be made worse by hasty, impatient and imperfect legislation."[17]

Kenner and other members of the legislature paid little or no attention to these critics. With an attitude which at times bordered on arrogance, the legislators confidently assumed that President Johnson would continue to control the Radicals in Congress, and they openly proclaimed their plans to challenge the much-disliked Freedmen's Bureau in Louisiana. Few of the South's legislators believed that there were any long-term dangers in their efforts to define the postwar status of the Negro, for Southerners simply could not imagine that anyone—in either North or South—sincerely favored extending full rights to the former slaves. Consequently, guided by a special joint legislative committee chaired by Kenner, all of the Black Code bills were passed by the lawmaking body. Governor Wells signed all but one into law.[18]

The opinion of Kenner and most other Southerners that the new laws regulating the status of the former slaves would not cause much of a disturbance was grossly in error. Northern Radicals bitterly attacked the measures as an attempt to re-establish a social and political system strikingly similar to what had existed before the Civil War. Since it was the restoration plan endorsed by President Andrew Johnson which permitted the Southern legislatures to pass such legislation, the laws presented the Radicals in the North with a golden opportunity to mobilize public opinion against the plan and to press for congressional control of Reconstruction.[19]

The position of Kenner and his colleagues in Louisiana was further undermined by a split between the lawmakers and Governor Wells and by an increase in racial violence in the state. Though he had shrewdly enlisted the support of influential ex-Confederates in his bid for political power, the governor soon discovered that the headstrong legislators had an agenda of their own. Relations between the Democratic body and the governor degenerated to such a point that, by the summer of 1866, he had joined the Radicals in their efforts to dislodge the Democrats from power. As the political situation deteriorated so too did the racial climate in Louisiana. As in the rest of the South, the end of the Civil War brought about an increase in violence directed towards Negroes. Frustrations resulting from the defeat were quickly transformed into violence against one of the most prominent symbols of the Northern victory—the freedmen. Thus, one postwar visitor to Louisiana claimed that the whites in the state governed "by the pistol and the rifle" and that he had observed "white men whipping colored men just the same as they did before the war."[20]

Events came to a head in Louisiana during the hot summer months of 1866. For opposite reasons, both the ex-Confederates, who were mostly Democrats, and the Radical Republicans wanted to change the state's 1864 constitution. The Democrats charged that the document, which had been adopted when much of the state was occupied by the Union forces and when many of the region's white males were away serving the Confederacy, was illegal. They hoped that a new charter would facilitate their efforts to reclaim their former position of ascendancy. Holding a totally different view were the Radical Republicans. They realized that their hopes for acquiring political power depended upon a transfer of the franchise from the Confederate veteran to the freedman. However, instead of calling a new constitutional convention, which surely would have been largely Democratic, the Radicals favored reconvening the 1864 convention, which by its nature did not include any Confederates.[21]

The actual catalyst which resulted in the Radical Republicans taking control of the Reconstruction process and gaining political control of Louisiana occurred on July 30 when a group of blacks in New Orleans attempted to march in support of the effort to reconvene the 1864 charter meeting. A number of armed white men attacked the group and in a bloody brawl, which General Philip H. Sheridan labeled "an absolute massacre," thirty-four blacks and three white Radicals were killed and another one hundred persons were injured. Radicals in both Louisiana and the North used the New Orleans riot to demonstrate to the moderate members of Congress the need for congressional action. In response, Congress increasingly turned away from President Johnson's plan to one of its own. The result was an intensified effort to win approval of the Fourteenth Amendment and the passage in March, 1867, of a series of Reconstruction Acts.[22]

By declaring that no legal governments existed in the seceded Southern states and that they would henceforth be governed under the authority of

Congress, the Federal legislation had the effect of drastically altering the political power structure of Louisiana and other states of the late Confederacy. The South was divided into five military districts, with Louisiana and Texas making up the Fifth District under the command of General Sheridan. In essence the military reconstruction of the South which resulted from the radicalization of the national government's reconstruction efforts reduced the ex-Confederate states to the status of conquered territories. Under the system of temporary military rule a drastic reorganization, based upon the expansion of Negro suffrage and disfranchisement of ex-Confederates, was forced upon the state governments of the South. By the time the reorganization of the voter rolls was completed, 73,230 Negroes and only 41,166 whites were qualified to vote in Louisiana. The new military authorities also removed Governor Wells from office and replaced him with Benjamin F. Flanders, a leader of the Radical forces in Louisiana. To solidify the new political order, General Sheridan pushed for constitutional changes which resulted in the adoption of a charter designed to give the Negro new political, civil, and social rights. Not unexpectedly, the election of state officials which coincided with the ratification of the 1868 Constitution resulted in a take-over of state government by the Republicans. The transfer of power in Louisiana was complete.[23]

However, as noted by Perry Howard in his study *Political Tendencies in Louisiana*, the new constitution and the reconstruction politics of the time resulted in more than a turnover in control of the state government. There was a change in the very substance of Louisiana politics. For what had been previously a contest between whites with opposing economic, political, and social interests now became a contest among whites for Negro support. Republican success in gaining the support of the former bondsmen together with the political corruption and governmental abuses which resulted from that alliance quickly led to a broadening of the breach between the races in Louisiana and to the formation of a counter-coalition between the poor whites and the remains of the planter-merchant oligarchy which had dominated the politics of the state for so long.[24]

Stunned and disappointed at the disastrous reversal of their political fortunes which accompanied the onset of a Radical Reconstruction, Kenner and many others among Louisiana's prewar power elite did not abandon totally their goal of restoring as much as possible the lifestyle and privileges they had enjoyed during the antebellum period. Excluded, at least temporarily, from the state's political power structure, Kenner and his peers continued to work at reviving some of the economic and societal trappings and traditions of the antebellum era. As demonstrated in the previous chapter, his forced retirement from the political arena enabled Kenner to spend considerable time and effort in restoring and improving his agricultural and business holdings.[25]

Stymied in their political recovery, Kenner and his peers found it far easier to re-establish some of the social trappings they had cherished in the prewar period. With social life in the parishes primarily one of simplicity, modesty, and unpretentiousness, it was in New Orleans, where gala social events had always been a staple of life for all classes, that social activities rapidly returned to their antebellum pace. Both residents and visitors to the city were able to escape from the economic and political problems which beset them by enjoying the many operas, concerts, plays, circuses, variety troupes, museums, balls, and sporting events which could be found in the Crescent City. Although he enjoyed most social activities that the city offered, his love of thoroughbred racing remained Kenner's principal recreational interest.[26]

Almost immediately upon his return to the state after the war, Kenner and some of the antebellum turfmen of the area began working in earnest to rebuild Louisiana's racing industry. Limited by a lack of money and fine horses, the horsemen at first limited their efforts to such modest activities as the reorganization of turfmen clubs, challenge matches, and charity races. However, as was the case with other facets of postwar life in the South, racing experienced great changes. Spurred on by the postwar disposition of urban residents to turn to commercial amusements for their entertainment, elaborate tracks were constructed to accommodate the throngs of spectators who transformed the sport of kings from an activity controlled by the privileged for their own amusement into a commercial venture with broad popular appeal. Yet, in spite of the broader spectator appeal which characterized the sport after the war, actual participation in racing generally remained the prerogative of individuals far wealthier than the majority of the population.[27]

Kenner's interest in the sport during the postwar period was two-fold. As before the war, he spent much time and money rebuilding his stable of thoroughbreds and training jockeys to ride his mounts. However, in spite of his determined efforts and those of his faithful trainer Graves, Kenner's stable never reached the degree of prominence it had held before the war.[28]

Though the war cost him his place among the nation's leading thoroughbred owners and racers, Kenner continued to have national influence in the development of the sport as a result of his prewar effort to develop a professional jockey corps. Among the few in the profession to gain celebrity, Kenner's former slave jockeys were looked upon by many as being among the nation's leading postwar professional jockeys.[29]

At least one successful postwar jockey greatly appreciated the training and opportunity he had obtained as one of Kenner's slave riders. When he and his former master met in Cincinnati shortly after the end of the war, the ex-slave, concerned about Kenner's reduced circumstances, reached in his pocket and offered his former owner several hundred dollars in cash in gratitude for the training he had received at Ashland. According to him, it was his prewar training which had enabled him to make the kind of money he was able to offer Kenner.[30]

In addition to his efforts to rebuild his private stable, Kenner also worked to restore the stature of the sport of thoroughbred racing in Louisiana to its prewar posture. This endeavor was centered around the attempt to restore the Metairie Course, the state's most famous and elaborate racetrack. Heading a group of distinguished community leaders which included his brother-in-law, former Rebel general Richard Taylor, former governor and Confederate general Paul O. Hebert, and Republican governor J. Madison Wells, Kenner reactivated the Metairie Jockey Club. Though the efforts of the group to operate the track and retain many of the aristocratic trappings that had characterized racing before the war received an enthusiastic reception from the community, the Civil War had so drained the state of its wealth and young manhood that it simply was not possible to recreate the success of the past. For seven years between 1865 and 1872 the club sponsored thirteen thoroughbred meetings, with varying degrees of success.[31]

Kenner remained active in thoroughbred racing through most of the rest of his life. However, he and his partners in the Metairie Association which owned the Metairie Course eventually realized that their dreams of returning the sport to its prewar aristocratic state would go unfulfilled. With the onset of the professional sportsman and the subsequent loss of control of the sport by the planters, Kenner and the other Metairie Association members began to consider alternative uses for the track. Disagreements among the members of the association and the board of directors over the track management led the board in 1872 to close the track—a surprising decision.[32]

Ever the businessman with a keen sense for opportunity, Kenner realized that the demise of the once-majestic race course offered him and his colleagues in the Metairie Association a chance for a prosperous business venture. Kenner and his partners figured that New Orleans was in need of a new type of cemetery—one patterned after the spacious rural cemeteries found in the eastern sections of the nation. Until that time, nearly all of the city's burial grounds were limited in size and were surrounded by wall vaults. Kenner and the other promoters decided that an area which offered a park-like setting with elegant tombs and monuments would prove popular with the community's wealthier families. Though not all of the members of the old Metairie Association made the transfer into the new Metairie Cemetery Association, Kenner quickly took advantage of the opportunity and served on the first board of the new business. Unlike his overly optimistic hopes for a revival of racing at the Metairie Course, Kenner's assessment of the business potential for a new cemetery proved accurate. Leading families of the community patronized the new cemetery, and to this day it remains a viable business and a major point of community interest.[33]

Besides his efforts to restore the social glamour previously associated with thoroughbred racing in Louisiana, Kenner also was instrumental in the effort of some of the social elite in New Orleans to revive the prestigious Boston Club. The oldest social club in New Orleans, the Boston Club was closed by Union soldiers during the war because of its members' Rebel sympathies. In December, 1865, Kenner and approximately sixty others met to reorganize the club. Kenner remained active in the group throughout the rest of his life and often participated in club activities.[34] Quickly regaining the social status it had held before the war, the Boston Club became a gathering place for many of the state's leading residents and visitors. Among the latter was Jefferson Davis, who often visited the club during his frequent stays in New Orleans.[35]

Though primarily a social organization, the Boston Club played an important role in the political events of the day. As in the period before the war, whenever Southerners met for social events the conversation of the men usually turned to politics. Such was the custom at the exclusive New Orleans Club. With most of its members drawn from the well-to-do families of the region, the club became a hub for some of the more reactionary elements of the white opposition to "Black Republican" Reconstruction in Louisiana.[36]

However, in spite of his friendship and association with many of the individuals who proposed taking drastic and even violent steps to overthrow the hated reconstruction governments, Kenner successfully maintained friendly relations with those on both sides of the controversy. Not only did he stay on good terms with his fellow Boston Club members, he also remained friendly with some of the most disliked Republican leaders of the time. Most notable was his ability to remain on good terms with Henry Clay Warmoth, one of Louisiana's most scorned and scandalous chief executives. A young Northerner, Warmoth was looked upon by most as the epitome of the corrupt carpetbagger. Yet, Kenner remained on good terms with him. Kenner was present on at least two occasions—the first, a dinner given by an old family friend Dr. Newton Mercer; and the second, a festive carnival event given at the Jockey Club for the visiting Grand Duke Alexis of Russia—which others of his social status chose to boycott because of Warmoth's presence.[37]

Just how close was the bond between the corrupt Republican governor and the prominent Democrat is not clear. As noted, Kenner at times was willing to risk the ire of his counterparts to attend engagements being boycotted by other Democrats. It appears that relations between Warmoth and Kenner were more than just political. Both men were prominent sugar planters and thus had considerable professional dealings. Furthermore, Kenner realized that in Reconstruction Louisiana it was necessary to cultivate good relations with local and state officials in order to succeed in many businesses. Kenner's determined efforts to regain his financial status necessitated much contact and business with state and local officials. One such example was his and Richard Taylor's involvement with the New Basin Canal Company, which held a state lease on the waterway. Despite the fact that the company never kept up its payments to the state and that it was even investigated by state officials, the leaseholders were never forced to make the payments they owed to the state.

Kenner also worked with the Republicans because he believed that no other road was open. He was concerned that the growing instances of violence, much of it racially related, would be counterproductive to the effort to return the Democrats to power. Remembering the Northern reaction to the instances of violence against blacks which had resulted in military control of state government, Kenner abandoned the hard line he once professed on the issue and urged the people of Louisiana to accept the former slaves into the political arena and to work on educating them to cast their ballots in the best interests of the South.[38]

Kenner was not alone in his belief that some political accommodation needed to be extended to the state's blacks. Largely promoted by businessmen from New Orleans who hoped it would stimulate an economic recovery, the endeavor eventually became known as the Unification Movement. However, despite the support of such distinguished Southerners as General P. G. T. Beauregard, General James Longstreet, and the sympathy of some of the conservative papers in New Orleans and the rest of the state, the movement never gained much popular support. More indicative of popular sentiment was a declaration by the *Shreveport Times* that "the hope of Louisiana is in the white race; in its increase and its dominion within her borders, and we hold as folly all political movements that have not that object in view."[39]

At the same time that the mood of conservative whites in the state was becoming increasingly belligerent, the Republican party was greatly weakened by an intra-party dispute. As the split within the Republican party grew in rancor with each side accusing the other of fraud and intimidation in their 1872 battle for the governorship of Louisiana, white conservative Democrats sought to take advantage of the chaotic situation by attempting to weaken the political power of the Negro in Louisiana and the support they gave to the Republicans. Encouraged by gains made by the national party in congressional elections and by the successful use of violence against blacks in other states, particularly Mississippi, Louisiana's Democrats increased their resolve to regain control of the state government.[40]

Since violence had marked every election in the state since the onset of Radical Reconstruction, it did not take much for the frustrated and resentful Democrats to promote through force their agenda of limiting the political influence of the state's blacks. Louisiana quickly became an armed camp which soon exploded into bloody massacres at Colfax and Coushatta. However, the most serious incident of armed conflict occurred in New Orleans on September 14, 1874. For some time before the violent incident, conservative whites across the state had been organizing in militant White Leagues. Emboldened by the successes of White League groups in other parts of Louisiana in driving "Black Republicans" from local offices, the Crescent City White League planned to take bold action. With hundreds of battle-hardened veterans from the Civil War arming themselves for a showdown, Kenner and other community leaders conferred with various leaders of the armed groups in an unsuccessful effort to avert violence. With over 3,500 armed men, the White Leaguers fought a brief but pitched battle with the forces of then Republican governor William P. Kellogg. Although the governor's force was commanded by former Confederate general James Longstreet, the White Leaguers overwhelmed Kellogg's troops and took control of New Orleans until ousted by federal troops, which were ordered to the scene by the president.[41]

Though the federal troops forced the White Leaguers to withdraw from their holdings, the "Battle of Liberty Place" marked a turning point in the Reconstruction politics of Louisiana. Following that bloody encounter, the power of the Radicals in the state ebbed. The size of the uprising shocked officials in Washington into the realization that, unless steps were taken to lessen the military occupation in Louisiana, full-scale open warfare between the Radicals and conservative whites might again break out.[42]

Emboldened by the limited success of the White League in weakening the power of the Republicans, the Democrats looked with hope to the elections of 1876. Kenner joined most Democrats in the state in supporting Confederate war hero Francis T. Nicholls for governor and Samuel J. Tilden for president. With their Republican opponents in disarray and their own ticket headed by the popular Nicholls, who would almost certainly win nearly all of the white vote in the campaign, the Democrats made a coordinated effort to win the votes of Louisiana's black voters. As with most elections of the time, tactics of intimidation were not uncommon. However, for the most part, Democrats attempted to attract black voters by down-playing racist comments, denouncing corruption, and promising to preserve the rights Negroes had gained since the end of the war.[43]

Kenner joined in the effort by Conservatives to win support among black voters of the state. So involved did he become in his support of the Democratic ticket that on election day he forfeited his vote so that he could work for his candidates. Because his varied business and political interests kept him busy in New Orleans a large part of the time, he had changed his official residence from Ashland to New Orleans. As such, his voting precinct was in the Crescent City but his target constituency—his black workers—was at Ashland. With five hundred to six hundred voters among the more than one thousand workers on his estate, Kenner returned to the plantation three or four days prior to the election to "win" as many votes for the Democratic gubernatorial nominee as possible. Little or no effort was made to win votes for the Democratic presidential nominee. Unlike other planters, Kenner did not overtly threaten his workers with the loss of their jobs if they did not vote for his candidate. Instead, he explained that if they voted for Nicholls and the latter were elected, the resulting "good laws, good government, and less taxes" would enable Kenner to prosper and thus to pay higher wages to his employees.[44]

Preliminary results of the voting caused great excitement among Kenner and his colleagues. The early count gave both the Democratic nominees for governor and president 52 percent of the vote to their Republican opponents' 48 percent. Unfortunately for Kenner and the Democrats, they soon discovered that their victory celebration was premature. By law and custom in Louisiana the official count of election results was performed by the Returning Board sometime after the balloting took place. The fact that the Returning Board was controlled by the Republicans and that the selection of the next president depended on the board's decision gave no solace to the Democrats. With Tilden needing to add only a single electoral vote, out of the twenty which remained in dispute, to the 184 votes he had already garnered in the presidential election in order for the Democrats to capture the White House, rumors were rife that the desperate Republicans would do whatever was necessary to assure that all the outstanding electoral votes were delivered to their presidential nominee, Rutherford B. Hayes.[45]

Not only were all numbers of the Returning Board partisan Republicans, but they were also men with very unsavory reputations. Heading the board was former governor J. Madison Wells, whose reputation was such that he had once been labeled by a fellow Republican as a "political trickster and dishonest man . . . [whose] conduct has been as sinous as the mark left in the dust by a snake."[46] Wells did not hesitate to capitalize on the situation. Shortly after convening the Returning Board, the ex-governor sent word to national party leaders that he had a difficult job on hand and that if he delivered the state's electoral votes to Hayes he would have to throw out a great many Democrat votes; such action, in turn, would place his life in danger from the angry Democrats. Because of these "dangers" he asked for at least $200,000 a piece for the two white members of the board and something less for the two black members.[47]

As rumors of the attempted bribe circulated in New Orleans, Kenner and a group of prominent Democrats, including his son-in-law Joseph L. Brent, attempted to save the situation for the Democrats by asking Wells what his price would be to count the votes in favor of the Democrats. Kenner invited

Wells to his office for a meeting on November 19, 1876. In testimony given before a congressional committee which later investigated the 1876 election in Louisiana, Kenner reported that he and his long-time acquaintance discussed the results of the election. Kenner argued that the Democrats had indeed received a majority of the votes in the election and that if Wells did not recognize that fact the state would continue to suffer both economically and politically. Though he did not challenge much of what Kenner said, Wells responded that he could not go against his party without suffering serious consequences.[48]

Wells finally broached the real issue at hand when Kenner asked him what political office he had been promised by the Republicans. Wells answered that he was not interested in holding another office because, at the age of sixty-eight, he was looking for something with more security—something that would enable him to retire in peace and prosperity to his home in Rapides Parish. The ex-governor added that since this was the biggest concern in his life, he would accept no political promises from either side. He had to have what he wanted in hand before doing anything. With the issue finally out in the open, Kenner pressed for an amount which would be needed to get Wells' support. However, the Republican played coy and said that he would have to consult with another member of the Returning Board before a price could be set.[49]

Over the next several days, Kenner met several times with Wells and other members of the Returning Board. In the meetings the Republicans usually pressed for large amounts of money which Kenner refused to pay, because "it was perfectly ridiculous and nonsensical to talk about so large a sum of money." The issue came to a head in the next meeting of the two sides. At that meeting, Wells presented his final offer. For $200,000 "in greenbacks cash in hand" he would deliver the election to the Democrats. When Kenner responded that the amount was still more than he could raise, the negotiations ended. Two days later the results of the election were promulgated by the Returning Board in favor of the Republican nominees.[50]

Any doubts as to how the official election totals were decided were removed several days after the results were announced. A chance meeting between the two men while they walked along the river levee in New Orleans afforded Kenner a final opportunity to challenge Wells on the issue. Kenner's account of the meeting, elucidated during his congressional testimony on the election, clearly reveals the political realities of the time. According to Kenner, he opened the conversation with the remark, "Well,

Wells, I must express my great astonishment and very great regret at what you have done." Without hesitation or any sign of concern, Wells simply responded, "What could I do? You had no money."[51]

Despite the Returning Board's decision in favor of the Republicans, the issue of who would control state government for the next four years was by no means settled. So many Louisianians refused to accept the decision of the Board that on inauguration day in January, 1877, two different administrations were sworn into office—a Republican one headed by S. B. Packard and a Democratic one with Francis T. Nicholls at its head. Fortunately for the Louisiana Democrats, the national Republican party was much more concerned with getting its man into the White House than its Louisiana surrogate into the governor's mansion. Realizing the strength of the Democratic position in Louisiana and anxious to secure the presidency, the national Republicans and Louisiana Democrats worked out a deal by which both sides got their wish. Rutherford B. Hayes obtained Louisiana's electoral votes and the presidency. Shortly thereafter, he appointed a commission to examine the Louisiana situation; to no one's surprise, the commission found in favor of the Democratic contenders. On April 24, 1877, President Hayes ordered all remaining federal troops out of New Orleans. Reconstruction was at last over in Louisiana.[52]

Though the withdrawal of federal troops cleared the way for the assumption of political power by the Redeemer Democrats, there remained areas of Republican power in the state. Most notably there were still many communities where black Republicans remained entrenched in local offices. The Redeemers quickly moved to eliminate these remaining segments of Republican power in Louisiana; their efforts culminated in a state election in 1878. In the election of that year the Redeemer Democrats took no chances and used every resource they had, including fraud, violence, and intimidation, to rout their opponents. Not only did this vote mark the death knell for the Republicans in Louisiana for decades to come, it also marked the final stage of the reassertion of white supremacy in the state.[53]

Not unexpectedly, among the ranks of the Redeemer Democrats seeking to re-establish the political ascendancy of the white planter-merchant (Bourbon) elite was Kenner. In the general election of November 5, 1878, Kenner at age sixty-five won election to the Louisiana senate. However, unlike all of his earlier elections to public office when he used Ashland as his legal residence, Kenner ran for a seat in the Fourth Senatorial District of Orleans Parish, using his home at 257 Carondelet Street as his residence.[54]

The legislative session of 1879 served as an important step in the ascent to power of the Bourbons, who dominated the political scene in Louisiana well into the twentieth century. After quickly brushing aside a challenge to his election by Charles Schenck, Kenner played an active role in the day-to-day activities of the lawmaking body. The most important piece of legislation considered during the session was the call for a constitutional convention. Kenner and his conservative colleagues realized that, despite their newly won power, the only way they could excise the Radical influences which had permeated the state during the Reconstruction period was by again changing Louisiana's charter. The 1868 constitution had been drafted by the Radicals primarily to limit the power of the white elite in the state and to benefit the carpetbaggers, scalawags, and politically naïve—yet powerful—black constituency. Determined to reverse what they considered to be the outrageous legislative enactments of the Radicals, the Redeemers looked for ways to overturn those policies without repeating the mistakes of the early postwar period which had resulted in harsh condemnation of their actions by people across the nation. As an enthusiastic supporter of the legislation calling for a new constitutional convention, Kenner introduced legislation allocating the $40,000 needed to pay for the meeting.[55]

When drafted by the convention and approved by the people, the Constitution of 1879 became the anchor of the conservative reaction to Reconstruction. Because Radical excesses had instilled in the Redeemers a deep suspicion of legislative bodies, the new organic law of Louisiana was filled with limitations against that branch of government. While duties of even minor public officials were sharply defined, the power of the governor was greatly expanded. The state's chief executive was accorded an item veto and the authority to appoint all state and local officials whose election was not specifically provided for in the new constitution. Hence, in many ways, the cure became worse than the disease. For example, so entrenched were the conservative policies of the new regime that many vital state services, including the public schools and most charitable institutions, were permitted to languish to a point of near collapse.[56]

In addition to the effort to revise the constitution, Kenner and the conservatives looked to the legislative session as an important tool for placing loyal Democrats in important governmental offices formerly held by the reconstruction forces. Most notable of these actions were Kenner's votes for Edward D. White for associate justice of the Louisiana Supreme Court and B. F. Jonas for United States senator.[57]

Kenner's support for Jonas was not given without some regret, for Kenner himself had hoped for and worked to win selection to the open Senate seat. Although he never had his name officially placed before the legislature, Kenner was among the few individuals given serious consideration by Democratic leaders. Unfortunately, as in his earlier try for a seat in the U.S. Senate in 1848, Kenner could not muster sufficient support to win the office. The selection of the state's new senator in 1879 followed a somewhat unusual process, even by Louisiana standards. With no one individual having a lock on the appointment, an unusually large number of politicians expressed an interest in the office. During the nomination and selection process, which ran for two weeks as opposed to the typical one or two days, as many as twenty legislators had their names placed in nomination for the senatorial seat. Confusing the situation even more was the fact that, in essence, two separate elections for the seat were taking place simultaneously. One was the official vote by legislators during a daily joint session of the legislature. But since Democrats were in the majority, most decisions on major issues were made by the Democrats in their caucus before the issue ever reached the floor for debate. Thus, the night before each vote was taken on the floor of the legislature, the Democrats would choose the person they would support the next day in the formal vote. Day after day and ballot after ballot, voting in the legislature and in the Democratic caucus continued with no single candidate gaining an advantage. Daily, names were added and deleted from the list of contenders. So frustrating did the situation become that one senator mockingly placed in nomination "the entire population of the state," and the press branded the session as a joke and a waste of money.[58]

It eventually took forty-eight different ballots of the caucus members to make the senatorial selection. In every caucus ballot Kenner remained in close contention, being among the top three vote-gatherers. Despite the solid support of a large number of legislators, Kenner was never able to win the support of more than thirty-two Democrats. This number was twenty short of the total needed to win the seat. The best Kenner could do was to collect enough support to finish second in the contest to the winner, B. F. Jonas, whom Kenner loyally supported on the floor of the legislature.[59]

Whether it was his disappointment in not winning the U.S. Senate seat or simply that he was tired of the political scene, Kenner's service in the 1879 legislature marked the end of his public career. With the old planter-merchant alliance back in power, Kenner focused his attention on his business and agricultural interests. Though no longer involved in seeking or holding elected public office, Kenner did not totally discontinue his lifelong custom of dedicating himself to the service of his state and community. He continued his leadership roles in the Louisiana Jockey Club, the Boston Club, and the Louisiana Sugar Planters' Association, and he also spent considerable time and effort serving on President Chester Arthur's tariff commission.

The last major project of Kenner's long and eventful career of community service involved his participation in the World's Industrial and Cotton Centennial Exposition, held in New Orleans in 1884. All across the South the end of Reconstruction introduced an era heralded as the "New South" of industrial progress. In an attempt to promote their economies, many of the South's larger cities competed to put on bigger and better industrial expositions. Not to be outdone by its rivals, the New Orleans business community planned the grandest of all the expositions. Initiated to commemorate the centennial of the first shipment of cotton from the United States to Europe in 1784, the city's business community planned to use the event to promote its vision of the long-hoped-for postwar commercial revival and industrial birth.[60]

Kenner enthusiastically supported the plan to promote the city and was deeply involved in the effort from its beginning. Among the original incorporators of the exposition, he was a member of the forty-person finance committee which worked to raise the large sums needed to put on the planned extravaganza. Kenner was also selected to serve on the twelve-man board of management which had the task of overseeing the development and implementation of the grand exposition. His particular area of responsibility was to chair the important building committee.[61]

Determined to put together an exposition second to no other, Kenner and the other planners constructed a setting which awed many of the visitors to the fair. On the 235-acre site, now occupied by Audubon Park, the building committee provided for the construction of fifteen buildings. The magnitude of the effort was exemplified by the exposition's main building. That structure alone contained twenty-five miles of walkways between exhibits. It was 1,378 feet long by 905 feet wide and covered more than thirty acres of the fair's area—approximately ten times the size of the main building at the Philadelphia Centennial Exposition of 1876. The music hall, located in the main building, seated eleven thousand people and six hundred musicians![62]

Unfortunately, in spite of the elaborate plans and grandiose buildings, the exposition failed to achieve most of its goals. Although the project received many favorable reviews, including one from the *New York Times* which praised the exposition for offering more items of interest than any previous world's fair, the one million visitors who attended were far fewer than the four million patrons the organizers had predicted. The fair also failed to meet its financial objectives. Having accumulated a debt of nearly a half million dollars, the exposition closed its doors on June 1, 1885.[63]

Though many factors contributed to the failure of the exposition, including the distance of the city from the population centers of the East, the lack of good cheap transportation facilities to and from the city, poor winter weather conditions, and a fear by visitors of New Orleans' reputation for yellow-fever epidemics, the project was also hampered by poor management. Among those who shared responsibility for the many problems of the fair were Kenner and his building committee. Despite the grand nature of the fair's structures, many problems were caused by long delays in their construction. Additionally, the nineteenth-century eclectic design of the buildings was disdained by some and was even condemned by at least one contemporary account as an "eyesore."[64]

The many problems associated with the exposition and the building committee marked one of the few times in his life that Kenner's ability did not match the task at hand. However, in spite of its shortcomings, the 1884 World's Industrial and Cotton Centennial Exposition did have a positive side for New Orleans and Louisiana. The fair marked an important turning point in the community's history by demonstrating to the rest of the country that the people of New Orleans were determined to put the many troubles of the previous decades behind them and begin to work for a new and prosperous future. Though the wished-for results were sometimes slow in coming, the fair nevertheless marked a point at which the community turned its attention from the past to that of the future. Thus, as a crucible of change, no more appropriate an event could have been found for Kenner to end his long career of public service.

XIII

"INTER PARES DUX"

Kenner remained active throughout the waning years of his life. Despite suffering from palsy, he maintained a full schedule until a short time before his death. Awaking each morning around 7:30, Kenner leisurely made his way to his office a short distance from his home, where he remained until approximately 1:00 p.m. when he usually lunched at the Boston Club. Afterwards he would return to his office for a few more hours of work before again visiting the club and then returning home for supper about 5:00 p.m. His evenings were usually spent either with his family or working in his library, often until early morning.[1]

Though his gradually worsening health had forced him in later years to cut back on his work schedule, Kenner's death at age seventy-four on Sunday morning, July 3, 1887, surprised and saddened the community. He was stricken shortly after awakening by what his doctors later termed "a fatal attack of heart disease." Kenner's family immediately summoned his three doctors, who upon their arrival realized that the old gentleman was beyond help. They were only able to make him comfortable during his final moments. Having converted to Roman Catholicism from Episcopalianism many years before, Kenner was given the church's last rites shortly before he breathed his last breath at 11:30 a.m.[2]

In spite of the fact that Kenner owned a tomb in the prestigious Metairie Cemetery, Nanine Kenner preferred to have her husband buried in her family's tomb in the Catholic cemetery in Donaldsonville, not far from his beloved Ashland. Built by Nanine's father of imported Italian marble for the high prewar price of $20,000, the immense tomb dominated the graveyard and was referred to by the community as "Le Monument." To accommodate the large number of people from New Orleans who wanted to attend the funeral, the family arranged for a special train to transport the body and mourners to Donaldsonville for the event.[3]

Kenner left his entire estate, including the plantations of Ashland, Hermitage, Bowden, Houmas, and Hollywood as well as several New Orleans properties, to his family. According to his will and Louisiana law, Nanine inherited half of the estate; the other half was divided among his two daughters, Blanche Simpson and Rosella Brent, and Kenner's young grandson, Duncan F. Kenner, Jr. The boy, who lived in Nashville, had inherited his share of Kenner's estate as a consequence of the death in 1881 of his father George, the brother of Blanche and Rosella. However, Nanine Kenner continued to hold usufruct on the various properties until her death on November 6, 1911.[4]

Mrs. Kenner and her son-in-law, General Joseph Brent, served as the estate's executors. Somewhat surprisingly, they either did not have the desire or the ability of Kenner to keep the estate's holdings together. Within a few years of Kenner's death most of the properties he had spent a lifetime acquiring and fighting to save had passed out of the hands of the family. Though considerable turmoil had resulted from an unsuccessful legal challenge by the guardians of Kenner's grandson to the division of the estate, the decisions were made largely for financial reasons. Because of poor crop yields on his plantations in the months before his death, Kenner had been forced to borrow large sums of money to meet his expenses. Though the estate's plantations yielded a modest profit of $10,500 the year after Kenner's death, Mrs. Kenner and Brent decided to sell off the Kenner holdings. Over the next few years nearly all of the Kenner properties were liquidated.[5]

Although not the last of Kenner's properties to be sold, Kenner's much-cherished Ashland was the most important. For some time before his death, the plantation had served as the home of Kenner's daughter Rosella and her husband, Joseph Brent. The Brents continued to live on the estate and to cultivate the land for almost two years after Kenner's death. The grand manor house and its 1,300 acres were finally sold at a sheriff's sale in 1889 for $85,000. Purchased by John Reuss, a sugar planter with extensive land holdings in the region, the name of the estate was changed to Belle Hélène in honor of his granddaughter. Now included on the National Register of Historic Places, the majestic home, in need of major preservation work, remained in the possession of the descendants of John Reuss until recently when ownership of the estate was transferred to the Shell Oil Company.[6]

Duncan Kenner's life spanned seven and a half of the most fateful decades in the history of Louisiana and the American South. Though other individuals may have, from time to time, been more instrumental in guiding the direction of the state and region, no other individual in nineteenth-century Louisiana maintained as high a position of leadership and influence for a greater period of time than Kenner. From the time he assumed a leadership role with the Whig party in Louisiana in the 1840s until his retirement four decades later, Kenner was involved with virtually every political issue of any consequence that occurred within the state. Although, Louisiana produced individuals, such as Slidell, Soulé, and Benjamin of the antebellum period and Francis T. Nicholls and Henry Clay Warmoth of the postwar era, who at one time or another ascended to greater levels of political power and influence than Kenner, none of his contemporaries remained among the state's most influential leaders as long as he did.

With the political and social setting of early nineteenth-century Louisiana influenced to a large extent by the Anglo-American versus Latin conflict, Kenner's background afforded him a unique opportunity to win acceptance and entrée into both sides of this parochial controversy. Likewise, Kenner's intelligence, integrity, and keen sense of humor, together with his reputation for sound judgement made establishing friendships and political alliances easy for him. With the politics and government of the state dominated by the planter-businessman throughout the antebellum period and for two generations after the Civil War, Kenner's wealth and property holdings placed him throughout his adult life at the center of the political power structure in Louisiana.[7]

Self-interest led Kenner during the antebellum period to support the political principles of the Whig party. Like the majority of sugar planters in the region, Kenner supported policies that would assist the sugar industry through tariff protection, internal improvements to protect their low-lying area from flooding, and support of the commercial and banking industry. Yet, in spite of his political concern for the needs of his industry and the social elite, Kenner did not abandon the common people of his constituency. As was typical throughout the old South, Kenner and other wealthy planters of the region often provided guidance and leadership for the common folk. As one Northerner observed, "every community had its great man, or its little great men, around whom his fellow citizens gathered when they want information, and to whose monologues they listen with a respect akin to humility."[8] Kenner relished the status and perquisites that members of the planter oligarchy enjoyed. Yet, ever cognizant of his class responsibilities, he looked upon his role of community leader as a profound duty, to be taken with great seriousness. His status as one of Louisiana's most important political figures kept Kenner popular with his constituents.

As a leading Whig legislator, Kenner was involved in most of the major political events of the antebellum period in Louisiana. Somewhat ironically, however, perhaps his most notable and enduring political accomplishments were those that benefited the common people of the state. Among the most significant of his efforts to address the needs of the lesser folk of Louisiana were his staunch support of free public education and constitutional reform. In the latter of these notable efforts, Kenner sought to broaden the electoral franchise, and, as presiding officer of the 1845 constitutional convention, he worked to liberalize even further the state's government and business environments. Unfortunately for his party, many of the constitutional reforms advocated by Kenner weakened the Whigs in Louisiana. The liberalized franchise led to an expansion of the Democratic party's political base, and the new constitutional guidelines for legislative apportionment split the state's Whigs into country and city factions.

Like most Louisianians, during much of the antebellum period Kenner seldom displayed much concern for national political issues. Economic issues which affected the state—banking regulations, the tariff, internal improvements, public lands, levee and drainage needs, and immigration legislation—were considered by most Louisianians to be more relevant to their interests than the political concerns of their neighboring states. However, once the debate over slavery caught the attention of the people of Louisiana, the situation changed. Always loyal to his personal feelings on an issue and never afraid to speak up for what he believed, Kenner's hard-line position in favor of states' rights and secession caused him to lose temporarily the support of his Ascension Parish constituents.

Yet, others in the state and South recognized Kenner's ability to contribute to their cause. Chosen to represent Louisiana in both the Confederate Provisional Congress and the two regular congresses, Kenner was in the forefront of those who worked to establish a sound economic program for the Rebel government. A strong supporter of Jefferson Davis, he promoted the idea that wartime conditions necessitated special arrangements such as the application of stringent confiscation and sequestration laws. However, a lack of similar feelings among many of his colleagues in the government as demonstrated by the petty and parochial nature of many of the issues handled by the Congress and its often acrimonious relations with the executive branch of the government muted the effectiveness of the Confederate legislature. Consequently, comparatively little notice or importance was given by contemporaries to the actions of Kenner and his congressional colleagues. Thus, despite playing a major role in the Confederate legislature, Kenner's contributions to the rebel cause in this area were largely unrecognized because of the muted role of the rebel Congress in the Confederacy's struggle for independence.[9]

Kenner's most memorable effort for the Confederate cause and perhaps the most notable of his entire political career was his illfated attempt to win recognition by the European powers for the South in exchange for the freeing of the slaves. Though his diplomatic mission to Europe had little chance for success because it came too late, it demonstrated initiative, a willingness for personal sacrifice, and an innovative effort which were all too rarely exhibited by the political leaders of the Confederacy. As evidenced by his readiness to forfeit his slaveholdings and by his support for confiscation and sequestration legislation, Kenner understood more clearly than most Confederate leaders the degree of personal sacrifice required for the South to achieve victory.

For years historians have debated to what degree internal problems contributed to the collapse of the Confederacy. Among the prominent theories on the subject are Frank L. Owsley's state-rights thesis, in which he maintained that the internal dissension between the centralizing influence of the administration and the resistance of state officials contributed to the South's defeat; David Donald's contention that the Confederates lacked discipline because Southerners refused to bend to the necessities of war by insisting upon retaining their democratic liberties; and most recently, in their work *Why the South Lost the Civil War*, the conclusions of historians Richard E. Beringer, Herman Hattaway, Archer Jones, and William N. Still, Jr. that it was a loss of morale and the will to resist further that decided the fate of the Confederacy.[10] All of these theories point to a deficit in the spirit of dedication to the Southern Cause among the people and leaders of the fledgling nation. By contrast, Kenner's devotion to the Rebel effort was complete. Despite the confiscation of his property by the enemy and the abandonment of his family home, Kenner remained devoted to the pursuit of Confederate independence. Unfortunately for the South, the depth and single-mindedness of his dedication for the Cause was not universally shared by all Confederates.[11]

During the postwar years, Kenner remained active on the Louisiana political scene. His efforts were instrumental in the successful efforts of Democrats to wrest control of state government from the Republicans. However, Kenner's most important postwar political contribution was his Black Code legislation. Although he and his colleagues considered these laws to be reasonable attempts to address several of the state's most pressing postwar problems, his legislation was bitterly condemned by Northerners. In the end the Black Codes in Louisiana and elsewhere were instrumental in providing radical elements in the North and Congress with the rationale to implement Radical Republican control in the states of the defunct Confederacy. Kenner's long political career and his numerous contributions to the political developments of his time, particularly his efforts at constitutional revision, his support of the Southern Cause, and his Black Code legislation, clearly earned him a place among the most prominent nineteenth-century political leaders of Louisiana and the Confederacy.

As important as they were, Kenner's political achievements were only one aspect of his contribution to the history and development of Louisiana and of the South. Like many Southern politicians, Kenner put considerably more effort into his thoroughbred racing and agricultural interests than he did into his political activities. In both of these areas, Kenner's achievements and contributions were unequaled by any of his contemporaries.

Given the sobriquet "Napoleon of the Louisiana turf" by his contemporaries, Kenner worked tirelessly throughout his life to develop the thoroughbred industry in Louisiana. As a breeder, racer, Jockey Club president, and member of the board of the state's premier course at the Metairie Race Track, Kenner was one of a handful of turf enthusiasts who laid the foundation for the sport in the state, where it remains today a multi-million dollar industry.

Horse racing was not the only Louisiana industry in which Kenner played a major role. Kenner's many contributions to the nation's sugar industry certainly qualify him as one of the greatest agriculturists of the nineteenth-century South. As one of America's largest sugar producers, Kenner steadfastly worked throughout his life to improve every aspect of the production and marketing of the nation's sugar crop. Kenner was among the earliest and strongest supporters of the application of scientific methods to the production of sugar. A prime mover in nearly all the great advances made by the industry during the century, including the all-important establishment of both the Sugar Planter's Association and the

Sugar Experimental Station, Kenner often brought changes to the industry by demonstrating on his plantations the latest improvements. Chief among these were the Rillieux double-effect pans, the McDonald hydraulic pressure regulator, and the use of the portable railroad to transport cane to the mill. Hence, his own practical success together with his leadership in promoting professional organizations and improved technology played a dominant role in forming the base upon which the nation's modern sugar industry continues to rest.

Though much has been written by such noted historians as Raimondo Luraghi and Eugene Genovese of the seigniorial characteristics of life on nineteenth-century sugar plantations, Kenner's lifestyle was more sophisticated and involved than that normally associated with the seigniorial philosophy. Kenner no doubt enjoyed the power, status, and good life of the sugar planters; yet he was first and foremost a tough-minded businessman determined to make the largest possible profit from his many enterprises. In true capitalist fashion, throughout his life Kenner invested his resources wherever he thought the best return from his investment could be achieved. Although his agrarian holdings remained his primary area of interest, yielding in most years his greatest financial returns, Kenner invested extensively in many different businesses. Even if one accepts the questionable premise that the capital-intensive and very technical aspects of the financing, growing, production, and marketing of the sugar crop were all characteristics of a seigneurial rather than a capitalist philosophy, Kenner's extensive portfolio of non-agricultural investments clearly denotes the lifelong interest of a most determined nineteenth-century capitalist.

Kenner's keen acumen for business and finances enabled him to succeed in many different ventures at the same time that many of his contemporaries succumbed to the multifarious and complex economic problems that afflicted the nineteenth-century South. A careful man who was always prudent and cautious in looking after his business interests, Kenner took to heart the sense of honor which characterized the dealings between members of the planter class. In both his political and business life, once he made an agreement he stuck to it no matter what the consequences. He developed such a respected reputation that, on the rare occasions in his public life that his word on an issue was challenged by another, little credence was afforded to the positions of Kenner's opponents.[12]

Kenner's sense of fairness was not limited to his fellow planters and business associates. Whether from an economic need to keep one's workers healthy and productive, Christian compassion, or from an aristocratic sense of noblesse oblige, Kenner governed his slaves with pragmatic paternalism. Although slaves were driven harder on Ashland and the other Kenner properties than they were on most other staple-producing plantations, considerable effort and money was expended by Kenner to keep his slaves healthy. Indeed, for those blacks involved with Kenner's thoroughbreds, no expense was spared in keeping them fit and happy. Yet for the majority of the Kenner slave force, life was largely one of hard work and monotonous routine in which the necessities of life, but few luxuries and privileges, were provided.

On the issue of slavery itself there is no evidence that Kenner ever seriously questioned the morality of the peculiar institution. Like the great majority of his planter colleagues, his traditional and conservative beliefs led him readily to accept slavery without giving much credence to the critics of the slave regime. He likely viewed criticism of the institution as a political attack rather than a moral challenge. Kenner no doubt was comfortable with the prevalent and self-serving view held by many slaveholders that their role of slavemaster was both duty and a burden. Anchored in a philosophy of paternal racism, Kenner looked upon Negroes as members of a backward, indolent race which needed the strict regimen of slavery to make them productive members of Southern society and upon the institution of slavery as the cornerstone of the Southern socioeconomic system and the natural social order of the South.[13]

Hence, Duncan Kenner in many ways actually lived and enjoyed the romantic and glamorous lifestyle about which so many writers of Southern fiction have written. Though the romantic mythologizing which has often embellished novels and films about the Old South has been justly criticized for presenting an unbalanced characterization of the societal makeup of the nineteenth-century South, the fact remains that the political, military, social, and economic events of the Old South were dominated and determined by a relatively small number of individuals whose roots were anchored in the South's plantations. However, despite the many contributions of these gentlemen leaders of the South to the development of America, the heinous legacy of their bondage of millions of black Americans often has distorted the character and motivations of the South's leadership class. It is hoped that this review of the life of one of nineteenth-century Louisiana's dominant figures has given insight not only into the character and driving events of the man Duncan Kenner but also into the remarkable rise and fall and partial resurgence of Louisiana's planter aristocracy.

Though there can be no argument that throughout most of his life Kenner, as did the vast majority of his contemporaries, uncritically accepted the flawed racial assumptions on which the Old South's society and culture were based, he was a man of great intelligence, ability, and accomplishment. As much as any other nineteenth-century son of the South, who personified the term "southern gentleman," Kenner contributed much to the society and times in which he lived. The breadth of his achievements across such a diverse spectrum of activities as state and national politics, diplomacy, large-scale commercial agriculture, science, business, and sport, perhaps is capsulized best by the simple epitaph which marks his final resting place— "Inter Pares Dux"—"A Leader Among Peers."

ENDNOTES

CHAPTER ONE

[1] Frederick Merk, *History of the Westward Movement* (New York, 1978), pp. 125, 134-135.

[2] A scarcity of reliable documents makes it difficult to determine with any degree of certainty facts concerning William Kenner's youth. It is likely that William was a descendant of one of the branches of the politically prominent Kenner family of Northumberland County in Virginia. However, except for the traditional statement (verified by entries in the family Bible) that he was born at Staunton in Augusta County, Virginia, one month before the Declaration of Independence was signed, little direct evidence has ever turned up about his heritage.

Though land records of the time list a Sarah Kenner as a property owner in the Natchez region, no documentation has ever been discovered which would tie her and William together. Hence, unlike many of his fellow migrants who maintained ties with their home communities and families, upon leaving Virginia, evidence suggest that William totally ended his connections with his relatives in his native state. Although many letters exist between him and his friends and in-laws in the Natchez region, no mention is ever made of his family roots in Virginia or of other blood relatives in Mississippi. Furthermore, it seems as if he never spoke with his children about their grandparents or any other of their Virginia relatives and family roots. This suggests that his departure from Virginia was not on very pleasant terms. However, his quick acquisition of wealth and acceptance by the political and social upper classes of his new home suggest that his departure from his home community was caused more by errant family feelings than any questionable or illegal activities. See Kenner Family Bible in possession of Mr. E. Schmidt; United States Congress, *American State Papers: Documents, Legislative and Executive of the Congress of the United States in Relation to the Public Lands, from the First Session of the First Congress to the First Session of the Twenty-Third Congress–March 4, 1789, to June 15, 1834*, Walter Lowrie, ed., vol. 1 (Washington: Duff Green, 1834), p. 785; Bringier Papers, Folder 4, Trist Wood Papers, The Urquhart Collection, Historic New Orleans Collection, New Orleans, Louisiana.

[3] William O. Lynch, "The Westward Flow of Southern Colonists before 1861," *Journal of Southern History* IX (1943), 303; Gilbert C. Din, "Proposals and Plans for Colonization in Spanish Louisiana, 1787-1790," *Louisiana History,* XI (1970), 197-213.

[4] A. E. Parkins, *The South: Its Economic-Geographic Development* (1938; reprint ed., Westport, Conn., 1970), pp. 107, 127; Clement Eaton, *A History of the Old South*, 2nd ed., (New York, 1966), p. 128.

[5] John Richardson Alden, *The South in the Revolution, 1763-1789*, vol. 3 in *A History of the South* (Baton Rouge, 1950), pp. 360, 363; Eaton, *Old South*, p. 176.

[6] Jack D. L. Holmes, "A Spanish Province, 1779-1798," in *A History of Mississippi*, 2 vols., Richard Aubrey McLemore, ed. (Hattiesburg, Miss., 1973), I, 159-60; Din, "Colonization in Spanish Louisiana," 211-212.

[7] Holmes, "A Spanish Province," 160, 168; Eaton, *Old South*, pp. 128-129.

[8] Holmes, "A Spanish Province," 160, 168; J. F. H. Claiborne, *Mississippi as a Province, Territory, and State* (1880; reprint ed., Spartanburg, S.C., 1978), p. 353; Certificate of Land Ownership, June 18, 1805, William Kenner Papers, Louisiana State University Archives, Baton Rouge.

[9] Robert V. Haynes, "The Formation of the Territory," in *A History of Mississippi*, 2 vols., Richard Aubrey McLemore, ed. (Hattiesburg, Miss., 1973), I, 188.

[10] Jack D. L. Holmes, "Stephen Minor: Natchez Pioneer," *Journal of Mississippi History* XLII (1980), 17, 21 (hereafter cited as "Natchez Pioneer"); Jack D. L. Holmes, "Genealogical and Historical Notes on Stephen Minor," *Louisiana Genealogical Register* XVI (1969), 113 (hereafter cited as "Genealogical Notes"); Haynes, "Formation of the Territory," 184.

[11] Haynes, "Formation of the Territory," 174, 187.

Endnotes

[12]*Ibid.*, 178, 180-181, 187; Mississippi Historical Records Survey, Works Progress Administration, *Transcription of County Archives of Mississippi, No. 2 Adams County (Natchez)*, vol. 1, *Minutes of the Court of General Quarter Sessions of the Peace, 1799-1801* (Jackson, 1942), p. 21.

[13]Holmes, "Natchez Pioneer," 21; Haynes, "Formation of the Territory," 187-188.

[14]Oscar T. Bark, Jr., and Hugh T. Lefler, *Colonial America*, 2nd ed. (New York, 1968), p. 247; Haynes "Formation of the Territory," 187; *Minutes of the Court*, pp. 21-22, 16, 28.

[15]Holmes, "Genealogical Notes," 114.

[16]Kenner Family Bible; Stanley C. Arthur, ed. and comp., and George Campbell Huchet de Kernion, collab., *Old Families of Louisiana* (1931; reprint ed., Baton Rouge, 1971), p. 158; Catherine Clinton, *The Plantation Mistress: Women's World in the Old South* (New York, 1982), pp. 60, 233.

[17]Quoted in Clinton, *Plantation Mistress*, p. 60.

[18]Folder 4, Bringier Papers, in Trist Wood Papers.

[19]Haynes, "Formation of the Territory," 187-88; John R. Skates, "Mississippi," in *The Encyclopedia of Southern History*, David C. Roller and Robert W. Twyman, eds., (Baton Rouge, 1979), p. 829.

[20]Thomas P. Abernethy, *The South in the New Nation, 1789-1819*, vol. 4 in *A History of the South* (Baton Rouge, 1961), p. 167.

[21]Abernethy, *The South in the New Nation*, 255-254; Merk, *History of the Westward Movement*, p. 137; John R. Kemp, *New Orleans* (Woodland Hills, Ca., 1981), p. 53.

[22]Abernethy, *The South in the New Nation*, 253-254.

[23]John G. Clark, *New Orleans, 1718-1812: An Economic History* (Baton Rouge, 1970), p. 303; New Orleans *Times-Democrat*, October 23, 1892; Catalogue of **New Orleans** Street Addresses, Louisiana State Museum, New Orleans ; Lewis E. Atherton, "John McDonogh–New Orleans Mercantile Capitalist," *Journal of Southern History* VII (1941), 458-459.

[24]Abernethy, *The South in the New Nation*, 254-255; Atherton, "John McDonogh," 458, 463; Mississippi Historical Records Survey, Works Progress Administration, *Transcription of County Archives of Mississippi*, No. 2 Adams County (Natchez), vol. 2, *Minutes of the County Court, 1802-1804* (Jackson, 1942), pp. 50, 104, 147, 184, 259; *Indirect Index to Land Conveyances, Adams County, Mississippi, From 1798*, State of Mississippi, Department of Archives and History, Jackson, Miss.; *Direct Index to Land Conveyances, Adams County, Mississippi, from 1798*, State of Mississippi, Department of Archives and History, Jackson, Miss.

[25]Atherton, "John McDonogh," 463.

[26]Abernethy, *The South in the New Nation*, 258; Kemp, *New Orleans*, p. 58; Dunbar Rowland, "Mississippi in the Transfer of the Louisiana Purchase by France to the United States," *Louisiana Historical Quarterly*, III (1930), 243; Pierce Butler, *The Unhurried Years: Memories of the Old Natchez Region* (Baton Rouge, 1948), p. 6; Holmes, "Genealogical Notes," 114.

[27]Kemp, *New Orleans*, p. 62; Louisiana Legislative Council, *The History and Government of Louisiana* (Baton Rouge, 1964), pp. 40-41; Henry Rightor, *Standard History of New Orleans, Louisiana* (Chicago, 1900), p. 95.

[28]Louisiana Legislative Council, *History and Government*, p. 41; Andrew Lipscomb, ed., *The Writings of Thomas Jefferson*, 20 vols. (Washington, D.C., 1904), XI, 6-37.

[29]New Orleans *Louisiana Gazette*, October 12, 1804; Clarence Edwin Carter, ed., *The Territorial Papers of the United States*, vol. 9, *The Orleans Territory* (Washington, D.C., 1940), 284-285.

[30] Louisiana Legislative Council, *History and Government*, p. 41; Albert Fossier, *New Orleans: The Glamour Period, 1800-1840* (New Orleans, 1957), p. 94; Joseph G. Tregle, Jr., "Early New Orleans Society: A Reappraisal," *Journal of Southern History* XVIII (1952), 23.

[31] Claiborne, *Mississippi as a Province*, p. 320. It is also possible that William Kenner even took an active part in the fighting during the war. The list of American forces at the battle of New Orleans at the Louisiana State Museum in New Orleans has as a member of Beale's Rifle Company an individual named Kenner. But since no first name is provided, there is no proof that this was indeed William Kenner.

[32] Hodding Carter and Betty Carter, *So Great a Good: A History of the Episcopal Church in Louisiana and of Christ Church Cathedral, 1805-1955* (Sewanee, Tenn., 1955), pp. 7-8; Georgia Fairbanks Taylor, "The Early History of the Episcopal Church in New Orleans, 1805-1840," *Louisiana Historical Quarterly*, XXII (1939), 449; Clement Eaton, *The Mind of the Old South* (1964; rev. ed., 1976), pp. 208-209.

[33] Mary Louise Christovich, Roulhac Toledano, Betsy Swanson, and Pat Holden, *New Orleans Architecture*, vol. 2, *The American Section (Faubourg St. Mary)* (Gretna, La., 1972), p. 163; Eaton, *History of the Old South*, pp. 357-358.

[34] Eaton, *Mind of the Old South*, pp. 72-73; Folder 2, Bringier Notes in Trist Wood Papers.

[35] Fossier, *New Orleans: The Glamour Period*, p. 60. Clark, *New Orleans, 1718-1812*, p. 336; Succession of William and Mary Kenner, 1826, in Jefferson Parish Court House, Gretna, La.; Craig A. Bauer, "From Burnt Canes to Budding City: A History of the City of Kenner, Louisiana," *Louisiana History*, XXIII (1982), 359; *Louisiana Gazette*, April 5, 1811.

[36] William Kenner to Stephen Minor, June 20, 1812, William Kenner Papers; Harnet T. Kane, *Plantation Parade: The Grand Manner in Louisiana* (New York, 1945), p. 188-189.

[37] Bauer, "From Burnt Canes to Budding City," 359-360.

[38] William Kenner to Stephen Minor, May 10, 1813, William Kenner Papers; Butler, *The Unhurried Years*, pp. 13-14; Bauer, "From Burnt Canes to Budding City," 360.

[39] Succession of William and Mary Kenner; Craig A. Bauer, "The History of the City of Kenner, Louisiana." (M.A. thesis, Southeastern Louisiana University, 1973), pp. 13-14..

[40] Clement Eaton, *Jefferson Davis* (New York, 1977), p. 38; William Kenner to John Minor, January 24, 1817, William J. Minor and Family Papers, Louisiana State University Archives, Baton Rouge.

[41] Kenner Family Bible; Folder 3, Bringier Notes in Trist Wood Papers; New Orleans *Daily Picayune*, October 23, 1892.

[42] *Ibid*.

[43] Kenner Family Bible; Folder 3, Bringier Notes in Trist Wood Papers; Butler, *The Unhurried Years*, p. 6; Eaton, *Jefferson Davis*, p. 27; Herman de Bachellé Seebold, *Plantation Homes and Family Trees*, 2 vols. (New Orleans, 1941), II, 87.

[44] Clinton, *Plantation Mistress*, p. 45; Folders 3, 4 Bringier Notes in Trist Wood Papers; Frank Lawrence Owsley, *Plain Folk of the Old South* (Baton Rouge, 1949), p. 92.

[45] Quoted in Edwin Adams Davis, *Louisiana: A Narrative History*, 3rd ed. (Baton Rouge, 1921), p. 5.

[46] William Kenner to Stephen Minor, June 19, 1814, William Kenner Papers; R. Claque to Stephen Minor, October 7, 1814, Kenner Family Papers, Louisiana State University Archives, Baton Rouge.

[47] R. Claque to Stephen Minor, October 7, 1814, Kenner Family Papers.

[48]*Ibid.*; Clinton, *Plantation Mistress*, p. 158.

[49]Mrs. Mary Farrar to Benjamin Farrar, October 18, 1814, Benjamin Farrar Papers, Manuscripts Division, Special Collection Division, Tulane University, New Orleans; Clinton, *Plantation Mistress*, p. 51.

[50]Mary Farrar to Benjamin Farrar, October 15, 1814, Benjamin Farrar Papers.

[51]Ann Farrar to Benjamin Farrar, January 4, 1815, Benjamin Farrar Papers.

[52]Clinton, *Plantation Mistress*, pp. 123-124.

[53]Quoted in Davis, *Louisiana*, p. 214.

[54]Stuart Grayson Noble, "Schools of New Orleans during the First Quarter of the Nineteenth Century," *Louisiana Historical Quarterly*, XIV (1931), 66; Eaton, *History of the Old South*, p. 417; Clinton, *Plantation Mistress*, p. 127.

[55]R. Claque to Stephen Minor, October 7, 1814, Kenner Family Papers.

[56]William Kenner to Stephen Minor, September 23, 1815, William Kenner Papers.

[57]Clinton, *Plantation Mistress*, pp. 130-133.

[58]William Kenner to Stephen Minor, September 12, 1815, William Kenner Papers; Clinton, *Plantation Mistress*, p. 135; Noble, "Schools of New Orleans," 69; Frances Kenner to William Kenner, May 1, 1818, Benjamin Farrar Papers.

[59]William Kenner to Jane Rapalje, February 13, 1822, Ellis-Farrar Papers, Louisiana State University Archives, Baton Rouge; Rightor, *Standard History of New Orleans*, p. 234.

[60]Quoted in Eaton, *Mind of the Old South*, p. 82; Davis, *Louisiana*, pp. 215-216.

[61]Quoted in Davis, *Louisiana*, p. 216.

[62]Noble, "Schools of New Orleans," 68-69.

[63]William Kenner to John Minor, August 9, 1816, William J. Minor and Family Papers.

[64]Butler, *The Unhurried Years*, p. 12; William Kenner to John Minor, November 17, 1819, William Kenner Papers.

[65]Butler, *The Unhurried Years*, p. 20; William Kenner to John Minor, November 17, 1819, William Kenner Papers.

[66]Frances Kenner to Jane Rapalje, March 11, 1822, and Undated Bill of Sale between Wade Hampton and William Kenner, William Kenner Papers; Historic American Buildings Survey Papers in possession of E. Schmidt, Metarie, La.

[67]William Kenner to John Minor, December 1, 1819, William Kenner Papers; Bauer, "From Burnt Canes to Budding City," 360.

[68]*Times-Democrat*, October 23, 1892; Anna Mercer to Benjamin Farrar, March 5, 1824, Benjamin Farrar Papers.

[69]Anna Mercer to Benjamin Farrar, March 22, 1824, Benjamin Farrar Papers; Sidney A. Marchand, *The Flight of a Century (1800-1900) in Ascension Parish, Louisiana* (Donaldsonville, La., 1936), pp. 59-60.

[70]Marchand, *Flight of a Century*, pp. 59-60.

CHAPTER TWO

[1] Last Will and Testament of William Kenner, July 23, 1823, Will Book Number 4, New Orleans Public Library, New Orleans.

[2] Bauer, "From Burnt Canes to Budding City," 360-361; Folder 3, Bringier Notes in Trist Wood Papers; List of Slaves Sold, n.d., William Kenner Papers; Kane, *Plantation Parade*, p. 189.

[3] Eaton, *History of the Old South*, pp. 422.

[4] Of the 192 students, only 76 were enrolled in the college proper. The other students were either members of the English and Scientific Departments, who were counted separately by the university, or were students enrolled in the school's primary or grammar schools.

[5] *A Catalogue of the Officers and Students of Miami University* (Oxford, Ohio, 1831), pp. 9, 14; Gordon D. Wilson, Archives Librarian, The Miami University Archives, Oxford, Ohio, to the author, May 10, 1976.

[6] Charles S. Sydnor, *The Development of Southern Sectionalism, 1819-1848*, vol. 5 in *A History of the South* (Baton Rouge, 1948), p. 67; *A Catalogue of Miami University*, pp. 12-13.

[7] Gordon D. Wilson to the author, May 10, 1976; Syndor, *Development of Southern Sectionalism*, p. 68.

[8] Diary of Duncan Farrar Kenner's Grand Tour of Europe in Duncan Farrar Kenner Papers, Historic New Orleans Collection, New Orleans (hereafter cited as Duncan Farrar Kenner Papers, HNOC).

[9] *Ibid.*

[10] George Mitchell, "The Ante-Bellum Political Career of Duncan Farrar Kenner," (M.A. thesis, Louisiana State University, 1936), p. 7; Seebold, *Plantation Homes*, II, 87; Eaton, *Jefferson Davis*, p. 168; *Daily Picayune*, July 4, 1887.

[11] Ascension Parish, La., Conveyance Records, 1770-1901, New Orleans Public Library, New Orleans.

[12] *Ibid.*; Betsy Swanson, *Historic Jefferson Parish: From Shore to Shore* (Gretna, La., 1975), p. 108.

[13] Swanson, *Historic Jefferson Parish*, p. 108; Bauer, "From Burnt Canes to Budding City," 361.

[14] Ascension Parish, La., Conveyance Records, 1770-1901; Bauer, "From Burnt Canes to Budding City," 361.

[15] Seebold, *Plantation Homes*, II, 87; Holmes, "Genealogical Notes," 113; Succession of Duncan Farrar Kenner, July 22, 1887, Duncan Farrar Kenner Papers, Louisiana State University Archives, Baton Rouge (hereafter cited as Succession of Duncan Farrar Kenner, LSU and Duncan Farrar Kenner Papers, LSU).

[16] Marchand, *Flight of a Century*, pp. 111, 113; Louisiana Legislative Council, *History and Government*, p. 47.

[17] Davis, *Louisiana*, p. 204.

[18] Succession of Duncan Farrar Kenner, LSU; *Times-Democrat*, October 23, 1892; Kenner Family Bible; P. A. Champomier, *Statement of the Sugar Crop Made in Louisiana, 1851* (New Orleans, 1852) p. 44; Kane, *Plantation Parade*, p. 191.

[19] Kane, *Plantation Parade*, p. 190; Notes on Mr. G. W. Graves, Rosella Kenner Brent Papers, Louisiana State University Archives, Baton Rouge.

Endnotes

[20]Folder 3, Bringier Notes in Trist Wood Papers; Notes on G. W. Graves, Rosella Kenner Brent Papers.

[21]Clinton, *Plantation Mistress*, p. 18.

[22]J. Carlyle Sitterson, *Sugar Country: The Cane Sugar Industry in the South, 1753-1950* (Lexington, Ky., 1953), p. 74.

[23]*Ibid.*; J. Frazer Smith, *White Pillars: Early Life and Architecture of the Lower Mississippi Valley Country* (New York, 1941), p. 217.

[24]Samuel Wilson, Jr., to the author, January 20, 1982; Kathleen H. McKee, "Belle Helene Plantation" (research paper, Architectural Archives, Special Collections Division, Tulane University), p. 2; Arthur Scully, Jr., *James Dakin, Architect: His Career in New York and the South* (Baton Rouge, 1973), p. 98.

[25]Samuel Wilson to the author, January 20, 1982; Scully, *James Dakin, Architect*, pp. 84, 98.

[26]Scully, *James Dakin, Architect*, p. 98.

[27]*Ibid.*, pp. 128-129.

[28]*Ibid.*, pp. 130.

[29]W. Darrell Overdyke, *Louisiana Plantation Homes: Colonial and Antebellum* (New York, 1965), p. 18.

[30]Overdyke, *Louisiana Plantation Homes*, 15-17; McKee, "Belle Helene Plantation," p. 24; Notes on G. W. Graves, Rosella Kenner Brent Papers.

[31]Overdyke, *Louisiana Plantation Homes*, p. 16; McKee, "Belle Helene Plantation," p. 17; Smith, *White Pillars*, p. 230; Interview with Mrs. Robert McKee, an heir to the Belle Helene Plantation, New Orleans, La., April 27, 1984.

[32]McKee, "Belle Helene Plantation," pp. 11, 15, 17, 20; Smith, *White Pillars*, p. 189.

[33]McKee, "Belle Helene Plantation," pp. 18, 20; Wesley F. Cooper, *Louisiana: A Treasure of Plantation Homes* (Natchez, 1961), p. 46.

[34]McKee, "Belle Helene Plantation," pp. 17, 20.

[35]*Ibid.*, pp. 20, 24; Overdyke, *Louisiana Plantation Homes*, p. 15; Cooper, *Louisiana: A Treasure of Plantation Homes*, p. 46.

[36]Smith, *White Pillars*, p. 154; Clarence John Laughlin, *Ghosts Along the Mississippi: An Essay in the Poetic Interpretation of Louisiana's Plantation Architecture* (New York, 1961), plate 62.

[37]Overdyke, *Louisiana Plantation Homes*, pp. 15, 35.

[38]*Ibid.*, p. 35; James C. Bonner, "Plantation Architecture of the Lower South on the Eve of the Civil War," *Journal of Southern History* XI (1945), 383-384.

[39]Overdyke, *Louisiana Plantation Homes*, p. 35; Notes on G. W. Graves, Rosella Kenner Brent Papers; Louisiana *Progress*, November 11, 1938; Plan of Ashland in possession of Mr. and Mrs. Robert McKee, New Orleans.

[40]Notes on G. W. Graves, Rosella Kenner Brent Papers; Plan of Ashland.

[41]Folder 3, Bringier Notes in Trist Wood Papers; Raimondo Luraghi, *The Rise and Fall of the Plantation South* (New York, 1978), p. 67.

CHAPTER THREE

[1] Sitterson, *Sugar Country*, p. 113; Walter Prichard, "Routine on a Louisiana Sugar Plantation Under the Slavery Regime," *Mississippi Valley Historical Review*, XIV (1927), 168-169.

[2] Sitterson, *Sugar Country*, pp. 116, 119; Prichard, "Routine on a Louisiana Sugar Plantation," 169; Ashland Plantation Record Book, February 18, 1852, Louisiana State University Archives, Baton Rouge.

[3] Ashland Plantation Record, January 13, 19, 1852.

[4] *Ibid.*, February 10, 18, 21, 1852; March 1, 20, 1852; Prichard, "Routine of a Louisiana Sugar Plantation," 169-170; Sitterson, *Sugar Country*, pp. 112, 114.

[5] Sitterson, *Sugar Country*, pp. 117-118; Ashland Plantation Record Book, January 20, 1852.

[6] Prichard, "Routine on a Louisiana Sugar Plantation," 170-171.

[7] *Ibid.*, Ashland Plantation Record Book, March 1, 20, 1852; J. Carlyle Sitterson, "Magnolia Plantation, 1852-1862: A Decade of a Louisiana Sugar Estate," *Mississippi Valley Historical Review*, XXV (1938), 204.

[8] Ashland Plantation Record Book, February 21; March 1; May 21, 1852.

[9] *Ibid.*, January 20, 1852; Prichard, "Routine on a Louisiana Sugar Plantation," 172.

[10] Prichard, "Routine on a Louisiana Sugar Plantation," 173.

[11] *Ibid.*, 173-174; Ashland Plantation Record Book, January 7; October 12, 1852.

[12] Ashland Plantation Record Book, October 17, 18, 1852; Pritchard, "Routine on a Louisiana Sugar Plantation," 174.

[13] Sitterson, *Sugar Country*, p. 134; Ashland Plantation Record Book, November 28, 1852; Prichard, "Routine on a Louisiana Sugar Plantation," 175.

[14] Prichard, "Routine on a Louisiana Sugar Plantation," 168; Plan of Ashland; Sitterson, *Sugar Country*, p. 135; Charles P. Roland, *Louisiana Sugar Plantations during the Civil War* (Leiden, 1957), pp. 3-4.

[15] Allen Begnaud, "The Louisiana Sugar Cane Industry: An Overview," in *Green Fields: Two Hundred Years of Louisiana Sugar* (Lafayette, La., 1980), pp. 35-36; Sitterson, *Sugar Country*, p. 148.

[16] Duncan Farrar Kenner to William J. Minor, January 22, 1846, Duncan Farrar Kenner Papers, LSU; Roland, *Louisiana Sugar Plantations*, p. 3; Ulrich Bonnell Phillips, *American Negro Slavery* (Baton Rouge, 1966), p. 246.

[17] Succession of Duncan Farrar Kenner, LSU; Ashland Plantation Record Book, July 1852.

[18] Ashland Plantation Record Book, July 7, 1852; J. Carlyle Sitterson, "The William J. Minor Plantations: A Study in Ante-Bellum Absentee Ownership," *Journal of Southern History* IX (1943), 65; Sitterson, *Sugar Country*, pp. 51-52.

[19] Eaton, *A History of the Old South*, pp. 224, 389; Sixth Census of the United States, 1840, Ascension Parish, Louisiana, Slave Schedules, Microfilm Copy in New Orleans Public Library, New Orleans; Seventh Census of the United States, 1850, Ascension Parish, Louisiana, Slave Schedules, Microfilm Copy in New Orleans Public Library, New Orleans; Eighth Census of the United States, 1860, Ascension Parish, Louisiana, Slave Schedules, Microfilm Copy in New Orleans Public Library, New Orleans; Richard E. Beringer, "A Profile of the Members of the Confederate Congress," *Journal of Southern History* XXXIII (1967), 535; William Kauffman Scarborough to the author, April 17, 1986.

Endnotes 299

[20]Folder 3, Bringier Notes in Trist Wood Papers.

[21]Sitterson, *Sugar Country*, pp. 60-61.

[22]*Ibid.*, pp. 96-97; Ashland Plantation Record Book, n.d.; Robert William Fogel and Stanley L. Engerman, *Time on the Cross: The Economics of American Negro Slavery* (Boston, 1974), p. 123.

[23]Fogel and Engerman, *Time on the Cross*, p. 124; Ashland Plantation Record Book, February 28; April 14, 1852; John W. Blassingame, *The Slave Community: Plantation Life in the Antebellum South* (New York, 1972), p. 94.

[24]Eugene D. Genovese, *Roll, Jordan, Roll: The World the Slaves Made* (New York, 1974); Ashland Plantation Journal, May, 1858, Historic New Orleans Collection, New Orleans.

[25]Sitterson, "Magnolia Plantation," pp. 199-200; Ashland Plantation Record Book, December 25, 1852.

[26]William Kauffman Scarborough, *The Overseer: Plantation Management in the Old South* (Baton Rouge, 1966), pp. 80-81; Kenneth M. Stampp, *The Peculiar Institution: Slavery in the Ante-Bellum South* (New York, 1956), pp. 54-55.

[27]Sitterson, *Sugar Country*, p. 99.

[28]*Ibid.*, pp. 91-92; Ashland Plantation Record Book, February 29; March 28, 1852.

[29]Genovese, *Roll, Jordan, Roll*, p. 544; Ashland Plantation Record Book, 1852.

[30]Stampp, *The Peculiar Institution*, pp. 282-283.

[31]Fogel and Engerman, *Time of the Cross*, pp. 111, 115; Ashland Plantation Record Book, February 29, 1852; List of Supplies, July, 1852.

[32]Spring Allocation List, 1859, Ashland Plantation Journal; Clothes Allocation, Winter, 1858; List of Slaves Receiving Clothing, July, 1854, Duncan Farrar Kenner Papers, LSU; Genovese, *Roll, Jordan, Roll*, p. 551.

[33]List of Winter Allocations, 1858; List of Spring Allocations, 1859, Ashland Plantation Journal; Fogel and Engerman, *Time on the Cross*, 116; Genovese, *Roll, Jordan, Roll*, p. 550.

[34]Sitterson, *Sugar Country*, p. 92; Plan of Ashland.

[35]Unfortunately, the slave schedule of the 1860 census does not provide additional data on the question of the number of slave dwellings at Ashland. For although the forms used in the collection of the data included a column for listing the number of slave houses, the census taker who performed the Ashland canvass did not accurately record the number of slave houses. The information in the census document concerning Duncan Farrar Kenner's slave force covers more than six pages. However, on only one of the pages is there a notation in the column for listing the number of slave houses. Next to where the census taker listed the page count of 78 slaves, he recorded that there were five slave houses. The number obviously referred to only one portion of the Kenner estate and therefore sheds little light on the question of the number and conditions of slave housing at Ashland.

[36]Eaton, *A History of the Old South*, p. 248; Fogel and Engerman, *Time on the Cross*, p. 115; Eighth Census of the United States, 1860, Ascension Parish, Louisiana, Slave Schedules.

[37]Sitterson, "The William J. Minor Plantations," 67; Eaton, *A History of the Old South*, p. 249; Ashland Plantation Record Book, January 3, 5; February 28; April 14, 1852; Fogel and Engerman, *Time on the Cross*, p. 121.

[38]Fogel and Engerman, *Time on the Cross*, p. 119; Sitterson, *Sugar Country*, p. 95; Ashland Plantation Record, February 10, 1852.

[39]Fogel and Engerman, *Time on the Cross*, p. 126.

⁴⁰Sitterson, *Sugar Country*, pp. 97, 105, 107.

⁴¹Ashland Plantation Record Book, May 24, 1852; Genovese, *Roll, Jordan, Roll*, p. 648.

⁴²Sitterson, *Sugar Country*, p. 103.

⁴³Genovese, *Roll, Jordan, Roll*, pp. 4-5.

⁴⁴John W. Blassingame, ed., *Slave Testimony: Two Centuries of Letters, Speeches, Interviews, and Autobiographies* (Baton Rouge, 1977), pp. 392-393.

⁴⁵Blassingame, *The Slave Community*, p. 145; Joe Gray Taylor, *Negro Slavery in Louisiana* (New York, 1963), pp. 194-195.

⁴⁶Blassingame, *Slave Testimony*, pp. 393; Seebold, *Plantation Homes*, II, 145, 150-151.

⁴⁷Blassingame, *Slave Testimony*, p. 392.

⁴⁸*Ibid.*

⁴⁹*Ibid.*, pp. 392-393.

⁵⁰*Ibid.*; Davis, *Louisiana*, p. 198.

⁵¹Blassingame, *Slave Testimony*, p. 393.

⁵²Seebold, *Plantation Homes*, II, 151.

⁵³Eaton, *Jefferson Davis*, p. 42.

⁵⁴*Ibid.*

⁵⁵Quoted in Scarborough, *The Overseer*, p. 93.

⁵⁶*Ibid.*, p. 96.

⁵⁷*Ibid.*, pp. 67-68.

⁵⁸Sitterson, *Sugar Country*, p. 54.

⁵⁹*Ibid.*, 54-55; Scarborough, *Overseer*, pp. 29, 38, 45.

⁶⁰Seventh Census of the United States, 1850, Ascension Parish, Louisiana, Population Schedules; see Ashland Plantation Record Book, 1852; Eighth Census of the United States, 1860, Ascension Parish, Louisiana, Population Schedules.

⁶¹Joseph Karl Menn, *The Large Slaveholders of Louisiana--1860* (New Orleans, 1964), p. 121; Rosella Kenner Brent Papers; Folder 3, Bringier Notes in Trist Wood Papers.

⁶²Scarborough, *Overseer*, pp. 35-36.

⁶³*Ibid*; Notes on G. W. Graves, Rosella Kenner Brent Papers.

⁶⁴Genovese, *Roll, Jordan, Roll*, pp. 365-366; Sitterson, *Sugar Country*, p. 90.

⁶⁵Sitterson, *Sugar Country*, p. 91; Notes on Henry Hammond, Rosella Kenner Brent Papers.

⁶⁶Pierre A. Champomier, *Statement of the Sugar Crop Made In Louisiana* (New Orleans, 1845-1862), 1851, 20; 1852, 14.

⁶⁷Sitterson, "The William J. Minor Plantations," 71; Prichard, "Routine on a Louisiana Sugar Plantation," 177.

Endnotes

[68]Sitterson, "Magnolia Plantation," pp. 202-203; Champomier, *Statement of the Sugar Crop, 1844-1862.*

[69]Champomier, *Statement of the Sugar Crop*, 1856, 13; 1857, 13.

[70]Ashland Plantation Record Book, 1852.

[71]*Ibid.*; Eaton, *History of the Old South*, pp. 357-358; Sitterson, *Sugar Country*, p. 197.

[72]Sitterson, "Magnolia Plantation," 204.

[73]Sitterson, *Sugar Country*, pp. 180, 196-197; Eighth Census of the United States, 1860, Ascension Parish, Louisiana, Population Schedules.

[74]Sitterson, *Sugar Country*, pp. 180-181; Eaton, *Mind of the Old South*, pp. 78-80.

[75]Luraghi, *Plantation South*, pp. 51-53; Eaton, *Mind of the Old South*, p. 76; Eaton, *History of the Old South*, p. 224.

CHAPTER FOUR

[1]Clinton, *Plantation Mistress*, p. 223; Sitterson, *Sugar Country*, pp. 70-71.

[2]Sitterson, *Sugar Country*, p. 71.

[3]Ezra J. Warner and W. Buck Yearns, *Biographical Register of the Confederate Congress* (Baton Rouge, 1975), p. 144.

[4]Davis, *Louisiana*, p. 201; Kemp, *New Orleans*, p. 75.

[5]Folders 1, 4, Bringier Notes in Trist Wood Papers; Christovitch, et al., *The American Section (Faubourg St. Mary)*, p. 148; New Orleans *Daily True Delta*, February 21, 1865; Succession of Duncan Farrar Kenner in New Orleans Public Library (hereafter cited as Succession of Duncan Farrar Kenner, NOPL).

[6]Stock Receipt, Southern Pacific Railroad, Duncan Farrar Kenner Papers, LSU; Miscellaneous Notes, Bringier Notes in Trist Wood Papers; Roseland Plantation Account Book, Kenner Family Papers.

[7]The term "Creole" is often used by writers to refer variously to all-white, all-French, all-Spanish, all-European, mixed French and Spanish, and upper class individuals who settled the region before the Americans obtained possession of the area. Despite the current wide-spread acceptance of this use of the term "Creole," during the antebellum period the term was most often used simply to designate anyone who was a native of Louisiana, regardless of race, ethnic origin, language, or social position. Hence, in this paper the term "*ancienne population*" shall be used to refer to those individuals who were descendants of the European settlers in Louisiana before the American regime. See Joseph G. Tregle, "Early New Orleans Society: A Reappraisal," *Journal of Southern History* XVIII (1952), 20-36; Joseph G. Tregle, "On That Word 'Creole' Again," *Louisiana History*, IX (1968), 193-198.

[8]Tregle, "On That Word 'Creole' Again," 198; Sitterson, *Sugar Country*, p. 69; Luraghi, *Plantation South*, p. 52; Davis, *Louisiana*, p. 229.

[9]Kemp, *New Orleans*, pp. 78-79.

[10]Tregle, "On That Word 'Creole' Again," 198.

[11]Charles L. Dufour, *Ten Flags in the Wind: The Story of Louisiana* (New York, 1967), p. 157.

[12]Sitterson, *Sugar Country*, p. 69; Davis, *Louisiana*, p. 229.

[13] Davis, *Louisiana*, p. 229.

[14] Kane, *Plantation Parade*, pp. 9-10; Sitterson, *Sugar Country*, p. 69.

[15] *Daily Picayune*, June 27, 1909; Grace King, *Creole Families of New Orleans* (New York, 1921), pp. 413-414.

[16] *Daily Picayune*, June 27, 1909; King, *Creole Families*, p. 416; Arthur and Huchet de Kernion, *Old Families*, pp. 426-429; Mark Mayo Boatner, *The Civil War Dictionary*, (New York, 1959), p. 835.

[17] Arthur and Huchet de Kernion, *Old Families*, pp. 426-429; Allan C. Ashcraft, "Richard 'Dick' Taylor," in *The Encyclopedia of Southern History*, pp. 1181-1182.

[18] Arthur and Huchet de Kernion, *Old Families*, pp. 426-429; Folders 3, 4, Bringier Notes, in Trist Wood Papers.

[19] Folders 1, 4, 26, Bringier Notes, in Trist Wood Papers; King, *Creole Families*, pp. 414-416.

[20] Clinton, *Plantation Mistress*, pp. 62-63.

[21] Kane, *Plantation Parade*, p. 190.

[22] Clinton, *Plantation Mistress*, p. 67.

[23] Folder 3, Bringier Papers in Trist Wood Papers; Certificate of Marriage of Duncan Farrar Kenner and Anne Guillelmine Bringier, June 1, 1839, Department of the Archives, Diocese of Baton Rouge, Baton Rouge.

[24] McKee, "Belle Helene Plantation," p. 3; Kane, *Plantation Parade*, p. 193.

[25] Clinton, *Plantation Mistress*, p. 44; Miscellaneous Notes, Bringier Notes in Trist Wood Papers.

[26] Clinton, *Plantation Mistress*, p. 45; Folder 4, Bringier Notes in Trist Wood Papers.

[27] Davis, *Louisiana*, p. 229; Eaton, *Jefferson Davis*, p. 27; Folders 3, 409, Bringier Notes in Trist Wood Papers.

[28] Folders 3, 409, Bringier Notes in Trist Wood Papers; Clinton, *Plantation Mistress*, 45.

[29] Clinton, *Plantation Mistress*, p. 156.

[30] Born in Maryland, Brent served during the war on the staff of Dick Taylor as Chief of Artillery and Ordnance. In 1863 he led the force which captured the Union ironclad *Indianola*. Later he was appointed a Brigadier General of Cavalry. At the time the war ended he was commander of the Southern forces in the front line of the West from Arkansas to the Gulf. After the war he practiced law in Baltimore and later returned to Louisiana, where he and Rosella took over the management of Ashland. See Boatner, *Civil War Dictionary*, p. 83.

[31] Folders 3, 409, Bringier Notes in the Trist Wood Papers.

[32] Clinton, *Plantation Mistress*, pp. 45-46.

[33] Eaton, *History of the Old South*, pp. 396-397; Eaton, *Jefferson Davis*, pp. 28-29.

[34] Clinton, *Plantation Mistress*, p. 18; Eaton, *History of the Old South*, p. 398.

[35] Clinton, *Plantation Mistress*, pp. 47-48.

[36] Quoted in Eaton, *History of the Old South*, pp. 398-399.

[37] Clinton, *Plantation Mistress*, p. 160; Sitterson, *Sugar Country*, p. 86.

Endnotes 303

[38] Sitterson, *Sugar Country*, p. 86; Clinton, *Plantation Mistress*, p. 160; New Orleans *Daily States*, July 4, 1887.

[39] Olive Isabell Arceneaux, "A Brief History of Public Education in Louisiana, 1805-1845" (M.A. thesis, Tulane University, 1938), pp. 77-78; Sitterson, *Sugar Country*, p. 84; Lester J. Cappon, "The Provincial South," *Journal of Southern History* XVI (1950), 19-20.

[40] Arceneaux, "Public Education," 49; Lionel C. Durel, "Creole Civilization in Donaldsonville, 1850, According to 'Le Vigilant'," *Louisiana Historical Quarterly*, XXXI (1948), 985; T. H. Harris, "The Story of Public Education in Louisiana" (M.A. thesis, Louisiana State University, 1924), p. 3; Seebold, *Plantation Homes*, I, 142.

[41] Noble, "Schools of New Orleans," 68; Eaton, *Mind of the Old South*, pp. 291-292.

[42] Edwin L. Jewell, *Crescent City Illustrated: The Commercial, Social, Political, and General History of New Orleans* (New Orleans, 1873), n.p.; Succession of Duncan Farrar Kenner, NOPL; Davis, *Louisiana*, pp. 224-225.

[43] G. U. Patrick, "Literature in the Louisiana Plantation Home" (Ph.D dissertation, Louisiana State University, 1935), pp. 153-158; Eaton, *Mind of the Old South*, pp. 246-247, 296-297; Durel, "Creole Civilization," p. 981.

[44] Sitterson, *Sugar Country*, pp. 78-79.

[45] Marchand, *Flight of a Century*, p. 67; Clinton, *Plantation Mistress*, p. 176.

[46] Sitterson, *Sugar Country*, pp. 76-77.

[47] Dufour, *Ten Flags in the Wind*, p. 151; Davis, *Louisiana*, p. 203.

[48] Marchand, *Flight of a Century*, p. 67; Durel, "Creole Civilization," 988-989; Davis, *Louisiana*, p. 203; Sitterson, *Sugar Country*, p. 110.

[49] Durel, "Creole Civilization," pp. 990-991.

[50] Succession of Duncan Farrar Kenner, NOPL; Sitterson, *Sugar Country*, p. 80; John Hervey, *Racing in America: 1665-1865*, 2 vols. (New York, 1944), II, 195; Folders 1, 3, 4, Bringier Notes in Trist Wood Papers.

[51] Fossier, *Glamour Period*, p. 452; Seebold, *Plantation Homes*, I, 139.

[52] Fossier, *Glamour Period*, pp. 471-472, 479; Sitterson, *Sugar Country*, p. 80-81.

[53] Dufour, *Ten Flags in the Wind*, p. 158; Stuart O. Landry, *History of the Boston Club* (New Orleans, 1953), p. 265.

[54] Landry, *Boston Club*, p. 61; Robert Douthat Meade, *Judah P. Benjamin: Confederate Statesman* (New York, 1943), p. 82; Rightor, *Standard History of New Orleans*, p. 607.

[55] Landry, *Boston Club*, p. 203.

[56] Fossier, *Glamour Period*, p. 464; Sitterson, *Sugar Country*, p. 81.

[57] Fossier, *Glamour Period*, pp. 461, 485.

[58] Jewell, *Cresent City Illustrated*, n.p.; Kemp, *New Orleans*, p. 85-86.

[59] Clinton, *Plantation Mistress*, pp. 176, 177-8.

[60] Louise Butler, "The Louisiana Planter and His Home," *Louisiana Historical Quarterly*, X (1927), 359-360.

[61] Quoted in Sitterson, *Sugar Country*, p. 81; Folder 1, Bringier Notes in Trist Wood Papers; Ruth Irene Jones, "Ante-Bellum Watering Places of Louisiana, Mississippi, Alabama, and Arkansas" (M.A. thesis, University of Texas, 1954), pp. 1-2; Butler, "Louisiana Planter," 360.

[62] Dale A. Somers, *The Rise of Sports in New Orleans, 1850-1900* (Baton Rouge, 1972), p. 9.

[63] *Ibid.*, pp. 24-25.

[64] *Ibid.*, pp. 27-28.

[65] *Ibid.*, p. 24.

[66] Fossier, *Glamour Period*, pp. 265-266; John Hervey, *Racing in America: 1665-1865*, 2 vols. (New York, 1944), I, 19; II, 182.

[67] Hervey, *Racing in America*, I, 182; Kane, *Plantation Parade*, p. 192.

[68] Plan of Ashland; Notes on G. W. Graves, Rosella Kenner Brent Papers.

[69] Quoted in Kane, *Plantation Parade*, p. 192.

[70] Jewell, *Crescent City Illustrated*, n.p.; Hervey, *Racing in America*, II, 195; Notes on Henry Hammond, Rosella Kenner Brent Papers; Somers, *Sports in New Orleans*, pp. 29-30.

[71] Somers, *Sports in New Orleans*, p. 30; Hervey, *Racing in America*, II, 194.

[72] Wilbur J. Cash, *The Mind of the South* (New York, 1941), p. 44; Somers, *Sports in New Orleans*, p. 30.

[73] Landry, *History of the Boston Club*, p. 59; Kane, *Plantation Parade*, p. 193.

[74] Somers, *Sports in New Orleans*, p. 29.

[75] Landry, *History of the Boston Club*, p. 59.

[76] *Ibid.*, pp. 59-60; Hervey, *Racing in America*, II, 195; Kane, *Plantation Parade*, p. 193.

[77] Sitterson, *Sugar Country*, p. 80.

[78] Somers, *Sports in New Orleans*, p. 30.

[79] Sitterson, *Sugar Country*, p. 79; Hervey, *Racing in America*, II, 200, 209, 243, 247, 353; Landry, *History of the Boston Club*, pp. 57-58; Fayette Copeland, *Kendall of the Picayune, Being His Adventures in New Orleans, on the Texan Santa Fe Expedition, in the Mexican War, and in the Colonization of the Texas Frontier* (Norman, Okla., 1943), p. 314; Notes on G. W. Graves, Rosella Kenner Brent Papers; *Daily States*, July 4, 1887.

[80] Hervey, *Racing in America*, II, 239; Somers, *Sports in New Orleans*, p. 33.

[81] Somers, *Sports in New Orleans*, p. 33.

[82] *Ibid.*, p. 34.

CHAPTER FIVE

[1] Eaton, *Jefferson Davis*, pp. 12, 47; Luraghi, *Plantation South*, p. 75.

[2] Luraghi, *Plantation South*, pp. 75, 77; Sitterson, *Sugar Country*, p. 88.

[3] Luraghi, *Plantation South*, pp. 75-76.

Endnotes

[4]Eaton, *Davis*, p. 47.

[5]Bauer, "From Burnt Canes to Budding City," 360; Davis, *Louisiana*, pp. 191-192; Louis Martin Sears, *John Slidell* (Durham, N.C., 1925), pp. 10, 13, 15.

[6]Jefferson Parish Police Jury Minutes, 1835, Jefferson Parish Courthouse, Gretna, La.; Butler, *Unhurried Years*, p. 48.

[7]*Daily Picayune*, September 5, 1844; Perry Howard, *Political Tendencies in Louisiana*, rev. edition (Baton Rouge, 1971), p. 23.

[8]Davis, *Louisiana*, pp. 190, 192; William H. Adams, *The Whig Party of Louisiana* (Lafayette, La., 1973), p. 2.

[9]Arthur Freeman, "Early Career of Pierre Soulé," *Louisiana Historical Quarterly*, XXV (1942), 1083; *Daily Picayune*, June 27, 1909.

[10]Mitchell, "Ante-Bellum Political Career," 9-10.

[11]*Ibid.*, 11; *Journal of the House of Representatives of the State of Louisiana, 1837*, p. 71; *Journal of the House of Representatives . . .1838*, p. 24.

[12]Davis, *Louisiana*, p. 210; Stephen A. Caldwell, *A Banking History of Louisiana* (Baton Rouge, 1935), pp. 38-39, 48, 54.

[13]Quoted in Butler, *The Unhurried Years*, p. 48; Howard, *Political Tendencies*, pp. 44-45, 419, 443; Mitchell, "Ante-Bellum Political Career," 16.

[14]Mitchell, "Ante-Bellum Political Career," 13-14.

[15]*Ibid.*, 15; Sidney A. Marchand, *The Story of Ascension Parish Louisiana* (Donaldsonville, La., 1931), 174; Adams, *Whig Party*, p. 149.

[16]Roger W. Shugg, *Origins of Class Struggle in Louisiana* (1939; reprint ed., Baton Rouge, 1972), pp.121-123.

[17]Howard, *Political Tendencies*, pp. 25, 40; Shugg, *Class Struggle*, p. 123.

[18]Howard, *Political Tendencies*, p. 48; Shugg, *Class Struggle*, p. 124.

[19]James Kimmins Greer, "Louisiana Politics, 1845-1861," *Louisiana Historical Quarterly*, XII (1929), 409; Howard, *Political Tendencies*, p. 45.

[20]Greer, "Louisiana Politics," 410; Adams, *Whig Party*, p. 114.

[21]*Journal of the Proceedings of the Convention of the State of Louisiana, Begun and Held in the City of New Orleans, January 14, 1845* (New Orleans: Besancon, Ferguson, and Co., 1845), p. 57, 115;Mitchell, "Ante-bellum Career," pp. 18-20.

[22]*Daily Picayune*, January 14, 16, 1845; *Official Report of the Debates in the Louisiana Convention* (New Orleans, 1845), p. 5, 127.

[23]*Proceedings and Debates of the Convention of Louisiana Which Assembled at the City of New Orleans, January 14, 1845* (New Orleans: Besancon, Ferguson, and Co., 1845), p. 21; Greer, "Louisiana Politics," 414.

[24]Howard, *Politcal Tendencies*, pp. 48-49; *Report of Debates*, pp. 839-849; Greer, "Louisiana Politics," 414; Mitchell, "Ante-Bellum Political Career," 21.

[25]*Report of Debates*, pp. 848-849; Greer, "Louisiana Politics," 415; Mitchell, "Ante-Bellum Politics," 22-23.

[26]Noble, "Schools of New Orleans," 70; Harris, "Public Education in Louisiana," 4; Davis, *Louisiana*, p. 214.

[27]*Report of Debates*, pp. 903-4.

[28]Arceneaux, "Education in Louisiana," 46.

[29]*Report on Debates*, pp. 906, 910; Shugg, *Origins of Class Struggle*, pp. 123-124; Alden L. Powell, "A History of Louisiana Constitutions," in *Project of a Constitution for the State of Louisiana with Notes and Studies*, prepared by the Louisiana State Law Institute (Baton Rouge, 1954), 326-327; Legislative Council, *History of Government*, p. 48.

[30]Shugg, *Origins of Class Struggle*, p. 122; Howard, *Political Tendencies*, p. 49.

[31]Howard, *Political Tendencies*, pp. 50-51; Greer, "Louisiana Politics," 412; Shugg, *Class Struggle*, pp. 132-133.

[32]Greer, "Louisiana Politics," 413; Mitchell, "Ante-Bellum Political Career," 20.

[33]*Report of Debates*, pp. 506-510, 945; *Journal of Proceedings*, pp. 141-142; Greer, "Louisiana Politics," 413; Mitchell, "Ante-Bellum Political Career," 20-21.

[34]*Report of Debates*, p. 929.

[35]Greer, "Louisiana Politics," 415-416; Adams, *Whig Party of Louisiana*, p. 148.

[36]Adams, *Whig Party of Louisiana*, p. 148; Howard, *Political Tendencies*, p. 48.

[37]Adams, *Whig Party of Louisiana*, p. 149.

CHAPTER SIX

[1]Mitchell, "Ante-Bellum Political Career," 26-28.

[2]Greer, "Louisiana Politics," 417; Davis, *Louisiana*, p. 192.

[3]Quoted in Adams, *Whig Party of Louisiana*, p. 151.

[4]Duncan Farrar Kenner to William Minor, January 22, 1846, Duncan Farrar Kenner Papers, LSU; Howard, *Political Tendencies*, pp. 54-55.

[5]*Daily Picayune*, February 18, 1846; *Baton Rouge Gazette*, February 21, 1846.

[6]T. Harry Williams, *The History of American Wars from 1745 to 1818* (New York, 1981), p. 155; *Louisiana Senate Journal, 1846*, pp. 42, 110-111; *Daily Picayune*, May 2, 1846; Davis, *Louisiana*, p. 196.

[7]Merk, *History of the Westward Movement*, pp. 325-326, 363-364; *Louisiana Senate Journal, 1846*, p. 6; Eaton, *History of the Old South*, p. 331.

[8]*Louisiana Senate Journal, 1847*, pp. 11-14; 54-58; *New Orleans Daily Delta*, February 10, 1847.

[9]*Daily Delta*, January 30, 1847.

[10]Davis, *Louisiana*, p. 217; Mitchell, "Ante-Bellum Political Career," p. 39.

[11]Jewell, *Crescent City Illustrated*, n.p.; Seebold, *Plantation Homes*, II, 87; Freeman, "Early Career of Pierre Soulé," 1086.

[12]Adams, *Whig Party of Louisiana*, p. 160; *Daily Delta*, January 16, 1848.

[13]*Baton Rouge Gazette*, November 20, 1847.

[14]Freeman, "Early Career of Pierre Soulé," 1095.

[15]Mitchell, "Ante-Bellum Political Career," 42.

[16]*New Orleans Weekly Delta*, January 31, 1848.

[17]Freeman, "Early Career of Pierre Soulé," 1094-1096; Mitchell, "Ante-Bellum Political Career," 43-44.

[18]Freeman, "Early Career of Pierre Soulé," 1095-1096; *Daily Delta*, January 25, 1848; Adams, *Whig Party of Louisiana*, p. 161.

[19]Freeman, "Early Career of Pierre Soulé," 1096; Mitchell, "Ante-Bellum Political Career," 46-47.

[20]Freeman, "Early Career of Pierre Soulé," 1096; Adams, *Whig Party of Louisiana*, pp. 161-162.

[21]Quoted in Freeman, "Early Career of Pierre Soulé," 1096.

[22]Quoted in *Daily Delta*, January 26, 1848.

[23]*Baton Rouge Gazette*, July 17, 1852.

[24]Quoted in Mitchell, "Ante-Bellum Political Career," 46.

[25]*Ibid.*, 43.

[26]*Louisiana Senate Journal, 1848*, pp. 38-39; Freeman, "Early Career of Pierre Soulé," 1098-1099.

[27]*Louisiana Senate Journal, 1848*, pp. 38-39.

[28]Freeman, "Early Career of Pierre Soulé," 1100.

[29]Greer, "Louisiana Politics," 557-558.

[30]Mitchell, "Ante-Bellum Political Career," 56; Freeman, "Early Career of Pierre Soulé," 1103.

[31]*Daily Delta*, February 2, 1848.

[32]Greer, "Louisiana Politics," 558; *Daily Picayune*, January 8, 1848.

[33]Freeman, "Early Career of Pierre Soulé," 1104-1105.

[34]Howard, *Political Tendencies*, pp. 56-57; David M. Potter, *The Impending Crisis, 1848-1861* (New York, 1976), pp. 82-83.

[35]Adams, *Whig Party of Louisiana*, p. 184.

[36]Greer, "Louisiana Politics," 564, 566.

[37]*Ibid.*, 566-567; Adams, *Whig Party of Louisiana*, p. 185.

[38]Adams, *Whig Party of Louisiana*, p. 186.

[39]*Ibid.*, pp. 188-189; Mitchell, "Ante-Bellum Political Career," 59, 62; Greer, "Louisiana Politics," 567.

[40]Adams, *Whig Party of Louisiana*, p. 190; Mitchell, "Ante-Bellum Political Career," 59-60.

⁴¹Eaton, *Davis*, p. 90; Davis, *Louisiana*, pp. 192-193.

⁴²Davis, *Louisiana*, p. 192; Jewel, *Crescent City Illustrated*, p. 11; "Kenner's Mission to Europe," *Tyler's Quarterly Historical and Genealogical Magazine*, IV (1923), 27.

⁴³*Daily Picayune*, October 30, 1849; Mitchell, "Ante-Bellum Political Career," 61-62.

⁴⁴Howard, *Political Tendencies*, p. 57; Adams, *Whig Party of Louisiana*, pp. 191-192; Mitchell, "Ante-Bellum Political Career," 64-65.

⁴⁵Mitchell, "Ante-Bellum Political Career," 67.

⁴⁶*Ibid.*, 68.

⁴⁷*Ibid.*, 69.

⁴⁸*Ibid.*, 70-71.

⁴⁹*Weekly Delta*, September 16, 1850; Mitchell, "Ante-Bellum Political Career," 71-72.

⁵⁰Mitchell, "Ante-Bellum Political Career," 73-75.

⁵¹*Ibid.*, 73-76.

⁵²*Ibid.*, 79, 85.

CHAPTER SEVEN

¹Greer, "Louisiana Politics," 587; William H. Adams, "The Louisiana Whigs," *Louisiana History*, XV (1974), 220.

²Adams, "Louisiana Whigs," 220-221; William Cooper, *The South and the Politics of Slavery 1828-1856* (Baton Rouge, 1978), pp. 238, 244.

³Adams, "Louisiana Whigs," 220; Richard H. Haunton, "Nashville Convention," in *Encyclopedia of Southern History*, David C. Roller and Robert W. Twyman, eds., (Baton Rouge, 1979), p. 877.

⁴Quoted in Greer, "Louisiana Politics," 574.

⁵*Ibid.*; Potter, *Impending Crisis*, pp. 94-95; Cooper, *Politics of Slavery*, p. 295.

⁶Quoted in Adams, "Louisiana Whigs," 219.

⁷Cooper, *Politics of Slavery*, pp. 274-276, 284.

⁸*Ibid.*, pp. 283-284; Eaton, *Jefferson Davis*, p. 72.

⁹Quoted in Adams, *Whig Party of Louisiana*, p. 200; Adams, "Louisiana Whigs," 221; Eaton, *Jefferson Davis*, p. 75.

¹⁰Greer, "Louisiana Politics," 575-578; Mitchell, "Ante-Bellum Political Career," 98.

¹¹Greer, "Louisiana Politics," 586-587.

¹²Howard, *Political Tendencies*, p. 69.

¹³*Daily Picayune*, November 2, 1851; Greer, "Louisiana Politics," 587-588; Adams, *Whig Party of Louisiana*, p. 211.

¹⁴Mitchell, "Ante-Bellum Political Career," 86; Adams, *Whig Party of Louisiana*, pp. 217-218; Greer,

Endnotes

"Louisiana Politics," 596; Powell, "History of Louisiana Constitutions," 339.

15Greer, "Louisiana Politics," 596-597.

16Mitchell, "Ante-Bellum Political Career," 91; Adams, *Whig Party of Louisiana*, p. 219; *Journal of the Convention to Form a New Constitution for the State of Louisiana* (New Orleans: Crescent Office, 1852), pp. 3-4.

17*Journal of the Convention*, pp. 3-5.

18Mitchell, "Ante-Bellum Political Career," 92.

19*Baton Rouge Gazette*, July 24, 1852.

20*Ibid.*; Greer, "Louisiana Politics," 598.

21Greer, "Louisiana Politics," 598; Mitchell, "Ante-Bellum Political Career," 95.

22Greer, "Louisiana Politics," 598-599; Pierce Butler, *Judah P. Benjamin* (Philadelphia, 1907), pp. 107, 110.

23Powell, "History of Louisiana Constitutions," 341-343; Greer, "Louisiana Politics," 599.

24Powell, "History of Louisiana Constitutions," 344-345; Greer, "Louisiana Politics," 600.

25Greer, "Louisiana Politics," 600.

26Shugg, *Origins of Class Struggle*, pp. 136-137; Edwin W. Edwards, "The Role of the Governor in Louisiana Politics: An Historical Analysis," *Louisiana History*, XV (1974), 108-109.

27Edwards, "Political Role of the Governor," 109; Ronald J. Millet, "Southwest Louisiana Enters the Railroad Age: 1800-1900," *Louisiana History*, XXIV (1983), 165.

28*Journal of the Convention*, p. 100

29Greer, "Louisiana Politics," 601; Adams, *Whig Party of Louisiana*, p. 221.

30Shugg, *Origins of Class Struggle*, p. 142; Greer, "Louisiana Politics," 603.

31Shugg, *Origins of Class Struggle*, p. 143; Greer, "Louisiana Politics," 603.

32Louisiana Legislative Council, *History and Government of Louisiana*, p. 53.

33Davis, *Louisiana*, p. 210; Millet, "Railroad Age," 165.

34Millet, "Railroad Age," 165; Bauer, "From Burnt Canes to Budding City," 362-363, 379.

35Adams, *Whig Party of Louisiana*, pp. 224-226; *Daily Picayune*, March 17, 1852.

36Cooper, *Politics of Slavery*, pp. 325-327.

37Adams, *Whig Party of Louisiana*, pp. 233-234, 237.

38*Ibid.*, p. 233.

39*Ibid.*, pp. 234, 239.

40*Weekly Delta*, November 24, 1852; *Daily Delta*, August 19, 1852; Mitchell, "Ante-Bellum Political Career," 97; Adams, *Whig Party of Louisiana*, p. 242.

41Adams, "Louisiana Whigs," 233.

⁴²*Ibid.*

⁴³*Ibid.*, 224; Cooper, *Politics of Slavery*, p. 342.

⁴⁴Mitchell, "Ante-Bellum Political Career," 97-98; Adams, *Whig Party of Louisiana*, pp. 257-258.

⁴⁵*New Orleans Bee*, June 10, 1854.

⁴⁶Marius Carriere, "Political Leadership of the Louisiana Know-Nothing Party," *Louisiana History*, XXI (1980), 186; Cooper, *Politics of Slavery*, p. 363.

⁴⁷Stephen B. Oates, *With Malice Towards None: The Life of Abraham Lincoln* (New York, 1977), p. 21; Cooper, *Politics of Slavery*, pp. 363-365; Howard, *Political Tendencies*, p. 75.

⁴⁸James H. Broussard, "Some Determinants of Know-Nothing Electoral Strength in the South, 1856," *Louisiana History*, VII (1966), 6.

⁴⁹*Senate Journal, 1854*, p. 107; Mitchell, "Ante-Bellum Political Career," 98; Cooper, *Politics of Slavery*, p. 353; Greer, "Louisiana Politics," 79-80.

⁵⁰David Potter, *Impending Crisis*, pp. 175-6; Eaton, *Davis*, pp. 87-88.

⁵¹Mitchell, "Ante-Bellum Political Career," 100; Greer, "Louisiana Politics," 91-92; Carrier, "Know-Nothing Party," 186; W. Darrell Overdyke, "History of the American Party in Louisiana," *Louisiana Historical Quarterly*, XVI (1933), 268.

⁵²Howard, *Political Tendencies*, p. 78; Greer, "Louisiana Politics," 95; Overdyke, "American Party in Louisiana," 275.

⁵³Overdyke, "American Party in Louisiana," 276; Greer, "Louisiana Politics," 95-96.

⁵⁴Overdyke, "American Party in Louisiana," 412; Mitchell, "Ante-Bellum Political Career," 101.

⁵⁵Quoted in Mitchell, "Ante-Bellum Political Career," 102-103.

⁵⁶*Ibid.*, 103.

⁵⁷Cooper, *Politics of Slavery*, pp. 366-367; Broussard, "Know-Nothing Electoral Strength," 15.

⁵⁸Greer, "Louisiana Politics," 105; Mitchell, "Ante-Bellum Political Career," 105.

⁵⁹Mitchell, "Ante-Bellum Political Career," 105; Baton Rouge *Weekly Advocate*, August 9, 1856.

⁶⁰Mitchell, "Ante-Bellum Political Career," 106.

⁶¹*Daily Delta*, September 28, 1856; Greer, "Louisiana Politics," 109; Overdyke, "American Party in Louisiana," 425.

⁶²*Weekly Advocate*, November 1, 1856.

⁶³*Ibid.*

⁶⁴*Ibid.*

⁶⁵Broussard, "Know-Nothing Strength in the South," 15-16.

⁶⁶Quoted in Avery O. Craven, *The Growth of Southern Nationalism, 1848-1861* (Baton Rouge, 1953), p. 246.

⁶⁷Cooper, *Politics of Slavery*, p. 370.

Endnotes

[68]Shugg, *Class Struggle in Louisiana*, pp. 150-151, 154; Mary Lilla McLure, "The Election of 1860 in Louisiana," *Louisiana Historical Quarterly*, IX (1926), 614.

[69]McLure, "Election of 1860," 614.

[70]Shugg, *Class Struggle in Louisiana*, p. 159.

[71]Mitchell, "Ante-Bellum Political Career," 109; Charles P. Roland, "Louisiana and Secession," *Louisiana History*, XIX (1978), 391-392.

[72]McLure, "Elections of 1860," 635, 638; Howard, *Political Tendencies*, p. 79.

CHAPTER EIGHT

[1]Quoted in Davis, *Louisiana*, p. 244.

[2]*Ibid*.

[3]McLure, "The Elections of 1860," 640-641.

[4]Eaton, *History of the Old South*, pp. 492-493.

[5]*Ibid.*, p. 494; Greer, "Louisiana Politics," 474.

[6]Eaton, *History of the Old South*, p. 494.

[7]*Ibid*.

[8]Quoted in Davis, *Louisiana*, p. 245; McLure, "Elections of 1860," 667.

[9]Howard, *Political Tendencies*, p. 91.

[10]McLure, "Elections of 1860," 667; Jefferson Davis Bragg, *Louisiana in the Confederacy* (Baton Rouge, 1941), p. 19; Davis, *Louisiana*, p. 245.

[11]William J. Minor to Mrs. William J. Minor, November 1, 1856, William J. Minor and Family Papers; Greer, "Louisiana Politics," 481; Sitterson, *Sugar Country*, p. 207.

[12]Roland, "Louisiana and Secession," 392; Bragg, *Louisiana in the Confederacy*, pp. 19-20.

[13]Roland, "Louisiana and Secession," p. 393; Howard, *Political Tendencies*, p. 95; Shugg, *Origins of Class Struggle*, p. 161.

[14]Shugg, *Origins of Class Struggle*, p. 162; Bragg, *Louisiana in the Confederacy*, p. 26.

[15]*Daily Picayune*, December 8, 1860; Bragg, *Louisiana in the Confederacy*, pp. 24, 26; Eaton, *History of the Old South*, pp. 508-509.

[16]The Ascension Parish totals were:

	votes
*Robert C. Martin, Cooperationist	458
*Thomas Cottman, Cooperationist	422
*Adolphe Verret, Cooperationist	370
*Edward Duffel, Cooperationist	348
E. J. McCall, Secessionist	261
L. D. Nichols, Secessionist	258
D. F. Kenner, Secessionist	234
R. L. Gibson, Secessionist	174

(* indicates candidates who won seats in the convention)

Source: Charles B. Dew, "The Long Lost Returns: The Candidates and Their Totals in Louisiana's Secession Election," *Louisiana History*, VIII (1969), 358-359.

[17] Jewell, *Crescent City Illustrated*, n.p.; Dew, "The Long Lost Returns," p. 358; Howard, *Political Tendencies*, p. 98.

[18] Quoted in Shrugg, *Origins of Class Struggle*, p. 167.

[19] Roland, "Louisiana and Secession," 397; Van D. Odom, "The Political Career of Thomas Overton Moore, Secession Governor of Louisiana," *Louisiana Historical Quarterly*, XXVI (1943), 999.

[20] Eaton, *History of the Old South*, p. 509; Roland, *Louisiana Sugar Plantations*, pp. 21-22.

[21] William H. Russell, *My Diary, North and South* (London, 1863), p. 260.

[22] *Daily Picayune*, January 31, 1861; Odom, "Career of Thomas Overton Moore," 1001-1002; Mitchell, "Ante-Bellum Political Career," 110; Charles L. Dufour, *The Night the War Was Lost* (Garden City, N.Y., 1960), p. 27.

[23] Charles Roland, *The Confederacy* (Chicago, 1960), pp. 16-17.

[24] *Ibid.*, p. 18; Allan Nevins, *Ordeal of the Union: Selected Chapters*, E. B. Long, intro. and comp. (New York, 1973), p. 149.

[25] Eaton, *Davis*, p. 125.

[26] *Ibid.*; Roland, *Confederacy*, pp. 20-21.

[27] Jefferson Davis, *The Rise and Fall of the Confederate Government*, 2 vols. (1881; reprint ed., New York, 1958), I, 238-239.

[28] Roland, *Confederacy*, p. 21.

[29] Duncan Farrar Kenner to A. B. Roman, February 9, 1861, Jean Ursin La Villebeuvre and Family Papers, Louisiana State University Archives, Baton Rouge.

[30] Roland, *Confederacy*, pp. 25-26; Bruce Catton, *The Coming Fury* (Garden City, N.Y., 1961), 208; Warner and Yearns, *Register of the Confederate Nation: 1861-1865* (New York, 1979), p. 64.

[31] Kenner to Roman, February 9, 1861.

[32] Bragg, *Louisiana in the Confederacy*, pp. 44-45.

[33] The Provisional Congress had five sessions: February 4, 1861, to March 16, 1861; April 29, 1861, to May 21, 1861 (at Montgomery) and July 20, 1861, to August 31, 1861; September 3, 1861; November 18, 1861, to February 17, 1862 (at Richmond).

[34] Wilfred Buck Yearns, *The Confederate Congress* (Athens, Ga., 1960), pp. 12-13; Warner and Yearns, *Biographical Register*, p. xvii; Thomas, *Confederate Nation*, p. 100.

[35] Notes on Henry Hammond, Rosella Kenner Brent Papers.

[36] Besides serving as attorney general, Benjamin also held the positions of secretary of war (September, 1861, to March, 1862) and secretary of state (March, 1862, until the end of the Confederacy). Thomas, *Confederate Nation*, p. 78; Richmond *Times-Dispatch*, May 26, 1912; Thomas Donaldson, Notes of a Conversation with Duncan Farrar Kenner, October 19, 1882, Duncan Farrar Kenner Collection, Manuscripts Division, Library of Congress, Washington, D.C. (hereafter cited as Donaldson Notes and Duncan Farrar Kenner Collection, LC); Meade, *Judah P. Benjamin*, 191.

[37] *Times-Dispatch*, May 26, 1912.

Endnotes

[38] E. Merton Coulter, *The Confederate States of America, 1861-1865* (Baton Rouge, 1950), pp. 117, 139-140.

[39] *Journal of the Congress of the Confederate States of America, 1861-1865*, 7 vols. (1905; reprint ed., New York, 1968), V, 99-102.

[40] Warner and Yearns, *Biographical Register*, pp. 144, 280; Coulter, *Confederate States of America*, p. 134.

[41] Yearns, *Confederate Congress*, p. 42.

[42] William J. Minor to T. J. Wells, November 19, 1861; January 1, 1862, William J. Minor and Family Papers.

[43] Warner and Yearns, *Biographical Register*, pp. 216, 230. The other members of the Louisiana Delegation to the First Congress were Charles J. Villere, John Perkins, Jr., Charles M. Conrad, Henry Marshall, and Lucius J. Dupre.

[44] Warner and Yearns, *Biographical Register*, p. 144; Jewell, *Crescent City Illustrated*, n.p.; Henry Putney Beers, *Guide to the Archives of the Government of the Confederate States of America* (Washington, 1968), pp. 23-25.

[45] Bragg, *Louisiana in the Confederacy*, pp. 267-268.

[46] *Journal of the Congress of the Confederate States*, V, 33, 45; United States War Department, *The War of the Rebellion: A Compilation of the Official Records of the Union and Confederate Armies*, 128 vols. (Washington, D.C., 1880-1901), Series 1, XXI, 1099 (hereafter cited as *Official Records*).

[47] J. G. Randall and David Donald, *The Civil War and Reconstruction*, 2nd ed., (Lexington, Mass., 1969), p. 256.

[48] *Ibid.*, p. 258; Coulter, *Confederate States of America*, p. 182; *Journal of the Congress of the Confederate States*, VI, 231.

[49] Randall and Donald, *Civil War*, pp. 259-260; Craig A. Bauer, "The Last Effort: The Secret Mission of the Confederate Diplomat, Duncan F. Kenner," *Louisiana History*, XXII (1981), 78; *Journal of the Congress of the Confederate States*, VI, 33-34.

[50] Quoted in Randall and Donald, *Civil War*, pp. 260.

[51] *Ibid.*; Margaret G. Myers, *A Financial History of the United States* (New York, 1970), pp. 169-170.

[52] William Kauffman Scarborough, ed., *The Diary of Edmund Ruffin*, vol. 2, *The Years of Hope: April, 1861-June, 1863* (Baton Rouge, 1976), p. 581

[53] Quoted in Coulter, *Confederate States of America*, p. 140.

[54] *Southern Historical Papers*, XLIV (1923), 51, 78, 91; *Journal of the Congress of the Confederate States*, VI, 121, 138, 274.

[55] Quoted in Coulter, *Confederate States of America*, p. 141.

[56] Eaton, *Davis*, p. 215.

[57] Roland, *Confederacy*, p. 61; *Journal of the Congress of the Confederate States*, V, 77, 419, 518; VI, 303; "Kenner's Mission to Europe," *Tyler's Quarterly Historical and Genealogical Magazine*, IV (1923), 24; Coulter, *Confederate States of America*, pp. 145-147.

[58] Quoted in Coulter, *Confederate States of America*, pp. 144.

⁵⁹Coulter, *Confederate States of America*, pp. 143-144; Richard E. Beringer, Herman Hattaway, Archer Jones, and William N. Still, Jr., *Why the South Lost the War* (Athens, Ga., 1983), p. 207.

⁶⁰Coulter, *Confederate States of America*, p. 145.

⁶¹*Ibid.*, p. 134; Warner and Yearns, *Biographical Register*, p. xx.

⁶²Warner and Yearns, *Biographical Register*, pp. xx-xxi; Beringer, "Confederate Congress," 531, 535; William K. Scarborough to the author, March 18, 1988.

⁶³Warner and Yearns, *Biographical Register*, p. 267; Coulter, *Confederate States of America*, pp. 134-135.

CHAPTER NINE

¹Walter Prichard, "The Effects of the Civil War on the Louisiana Sugar Industry," *Journal of Southern History*, V (1939), 319; Sitterson, *Sugar Country*, p. 207.

²Sitterson, *Sugar Country*, pp. 207-208.

³*Ibid.*, p. 205; Russell, *My Diary North and South*, p. 260.

⁴Kenner Family Papers; Roland, *Louisiana Sugar Plantations*, p. 26.

⁵Roland, *Louisiana Sugar Plantations*, pp. 30-31; Third Special Agency, Record Group 366, Judicial and Fiscal Branch, Civil Archives Division, National Archives, Washington, D.C. (hereafter cited as Record Group 366, NA); Russell, *My Diary North And South*, p. 265.

⁶Roland, *Louisiana Sugar Plantations*, pp. 38-40; Russell, *My Diary North and South*, p. 279.

⁷*Daily Delta*, January 2, 1861; Roland, *Louisiana Sugar Plantations*, pp. 39-40.

⁸Roland, *Louisiana Sugar Plantations*, p. 42; Dufour, *The Night the War Was Lost*, pp. 45, 63.

⁹John D. Winters, *The Civil War in Louisiana* (Baton Rouge, 1963), p. 71; see Memoir of Kenner's Daughter, Mrs. Rosella Kenner Brent, in Seebold, *Plantation Homes*, I, 142.

¹⁰Seebold, *Plantation Homes*, I, 142; Dufour, *Night the War Was Lost*, p. 212.

¹¹Seebold, *Plantation Homes*, I, 142.

¹²*Ibid.*

¹³*Ibid.*, 141-142.

¹⁴*Ibid.*, 144.

¹⁵*Ibid.*; Permit for Mr. Kenner to Visit New Orleans, War Department Collections of Confederate Records, Record Group 109, National Archives, Washinton D.C. (hereafter cited as Record Group 109, NA).

¹⁶Roland, *Louisiana Sugar Plantations*, p. 50; Winters, *Civil War in Louisiana*, pp. 103-104; Seebold, *Plantation Homes*, I, 142.

¹⁷Seebold, *Plantation Homes*, I, 142; Recollections of Rosella Kenner Brent, Typescript in Rosella Kenner Brent Papers.

¹⁸Recollections, Rosella Kenner Brent Papers.

Endnotes 315

[19]*Ibid.*

[20]*Ibid.*

[21]*Ibid.*

[22]*Ibid.*

[23]Quoted in Roland, *Louisiana Sugar Plantations*, p. 72; Seebold, *Plantation Homes*, Vol. 1, 147; Michael P. Musick, Military Archives Division, National Archives and Records Service, Washinton D.C., to the author, August 12, 1980.

[24]Seebold, *Plantation Homes*, I, 146.

[25]*Ibid.*

[26]*Ibid.*, I, 147; Recollections, Rosella Kenner Brent Papers.

[27]Seebold, *Plantation Homes*, I, 147; Recollections, Rosella Kenner Brent Papers; Roland, *Louisiana Sugar Plantations*, p. 70.

[28]Seebold, *Plantation Homes*, I, 147-148; Recollections, Rosella Kenner Brent Papers.

[29]Seebold, *Plantation Homes*, I, 148.

[30]*Ibid.*

[31]*Ibid.*, I, 149; Recollections, Rosella Kenner Brent Papers.

[32]Seebold, *Plantation Homes*, I, 148; Recollections, Rosella Kenner Brent Papers.

[33]Recollections, Rosella Kenner Brent Papers.

[34]Seebold, *Plantation Homes*, I, 150.

[35]Recollections, Rosella Kenner Brent Papers; Seebold, *Plantation Homes*, I, 150.

[36]Recollections, Rosella Kenner Brent Papers; Seebold, *Plantation Homes*, I, 151.

[37]Seebold, *Plantation Homes*, I, 151.

[38]Bragg, *Louisiana in the Confederacy*, p. 148; Edwin C. Bearss, ed., *A Louisiana Confederate: Diary of Felix Pierre Poché* (Natchitoches, La., 1972), pp. 33, 49; Folder 2, Bringier Notes in Trist Wood Papers.

[39]Bearss, ed., *A Louisiana Confederate*, p. 49; *Progress*, November 11, 1938.

[40]Sitterson, *Sugar Country*, p. 214.

[41]Quoted in Roland, *Louisiana Sugar Plantations*, p. 51.

[42]Bauer, "From Burnt Canes to Budding City," 365.

[43]Marchand, *Story of Ascension Parish*, pp. 63, 66, 70, 71; Folder 3, Bringier Notes in Trist Wood Papers.

[44]Roland, *Louisiana Sugar Plantations*, pp. 72-73; Davis, *Louisiana*, p. 263.

[45]Folder 3, Bringier Notes in Trist Wood Papers; Roland, *Louisiana Sugar Plantations*, pp. 73; *Daily True Delta*, February 21, 1865.

[46]Roland, *Louisiana Sugar Plantations*, pp. 73-74; Sitterson, *Sugar Country*, p. 226.

[47] Joe Gray Taylor, *Louisiana Reconstructed: 1863-1877* (Baton Rouge, 1974), pp. 32, 36.

[48] *Ibid.*, p. 36; Plantation Rental Log, Record Group 366, NA; Joseph G. Tregle, Jr., "Thomas J. Durant, Utopian Socialism, and the Failure of Presidential Reconstruction in Louisiana," *Journal of Southern History*, XLV (1979), 497.

[49] Quoted in Sitterson, *Sugar Country*, p. 220.

[50] *Ibid.*, p. 221; Roland, *Louisiana Sugar Plantations*, pp. 82, 88.

[51] Little is known of Russell. Because of the way he and Graves worked on both of Kenner's Ascension Parish plantations, it is likely that he was either a close family friend or perhaps a partner, possibly from the North, who was brought in to help supply Graves with needed capital. The practice of bringing in Northern partners was not uncommon among sugar planters in the Union-occupied area of Southeast Louisiana. See Roland, *Louisiana Sugar Plantations*, pp. 89-90.

[52] In 1864 Bowden was leased to Graves for a $20,000 bond and a rental rate of ten dollars per bale of "400th" cotton and four dollars per hogshead of sugar; Ashland was rented to Russell for $15,000 dollars and the same rent as Bowden. For an undetermined reason, records for 1865 list Graves and Russell as having switched positions in the management of Kenner's two estates, with Graves being listed as the renter of Ashland and Russell of Bowden. The bond requirements for both estates were $5,000 apiece and the rent for both properties was simply listed as "one eighth products." See Plantation Rental Log; *Daily True Delta*, August 19, 1865.

[53] Sitterson, *Sugar Country*, pp. 216-217.

[54] Plantation Registry, April 17, June 14, 1865, Record Group 366, NA.

[55] Joseph Diggs to probably Benjamin F. Flanders, October 26, 1864, Record of Reports, Plantation Bureau, Record Group 366, NA.

[56] Joseph Diggs to Captain S. W. Cozzens, July 29, 1864, Record of Reports.

[57] Sitterson, *Sugar Country*, pp. 221-222; Roland, *Louisiana Plantations*, p. 115.

[58] Notes on Henry Hammond, Rosella Kenner Brent Papers.

[59] Duncan Farrar Kenner, John Pettus, A. G. Brown, W. P. Harris, and E. Barksdale to Jefferson Davis, June 10, 1863, *Official Records*, Series 1, LII, 498.

[60] Jefferson Davis to Kenner, Pettus, Brown, Harris, and Barksdale, *Official Records*, Series 1, LII, 498.

[61] Duncan Farrar Kenner to Governor Thomas O. Moore, September 25, 1864, Thomas Moore Papers, Louisiana State University Archives, Baton Rouge, La.; Herman Hattaway and Archer Jones, *How the North Won: A Military History of the Civil War* (Urbana, Ill., 1983), p. 623.

[62] Hattaway and Jones, *How the North Won*, p. 641.

[63] Arthur W. Bergeron, "General Richard Taylor as a Military Commander," *Louisiana History*, XXIII (1982), p. 46.

[64] Quoted by Richard Taylor in a communication to Edmund Kirby Smith, April 3, 1864, in *Official Records*, Series 1, XXXIV, 519.

[65] *Ibid.*

[66] Robert L. Kerby, *Kirby Smith's Confederacy: The Trans-Mississippi South, 1863-1865* (New York, 1972), 320-321; Bergeron, "Taylor as a Military Commander," 47.

Endnotes 317

⁶⁷Duncan Farrar Kenner to Judah P. Benjamin, July 31, 1864, Duncan Farrar Kenner Papers, HNOC. Emphasis added by Kenner.

⁶⁸Bergeron, "General Richard Taylor," 47.

CHAPTER TEN

¹Bauer, "The Last Effort," 67.

²*Ibid.*, 68.

³*Ibid.*; James Morton Callahan, *The Diplomatic History of the Southern Confederacy* (Baltimore, 1901), p. 240; Norman A. Graebner, "Northern Diplomacy and European Neutrality," in *Why the North Won the Civil War*, David Donald, ed. (New York, 1962), pp. 55-78.

⁴See Kinley J. Brauer, "The Slavery Problem in the Diplomacy of the American Civil War," *Pacific Historical Review*, XLVI (1963), 439-469; and Joseph M. Hernon, Jr., "British Sympathies in the American Civil War: A Reconsideration," *Journal of Southern History*, XXIII (1967), 356-367.

⁵United States War Department, *Official Records of the Union and Confederate Navies in the War of the Rebellion*, Series 2, III, 214-216, (hereafter cited as *O.R.N.*); Brauer, "Slavery Problem in the Diplomacy," 441, 446.

⁶Quoted in Meade, *Judah P. Benjamin*, p. 263.

⁷John Slidell to Robert M. T. Hunter, February 11, 1862, *O.R.N.*, Series 2, III, 336; Frank Lawrence Owsley, *King Cotton Diplomacy: Foreign Relations of the Confederate States of America*, 2nd ed., Harriet C. Owsley, ed. (Chicago, 1959), p. 530.

⁸Quoted in Brauer, "Slavery Problems in Diplomacy," 448.

⁹*Ibid.*, 455-456.

¹⁰Owsley, *King Cotton Diplomacy*, p. 531.

¹¹Callahan, *Diplomatic History*, p. 246.

¹²Donaldson Notes, p. 4.

¹³*Ibid.*; Meade, *Judah P. Benjamin*, p. 264.

¹⁴Callahan, *Diplomatic History*, pp. 246-247; Robert F. Durden, *The Gray and the Black: The Confederate Debate on Emmancipation* (Baton Rouge, 1972), p. 3.

¹⁵Callahan, *Diplomatic History*, pp. 246-247; Durden, *Gray and the Black*, pp. 29-30, 74-75.

¹⁶Durden, *Gray and the Black*, pp. 68-69, 101-103.

¹⁷Durden, *Gray and the Black*, pp. 101, 143; Callahan, *Diplomatic History*, p. 248; Donaldson Notes, p. 4; Judah P. Benjamin to John Slidell, and Benjamin to James Mason, December 27, 1864, *O.R.N.*, Series 2, III, 1253-1256.

¹⁸Callahan, *Diplomatic History*, pp. 246-247.

¹⁹Donaldson Notes, p. 4; J. L. Brent Manuscript Notes in Duncan Farrar Kenner File, Special Collections Division, Tulane University Library, New Orleans.

²⁰Donaldson Notes, p. 5.

[21] Callahan, *Diplomatic History*, p. 249.

[22] John Bigelow, "The Confederate Diplomatists and Their Shirt of Nessus: A Chapter of Secret History," *Century Magazine* (1891), 126; Brent Notes, p. 4.

[23] Benjamin to Slidell and Benjamin to Mason, December 27, 1864, *O.R.N.*, Series 2, III, 1253-1256.

[24] *Ibid*.

[25] *Ibid*.

[26] Coulter, *Confederate States of America*, p. 169.

[27] Thomas, *Confederate Nation*, p. 286; B. S. Baruc to Trenholm, December 9, 1864; Trenholm to Baruc, December 13, 1864; Trenholm to Davis, January 3, 1865, George A. Trenholm Papers, Library of Congress, Washington, D.C.

[28] Trenholm to Davis, January 3, 1865; Trenholm to Kenner, January 4, 1865, Trenholm Papers.

[29] Trenholm to Frazier and Company, January 11, 1865; Trenholm to John B. LaFitte, January 9, 1865, Trenholm Papers.

[30] Trenholm to John B. LaFitte, January 9, 1865, Trenholm Papers; Donaldson Notes, p. 6.

[31] Donaldson Notes, p. 7.

[32] *Ibid*.

[33] *Ibid*.; Bigelow, "Confederate Diplomatists," 126.

[34] John B. Jones, *A Rebel War Clerk's Diary*, Earl Schenck Miers, cond., annot. and ed. (New York, 1958), pp. 393-395; Donaldson Notes, p. 8.

[35] Donaldson Notes, p. 9.

[36] *Ibid*., p. 10.

[37] *Ibid*., p. 13.

[38] *Ibid*., pp. 15-16.

[39] *Ibid*., p. 17.

[40] *Ibid*., pp. 17-18.

[41] *Ibid*., p. 18.

[42] *Ibid*., pp. 18-19.

[43] *Ibid*., pp. 19-20.

[44] *Ibid*., p. 20; Landry, *History of the Boston Club*, p. 79.

[45] Donaldson Notes, p. 20.

[46] *Ibid*., p. 21.

[47] *Ibid*., p. 22; W. W. Henry Typescript prepared for J. M. Callahan, in Duncan Farrar Kenner Collection, LC, p. 3.

[48] Donaldson Notes, p. 22.

[49] *Ibid*.

Endnotes 319

[50]*Ibid.*, p. 22-23; Henry Typescript, p. 3.

[51]Donaldson Notes, p. 23.

[52]*Ibid.*; Warner and Yearns, *Biographical Register of the Confederate Congress*, pp. 86-87.

[53]Bigelow, "Confederate Diplomatists," 126; Henry Typescript, p. 3.

[54]Donaldson Notes, p. 26-27.

[55]*Ibid.*; Warner and Yearns, *Biographical Register of the Confederate Congress*, pp. 86-87.

[56]*Ibid.*; Grady Daniel Price, "The Secret Mission of Duncan F. Kenner, Confederate Minister Plenipotentiary to Europe in 1865" (M.A. thesis, Tulane University, 1929), appendix.

[57]Donaldson Notes, p. 24; Henry Typescript, p. 3.

[58]Donaldson Notes, p. 25.

[59]Owsley, *King Cotton Diplomacy*, p. 536.

[60]Donaldson Notes, p. 25; Henry Typescript, p. 4; Callahan, *Diplomatic History*, pp. 264-265.

[61]Donaldson Notes, p. 25; Henry Typescript, p. 4.

[62]*Ibid.*; Benjamin to John Slidell, December 27, 1864, James M. Mason Papers, Library of Congress, Washington, D.C.

[63]Owsley, *King Cotton Diplomacy*, p. 537; Price, "Secret Mission," 31.

[64]Price, "Secret Mission," 31; Callahan, *Diplomatic History*, pp. 265-266.

[65]Coulter, *Confederate States of America*, p. 190; Donaldson Notes, 25.

[66]Owsley, *King Cotton Diplomacy*, p. 537; Ephraim Douglas Adams, *Great Britain and the American Civil War*, 2 vols. (New York, 1924), I, 249.

[67]Adams, *Great Britain and the American Civil War*, pp. 249-250; Mason to Slidell, March 4, 1865; Slidell to Mason, March 5, 6, 1865, James M. Mason Papers; Owsley, *King Cotton Diplomacy*, p. 538.

[68]Slidell to Mason, March 6, 1865; Mason to Benjamin, March 31, 1865, James M. Mason Papers; Owsley, *King Cotton Diplomacy*, p. 538; Lynn M. Case and Warren F. Spencer, *The United States and France: Civil War Diplomacy* (Philadelphia, 1970), p. 565.

[69]George A. Trenholm to Duncan Farrar Kenner, January 4, 1865, Trenholm Papers; Callahan, *Diplomatic History*, p. 266.

[70]Coulter, *The Confederate States of America*, p. 169; Trenholm to Kenner, January 4, 1865, Trenholm Papers.

[71]Baruc to Trenholm, December 9, 1864; Baruc to Kenner, March 17, 1865; Kenner to Baruc, March 18, 1865, Trenholm Papers.

[72]Owsley, *King Cotton Diplomacy*, p. 538; Meade, *Judah P. Benjamin*, p. 310.

[73]*Ibid.*; Randall and Donald, *The Civil War*, p. 361.

[74]The Hampton Roads Conference was held on February 3, 1865. Attending the meeting were President Lincoln and Secretary Seward on one side and a Confederate commission of Vice-President Stephens, former Associate Justice of the United States Supreme Court John A. Campbell, and Rebel Senator R. M. T. Hunter on the other side. The conference was an attempt to arrange an armistice between the

warring sides. Nothing ever resulted from the meeting. Roland, *The Confederacy*, pp. 181-182.

[75] Mason to Benjamin, Number 20, March 31, 1865, *O.R.N.*, Series 2, III, 1276.

[76] *Ibid.*

[77] *Ibid.*

[78] *Ibid.*; Owsley, *King Cotton Diplomacy*, pp. 539-540.

[79] Owsley, *King Cotton Diplomacy*, p. 540.

[80] Mason to Benjamin, Number 20, March 31, 1865, James M. Mason Papers; *O.R.N.*, Series 2, III, 1276.

[81] *Ibid.*

[82] *Ibid.*, 1276-1277.

[83] An ironic coincidence of Kenner's appearance and oath-taking at the United States Legation in Paris involved the American diplomat, John Bigelow, who gave the oath to Kenner. Though Kenner and Bigelow were never friends, more than twenty years after the two men met in Paris, members of the Kenner and Bigelow families again met–but under far different circumstances. In 1888, Kenner's nephew, Butler Kenner Harding married Aussie Bigelow, the daughter of the American diplomat. See Kenner Family Papers.

[84] Bigelow, "The Confederate Diplomatists," 125; Duncan Farrar Kenner, "Oath of allegiance and request for pardon, June 1865," Diplomatic Branch, Civil Records Division, Record Group 84, National Archives, Washington, D.C. (hereafter cited as Record Group 84, NA); Donaldson Notes, p. 27.

[85] Graebner, "Northern Diplomacy," 66; Owsley, *King Cotton Diplomacy*, p. 549.

[86] Eaton, *Jefferson Davis*, p. 172; Coulter, *Confederate States of America*, p. 189; Meade, *Judah P. Benjamin*, p. 262; Bauer, "The Last Effort," 94-95.

CHAPTER ELEVEN

[1] John Samuel Ezell, *The South Since 1865* (New York, 1963), pp. 34-35.

[2] *Ibid.*; John Hope Franklin, *Reconstruction After the Civil War* (Chicago, 1961), p. 27.

[3] *Ibid.*, pp. 29-30.

[4] Quoted in Ezell, *South Since 1865*, p. 38.

[5] John Bigelow to William H. Seward, June 21, 1865 and Enclosure No. 2, Memorandum of facts in the case of D. F. Kenner . . . , Record Group 84, NA.

[6] Duncan Farrar Kenner to President Andrew Johnson, August 24, 1865, Records of the Adjutant General's Office, Record Group 94, National Archives, Washington, D.C. (hereafter cited as Record Group 94, NA); William Seward to Thomas Cottman, June 8, 1865, Duncan Farrar Kenner Papers, Archives and Records Collection, Louisiana State Museum, New Orleans (hereafter cited as Duncan Farrar Kenner Papers, LSM); Taylor, *Louisiana Reconstructed*, p. 22; Mark W. Summers, "The Moderates Last Chance: The Election of 1865," *Louisiana History,* XXIV (1983), 51.

[7] Taylor, *Louisiana Reconstructed*, p. 28; Shugg, *Origins of Class Struggle*, p. 211; Recommendation for Executive Clemency signed by J. Madison Wells, L. E. Forestall, J. Burnside, Wm. G. Fike, and Ths. Cottman, n.d., and Duncan Farrar Kenner to Robert Schenck, September 14, 1865, Record Group 94, NA.

Endnotes 321

[8] Duncan Farrar Kenner to Robert Schenck, September 14, 1865 and Thomas Cottman to Robert Schenck, September 13, 1865, Record Group 94, NA; Boatner, *Civil War Dictionary*, p. 725.

[9] Governor J. Madison Wells to President Andrew Johnson, September 23, 1865, Record Group 94, NA; Address of John Dymond, January 14, 1909, Trist Wood Papers.

[10] Duncan Farrar Kenner Amnesty Papers, October 4, 1865, and Duncan Farrar Kenner to William H. Seward, October 5, 1865, Duncan Farrar Kenner Papers, LSM; Acting Attorney General J. Hubley Ashton to William H. Seward, October 4, 1865, Record Group 59, National Archives, Washington, D.C.

[11] Quoted in Ezell, *South Since 1865*, p. 30; Winters, *Civil War in Louisiana*, p. 428; Sitterson, *Sugar Country*, p. 226.

[12] Sitterson, *Sugar Country*, pp. 231-232.

[13] Notes on Henry Hammond, Rosella Kenner Brent Papers.

[14] *New Orleans Times*, October 21, 1865; C. A. Werdtlig to General E. R. S. Canby, November 7, 1865, Record Group 109, NA; William Fowlin to Thomas W. Conway, October 5, 1865, Brent Collection, Archives and Manuscript Collection, Louisiana State Museum, New Orleans (hereafter cited as Brent Collection, LSM); E. Merton Coulter, *The South During Reconstruction, 1865-1877* (Baton Rouge, 1947), p. 73.

[15] Sitterson, *Sugar Country*, pp. 233, 301-302; Roland, *Louisiana Sugar Plantations*, p. 139; John Alfred Heitman, *The Modernization of the Louisiana Sugar Industry, 1830-1910* (Baton Rouge, 1987), p. 49; Taylor, *Louisiana Reconstructed*, p. 365.

[16] Ruhamah Riske Kenner to Philip Minor Kenner, August 23, 1868, Kenner Family Papers.

[17] Ruhamah Riske Kenner was the widow of Duncan's brother, William Butler, who had died in the yellow fever epidemic of 1853.

[18] Ruhamah Riske Kenner to Philip Minor Kenner, August 23, 1868, Kenner Family Papers.

[19] Kenner's efforts to assist his nephew's family were not wasted. The situation at Roseland improved to such a degree that in February, 1878, the family was able to acquire Kenner's half-interest in the property and to assume ownership of the plantation. See C. K. Harding to P. M. Kenner, 20th day of an unknown month, 1871, and Roseland Plantation Account Book, Kenner Family Papers; Folder 246, Trist Wood Papers; Claim of Title of Roseland Plantation in the possession of E. Schmidt.

[20] Act of Sale of the Hermitage, February 12, 1869, Trist Wood Papers.

[21] Though they were the majority purchasers of the Melpomene property, Nanine and Duncan were joined in the purchase of the estate by several other relatives, including Nanine's sisters, Octavie Thomas (the wife of C.S.A. Brigadier General and U.S. Minister to Venezuela Allen Thomas), Myrthe Taylor (the wife of C.S.A. General Richard Taylor), and her daughter Betty Taylor. Trist Wood Papers.

[22] Melpomene Notes, Trist Wood Papers.

[23] Scully, *James Dakin*, p. 56; Succession of Duncan Farrar Kenner, NOPL; Taylor, *Louisiana Reconstructed*, p. 343.

[24] Succession of Duncan Farrar Kenner, NOPL; Louis Bringier to Stella, February 24, 1870, L.A. Bringier and Family Papers, LSU; Plantation Account Notes, 1887-1888 and other miscellaneous undated notes, Duncan Farrar Kenner Papers, LSU; and Miscellaneous Undated Notes, Duncan Farrar Kenner Papers, LSU; Folders 2 and 4, Bringier Notes, Trist Wood Papers.

[25] Succession of Duncan Farrar Kenner, NOPL; Office of Louisiana Levee Company and Statement

of Claim by New Orleans, St. Louis, and Chicago Railroad, February 1, 1875, Brent Collection, LSM; Heitman, *Modernization of the Louisiana Sugar Industry*, p. 80.

[26]Succession of Duncan Farrar Kenner, NOPL; Duncan Farrar Kenner Papers, LSU; Jon L. Wakelyn, *Biographical Dictionary of the Confederacy* (Westport, Conn., 1977), p. 272; *Soard's New Orleans Directory* (1879), p. 752, (1881), p. 820; Jewell, *Crescent City Illustrated*, n.p.

[27]Succession of Duncan Farrar Kenner, NOPL

[28]*Ibid.*; S. H. Zilman to Duncan Farrar Kenner, January 19, 1880, Brent Collection, LSM; Wakelyn, *Biographical Dictionary*, p. 272; Leonard V. Huber, *New Orleans: A Pictorial History* (New York, 1980), p. 135.

[29]Memorandum of an Agreement between Richard Taylor and Duncan Farrar Kenner, January 21, 1867, and Answer to Interrogation . . . Propounded to Duncan Farrar Kenner, n.d., Duncan Farrar Kenner Papers, LSU; Huber, *New Orleans*, p. 230; Jackson Beauregard Davis, "The Life of Richard Taylor," *Louisiana Historical Quarterly*, XXIV (1941), 116.

[30]Duncan Farrar Kenner to James McCloskey, May 25, 1868; Duncan Farrar Kenner to Richard Taylor, July 18, 1869, and April 10, 1870, Duncan Farrar Kenner Papers, LSU.

[31]Davis, "Life of Richard Taylor," 116.

[32]Sitterson, *Sugar Country*, pp. 233, 235.

[33]Taylor, *Louisiana Reconstructed*, p. 365.

[34]Garnie William McGinty, *A History of Louisiana*, 4th ed. (New York, 1949), p. 260; East Baton Rouge Police Jury Statement of Permission for Rice Flume, Duncan Farrar Kenner Papers, LSU; Alcée Bouchereau, *Statement of the Sugar and Rice Crops Made in Louisiana*, 1886, p. 28; Ezell, *South Since 1865*, pp. 128-129.

[35]Sitterson, *Sugar Country*, pp. 264, 310; Heitman, *Modernization of the Louisiana Sugar Industry*, p. 66.

[36]Sitterson, *Sugar Country*, p. 281; Heitman, *Modernization of the Louisiana Sugar Industry*, p. 111.

[37]Bringier Pulverizing Cultivator, Agreement for Eureka Decorticating Machines, November 27, 1883, Duncan Farrar Kenner Papers, LSU; Application for Patent, May 18, 1887, Duncan Farrar Kenner Papers, LSU; "Decorticator for Ramie," United States Patent Office, Numbers 409, 847, August 27, 1889.

[38]Sitterson, *Sugar Country*, p. 252.

[39]*Ibid.*, p. 253; *Soard's New Orleans Directory*, p. 752.

[40]Sitterson, *Sugar Country*, pp. 253-254; Heitman, *Modernization of the Louisiana Sugar Industry*, p. 74.

[41]Quoted in Sitterson, *Sugar Country*, p. 254; Heitman, *Modernization of the Louisiana Sugar Industry*, p. 113.

[42]Heitman, *Modernization of the Louisiana Sugar Industry*, pp. 139-142

[43]*Ibid.*, pp. 145-146, 172-173; Sitterson, *Sugar Country*, p. 255.

[44]Heitman, *Modernization of the Louisiana Sugar Industry*, p. 174-175.

[45]*Ibid.*, p. 90; Sitterson, *Sugar Country*, pp. 175, 325.

Endnotes

[46]Hietman, *Modernization of the Louisiana Sugar Industry*, pp. 91-92.

[47]*Ibid.*, pp. 78, 93-94; Sitterson, *Sugar Country*, pp. 324-325.

[48]Quoted in Myers, *A Financial History of the United States*, pp. 235-236.

[49]George Frederick Howe, *Chester A. Arthur: A Quarter-Century of Machine Politics* (New York, 1934), pp. 220-221.

[50]Copy of Speech by John Dymond, January 14, 1909, Trist Wood Papers; John Smith Kendall, *History of New Orleans*, 3 vols. (Chicago, 1922), II, 779-780; Charles Folger to Duncan Farrar Kenner, June 22, 1882, Brent Collection, LSM; President Chester A. Arthur to the United States Senate, Nomination of Duncan Farrar Kenner to the Tariff Commission, May 15, 1882, Legislative, Judicial and Fiscal Branch, Civil Archives Division, National Archives, Washington, D.C.; Howe, *Chester A. Arthur*, pp. 220-221.

[51]Judge Emil Rost to Reginold Dykers, Esq., January 13, 1909, Trist Wood Papers; *Daily States*, June 8, 1882.

[52]Myers, *Financial History of the United States*, pp. 235-236; Heitman, *Modernization of the Louisiana Sugar Industry*, pp. 94-95.

[53]John Dymond to Duncan Farrar Kenner, October 30, 1882, Brent Collection, LSM; Heitman, *Modernization of the Louisiana Sugar Industry*, p. 95.

[54]Myers, *Financial History of the United States*, p. 236.

[55]*Ibid.*; Heitman, *Modernization of the Louisiana Sugar Industry*, pp. 95, 97.

CHAPTER TWELVE

[1]New Orleans *Daily Southern Star*, October 21, 1865.

[2]Joe Gray Taylor, *Louisiana: A History* (Nashville, 1984), pp. 102-103.

[3]Howard, *Political Tendencies*, p. 120; Taylor, *Louisiana Reconstructed*, p. 66; Eric Foner, *Reconstruction: America's Unfinished Revolution, 1863-1877* (New York, 1988), p. 182.

[4]Taylor, *Louisiana Reconstructed*, p. 71; Franklin, *Reconstruction*, p. 43; Summers, "The Moderates' Last Chance," pp. 56-57.

[5]Summers, "The Moderates' Last Chance," 64; Taylor, *Louisiana Reconstructed*, p. 73.

[6]*Daily Picayune*, November 24, 1865; Summers, "The Moderates' Last Chance," 66; Howard, *Political Tendencies*, p. 122.

[7]*Daily Picayune*, November 24, December 1, 1865; Summers, "The Moderates' Last Chance," 66.

[8]Franklin, *From Slavery to Freedom*, p. 303; Bauer, "From Burnt Canes To Budding City," 365; Taylor, *Louisiana Reconstructed*, p. 99.

[9]*Daily Picayune*, November 24, December 14, 15, 1865; Eric Foner, *Reconstruction*, p. 209; Roland P. Constantin, "The Louisiana 'Black Code' Legislation of 1865" (M.A. thesis, Louisiana State University, 1956), pp. 53-54; Shugg, *Origins of Class Struggle*, p. 213.

[10]Foner, *Reconstruction*, pp. 208-209; Coulter, *South During Reconstruction*, p. 39; Kenneth M. Stampp, *The Era of Reconstruction: 1865-1877* (New York, 1965), p. 79.

[11]Duncan Farrar Kenner to Robert Schenck, September 14, 1865, Record Group 94, NA.

[12]Constantin, "'Black Code' Legislation," 59.

[13] Leon F. Litwack, *Been in the Storm So Long* (New York, 1979), p. 533.

[14] Duncan Farrar Kenner to Robert Schenck, September 14, 1865, National Archives.

[15] See above pages 181-182.

[16] *New Orleans Tribune*, November 28, 1865.

[17] *Daily Picayune*, November 28, 1865; Constantin, "'Black Code' Legislation," 63-64.

[18] Constantin, "'Black Code' Legislation," 84, 87-88, 94; Joe Gray Taylor, "New Orleans and Reconstruction," *Louisiana History*, IX (1968), 195.

[19] Howard, *Political Tendencies*, p. 122; Franklin, *From Slavery to Freedom*, pp. 303-304.

[20] Quoted in Foner, *Reconstruction*, p. 119; Taylor, *Louisiana Reconstructed*, p. 82.

[21] Howard, *Political Tendencies*, pp. 123-124; Shugg, *Origins of Class Struggle*, p. 216.

[22] Foner, *Reconstruction*, p. 263; Taylor, "New Orleans and Reconstruction," 195.

[23] Dufour, *Ten Flags in the Wind*, pp. 184-185; Shugg, *Origins of Class Struggle*, p. 219; Randall and Donald, *Civil War and Reconstruction*, p. 595; Davis, *Louisiana*, p. 270.

[24] Howard, *Political Tendencies*, p. 127.

[25] Jewell, *Crescent City Illustrated*, n.p.

[26] Davis, *Louisiana*, p. 278; Somers, *Sports in New Orleans*, p. 91.

[27] Somers, *Sports in New Orleans*, pp. 91-92.

[28] *Ibid.*, 111.

[29] *Ibid.*; Folder 3, Bringier Notes in Trist Wood Papers.

[30] Folder 3, Bringier Notes in Trist Wood Papers.

[31] Somers, *Sports in New Orleans*, pp. 92-93, 108; Henri A. Gandolfo, *Metarie Cemetery: An Historical Memoir* (New Orleans, 1981), p. 15.

[32] Gandolfo, *Metarie Cemetery*, p. 15; Mary Louise Christovich, Peggy McDowell, and Leonard V. Huber, *New Orleans Architecture*, vol. 3, *The Cemeteries* (Gretna, La., 1974), pp. 50-51.

[33] Gandolfo, *Metarie Cemetery*, p. 15; Christovich, et al., *Cemeteries*, pp. 50-51; Duncan Farrar Kenner to D. D. Withers, May 16, 1872, Duncan Farrar Kenner Papers, LSU.

[34] Among Kenner's activities were membership on the committee to find a new building for the club, the library committee, the bondholders committee, and the executive committee. Landry, *History of the Boston Club*, pp. 88, 117, 118, 121.

[35] Ibid., pp. 63, 64, 86, 169.

[36] *Ibid.*, pp. 115-116.

[37] *Ibid.*, p. 105; Heitman, *Modernization of the Louisiana Sugar Industry*, p. 130.

[38] *Ibid.*, pp. 105-106; Edward Larocque Tinker, *Creole City: Its Past and Its People* (New York, 1953), p. 119; Stuart Omer Landry, *The Battle of Liberty Place: The Overthrow of Carpet-Bag Rule in New Orleans--September 14, 1874* (New Orleans, 1955), p. 9.

[39] Quoted in Taylor, *Louisiana Reconstructed*, p. 278.

Endnotes

[40]*Ibid.*, p. 280; Shugg, *Origins of Class Struggle*, pp. 230-231.

[41]Foner, *Reconstruction*, p. 551; Landry, *Battle of Liberty Place*, p. 179; Dufour, *Ten Flags in the Wind*, pp. 208-209.

[42]Foner, *Reconstruction*, p. 551; Howard, *Political Tendencies*, p. 143; Davis, *Louisiana*, p. 271.

[43]Taylor, *Louisiana Reconstrcuted*, pp. 485-487.

[44]Testimony of Duncan F. Kenner, U.S. Congress, Miscellaneous Documents, 42 (44-2), MDCCLXII, pp. 380-381.

[45]Taylor, *Louisiana Reconstructed*, pp. 490-491; Keith Ian Polakoff, *Politics of Inertia* (Baton Rouge, 1973), pp. 210-213.

[46]Quoted in Polakoff, *Politics of Inertia*, p. 212.

[47]Walter McGehee Lowrey, "The Political Career of James Madison Wells," *Louisiana Historical Quarterly*, XXXI (1948), 1106.

[48]Testimony of Duncan Farrar Kenner, 376; Unsigned Personal Notes in Kenner's Handwriting on Stationary from Welker's Hotel, Washington, D.C., 1877, Duncan Farrar Kenner Collection, LSM (hereafter cited as Unsigned Personal Notes).

[49]Testimony of Duncan Farrar Kenner, 376.

[50]*Ibid.*, pp. 376-378; Unsigned Personal Notes.

[51]Wells, in his testimony before the congressional committee, claimed that Kenner offered on four occasions $200,000 for his support for the Democrats, but that his party loyalty prevented him from taking the money. Given Kenner's reputation and the fact that Wells had approached others, including leaders of both national parties, for compensation, little credence has even been afforded the ex-governor's account. U. S. Congress, "Testimony of Duncan F. Kenner," 42 (44-2), MDCCLXII, p. 378; Unsigned Personal Notes; Lowrey, "Political Career of James Madison Wells," 1107; Polakoff, *Politics of Inertia*, p. 213.

[52]Dufour, *Ten Flags in the Wind*, p. 214.

[53]Otis Arnold Singletary, "The Reassertion of White Supremacy in Louisiana" (M.A. thesis, Louisiana State University, 1949), pp. 67-70.

[54]*Official Journal of the Proceedings of the Senate of the State of Louisiana, at the Regular Session Begun and Held In New Orleans, January 6, 1879* (New Orleans, The Democrat Publishing Company, 1879), p. 4 (hereafter cited as *Proceedings of the Senate*, 1879).

[55]*Ibid.*, p. 7; Adams, *Louisiana*, p. 286; *Daily Picayune*, January 10, 1879.

[56]Adams, *Louisiana*, p. 286; Howard, *Political Tendencies*, p. 154.

[57]*Proceedings of the Senate*, 1879, pp. 7, 21. Robert B. Highsaw, "Edward Douglass White," in *The Encyclopedia of Southern History*, David C. Roller and Robert W. Twyman, eds. (Baton Rouge, 1979), 1337. White would eventually go on to become a United States Senator and Chief Justice of the United States Supreme Court.

[58]*Daily Picayune*, January 15, 16, 18, 24, 1879.

[59]*Ibid.*, January 24, 30, 1879.

[60]Samuel C. Shepherd, Jr., "A Glimmer of Hope: The World's Industrial and Cotton Centennial Exposition, New Orleans, 1884-1885," *Louisiana Historical Quarterly*, XXVI (1985), 272-273; Kemp,

New Orleans, pp. 122-123.

[61]*Times-Democrat*, May 8, 16, 22, 23, 1883; Warner and Yearns, *Biographical Register*, p. 145.

[62]Shepherd, "A Glimmer of Hope," 279.

[63]*Ibid.*, 278-279; Kemp, *New Orleans*, pp. 126-127.

[64]Kemp, *New Orleans*, pp. 125-127.

CHAPTER THIRTEEN

[1]Seebold, *Plantation Homes*, II, 88; *Daily States*, July 4, 1887.

[2]*Daily States*, July 4, 1887; *Daily Picayune*, July 4, 1887.

[3]Folder 3, Bringier Notes in Trist Wood Papers; Succession of Duncan Farrar Kenner, NOPL.

[4]Folder 3, Bringier Notes in Trist Wood Papers; Succession of Duncan Farrar Kenner, NOPL; J. L. Brent to Mrs. Alexander, July 6, 1887, and Undated Newspaper Article in Duncan Farrar Kenner Papers, LSU.

[5]Executor Cash Statement, March 25, 1888, and J. L. Brent to Mrs. Alexander, July 6, 1887, Duncan Farrar Kenner Papers, LSU; Folder 3, Bringier Notes in Trist Wood Papers.

[6]McKee, "Belle Helene Plantation," p. 4; New Orleans *Times-Picayune*, January 9, 1983; Baton Rouge *Advocate*, July 28, 1992.

[7]Seebold, *Plantation Homes*, II, 88.

[8]Quoted in Eaton, *Mind of the Old South*, p. 307.

[9]Warner and Yearns, *Confederate Congress*, pp. xxi, 144.

[10]For an additional perspective on the reason for the South's defeat see Grady McWhiney and Perry D. Jamieson, *Attack and Die: Civil War Military Tactics and the Southern Heritage* (Alabama, 1982), p. xv. The authors contend that it was the South's celtic heritage of boldness on the battlefield which caused the Confederacy's defeat by bleeding itself to death by wasteful frontal assaults.

[11]Beringer, Hattaway, Jones, and Still, *Why the South Lost*, pp. 7, 8, 34.

[12]Newspaper Obituary, July 4, 1887, in Duncan Farrar Kenner Papers, LSU.

[13]For additional discussion of the planter/slave relationship see William K. Scarborough, "Slavery–The White Man's Burden," in *Perspectives and Irony in American Slavery*, Harry P. Owens, ed. (Jackson, 1976), pp. 103-135.

BIBLIOGRAPHY

PRIMARY SOURCES

Manuscript Records

Diocese of Baton Rouge, Department of Archives, Baton Rouge, Louisiana

    Certificate of Marriage of Duncan Farrar Kenner and Anne Guillelmine Bringier.

Jefferson Parish Court House. Gretna, La.

    Succession of William and Mary Kenner.

Historic New Orleans Collection, New Orleans, La.

    Ashland Plantation Journal, 1858.
    Duncan Farrar Kenner Papers.
    The Urquhart Collection, Trist Woods Papers.

Library of Congress, Manuscript Division, Washington, D.C.

    Duncan Farrar Kenner Collection.
    James M. Mason Papers.

Louisiana State Museum, Archives and Manuscript Collection, New Orleans, La.

    Brent Collection.
    Catalogue of New Orleans Street Addresses.
    Duncan Farrar Kenner Papers.

Louisiana State University Archives, Baton Rouge, La.

    Ashland Plantation Record Book.
    Rosella Kenner Brent Papers.

Louis A. Bringier and Family Papers.
Ellis-Farrar Papers.
Duncan Farrar Kenner Papers.
William Kenner Papers.
Kenner Family Papers.
William J. Minor and Family Papers.
Thomas Moore Papers.
Jean Ursin La Villebeuvre and Family Papers.

National Archives, Washington, D.C.

Diplomatic Branch, Civil Archives Division. Record Group 84.
Judicial and Fiscal Branch, Civil Archives Division. Record Group 366. Third Special Agency.
Legislative, Judicial, and Fiscal Branch, Civil Archives Division. Nomination of Duncan Farrar Kenner to Tariff Commission.
Records of the Adjutant General's Office. Record Group 94. War Department Collection of Confederate Records. Record Group 109.

New Orleans Public Library, New Orleans, La.

Ascension Parish, La. Conveyance Records, 1770-1901.
Will Book Number 4, Last Will and Testament of William Kenner.
Succession of Duncan Farrar Kenner.

State of Mississippi, Department of Archives and History, Jackson, Mississippi

Direct Index to Land Conveyances, Adams County, Mississippi, From 1798.
Indirect Index to Land Conveyances, Adams County, Mississippi, From 1798.

Tulane University, Manuscript Department, Special Collections Division, New Orleans, La.

Benjamin Farrar Papers.
Duncan Farrar Kenner File.

Bibliography

Public Documents

Constitution of the Confederate States.

Constitution for the Provisional Government.

Eighth Census of the United States, 1860. Ascension Parish, Louisiana. Slave and Population Schedules. Microfilm copy in New Orleans Public Library, New Orleans, La.

Work Projects Administration. *Transcription of Parish Records of Louisiana, No. 26, Jefferson Parish (Gretna). Series 1. Police Jury Minutes.* Gretna, Louisiana: Jefferson Parish Police Jury, 1939.

Journal of the Congress of the Confederate States of America, 1861-1865. 7 vols. 1905; reprint ed., New York: Kraus Reprint Co., 1968.

Journal of the Convention to Form a New Constitution for the State of Louisiana. New Orleans: Crescent Office, 1852.

Journal of the Proceedings of the Convention of the State of Louisiana, Begun and Held in the City of New Orleans January 14, 1845. New Orleans: Besancon, Ferguson, and Co., 1845.

Journal of the House of Representatives of the State of Louisiana. New Orleans: attributed to Jerome Bayon, 1837.

Journal of the House of Representatives of the State of Louisiana, Second Session of the Thirteenth Legislature. New Orleans: attributed to Jerome Bayon, 1838.

Journal of the Senate. First Session of the First Legislature of the State of Louisiana. New Orleans: attributed to Van Benthuysen and Besancon, 1846.

Journal of the Senate of the State of Louisiana, Session 1846-7–Continued. New Orleans: W. Van Benthuysen.

Journal of the Senate of the State of Louisiana, Session 1848. New Orleans: The Louisiana Courier, 1848.

Mississippi Historical Records Survey, Works Progress Administration. *Transcription of County Archives of Mississippi, No. 2 Adams County (Natchez)*. Vol. 1: *Minutes of the Court of General Quarter Sessions of the Peace 1799-1801*. Jackson: Board of Supervisors, Adams County, 1942.

Official Journal of the Proceedings of the Senate of the State of Louisiana, at the Regular Session Begun and Held In New Orleans, January 1, 1879. New Orleans: The Democratic Publishing Company, 1879.

Official Report of Debates in the Louisiana Convention. New Orleans: J. Bayon, 1845.

Proceedings and Debates of the Convention of Louisiana which Assembled at the City of New Orleans, January 14, 1845. New Orleans: Besancon, Ferguson, and Co., 1845.

"Proceedings of the Confederate Congress." *Southern Historical Society Papers*, Vols. 44-52 (1923-59).

Seventh Census of the United States, 1850. Ascension Parish, Louisiana. Slave and Population Schedules. Microfilm copy in New Orleans Public Library, New Orleans, La.

Sixth Census of the United States, 1840. Ascension Parish, Louisiana. Slave and Population Schedules. Microfilm copy in New Orleans Public Library, New Orleans, La.

United States Congress. *American State Papers: Documents, Legislative and Executive of the Congress of the United States in Relation to the Public Lands, From the First Session of the First Congress to the First Session of the Twenty-third Congress–March 4, 1789, to June 15, 1834*. Walter Lowrie, ed., Vol. 1. Washington: Duff Green, 1834.

United States Congress. House Miscellaneous Documents. 42 (44-2) Vol. 1762, 376-387.

United States Patent Office, "Decorticator for Ramie," No. 409,847, August 27, 1889.

The War of the Rebellion: A Compilation of the Official Records of the Union and Confederate Armies. 128 vols. Washington, D.C.: United States Government Printing Office, 1880-1901.

Official Records of the Union and Confederate Navies in the War of the Rebellion. 30 vols. Washington: United States Government Printing Office, 1894-1927.

Private Holdings

Mr. and Mrs. Robert McKee, New Orleans, La.

    Miscellaneous Photographs.
    Plan of Ashland: Estate of Duncan Farrar Kenner
    Subdivision of Belle Helene Plantation

Mr. Engel H. Schmidt, Metairie, La.

    Historic American Survey Papers
    Kenner Family Bible
    Miscellaneous Photographs

SECONDARY SOURCES

Books

Abernethy, Thomas P. *The South in the New Nation, 1789-1819.* Vol. 4 in *A History of the South.* Baton Rouge: Louisiana State University Press, 1961.

Adams, Ephraim Douglas. *Great Britain and the American Civil War.* 2 vols. New York: Russell and Russell, 1924.

Adams, William H. *The Whig Party of Louisiana.* Lafayette, La.: University of Southwestern Louisiana, 1973.

Alden, John Richard. *The South in the Revolution, 1763-1789.* Vol. 3 in *A History of the South.* Baton Rouge: Louisiana State University Press, 1957.

Arthur, Stanley C. and Huchet de Kernion, George C. *Old Families of Louisiana.* 1931; reprint ed., Baton Rouge: Claitor's Publishing Division, 1971.

Ashcraft, Allan C. "Richard 'Dick' Taylor." In *The Encyclopedia of Southern History*, David C. Roller and Robert W. Tyman, eds., pp. 1181-1182. Baton Rouge: Louisiana State University Press, 1979.

Barck, Oscar T., Jr. and Lefler, Hugh T. *Colonial America.* 2nd ed. New York: Macmillan Co., 1968.

Beers, Henry Putney. *Guide to the Archives of the Government of the Confederate States of America.* Washington: National Archives, 1968.

Begnaud, Allen. "The Louisiana Sugar Cane Industry: An Overview." In *Green Fields: Two Hundred Years of Louisiana Sugar*, pp. 29-50. Lafayette, La.: The Center for Louisiana Studies. The University of Southwestern Louisiana, 1980.

Beringer, Richard E.; Hattaway, Herman; Jones, Archer; and Still, William N., Jr. *Why the South Lost the Civil War*. Athens, Ga.: University of Georgia Press, 1986.

Bigelow, John. "The Confederate Diplomatists and Their Shirt of Nessus: A Chapter of Secret History." *Century Magazine* (1891), 113-126.

Blassingame, John W., *The Slave Community: Plantation Life in the Antebellum South*. New York: Oxford University Press, 1972.

Boatner, Mary Mayo. *The Civil War Dictionary*. New York: David McKay Co., Inc., 1959.

Bouchereau, Alcée. *Statement of the Sugar and Rice Crops Made in Louisiana*, New Orleans: A. Bouchereau, 1886.

Bragg, Jefferson Davis. *Louisiana in the Confederacy*. Baton Rouge: Louisiana State University Press, 1941.

Butler, Pierce. *Judah P. Benjamin*. Philadelphia: G. W. Jacobs and Co., 1907.

_____. *The Unhurried Years: Memories of the Old Natchez Region*. Baton Rouge: Louisiana State University Press, 1948.Bearss, Edwin C., ed. *A Louisiana Confederate: Diary of Felix Pierre Poche*. Natchitoches, La.: Louisiana Studies Institute. Northwestern State University, 1972.

Caldwell, Stephen A. *A Banking History of Louisiana*. Baton Rouge: Louisiana State University Press, 1935.

Callahan, James Morton. *The Diplomatic History of the Southern Confederacy*. Baltimore: The Johns Hopkins Press, 1901.

Carter, Clarence Edwin, ed. *The Territorial Papers of the United States*. Vol. IX. *The Orleans Territory*. Washington, D.C.: Department of State, 1940.

Carter, Hodding, and Carter, Betty Werlein. *So Great A Good: A History of the Episcopal Church in Louisiana and of Christ Church Cathedral, 1805-1955*. Sewanee, Tenn.: The University Press, 1955.

Case, Lynn M., and Spencer, Warren F. *The United States and France: Civil War Diplomacy.* Philadelphia: University of Pennsylvania Press, 1970.

Cash, Wilbur J. *The Mind of the South.* New York: Vintage Books, 1941.

A Catalogue of the Officers and Students of Miami University. Oxford, Ohio: Miami University, 1831.

Catton, Bruce. *The Coming Fury.* Garden City, N.Y.: Doubleday and Co., Inc., 1961.

Champomier, Pierre A. *Statement of the Sugar Crop Made in Louisiana, 1844-1861.* New Orleans: Cook, Young, and Co., 1845-1862.

Christovich, Mary Louise; Toledano, Roulhac; Swanson, Betsy; and Holden, Pat. *New Orleans Architecture.* Vol 2. *The American Sector (Faubourg St. Mary).* Gretna, La.: Pelican Publishing Co., 1972.

_____; McDowell, Peggy; and Huber, Leonard V. *New Orleans Architecture.* Vol. 3. *The Cemeteries.* Gretna, La.: Pelican Publishing Co., 1974.

Clark, John G. *New Orleans, 1718-1812: An Economic History.* Baton Rouge: Louisiana State University Press, 1970.

Claiborne, J. F. H. *Mississippi As A Province, Territory, and State.* 1880; reprint ed., Spartanburg, S.C.: The Reprint Co., 1978.

Clinton, Catherine. *The Plantation Mistress: Woman's World in the Old South.* New York: Pantheon Books, 1982.

Cooper, William J. *The South and the Politics of Slavery, 1828-1856.* Baton Rouge: Louisiana State University Press, 1978.

Copeland, Fayette. *Kendall of the Picayune, Being His Adventures in New Orleans, on the Texan Santa Fe Expedition, in the Mexican War, and in the Colonization of the Texas Frontier.* Norman, Okla.: University of Oklahoma Press, 1943.

Coulter, E. Merton. *The Confederate States of America, 1861-1865.* Vol. 7 in *A History of the South.* Baton Rouge: Louisiana State University Press, 1950.

―――――. *The South During Reconstruction 1865-1877.* Vol. 8 in *A History of the South.* Baton Rouge: Louisiana State University Press, 1947.

Craven, Avery O. *The Growth of Southern Nationalism, 1848-1861.* Vol. 6 in *A History of the South.* Baton Rouge: Louisiana State University Press, 1953.

Crook, D. P. *The North, the South, and the Powers: 1861-1865.* New York: John Wiley and Sons, 1974.

Davis, Edwin Adams. *Louisiana: A Narrative History.* 3rd ed. Baton Rouge: Claitor's Publishing Division, 1971.

Davis, Jefferson. *The Rise and Fall of the Confederate Government.* 2 vols. 1881; reprint ed., New York: Thomas Yoseloff, 1958.

Dufour, Charles L. *The Night the War Was Lost.* Garden City, N.Y.: Doubleday, 1960.

―――――. *Ten Flags In the Wind: The Story of Louisiana.* New York: Harper and Row, 1967.

Durden, Robert F. *The Gray and the Black: The Confederate Debate on Emancipation.* Baton Rouge: Louisiana State University Press, 1972.

Eaton, Clement. *A History of the Old South.* 2nd ed. New York: Macmillan Co., 1966.

―――――. *Jefferson Davis.* New York: The Free Press, 1977.

―――――. *The Mind of the Old South.* Rev. ed. Baton Rouge: Louisiana State University Press, 1976.

Ezell, John Samuel. *The South Since 1865.* New York: Macmillan Co., 1963.

Fogel, Robert William and Engerman, Stanley L. *Time on the Cross: The Economics of American Negro Slavery.* 2 vols. Boston: Little, Brown and Co., 1974.

Foner, Eric. *Reconstruction: America's Unfinished Revolution, 1863-1877.* New York: Harper and Row Publishers, 1988.

Fossier, Albert. *New Orleans: The Glamour Period, 1800-1840.* New Orleans: Pelican Publishing Co., 1957.

Franklin, John Hope. *From Slavery to Freedom: A History of Negro Americans.* 3rd ed. New York: Alfred A. Knopf, 1967.

_____. *Reconstruction After the Civil War.* Chicago: University of Chicago Press, 1961.

Gandolfo, Henri A. *Metairie Cemetery: An Historical Memoir.* New Orleans: Stewart Enterprises, Inc., 1981.

Genovese, Eugene D. *Roll, Jordan, Roll: The World The Slaves Made.* New York: Pantheon Books, 1974.

Graebner, Norman A. "Northern Diplomacy and European Neutrality." In *Why the North Won the Civil War*, David Donald, ed., pp. 55-78. New York: Collier Books, 1972.

Hattaway, Herman and Jones, Archer. *How the North Won: A Military History of the Civil War.* Urbana, Ill.: University of Illinois Press, 1983.

Haynes, Robert V. "The Formation of the Territory." In *A History of Mississippi*, Richard Aubrey McLemore, ed., 2 vols., I, 174-216. Hattiesburg, Miss.: University and College Press of Mississippi, 1973.

Haunton, Richard H. "Nashville Convention." In *The Encyclopedia of Southern History*, David C. Roller and Robert W. Twyman, eds., p. 877. Baton Rouge: Louisiana State University Press, 1987.

Heitman, John Alfred. *The Modernization of the Louisiana Sugar Industry, 1830-1910.* Baton Rouge: Louisiana State University Press, 1987.

Hervey, John. *Racing In America, 1665-1865.* 2 vols. New York: The Jockey Club, 1944.

Highshaw, Robert B. "Edward Douglas White." In *The Encyclopedia of Southern History*, 1337. Baton Rouge: Louisiana State University Press, 1979.

Holmes, Jack D. L. "A Spanish Province, 1779-1798." In *A History of Mississippi*, Richard Aubrey McLemore, ed., 2 vols., I 158-173. Hattiesburg: University and College Press of Mississippi, 1973.

Howard, Perry H. *Political Tendencies in Louisiana.* Rev. and enl. ed. Baton Rouge: Louisiana State University Press, 1971.

Howe, George Frederick. *Chester A. Arthur: A Quarter-Century of Machine Politics.* New York: Dodd, Meade and Co., 1934.

Huber, Leonard V. *New Orleans: A Pictorial History.* New York: Bonanza Books, 1980.

Jewell, Edwin L. *Crescent City Illustrated: The Commercial, Social, Political and General History of New Orleans.* New Orleans: Edwin L. Jewell, 1873.

Jones, John B. *A Rebel War Clerk's Diary.* Earl Schenck Miers, cond., ed., and annot. New York: Sagamore Press, 1958.

Kane, Harnett T. *Plantation Parade: The Grand Manner in Louisiana.* New York: William Morrow and Co., 1945.

Kemp, John R. *New Orleans.* Woodland Hills, Ca.: Windsor Publications, Inc., 1981.

Kendall, John Smith. *A History of New Orleans.* 3 vols. Chicago: Lewis Publishing Co., 1922.

Kerby, Robert L. *Kirby Smith's Confederacy, 1863-1865.* New York: Columbia University Press, 1972.

King, Grace. *Creole Families of New Orleans.* New York: Macmillan Co., 1921.

Landry, Stuart Omer. *The Battle of Liberty Place: The Overthrow of Carpet-Bag Rule in New Orleans--September 14, 1874.* New Orleans: Pelican Publishing Co., 1955.

_____. *History of the Boston Club.* New Orleans: Pelican Publishing Co., 1938.

Laughlin, Clarence John. *Ghosts Along the Mississippi: An Essay in the Poetic Interpretation of Louisiana's Plantation Architecture.* New York: Bonanza Books, 1979.

Lipscomb, Andrew A., ed. *The Writings of Thomas Jefferson.* 20 vols. Washington, D.C.: Thomas Jefferson Memorial Association, 1904.

Litwack, Leon F. *Been in the Storm So Long: The Aftermath of Slavery.* New York: Alfred A. Knopf, 1979.

Louisiana Legislative Council. *The History and Government of Louisiana.* Baton Rouge: Louisiana Legislative Council, 1964.

Luraghi, Raimondo. *The Rise and Fall of the Plantation South.* New York: New Viewpoints, 1978.

McGinty, Garnie William. *A History of Louisiana.* 4th ed. New York: Exposition Press, 1949.

Marchand, Sidney A. *The Flight of a Century (1800-1900) In Ascension Parish Louisiana.* Donaldsonville, La.: N.p., 1936.

_____. *The Story of Ascension Parish Louisiana.* Baton Rouge: J. E. Ortlieb Printing Co., 1931.

Meade, Robert Douthat. *Judah P. Benjamin: Confederate Statesman.* New York: Oxford University Press, 1943.

Menn, Joseph Karl. *The Large Slaveholders of Louisiana--1860.* New Orleans: Pelican Publishing Co., 1964.

Merk, Frederick. *History of the Westward Movement*. New York: Alfred A. Knopf, 1978.

Myers, Margaret G. *A Financial History of the United States*. New York: Columbia University Press, 1970.

Nevins, Allan. *Ordeal of the Union: Selected Chapters*. E. B. Long, intro. and comp. New York: Charles Scribner's Sons, 1973.

Oates, Stephen B. *With Malice Toward None: The Life of Abraham Lincoln*. New York: Harper and Row, 1977.

Overdyke, W. Darrell. *Louisiana Plantation Homes: Colonial and Ante Bellum*. New York: Architectural Book Publishing Co., Inc., 1965.

Owsley, Frank Lawrence. *King Cotton Diplomacy: Foreign Relations of the Confederate States of America*. 2nd ed. Harriet C. Owsley, ed. Chicago: The University of Chicago Press, 1959.

_____. *Plain Folk of the Old South*. Baton Rouge: Louisiana State University Press, 1949.

Parkins, A. E. *The South: Its Economic-Geographic Development*. 1938; reprint ed., Westport, Conn.: Greenwood Press, 1970.

Polakoff, Keith Ian. *The Politics of Inertia: The Election of 1876 and the End of Reconstruction*. Baton Rouge: Louisiana State University Press, 1973.

Potter, David M. *The Impending Crisis, 1848-1861*. New York: Harper and Row, 1976.

Powell, Alden L. "A History of Louisiana Constitutions." In *Project of a Constitution for the State of Louisiana With Notes and Studies*. Prepared by the Louisiana State Law Institute, pp. 273-553. Baton Rouge: Wade O. Martin, Jr., 1954.

Randall, J. G. and Donald, David. *The Civil War and Reconstruction*. 2nd ed. Lexington, Massachusetts: D.C. Health and Co., 1969.

Rightor, Henry. *Standard History of New Orleans, Louisiana.* Chicago: Lewis Publishing Co., 1900.

Roland, Charles. *The Confederacy.* Chicago: The University of Chicago Press, 1960.

_____. *Louisiana Sugar Plantations During the American Civil War.* Leiden, Netherlands: E.J. Brill, 1957.

Russell, William H. *My Diary, North and South.* London: Bradley and Evans, 1863.

Scarborough, William Kauffman, ed. *The Diary of Edmund Ruffin.* Vol. 2. *The Years of Hope: April, 1861-June, 1863.* Baton Rouge: Louisiana State University Press, 1976.

_____. *The Overseer: Plantation Management in the Old South.* Baton Rouge: Louisiana State University Press, 1966.

_____. "Slavery–The White Man's Burden." In *Perspectives and Irony in American Slavery*, Harry P. Owens, ed., pp. 103-135. Jackson: University Press of Mississippi, 1976.

Scully, Arthur, Jr. *James Dakin, Architect: His Career in New York and the South.* Baton Rouge: Louisiana State University Press, 1973.

Sears, Louis Martin. *John Slidell.* Durham, N.C.: Duke University Press, 1925.

Seebold, Herman de Bachellé. *Old Louisiana Plantation Homes and Family Trees.* 2 vols. New Orleans: Herman de Bachellé Seebold, 1941.

Shugg, Roger W. *Origins of Class Struggle in Louisiana.* 1939; reprint ed., Baton Rouge: Louisiana State University, 1972.

Sitterson, J. Carlyle. *Sugar Country: The Cane Sugar Industry in the South, 1753-1950.* Lexington: University of Kentucky Press, 1953.

Skates, John R. "Mississippi." In *The Encyclopedia of Southern History*, David C. Roller and Robert W. Twyman, eds., pp. 825-836. Baton Rouge: Louisiana State University Press, 1979.

Smith, J. Frazer. *White Pillars: Early Life and Architecture of the Lower Mississippi Valley Country*. New York: Bramhall House, 1941.

Somers, Dale A. *The Rise of Sports in New Orleans, 1850-1900*. Baton Rouge: Louisiana State University Press, 1972.

Soards' New Orleans City Directory. New Orleans: L. Soards and Co., 1879-1881.

Stampp, Kenneth M. *The Era of Reconstruction: 1865-1877*. New York: Vintage Books, 1865.

_____. *The Peculiar Institution: Slavery in the Ante-Bellum South*. New York: Vintage Books, 1956.

"Stephen Minor." In *Encyclopedia of Mississippi History: Comprising Sketches of Countries, Towns, Events, Institutions and Persons*, Dunbar Rowland, ed., 2 vols., II, 247-249. Madison: Selwyn A. Brant, 1907.

Sydnor, Charles S. *The Development of Southern Sectionalism, 1819-1848*. Vol. 5 in *A History of the South*. Baton Rouge: Louisiana State University Press, 1948.

Swanson, Betsy. *Historic Jefferson Parish: From Shore to Shore*. Gretna: Pelican Publishing Co., 1975.

Taussig, F. W. *The Tariff History of the United States*. 8th ed. New York: G. P. Putnam's Sons, 1931.

Taylor, Joe Gray. *Louisiana: A History*. New York: W. W. Norton and Co., 1984.

_____. *Louisiana Reconstructed: 1863-1877*. Baton Rouge: Louisiana State University Press, 1974.

_____. *Negro Slavery in Louisiana*. New York: Negro Universities Press, 1963.

Thomas, Emory M. *The Confederate Nation, 1861-1865*. New York: Harper and Row, 1979.

Tinker, Edward Larocque. *Creole City: Its Past and Its People*. New York: Longmans, Green and Co., 1953.

Wakelyn, Jon L. *Biographical Dictionary of the Confederacy*. Westport, Conn.: Greenwood Press, 1977.

Warner, Ezra J., and Yearns, W. Buck. *Biographical Register of the Confederate Congress*. Baton Rouge: Louisiana State University Press, 1975.

White, M. J. "Duncan Farrar Kenner." Vol. 10, *Dictionary of American Biography*. 1928; reprint ed., New York: Charles Scribner's Sons, 1936.

Williams, T. Harry. *The History of American Wars From 1745 to 1918*. New York: Alfred A. Knopf, 1981.

Winters, John D. *The Civil War in Louisiana*. Baton Rouge: Louisiana State University Press, 1963.

Yearns, Wilfred Buck. *The Confederate Congress*. Athens, Ga.: University of Georgia Press, 1960.

Articles

Adams, William H. "The Louisiana Whigs." *Louisiana History*, XV (1974), 213-228.

Atherton, Lewis E. "John McDonogh--New Orleans Mercantile Capitalist." *Journal of Southern History*, VII (1941), 451-481.

Bauer, Craig A. "From Burnt Canes to Budding City: A History of the City of Kenner, Louisiana." *Louisiana History*, XXIII (1982), 353-381.

_____. "The Last Effort: The Secret Mission of the Confederate Diplomat, Duncan F. Kenner." *Louisiana History*, XXII (1981), 67-95.

Bergeron, Arthur W. "General Richard Taylor as a Military Commander." *Louisiana History*, XXIII (1982), 35-47.

Beringer, Richard E. "A Profile of the Members of the Confederate Congress." *Journal of Southern History*, XXXIII (1967), 518-540.

Blumenthal, Henry. "Confederate Diplomacy: Popular Notions and International Realities." *Journal of Southern History*, XXXII (1966), 151-171.

Bonner, James C. "Plantation Architecture of the Lower South on the Eve of the Civil War." *Journal of Southern History*, XI (1945), 370-388.

Broussard, James H. "Some Determinants of Know-Nothing Electoral Strength in the South, 1856." *Louisiana History*, VII (1966), 5-20.

Butler, Louise. "The Louisiana Planter and His Home." *Louisiana Historical Quarterly*, X (1927), 355-363.

Cappon, Lester J. "The Provincial South." *Journal of Southern History*, XVI (1950), 5-24.

Carriere, Marius. "Political Leadership of the Louisiana Know-Knothing Party." *Louisiana History*, XXI (1980), 183-195.

Davis, Jackson Beauregard. "The Life of Richard Taylor." *Louisiana Historical Quarterly*, XXIV (1941), 49-126.

Dew, Charles B. "The Long Lost Returns: The Candidates and Their Totals in Louisiana's Secession Election." *Louisiana History*, VIII (1969), 353-369.

Din, Gilbert C. "Proposals and Plans for Colonization in Spanish Louisiana, 1887-1790." *Louisiana History*, XI (1970), 197-213.

Durel, Lionel C. "Creole Civilization in Donaldsonville, 1850, According to 'Le Vigilant'." *Louisiana Historical Quarterly*, XXXI (1948), 981-994.

Edwards, Edwin W. "The Role of the Governor in Louisiana Politics: An Historical Analysis." *Louisiana History*, XV (1974), 101-116.

Freeman, Arthur. "Early Career of Pierre Soulé." *Louisiana Historical Quarterly*, XXV (1942), 971-1127.

Greer, James Kimmins. "Louisiana Politics, 1845-1861." *Louisiana Historical Quarterly*, XII (1929), 381-425, 555-610; XIII (1930), 67-116, 257-303, 444-483, 617-654.

Hernon, Joseph M. Jr. "British Sympathies in the American Civil War: A Reconsideration." *Journal of Southern History*, XXXIII (1967), 356-367.

Holmes, Jack D. L. "Genealogical and Historical Notes on Stephen Minor." *Louisiana Genealogical Register*, XVI (1969), 106-115.

_____. "Stephen Minor: Natchez Pioneer." *Journal of Mississippi History*, XLII (1980), 17-26.

"Incorporators of Various Churches, Schools, and Libraries as Shown by Acts of the Orleans Territory and Louisiana State Legislatures." *The Louisiana Genealogical Register*, XIX (1972): 324-326.

"Kenner's Mission to Europe." *Tyler's Quarterly Historical and Genealogical Magazine*, IV (1923), 23-27.

Lowrey, Walter McGehee. "The Political Career of James Wells." *Louisiana Historical Quarterly*, XXXI (1948), 995-1123.

McLure, Mary Lilla. "The Election of 1860 in Louisiana." *Louisiana Historical Quarterly*, IX (1926), 601-702.

Millet, Ronald J. "Southwest Louisiana Enters the Railroad Age: 1880-1900." *Louisiana History*, XXIV (1983), 165-183.

Noble, Stuart Grayson. "Schools of New Orleans During the First Quarter of the Nineteenth Century." *Louisiana Historical Quarterly*, XIV (1931), 65-78

Odom, Van D. "The Political Career of Thomas Overton Moore, Secession Governor of Louisiana." *Louisiana Historical Quarterly*, XXVI (1943), 975-1054.

Overdyke, W. Darrell. "History of the American Party in Louisiana." *Louisiana Historical Quarterly*, XVI (1933), 256-277.

Prichard, Walter. "The Effects of the Civil War on the Louisiana Sugar Industry." *Journal of Southern History*, V (1939), 315-332.

_____. Routine on a Louisiana Sugar Plantation Under the Slavery Regime." *Mississippi Valley Historical Review*, XIV (1927), 168-178.

Roland, Charles P. "Louisiana and Secession." *Louisiana History*, XIX (1978), 389-399.

Rowland, Dunbar. "Mississippi in the Transfer of the Louisiana Purchase by France to the United States." *Louisiana Historical Quarterly*, XIII (1930), 235-245.

Shepherd, Samuel C., Jr. "A Glimmer of Hope: The World's Industrial and Cotton Centennial Exposition, New Orleans, 1884-1885." *Louisiana History*, XXVI (1985), 271-290.

Sitterson, J. Carlyle. "Magnolia Plantation, 1852-1862: A Decade of a Louisiana Sugar Estate." *Mississippi Valley Historical Review*, XV (1938), 197-210.

_____. "The William J. Minor Plantations: A Study in Ante-Bellum Absentee Ownership." *Journal of Southern History*, IX (1943), 59-74.

Summers, Mark W. "The Moderates' Last Chance: The Election of 1865." *Louisiana History*, XXIV (1983), 49-69.

Taylor, Georgia Fairbanks. "The Early History of the Episcopal Church in New Orleans, 1805-1840." *Louisiana Historical Quarterly*, XXII (1939), 428-478.

Taylor, Joe Gray. "New Orleans and Reconstruction." *Louisiana History*, IX (1968), 189-208.

Tregle, Joseph G., Jr. "Early New Orleans Society: A Reappraisal." *Journal of Southern History*, XVIII (1952), 20-36.

———. "On That Word 'Creole' Again: A Note." *Louisiana History*, XXIII (1982), 193-198.

———. "Thomas J. Durant, Utopian Socialism, and the Failure of Presidential Reconstruction in Louisiana." *Journal of Southern History*, XV (1979), 485-512.

Newspapers

Baton Rouge *Advocate*, 1992.

Baton Rouge Gazette, 1846-1852.

Baton Rouge *Weekly Advocate*, 1856.

Louisiana *Progress*, 1938.

New Orleans *Daily Picayune*, 1846-1865, 1909.

New Orleans *Daily Southern Star*, 1865.

New Orleans *Daily States*, 1882-1887.

New Orleans *Daily True Delta*, 1865.

New Orleans *Louisiana Gazette*, 1804-1811.

New Orleans Bee, 1854.

New Orleans Daily Delta, 1847-1861.

New Orleans States, 1952.

New Orleans Times, 1865.

New Orleans Tribune, 1865.

New Orleans Weekly Delta, 1848-1856.

New Orleans *Times-Democrat*, 1883-1892.

New Orleans *Times-Picayune*, 1975-1983.

Richmond *Times-Dispatch*, 1912.

Dissertations, Theses, and Papers

Arceneaux, Olive Isabel. "A Brief History of Public Education in Louisiana, 1805-1845." M.A. thesis, Tulane University, 1938.

Bauer, Craig A. "The History of the City of Kenner, Louisiana." M.A. thesis, Southeastern Louisiana University, 1973.

Constantin, Roland P. "The Louisiana 'Black Code' Legislation of 1865." M.A. thesis, Louisiana State University, 1956.

Harris, T. H. "The Story of Public Education in Louisiana." M.A. thesis, Louisiana State University, 1924.

McKee, Kathleen H. "Belle Helene Plantation." Research paper, Architectural Archives, Special Collections Division, Tulane University.

Mitchell, George. "The Ante-Bellum Political Career of Duncan Farrar Kenner." M.A. thesis, Louisiana State University, 1936.

Patrick, G. U. "Literature in the Louisiana Plantation Home." Ph.D. dissertation, Louisiana State University, 1935.

Price, Grady Daniel. "The Secret Mission of Duncan F. Kenner, Confederate Minister Plenipotentiary To Europe in 1865." M.A. thesis, Tulane University, 1929.

Singletary, Otis Arnold. "The Reassertion of White Supremacy in Louisiana." M.A. thesis, Louisiana State University, 1949.

Correspondence

Scarborough, William K., to the author, April 17, 1986.

Wilson, Gordon D. Archives Librarian, The Miami University Archives, Oxford, Ohio, to the author, May 10, 1976.

Wilson, Samuel, Jr., to the author, January 20, 1982.

Index

Abolitionists, 152, 172
Acklen, A. S., 61
Adams, Charles Francis, 213
Adams, Christopher, 118
Adams, D. W., 176
Adams, John, 7
Adams, John Quincy, 187
Adams, W. R., 176
Adams County, Miss., 7
African-Americans, see also
    Slavery, 263-266, 274
    as free persons of color, 138
    as sharecroppers, 251
    view of, by Duncan Farrar Kenner, Sr., 290-291
Alabama, 171, 178
Alexandria, La., 84, 86
Algiers, La., 127
America, The, 227, 228
American party, see Know-Nothing party
American Revolution, 3, 5, 21
Anderson, Robert, 29
Antel, A. C., 63
Appomattox Courthouse, Va., 235
Arkansas, 191, 252
Arthur, Chester, 257, 281
Ascension Parish, La., 16, 32-34, 36, 42, 52, 63, 64, 75, 78, 83, 85, 100-103, 112, 113, 136, 147, 151, 172-174, 183, 191, 201, 203, 204, 206, 243, 244, 247, 260, 286
    police jury, 244
Ashland Plantation, 33, 36-60, 63, 65-69, 78, 80, 82, 84, 85, 93, 102, 189, 193-197, 201-205, 242, 243, 250-252, 271, 275, 283, 284, 290
    Civil War's effect upon, 193-197, 201-205
    confiscation of property at, by Union troops, 195-198
    damaged by flooding (1851-52), 65-66
    Reconstruction period, 238-259
    sugar production levels at, 66-67
Assumption Parish, La., 172, 173, 260
Atlanta, Ga., 207
Attakapas country, 85
Austria, 213

Baldwin, Rep., 118, 120, 121
Baltimore, Md., 171, 224
Bancroft, George, 84
Banks, Nathaniel P., 76, 202, 203, 208, 209, 211, 261
Baptist church, 14, 82
Baruc, B. S., 220, 232
Baton Rouge, La., 14, 37, 86, 114, 124, 136, 142, 143, 193, 198, 200
    Daily Comet, 151
    Democratic Advocate, 119
    Gazette, 116, 117, 119, 137
    Old State Capitol in, 36
    secession convention in, 174-176, 240
    Weekly Advocate, 151
Battles,
    Antietam, 237
    Gettysburg, 237
    Mansfield, 208, 209
    New Orleans, 89, 100, 101
    Pleasant Hill, 208, 209
    Sabine Crossroads, 76
Bauer, Betsy, 2
Bauer, Joyce, 2
Bauer, Rudy, 2
Bay Saint Louis, Miss., 91, 246
Bayous,
    Lafourche, 33, 35, 85, 127, 199
    Teche, 35, 85
Beauregard, P. G. T., 274
Bell, John, 118, 172, 174
Belle Cheney Springs, La., 193
Belle Grove Plantation, 18, 32, 36, 66, 143
Bellechasse Plantation, 71
Bengaman, Adam L., 94
Benjamin, Judah P., 71, 88, 104, 117, 123, 130, 137-139, 152, 153, 181, 182, 212, 214-219, 221, 233, 236, 238, 285
Beringer, Richard E., 287
BerlÈ, E., 232
Bermudez, Joachim, 126
Bienvenue, Rep., 119
Bigelow, John, 239, 240
Black Code, 263, 264, 266, 267, 288
Bladensburg, Md., 223
Bonaparte, Napoleon, 11, 12
Bordelon, Louis, 145
Boston, Mass., 258
Bowden Plantation, 64, 75, 201, 203-205, 250, 252, 284
Brag, Mr., 194, 195
Braud, J. A., Jr., 63
Brazil, 73

349

Breckinridge, John C., 171, 172, 174
Brecks, George, 57
Brent, Joseph Lancaster, 80, 276, 284
Brent, Rosella, 284
Bringier Pulverizing Cultivator, 252
Bringier, AmÈdÈe, 193, 246
Bringier, Anne Guillelmine "Nanine," 34, 36, 76-83, 93, 100, 101, 190-192, 195, 196, 198, 199, 245, 246, 283, 284
Bringier, Anne Octavie, 75
Bringier, Emmanuel Marius, 75
Bringier, Louis, 252
Bringier, Louise FranÁoise, 75
Bringier, Louise Marie MyrthÈ, 76
Bringier, M. S., 191
Bringier, Marie Elizabeth AglaÈ, 75
Bringier, Martin, 79
Bringier, Michel Doradou, 37, 48, 75
Bringier, Mrs. M. D., 192, 246
Bringier, Rosella, 75, 100
Bringier, Stella, 246
Brown, James, 17
Brown, John, 157
Brown, Shepherd, 10
Bruce, Mr., 17
Brussels, Belgium, 229
Buchanan, James, 143, 154, 156, 171
Bullard, Henry A., 129
Bullitt, Alexander, 123
Bunyan, John, 84
Burke, Glendy, 151
Burnside, John, 191
Burthe, Leon, 151
Butler, Benjamin Franklin, 193, 201, 202
Butler, Louise, 89
Byron, Lord, 84

Caldwell Parish, La., 101
Calhoun, John C., 134, 187
California, 133
Camp, R. C., 225
Canby, General, 209
Cannes Br°lÈes District, La., 16, 17
Carlos IV, 11
Cash, W. J., 94
Cass, Lewis, 123, 143
Catahoula Parish, La., 107
Catholic church, 14, 82
Cervantes, Miguel de, 84
Charleston, S. C., 170, 221

Chew, B., 15
Cholera, 55
Ciccarelli, Orazio, 2
Cincinnati, Ohio, 18, 33, 34, 271
   Grocers' Association, 256
Citizens Bank of Louisiana, 101, 102, 106
Civil War, 59, 61, 72, 73, 75, 87, 97, 116, 123, 156, 271, 285
   casualties among Louisiana soldiers, 242
   Confederate diplomacy in England, 229-237
   Confederate political history, 176-221
   Duncan Farrar Kenner's journey to New York City during, 221-227
   Kenner family during the early, 189-210
Claiborne, Ferdinand Leigh, 14
Claiborne, William C. C., 9, 12, 13, 18
Claque, R., 21
Clark, Daniel, 7, 84
Clarkesville, Tenn., 7
Clay, Henry, 133-135, 187
Clermont Plantation, 63
Clinton, Catherine, 8, 80, 81
Cobb, Howell, 177
Cochrane, Dr., 19
Compromise of 1850, 133-135, 143, 144, 146, 149, 157
Concord Plantation, 8, 17
Confederate States of America,
   army, 75
   collapse of, 235-238
   Congress, 176-189, 191, 193, 199, 200, 206, 215-218, 220, 286, 287
   Constitution, 178, 179
   Department of Alabama, Mississippi, and East Louisiana, 76
   Treasury Department, 232
Conrad, Charles M., 104, 127, 137, 176, 181
Conrad, Glenn R., 2
Conservatives, 261, 275
Constitutional Union Party, 171
Cooper, James Fenimore, 84
Corcoran, W. W., 229
Corn, 45, 53, 175, 204
Corneille, 88
Cottman, Thomas, 240
Cotton, 33, 175, 217, 220, 263
Coulter, E. Merton, 184, 187
Couper, John, 23
Cranston, Mr., 227

Creoles, 72, 77
  cuisine, 10
  definition of, 13
Crescent City Oil Company, 248, 253
Crittenden, John J., 148
Cuba, 252, 256
Cunard Ship Line, 226-227

Dakin, Charles, 35, 36
Dakin, James, 35, 36, 38
Dakin and Dakin, Architects, 37
Davis, Eliza, 18
Davis, Jefferson, 61, 104, 177-178, 181, 186, 210, 212-217, 221, 227, 229, 230, 234, 238, 286
De Bow's Review, 85
Declouet, Alexander, 124, 127, 176
Declouet Rangers, 125, 126
Delaware, 154
DeLeon, Edwin, 212
Democratic party, see also Conservatives, 75, 100-102, 104, 110-114, 116-125, 130-132, 134-137, 142-146, 148, 150-153, 155, 171, 174, 257, 261, 267, 268, 273, 274, 276, 278-280, 288
  Southern faction, 152
Department of Alabama, Mississippi, and East Louisiana, 210
Derbigny, Pierre, 148, 149
Dick, John, 17
Diggs, Joseph, 204, 205
District of Columbia, 133
Donald, David, 287
Donaldsonville, La., 32, 83, 84, 86, 87, 114, 146, 193, 195, 201, 246, 283, 284
  Ascension Catholic Church in, 86
  Ascension Parish Courthouse in, 86
  theatrical productions in, 86
  Vigilant, 153
  Volunteer Company of Cannoneers of, 101
Donoughmore, Earl of, 235
Douglas, Stephen A., 143, 146, 150, 156, 170-174
Downs, Solomon, 110, 134
Doyal, Henry, 194, 201
DuBourg, Elizabeth Aglae, 75
Dubourg, Louis Guillaume, 76
Dumas, Alexandre, 84
Duncan, Currie, 30

Duncan, Mrs. Currie, 30
Duncan, George Currie, 17
Duncan, Mrs. George Currie, 102
Duncan, Stephen, 18
Dymond, John, Sr., 253, 257
Dysentery, 55

East Baton Rouge Parish, La., 247
Edinburgh, Schotland, 30
Edison, Thomas, 249
Education, 21-24
Elam, James, 117
Ellicott, Andrew, 7
Ellis, Martha, 8
Emancipation Proclamation, 202
Engerman, Stanley L., 50, 53, 54, 56
Episcopal church, 14, 23, 82
Eureka Decorticating Machines, 252
Eustis, George, 104

Farragut, David G., 192
Farrar, Ann, 18, 20
Farrar, Anna, 16
Farrar, Benjamin, 12, 18, 20, 24, 25
Farrar, Mary, 18, 20. 25
Fashion Plantation, 76
Feliciana Parish, La., 104
Figs, 33
Fillmore, Millard, 105, 135, 143, 146, 152-154
Fillmore Rangers, 152
Fitzhugh, George, 239
Flanders, Benjamin F., 269
Flint, Timothy, 73
Flood, Dr., 19
Florida, 176
Florida Parishes, 138
Fogel, Robert W., 50, 53, 54, 56
Folger, Charles, 257
Foote, Henry Stuart, 181, 185, 227
Forts,
  Fisher, 220, 221
  Jackson, 175
  Johnson, 222
  St. Philip, 175
Fourage, Madame, 14
France, 213, 216-219
Franco-Confederate Bank, 219
Frazier and Trenholm Company, 220
Free Soil party, 123

Free Soilers, 150, 152, 154
Freedmen's Bureau, 244, 263, 267
Fremont, John C., 152, 154, 155
Fugitive Slave Act, 144

Gallier, James, Jr., 35, 36
Gallier, James, Sr., 35, 36
Garcia, Felix, 119
GayarrÈ, Charles, 24, 115
Genovese, Eugene, 289
Georgia, 176, 178, 185, 235, 242, 251
Gibbon, Edward, 84
Goldsmith, Oliver, 84
Gordon, Louise, 246
Gordon, Martin, Jr., 67, 75, 203, 205, 246
Gordon, Martin, Sr., 91, 101
Grant, Ulysses S., 209, 211
Graves, George Washington, 93, 95, 189, 194, 195, 197, 198, 202, 203, 243, 270
Great Britain, 216-219, 230, 235, 236
Gregg, Josiah, 19
GrimkÈ, Angelina, 81
GrimkÈ, Sarah, 81
Grymes, John R., 88
Guice, John, 2
Gulf of Mexico, 85, 175, 190

Hahn, Michael, 241
Hammond, Henry, 65, 94, 180, 181, 199, 206, 243, 244
Hampton Roads, Va., 233
Hampton, Wade, 25, 239
Hardtimes Plantation, 65
Harper's Ferry, Va., 157
Harper's Magazine, 85
Harper, Glenn, 2
Hattaway, Herman, 287
Hawkins, Abe, 94, 96
Hay, 45
Hayes, Rutherford B., 276, 278
Hays, Harry T., 183
Hebert, Paul O., 145, 271
Henderson, Stephen, 10, 15, 16
Hermitage Plantation, 48, 75, 78, 193, 201, 246, 247, 252, 254, 255, 284
Hildreth, D. M., 225-227
Hill, D. H., 183
Hilton, Robert B., 188
Historic New Orleans Collection, 2
Hollywood Plantation, 247, 284

Homer, La., 86
Hood, John, 207
Houma, La., 199
Houmas Plantation, 247, 251, 284
Howard, Henry, 35, 36
Howard, Perry, 269
Howell, 221, 223-227
Humphreys, John B., 17
Hunt, Randall, 88, 117, 130
Hunt, Theodore G., 127, 128, 147
Hunter, Robert M. T., 213

Iberville Parish, La., 118, 141
Illinois, 171
Index, The, 230
Indians, 4
Indigo, 33
Influenza, 51, 55
Iowa, 154

Jackson, Andrew, 99, 100, 123, 244, 267
Jackson, La., 105
Jackson, Miss., 206
    Mississippian, 215
Jefferson, Thomas, 9, 12, 13, 75, 100
Jefferson City Gaslight Company, 249
Jefferson Parish, La., 18, 31, 32, 91, 127, 128, 141, 142, 149, 245
Jefferson Parish, Police Jury, 99
Johnson, Alex, 7
Johnson, Andrew, 238, 239, 241, 242, 263
Johnson, Henry, 117
Johnson, Isaac, 113
Johnston, Joseph, 207
Jonas, B. F., 280
Jones, Archer, 287
Jones, Charlotte, 33, 59
Jones, Mr., 122
Judice, Robert, 2
Judice, Susan, 2

Kansas, 149, 157
Kansas-Nebraska Act, 146, 149, 150
Keith, John A., 195, 196, 198
Kellogg, William Pitt, 257, 275
Kendall, George W., 96
Kenner Guards, 125, 126
Kenner, Alexander, 59, 60
Kenner, D. Ella, 245, 248
Kenner, Duncan Farrar, Jr., 79, 80, 284

Kenner, Duncan Farrar, Sr.,
  as a planter, 32, 33, 43-69
  attitude of, toward African-Americans, 290-291
  attitude toward the Missouri Compromise, 134-144, 148, 153
  birth of, 18
  Boston Club membership of, 88, 225, 226, 272, 273, 281, 283
  care of slaves owned by, 290
  Civil War journey to New York City, 221-227
  Confederate agent in England, 229-237
  Confederate Congressman, 176-189, 191, 193, 199, 200, 206
  diplomatic mission to Europe (1865), 211-237
  disguised as A. B. Kinglake, 221-228
  domestic affairs of, during the Civil War, 189-210
  domestic life of, 76-97
  early childhood of, 19-27
  early political career of, 98-130
  education of, 28-30
  gambling losses of, 88
  grand tour of, 30-31
  Greek Revival home of, 34-42, 78
  horse racing interests of, 59, 65, 72, 78, 88, 91-98, 189, 191, 197, 198, 242, 270, 271, 288, 290
  legal training of, 31
  literary interests of, 84-85
  marriage of, 34, 77
  New Orleans townhouse of, 42, 84, 87
  non-agricultural business interests of, 70-74
  postbellum political activities of, 260-282
  presidential pardon for, 241-242
  Reconstruction difficulties of, 238-259
  religious background of, 82
  secession crisis and, 169-188
Kenner, Frances Ann, 17, 18, 22, 23
Kenner, Frances Rosella, 80, 197
Kenner, George, 18, 32, 33, 49, 59, 60, 64, 80, 93
Kenner, George Currie Duncan, 80, 198, 284
Kenner, Maria, 17
Kenner, Martha, 17, 18, 22, 23, 26
Kenner, Martha Blanche, 80
Kenner, Mary Minor, 8, 12, 14, 17-21

Kenner, Philip Minor, 190, 245
Kenner, Rodham, 92
Kenner, Ruhamah Riske, 18, 245
Kenner, Stephen Minor, 18, 32, 78, 92, 99, 142
Kenner, William, 3-26, 31, 32, 71, 73, 74, 76, 92, 99, 245
Kenner, William Butler, 18, 32, 66, 142, 143
Kennerville, La., 32, 143, 201, 245
Kentucky, 4, 18, 103, 154, 241
King, T. Floyd, 255
Kinglake, A. B., see Kenner, Duncan Farrar, Sr.
Kirby Smith, Edmund, 208-210, 239
Know-Nothing party, 147-155, 157, 261, 262
Kossuth, Louis, 144

Lafayette (suburb of New Orleans), La., 128
Lafourche Parish, La., 141, 173
Lake Pontchartrain, 16, 85
Landry, J. Aristide, 147
Lanier, Sidney, 242
Latrobe, Benjamin Henry B., 73
Laurel Hill Plantation, 24
Laussat, Pierre ClÈment, 11
Lawrence, Effingham, 63
Lee, Robert E., 98, 211, 212, 235, 239
Leruth, Michael Joseph, 252
Lincoln, Abraham, 171-173, 207, 211, 237-239
Lintot, Catherine, 8
Linwood Plantation, 16-18, 25, 26, 28, 32, 33
Liverpool, England, 15, 17, 220, 225
Livestock, 48, 49
Livingston, Edward, 14
London, England, 226, 232
  Telegraph, 230
Longstreet, James, 274, 275
Louisiana
  Civil War casualties among soldiers from, 242
  Constitution of 1812, 104, 106
  Constitution of 1845, 37, 112, 135-141
  Constitution of 1852, 135-142
  Constitution of 1864, 262
  Constitution of 1879, 279
  Cotton Manufacturing Company, 248
  Department of Internal Improvements, 150
  Jockey Club, 281, 288
  Legislative Council of, 142

Legislative Council, 12-14, 142
Levee Company, 247, 248
   Roman Catholic population of, 148
   Scientific Agricultural Association, 255
   State University, 2
   Sugar Planters' Association, 253-258, 281, 288
   Sulphur Mining Company, 248
   Superior Court of, 12
   Supreme Court, 280
Lovell, Mansfield, 193
Ludlow, Israel, 34
Luraghi, Raimondo, 289
Lynchburg, Va., *Virginian,* 216

McClellan, George, 207
McCloskey, James, 249, 250
McCrary, Mr., 241, 242
McDonald, John, 252
McDonogh, John, 5, 10, 14
McKee, Joan, 2
McKee, Robert, 2
Madewood Plantation, 36
Magnolia Plantation, 63, 254
Mann, A. Dudley, 212, 217, 229
Marigny, Bernard, 105, 109
Marquardt, Ronald, 2
Marshall, Henry, 176
Martin, Senator, 121
Maryland, 222
Mason, James, 216-218, 229-235
Matagorda County, Tex., 18, 34, 49
Mayo, G., 107
Mazureau, Etienne, 25, 28, 99, 126
Measles, 55
Melhado, Professor, 192
Melpomene Estate, 246
Memminger, Christopher G., 184
Menlo Park, N. J., 249
Mercer, Newton, 273
Mercer, William N., 16
Merchant's Bank, 232
Merrick, 221, 223
Metairie Association, 97, 271, 272
Metairie, La.,
   Cemetery Association, 272, 283
   Jockey Club, 96, 271
   race course in, 91, 96, 97, 271, 272, 288
Metairie Ridge, La., 91
Methodist church, 14, 82

Metternich, Klemens von, 31
Mexican War, 131, 143
Mexico, 114, 123, 233, 248
Miami University of Ohio, 29, 30, 241
Michel, J. J., 151
Michigan, 123
Milton, John, 84
Minden, La., 86
Minor, Duncan, 190
Minor, John, 15, 24
Minor, Philip, 32
Minor, Stephen, 6-8, 15, 16, 20, 99, 195, 196
Minor, Theophilus, 16, 32
Minor, William J., 48, 62, 83, 94, 96, 97, 113, 173, 182, 191, 195
Minor, William, Jr., 199
Mississippi, 176, 252
Mississippi Sound, 191
Mississippi Territory, 3, 12, 14
Missouri Compromise, 134-144, 148, 153
Mobile, Ala., 96
   Register, 216
Monaco, 31
Montgomery, Ala., Confederate convention at, 176, 178, 180
Moore, Thomas Overton, 84, 157, 173, 175, 207
Morehead, Charles S., 148
Morgan, Benjamin, 16
Motley, John Lothrop, 213
Moundville, La., 200
Myers, Abraham C., 183
Myles, Isaac A., 118, 119, 121, 122

Napoleon III, 231, 232
Nashville, Tenn., 80, 284
   Convention (1850), 132, 133
Nassau, Bahama Islands, 220
Natchez, Miss., 3-11, 18, 20, 22, 24, 63, 74, 90, 193
   Light Infantry, 190
   Trace, 4
Natchitoches, La., 200
Nebraska, 147, 149
Nevitt, John, 63
New Basin Canal, 250, 273
New Dalton Plantation, 75
New Hope Plantation, 75
New Mexico, 133
New Orleans Pacific Railroad Company, 248

New Orleans, Jackson, and Great Northern Railroad, 142
New Orleans, La., 3, 5, 6, 8-19, 24, 29, 31, 83, 85, 100, 101, 105-06, 108, 109, 113, 123, 126, 128, 135, 140, 143, 147, 172, 175, 260, 274
   Arsenal Building in, 36
   Audubon Park in, 91, 255
   banks in, 15
   Bar Association of, 116
   Battle of Liberty Place in, 275
   Bee, 148
   Boston Club in, 88, 225, 226, 272, 273, 281, 283
   Bulletin, 119, 134
   Cabildo in, 15
   Canal Bank of, 248
   Catholic Asylum of, 101
   Club, 272
   Crescent, 155
   Daily Delta, 115-117, 134, 145, 191
   Daily Picayune, 120, 123, 176, 267
   Eclipse Course in, 91
   First Ward of, 138
   frauds and riots in (1856), 151
   French character of, 87
   Gaslight Company, 249
   horse racing around, 91-97
   Jews in, 14, 15
   Jockey Club, 92
   libraries in, 84
   Louisiana Course in, 91
   Mardi Gras celebration in, 89
   Mechanic's Institute, 261
   morality in, 10
   Mr. Shute's school in, 23
   opera in antebellum, 88
   Pelican Club of, 88
   Pickwick Club of, 88
   Place d'Armes in, 15
   planters' townhouses in, 42, 84, 87
   polyglot population of, 10
   port of, 101
   Produce Exchange, 248
   Protestants in, 14
   Public Service, 249
   riot of 1867 in, 268
   Saint Charles Hotel in, 253
   Saint Charles Theater in, 87
   slave market in, 50
   theatrical productions in, 86
   ThÈ,tre d'OrlÈans in, 87-88
   Tribune, 266
   Union occupation of, 193
   University of Louisiana in, 116
   Vieux CarrÈ of, 10, 25, 28
   Weekly Delta, 144
   White League in, 274, 275
   World's Industrial and Cotton Centennial Exposition at (1884), 281, 282
New Orleans, The, 16
New River, La., 197
New York, N.Y., 15, 91, 221, 225-227, 240, 258
   Times, 282
   Tribune, 228
New Zatoma, 67
Newport, R.I., 90
Nicholls, Francis T., 275, 276, 278, 285
North Carolina, 133
Norton, M. O. H., 225

Oakland Plantation, 16-19, 26, 28, 31-33, 66, 245, 246, 263
Oldham, John, 25
Olmsted, Frederick Law, 61
Opelousas, La., 193, 199, 200
Oranges, 33
Oregon, 114
Orleans Light Horse Company, 190
Orleans Parish, La., 118, 127, 141, 279
Orleans Territory, 12, 99
   Legislative Council of, 99
Ouachita Parish, La., 110
Owsley, Frank L., 287
Oxford, Ohio, 29
Oxley, Charles, 17

Packard, S. B., 278
Packard, Stephen B., 257
Palmerston, Henry, 233-235
Panic of 1837, 104, 106
Parham, William, 119-121
Paris, France, 213, 229, 230, 236, 239, 240
Pasture Plantation, 32, 66, 143
Peaches, 33
Peas, 53
Pennsylvania, 6, 235
Perkins, John, Jr., 176, 188
Peters, Samuel J., Jr., 133

Petersburg, Va., 211
Pettus, John J., 206
Philadelphia, Pa., 224, 228
   Centennial Exposition (1876), 282
   Mrs. Mallon's Seminary in, 22, 23, 30
   United States Bank of, 15
Pierce, Franklin, 143, 144, 149, 150, 156
Plantation Bureau, 204
Planter's Crescent Oil Company, 248
Planters Fertilizer and Manufacturing
   Company, 248
Plaquemine, La., 86
Plaquemines Parish, La., 63, 71, 254
PlauchÈ, John B., 124, 125, 127
Plums, 33
Pointe CoupÈe Parish, La., 141
Polk, James K., 114, 115
Port Tobacco, Md., 222
Porter, Alexander, 96
Postl, Karl, 21, 106
Potatoes, 45, 53
Pratt, T. G., 148
Presbyterian church, 82
Prescott, W. H., 84
Preston, Isaac T., 104

Racine, 88
Randall, J. A., 63
Rapides Parish, La., 240
Reconstruction, 94, 142, 238-259
Reconstruction Acts, 268
Red River Campaign (1864), 76, 208-211
Republican party, 147, 170, 172, 255-258,
   261, 268, 273, 274, 277, 278, 288
Reuss, John, 284
Rhett, Robert Barnwell, 178
Rice, 251, 252
Richmond, Va., 171, 180, 181, 183, 188, 191,
   193, 199, 206, 211, 215, 220, 221, 244
   Enquirer, 215, 216
Rillieux, Norbert, 47, 48, 289
Rivers,
   Alabama, 14
   Amite, 201
   Cane, 200
   Caney, 34
   Mississippi, 4, 6, 18, 33-35, 42, 46, 76, 85,
      99, 141, 175, 190, 192, 193, 200, 206,
      210, 214, 251, 252
   Ohio, 3, 4

Potomac, 221, 222
Red, 141
Roland, Charles, 200
Roman, A. B., 178
Rome, Italy, 30
Roseland Plantation, 17, 245
Rost, Pierre, 212
Rothschild, Baron, 31
Rougeau, Mr., 86
Rouquette, D., 84
Ruffin, Edmund, 185, 186
Russell, John, 229-231, 234
Russell, W. P., 203
Russell, William Howard, 175, 176, 190
Russell, William, 86

Sabine Parish, La., 118
Saint Catherine's Creek, 6
Saint Charles Parish, La., 17, 76, 247
Saint Francisville, La., 84, 114
Saint James Parish, La., 52, 75, 103, 136
Saint John the Baptist Parish, La., 111, 136
Saint Louis, Mo., 59
Saint Martin Parish, La., 33
Saint Simon's Island, Ga., 23
Sargent, Winthrop, 7, 9, 13
Saxe-Weimar, Duke of, 73
Scarborough, William K., 2, 62
Schenck, Robert, 241, 265, 279
Schmidt, Engel H., 2
Scott, Walter, 84
Scott, Winfield, 143, 144, 146
Scully, Arthur, 36
Segoud, Jerry, 197
Semmes, Thomas J., 182
Seward, William Henry, 212, 213, 240
Sewell, Leonard, 252
Shakespeare, William, 84
Shell Oil Company, 284
Shepherd, R. D., 15
Sheridan, Philip H., 268, 269
Sherman, William T., 207, 209, 217, 235
Ship Island, 191, 192
Shreveport, La., 86
   Times, 274
Shugg, Roger, 142, 263
Simms, William Gilmore, 84
Simpson, Blanche, 284
Sitterson, J. Carlyle, 50, 57, 243, 244
Slavery, 17, 28, 31, 43-65, 70, 73, 82, 98, 131,

133, 134, 138, 139, 149, 188, 214, 235, 260, 290
Confederate debate of emancipation of slaves, 214-216
Confederate diplomacy and, 213-214
Confederate effort to secure diplomatic recognition in return for abolition of slavery, 229-237
during the Civil War, 190, 193, 194, 197, 200, 202, 204
slave jockeys, 94
Slidell, John, 31, 88, 92, 99, 100, 117-122, 156, 157, 170, 171, 173, 213, 216-218, 229-232, 236, 285
Smallpox, 55
Smuggling, 203
SoulÈ, Pierre, 88, 104, 105, 119-122, 134, 156, 157, 170-173, 236, 285
South Carolina, 81, 174, 176, 178, 242
Southampton, England, 228, 229
Southdown Plantation, 199
Southern Cultivator, 41
Southern Literary Messenger, 85
Southern Pacific Railroad, 72, 248
Sparrow, Edward, 176, 188
Speed, James, 241
Spirit of the Times, 85
Stampp, Kenneth, 53, 61, 264
Staples, Col., 121, 122
Stephens, Alexander H., 148, 178, 185, 212, 238, 239
Steward, J. Ross, 248
Still, William N., 287
Stowe, Harriet Beecher, 157
Stuttgart, Germany, 228
Sugar Experimental Station, 91, 288-289
Sugar industry, 33, 43-48, 57, 63, 64, 66-67, 104, 175, 190, 197, 203, 204, 245, 251-259, 288-289

Tariff Act of 1883, 258
Taylor, Myrthe Bringier, 192
Taylor, Richard "Dick," 76, 176, 192, 208, 209, 211, 249, 250, 271, 273
Taylor, Zachary, 114, 123, 125, 126, 133, 135, 143
Tehuantepec Inter-Ocean Railroad, 248
Ten Broeck, Richard, 97
Tennessee, 4, 154, 171, 227, 238
Terrebonne Parish, La., 191, 260

Texas, 209
Tezcuco Plantation, 75, 246
Thibodaux, Bannon, 123
Thibodaux, La., 86, 152
Thomas, Allen, 75, 192
Tilden, Samuel J., 275
Toombs, Robert A., 148, 177
Touro, Judah, 15
Trans-Mississippi Department, 206, 208, 209
Treaties,
　Guadalupe Hidalgo, 75
　Paris (1783), 3
　Pinckney's (1795), 9
　San Lorenzo, 6
Trenholm, George A., 219, 232
Trist, Hore Browse, 64, 75, 100
Trist, Nicholas P., 75
Troy, N.Y., 36
Tulane University, Howard-Tilton Memorial Library at, 2
Tureaud, Aglae, 246
Tureaud, Benjamin, 75, 91, 199-200
Turnips, 53
21st Indiana Infantry, 195
Typhoid, 190

Unification Movement, 274
Union Tie and Compress Company, 248
United States,
　Bank, 100
　Congress, 11, 14, 104, 114, 119, 123, 127, 128, 131-134, 146, 147, 149, 154, 176, 186, 187, 195, 240, 241, 255, 256, 258, 261, 263, 264, 267, 269, 288
　Constitution, 177
　Department of Agriculture, 254, 255
　House of Representatives, 171
　National Archives, 2
　Senate, 99, 119, 130, 136, 156, 258, 280, 281
　Supreme Court, 170
　Tariff Commission of 1882, 257-259
University of North Carolina, 30
University of Southern Mississippi, 2
Utah, 133

Van Buren, Martin, 123
Venezuela, 75
Vicksburg, Miss., 206, 207
Vidalia, La., 255

Vienna, Austria-Hungary, 31
Virginia, 18, 75, 90, 92-94, 178, 180, 191, 242
Voltaire, 88

Wade, W. G., 44, 49-51, 57, 63
Walker, Joseph, 124-127, 132
War of 1812, 18, 71
Warmoth, Henry Clay, 254, 285
Washington, D. C., 155, 223, 235, 241, 256, 257, 260, 262, 275
Washington, La., 200
Washington Parish, La., 118, 121
Waterloo Plantation, 195, 196
Watkins, Rep., 119
Webster, Daniel, 134, 187
Wells, James Madison, 94, 240, 241, 260-262, 267, 269, 277
Wells, Thomas Jefferson, 94, 95, 97, 157
West Feliciana Parish, La., 113, 138, 141
West Florida, Spanish, 3
West Indies, 43
Whig party, 100, 103, 104, 110-114, 116-120, 123-131, 133-149, 240, 261, 285, 286
   national conventions of the, 143-144
   Northern faction of the, 143, 148
   Southern faction of the, 143, 148, 149, 155
White, Edward D., 280
White, Maunsel, 14, 23, 118, 119
White Hall Plantation, 75, 101
White Sulphur Springs, Va., 90
Whooping cough, 55
Wickliffe, Robert C., 150, 169
Wilkins, James C., 6
Wilkinson, James, 12
Wilmington, N.C., 220, 221
Wilmot Proviso, 132, 133
Wisconsin, 201
Woodlawn Plantation, 36
World War II, 143

Yancey, William Lowndes, 178, 185, 212
Yellow fever, 55, 143
Zilman, S. H., 249

www.ingramcontent.com/pod-product-compliance
Lightning Source LLC
Chambersburg PA
CBHW071555080526
44588CB00010B/919